THE ICONIC CASES IN CORPORATE LAW

Edited by

Jonathan R. Macey

*Deputy Dean and Sam Harris Professor of Corporate Law,
Corporate Finance and Securities Law, Yale University
and Professor in the Yale School of Management*

Contributors

Stephen M. Bainbridge
*William D. Warren Professor of Law,
UCLA School of Law*

Logan Beirne
Yale Law School 2008

James D. Cox
*Brainerd Currie Professor of Law,
Duke University*

Jill E. Fisch
*T.J. Maloney Professor of Business
Law, Fordham University*

Vikramaditya Khanna
*Professor of Law, University of
Michigan Law School*

Donald C. Langevoort
*Thomas Aquinas Reynolds Professor of
Law, Georgetown University Law
Center*

Fred S. McChesney
*Class of 1967 James B. Haddad
Professor of Law, Northwestern
University; Professor, Kellogg School of
Management*

Geoffrey P. Miller
*Stuyvesant P. Comfort Professor of
Law, New York University*

Douglas K. Moll
*Beirne, Maynard & Parsons, L.L.P.
Professor of Law, University of
Houston Law Center*

Hillary A. Sale
*F. Arnold Daum Professor of Corporate
Finance and Law, University of Iowa
College of Law*

David A. Skeel, Jr.
*S. Samuel Arsht Professor of Corporate
Law, University of Pennsylvania*

Lynn A. Stout
*Paul Hastings Professor of Corporate
and Securities Law and Principal
Investigator for the UCLA-Sloan
Research Program on Business
Organizations, UCLA School of Law*

Eric Talley
*Professor of Law, University of
California at Berkeley*

Robert B. Thompson
*New York Alumni Chancellor's Chair
in Law and Professor of Management,
Vanderbilt University*

AMERICAN CASEBOOK SERIES®

THOMSON ™ WEST

Mat # 40599019

American Casebook Series and West Group are trademarks registered in the U.S. Patent and Trademark Office.

© 2008 Thomson/West
610 Opperman Drive
P.O. Box 64526
St. Paul, MN 55123
1–800–313–9378

Printed in the United States of America

ISBN: 978–0–314–18048–3

 TEXT IS PRINTED ON 10% POST
CONSUMER RECYCLED PAPER

Introduction

As the title of this book implies, in this volume are gathered together what I regard to be the most important (iconic) cases in corporate law. Each chapter includes one (or at most two, or three) iconic cases in a particular, critical area of law. The cases selected for this volume span the twentieth century from beginning to end. The cases discussed in this book constitute not just important judicial decisions concerning corporate law, they also have become part of the legal canon.

Just mentioning the names of the cases discussed in these chapters from *Dodge v. Ford Motor Company* to *In re Caremark Derivative Litigation* conveys valuable information to corporate lawyers. Law is a language as well as a system of rules, and the cases in this volume are each an important part of that language. Thus, this book provides both a useful guide for students of corporate law, as well as an important introduction to the corporate law canon for lawyers who work in other sub-specialties.

The book begins with Lynn Stout's interesting and provocative treatment of the famous but still controversial *fin de seicle* opinion of the Michigan Supreme Court in *Dodge v. Ford Motor Company* (1900) which articulates a clear, but perhaps unattainable role for law in the governance of U.S. corporations.

Next, in *Meinhard v. Salmon* (1928), Geoffrey Miller provides interesting new historical evidence of an agreement between the plaintiff and the defendant in this spectacular case which expounds prosaically on the nature of fiduciary duties in various forms of business organizations. Although the business in *Meinhard v. Salmon* was a joint venture, the analysis and doctrine espoused in that case are still highly relevant today for all sorts of business enterprises, including corporations, limited liability companies, and all forms of partnerships.

The legal doctrine and theory that still govern executive compensation find early expression in the iconic case *Rogers v. Hill* (1933) which Jim Cox and Eric Talley discuss in their timely and important chapter. From there, the authors proceed to the latest statement of the Delaware Supreme Court, which came in *In re Walt Disney Derivative Litigation* (2006). As Professors Cox and Tally point out, this opinion, which has clear roots in *Rogers v. Hill*, illustrate not only how difficult it is for corporate law to insert itself in the executive compensation wars, but also how the newly emergent conception of the fiduciary duty of good faith has entered into the analysis in recent years.

No issues in corporate law are more controversial than the issues of shareholder voting and the role of shareholder activists in the governance of the U.S. public company. Jill Fisch ably tackles these issues in her important chapter on *SEC v. Transamerica Corporation* (1947). Despite the fact that this is a decision by a federal court, interpreting proxy rules adopted by a federal administrative agency, the United States Securities and Exchange Commission, pursuant to Congress's authorization in the Securities Exchange Act of 1933, Transamerica still can lay a claim to being a building block of U.S. corporate law. This case clearly is a harbinger for the future as the federal government. For some time now, culminating in the passage of the Sarbanes-Oxley Act of 2002, both the SEC and Congress have steadily been usurping the states' traditional role as the primary source of law concerning the internal affairs and governance of U.S. corporations.

During the 1970s, corporate law jurisprudence continued to struggle mightily with the myriad issues of fairness and fiduciary duty that emerge in the context of the relationship between majority and minority shareholders. Often, but not always, this relationship presents itself in the context of the closely-held corporation. Besides the closely-held corporation context, we also observe majority investors interacting with minority investors in the context of parent corporations who have controlling interests in subsidiaries where that controlling interest represents something less than 100% ownership in the subsidiary. It is in this context that Robert Thompson explores the obligations of a majority shareholder to minority investors in *Sinclair Oil v. Levien* (1971), where the controlling majority shareholder was a multinational oil company, the subsidiary corporation, Sinven, did oil exploration and drilling in Venezuala, and its minority shares traded on the American Stock Exchange, which is where the plaintiff, Francis Levin, acquired his block of shares.

As Professor Thompson observes, the case involves analysis of three actions by the majority shareholder, Sinclair. The plaintiffs alleged that Sinclair was paying excessive dividends, excluding them from business opportunities being pursued by the parent outside of Venezuela and causing one of its wholly owned subsidiaries, Sinclair International to harm Sinven by failing to pay for oil acquired from Sinven in a timely manner and by opportunistically failing to purchase oil from Sinven as required by a prior agreement between Sinven and Sinclair International whenever oil prices declined to a point at which it was not advantageous for Sinclair International to abide by the contract.

This case provides the decision rule in corporate law for determining when the deferential business judgment rule will apply to dealings between majority and minority shareholders and when the non-deferential intrinsic fairness standard will apply. The court establishes a deceptively simple rule. Where the majority shareholder receives a benefit that comes to the "exclusion and detriment" of the minority shareholder, the tough intrinsic fairness standard will apply. But where the majority shareholder and the minority share the benefits of a particular corporate action such that the minority has not been excluded or harmed by the action, the deferential business judgment rule will apply, and the directors will be presumed to have "acted on an informed basis, in good faith and in the honest belief that the action taken was in the best interests of the company." *Sinclair Oil Corp. v. Levien*, 280 A.2d 717, 720 (Del. 1971). While the case presents a clear and succinct description of a legal principle, the decision ultimately is disappointing because the decision does not carefully apply the legal test it develops to the facts of the case before it. In particular, while the decision seems clearly correct, it would provide greater clarity if the court had clearly explained why Sinclair's exploration activities outside of Venezuela did not provide the parent with a benefit that was to the exclusion and detriment of the plaintiff minority shareholders who asserted that these opportunities should have been shared with them.

In the second case in this book that deals with fiduciary duties to minority shareholders, Professor Douglas Moll addresses a case by the Massachusetts Supreme Court, *Donahue v. Rodd Electrotype* (1975), which deals with fiduciary duties to minority shareholders in a closely held corporation in the context of a decision by the corporation to repurchase the shares of a family-member of the majority faction, while declining to repurchase the shares of the closely-held corporation's minority shareholder. As Professor Moll ably demonstrates, as a result of *Donahue* and cases like it, in many jurisdictions, though not in Delaware, courts articulate a different and higher standard of conduct for majority shareholders in closely held corporations than is required of publicly held corporations.

Like *Sinclair Oil v. Levien*, Donahue is not without its analytical difficulties. In particular, it is not clear how effective the decision really is in protecting minority shareholders. The repurchase by the majority was designed with one goal in mind: cashing out a family member of the majority shareholder faction. While the decision cuts off the one avenue for playing favorites by funneling money to a particular shareholder, it by no means cuts off all of them. By this I mean that the *Donahue* decision applies in the specific context of a share repurchase, but there are other ways of funneling money out of the corporation to particular favored shareholders. Retirement schemes, consulting arrangements, and employment opportunities for some, but not all shareholders all are alternative mechanisms by which majority shareholders can receive advantages on a discriminatory basis. As the dissent in *Donahue* observes, it is far from clear the rule that is formulated to deal with the narrow facts of a close corporation's purchase of a controlling shareholder's stock cannot easily be made to apply more broadly "to all of operations of the corporation as they affect minority shareholders."

As Professor Moll ably shows, *Donahue v. Rodd Electrotype* cannot be read without also considering the very different approach to the treatment of minority shareholders in closely held corporations provided in Delaware as exemplified by *Nixon v. Blackwell* (1993). Unlike the Massachusetts Supreme Court, in *Nixon* the Delaware Supreme Court refused to create a broad and special common-law remedy for oppression of minority shareholders in close corporations for two reasons. First, minority shareholders in Delaware easily can protect themselves by entering into contractual arrangement, particularly buy-sell arrangements that protect them from abuse by majorities. In addition, in Delaware the legislature already has provided protection to minority shareholders in closely held corporations in that it has enacted in entire set of special statutory provisions that can be utilized by investors in close corporations if they so choose.

The final iconic case from the 1970s is *Kamin v. American Express* (1976), another case that deals with judicial protection of directors' decisions under the business judgment rule. There is some dispute about what the case stands for. Some think that the opinion still represents what the law is; others think that it represents what the law ought to be; still other commentators think that Kamin represents what the law once was, but (thankfully) no longer is. The case involves a decision by the board of directors of American Express to distribute to their shareholders, as a dividend, roughly two million shares of stock owned by American Express in a company called Donaldson, Lufken and Jenrette, Inc. The shares were acquired by Amex for $29.9 million and had plummeted in value to approximately $4 million when they were sold. The plaintiffs argued that the directors decided to distribute the shares as an in-kind dividend, rather than simply to sell the shares, harmed American Express by depriving the Company of a large tax savings they would enjoy upon realization of the loss. The plaintiffs asserted that the decision was imprudent, and insinuated that the directors distributed the shares rather than sell them in order to make the company's books look better, cosmetically. The court was persuaded to side with the directors on the grounds that the objections raised by the plaintiffs to the proposed in-kind dividend payment were carefully considered by the American Express board and specifically rejected.

Undoubtedly, the case represents an exercise of poor judgment by the American Express directors, not to mention a rejection of modern financial theory, which teaches that actual financial results (as represented by the market value of the DLJ shares) is what matters in valuing Amex's investment, and that the cosmetic accounting treatment on DLJ's books is not relevant to markets or investors.

Most objective observers would probably conclude that what the directors of American Express did was misguided. However misguided the decision to distribute the stock rather than sell it might have been, the Amex directors said that they thought that they were acting in the Corporation's best interests, and the court believed them. Sometimes, it seems, courts take directors at their word when they say that they have carefully considered some alternative (as in *Kamin* and in the *Disney* cases discussed above), and sometimes they don't (as in *Smith v. Van Gorkom* discussed below). Because the court believed them, then even though the decision was misguided (even stupid), the business judgment rule protected the directors from liability because their decision was deliberated with sufficient care, and because the directors, at least arguably, believed that there was a reasonable justification for doing what they did and because a majority of the directors making the decision were not motivated by personal gain or other self interest.

The 1980s was the decade of corporate greed, and hostile takeovers and insider trading, both of which occurred with abundance during that turbulent decade, represents that greed. Steven Bainbridge ably chronicles the development of insider trading jurisprudence from its early beginnings in cases like *Cady, Roberts & Co.* (1961), which involved tipping by insiders on confidential information about a cut in a corporation's dividend payout and *SEC v. Texas Gulf Sulphur* (1968), which involved rampant buying of securities by its insiders on the eve of its announcement of a huge mineral strike. In a moment of high judicial activism, the Second Circuit in *Texas Gulf Sulphur* imposed a broad fairness requirement on market participants, announcing that there must be "equal access" to information before someone with privileged access to that information can trade. Three cases, *Chiarella v. United States* (1980), *Dirks v. SEC* (1983) and *United States v. O'Hagan* (1997), describe the legal rules concerning insider trading that have been developed by the U.S. Supreme Court. As Professor Bainbridge observes, the old equal access to information approach has been disbanded in favor of a much more sensible and rigorous approach based on fiduciary duties. We see, however, that the Court has not completely clarified the applicable legal standard as it has embraced the controversial misappropriation theory as a basis for imposing liability on securities traders where traders use misappropriated inside information, even where they do not trade with people to whom they owe any duties.

After several consecutive losses in the Supreme Court (including losses in both *Chiarella* and *Dirks*), the SEC successfully urged the Supreme Court in *O'Hagan* to adopt the misappropriation theory as a basis for imposing liability under the regulations governing insider trading. The misappropriation theory posits that a person who breaches a fiduciary duty to one group of shareholders by misappropriating confidential information that belongs to that group for personal gain, the defendants that misappropriation will satisfy the fraud requirement necessary to impose insider trading liability on the defendants even if they did not trade with that group. Professor Bainbridge ably pierces through the myriad doctrinal complexities in the iconic insider trading cases and shows that the basic choice among legal rules involves selecting either a rule that attempts to give all traders equal access to information or a rule that seeks to protect market participants' property rights in information. Professor Bainbridge is on very solid ground, in my view, in favoring the property rights approach to insider trading law as a normative matter. I would add that the federal courts and particularly the Supreme Court consistently have endorsed the property rights approach. The SEC however has, more or less consistently endorsed the equal access approach, which though it may not be analytically sound is at least consistent and internally coherent. Congress has never settled on a particularly consistent approach, and it is the mish-mash of these views that has resulted in a legal landscape littered with confused, inconsistent and doctrinally incoherent rules.

Yet another set of iconic cases from the turbulent 1980s deal with the controversial issue of shareholder derivative litigation, a subject addressed carefully and interestingly by Professor David Skeel who manages not only to describe the iconic cases, *Aronson v. Lewis* (1984) and *Zapata v. Maldonado* (1981), but also to explain the ancient origins and the evolution of the derivative lawsuit through time. Professor Skeel brilliantly explains the relationship between derivative lawsuits and securities law class actions, the political and social dimensions of the derivative lawsuit, and the agency problems that plague the use of the derivative lawsuits as a mechanism for controlling corporate deviance.

A derivative lawsuit is a lawsuit brought by a creditor or a shareholder to assert some right by or on behalf of the corporation. In essence, every derivative lawsuit involves two lawsuits in one. The first phase of the derivative lawsuit is a struggle by the outside investor against the company's board of directors with the prevailing party winning the right to commandeer the critical decision about whether proceeding with the lawsuit is in the best interests of the corporation. The second phase of the derivative lawsuit is the suit to redress whatever underlying wrong has allegedly harmed the corporation and motivated the litigation in the first place. The derivative lawsuit is shrouded in both complexity and controversy. Professor Skeel's chapter may well be the most succinct treatment of this important facet of corporate law, and is certainly the most important treatment of the derivative suit since the so-called Wood Report commissioned by the New York Chamber of Commerce (published in 1944 and thoroughly discussed by Professor Skeel.)

The next three chapters, by Vic Khanna, Logan Beirne & Jonathan Macey, and Fred McChesney, all deal with important aspects of the market for corporate control. Vic Khanna's chapter contains a brilliant treatment of the iconic case *Weinberger v. UOP* (1983). Weinberger presents the still salient issue of how majority shareholders should go about removing (cashing out) minority shareholders to that the majority can gain 100% ownership of a corporation that it already controls. The difficult problem with these transactions is that it often is in the best interests of both the majority and the minority shareholders for the corporation to "cash out" their minority interests. The sale of shares generally permits the minority shareholders to obtain a significant premium for the shares above what they could get in a non-control market transaction. At the same time, a buyout provides greater freedom of action for the majority, and also enables the majority to capture all, rather than only a fraction, of the gains associated with new investment in the company. Starting with *Weinberger*, Professor Khanna explains the difference between a cash-out merger and the alternative strategy for freezing out the minority interest, which is for the majority to effectuate a tender offers for most of the minority shares followed by a "clean up operation" in the firm of a short-form merger for any shares remaining in minority hands after the tender offer. Professor Khanna's chapter contains an interesting and important analysis of why these two strategies for ridding a company of its minority shareholders are treated so differently by courts under Delaware law, with cash-mergers being subjected to an entire fairness test, while tender offer/cash out mergers are treated far more deferentially under a business judgment standard.

Logan Beirne and I combined to present an analysis of three cases, *Unocal v. Mesa Petroleum* (1985), *Moran v. Household International* (1985) and *Revlon v. MacAndrews & Forbes Holdings, Inc.* (1985). These cases, taken together, often are referred to as the "takeover trilogy" because they contain virtually a complete statement of the Delaware law governing the conduct of boards of directors in the context of control contests.

While every case in this book is iconic, it must be admitted that some cases are even more iconic than others. *Smith v. Van Gorkom* (1988), also known as the "Trans Union case", can make a sold claim on being the most iconic case in this book. The subject of thousands of board room discussions, hundreds of law review articles, dozens of symposia by legal academics and practitioners of corporate law, and even a statute or two, this case truly shook the corporate law world to its very roots in holding that the directors of the Trans Union Corporation were grossly negligent in the way that they approved a cash-out merger proposal. Fred McChesney points out the deep flaws in the Court's reasoning, and goes on to show how Delaware law managed to correct this error in future statutes and decisions even without ever explicitly over-ruling it.

As Donald Langevoort shows in his chapter on *Basic v. Levinson* (1988), this case deserves treatment as an iconic case for two reasons. First, the decision provides an unusually rich and textured treatment of the meaning of the ubiquitous legal idea of "materiality" in the interesting context of when, if ever, preliminary merger discussions between a bidder and a target company's management are material. Second, *Basic v. Levinson* confronts the issue of whether modern financial theory, in the form of the Efficient Capital Markets Hypothesis, can be used as a tool for satisfying the reliance requirement of SEC Rule 10b-5. While this case deals with federal securities law rather than with state corporate law, the case fully merits inclusion in this volume, in my view, because of the profound implications of the decision on the quotidian conduct of corporate managers in dealing with merger proposals, and in dealing with inquiries from the financial press on a host of other issues.

The last iconic case in this book is by Hillary Sale, who writes about the evolving concept of the fiduciary duty of good faith under Delaware law, particularly in the context of directors' obligations of ongoing monitoring and oversight. Professor Sale's chapter features *In re Caremark International, Inc., Derivative Litigation* (1996), as well as the opinion of the Delaware Supreme Court in *Stone v. Ritter* (2006) which clarifies that monitoring and oversight are key components of the fiduciary duty of good faith which in turn is part of the fiduciary duty of loyalty.

Jonathan R. Macey

April, 2008

Summary of Contents

*

Table of Contents

_____

THE ICONIC CASES IN CORPORATE LAW

*

Chapter 1

WHY WE SHOULD STOP TEACHING
DODGE v. FORD

By
Lynn A. Stout*

A. INTRODUCTION

What is the purpose of a corporation? To many people the answer to this question seems obvious: corporations exist to make money for their shareholders. Maximizing shareholder wealth is the corporation's only true concern, its *raison d'etre*. Devoted corporate officers and directors should direct all their efforts toward this goal.

Some find this picture of the corporation as an engine for increasing shareholder wealth to be quite attractive. Nobel Prize-winning economist Milton Friedman famously praised this view of corporate purpose in his 1970 essay in the New York Times, *The Social Responsibility of Business Is to Increase Its Profits*.[1] To others, the idea of the corporation as a relentless profit-seeking machine seems less appealing. In 2004, Joel Bakan published *The Corporation: The Pathological Pursuit of Profit and Power,* a book accompanied by an award-winning film documentary of the same name. Bakan's thesis is that corporations are indeed dedicated to maximizing shareholder wealth, without regard to law, ethics, or the interests of society. This means, Bakan argues, corporations are dangerously psychopathic entities.

Whether viewed as cause for celebration or for concern, the idea that corporations exist only to make money for shareholders is rarely subject to challenge.[2] Much of the credit—or perhaps more accurately, the

* Paul Hastings Professor of Corporate and Securities Law and Principal Investigator for the UCLA–Sloan Research Program on Business Organizations, UCLA School of Law. Do not cite or quote without permission.

1. Milton Friedman, The Social Responsibility of Business Is To Increase Profits,

New York Times Sunday Magazine, September 13, 1970.

2. Although there is a tradition of scholarly debate on this point among legal academics, it has attracted little attention outside the pages of specialized journals. See Lynn A. Stout, Bad and Not–So–Bad Argu-

1

blame—for this state of affairs can be laid at the door of a single judicial opinion. That opinion is the 1919 Michigan Supreme Court decision in *Dodge v. Ford Motor Co.*[3]

B.   *DODGE v. FORD* ON CORPORATE PURPOSE

The facts underlying *Dodge v. Ford* are familiar to virtually every student who has taken a course in corporate law. Famed industrialist Henry Ford was the founder and majority shareholder of the Ford Motor Company. Brothers John and Horace Dodge were minority investors in the firm. The Dodge brothers brought a lawsuit against Ford claiming that he was using his control over the company to restrict dividend payouts, even though the company was enormously profitable and could afford to pay large dividends to its shareholders. Ford defended his decision to withhold dividends through the provocative strategy of arguing that he preferred to use the corporation's money to build cheaper, better cars and to pay better wages. The Michigan Supreme Court sided with the Dodge brothers and ordered the Ford Motor Company to pay its shareholders a special dividend.

In the process, the Michigan Supreme Court made an offhand remark that is regularly repeated in corporate law casebooks today:

> "There should be no confusion .... A business corporation is organized and carried on primarily for the profit of the stockholders. The powers of the directors are to be employed for that end. The discretion of the directors is to be exercised in the choice of means to attain that end, and does not extend to ... other purposes."[4]

As will be discussed in greater detail below, this statement was judicial *dicta*, quite unnecessary to reach the Court's desired result. Nevertheless, this quotation from *Dodge v. Ford* is almost invariably cited as evidence that corporate law requires corporations to have a "profit maximizing purpose" and that "managers and directors have a legal duty to put shareholders' interests above all others and no legal authority to serve any other interests."[5] Indeed, *Dodge v. Ford* is routinely employed as the *only* legal authority cited for this proposition.[6]

But what if the opinion in *Dodge v. Ford* is incorrect? What if the Michigan Supreme Court's statement of corporate purpose is a misinterpretation of American corporate doctrine? Put bluntly, what if *Dodge v. Ford* is bad law?

This Essay argues that *Dodge v. Ford* is indeed bad law, at least when cited for the proposition that the corporate purpose is, or should

ments for Shareholder Primacy, 75 S. Cal. L. Rev. 1189, at 1189–90 (2002).

3. Dodge v. Ford Motor Co., 170 N.W. 668 (Mich. 1919).

4. Id. at 684.

5. Robert C. Clark, Corporate Law (1986) at 679; Joel Bakan, The Corporation:

The Pathological Pursuit of Profit and Power (2004), at 36.

6. See, e.g. id.; Lawrence E. Mitchell, A Theoretical and Practical Framework for Enforcing Corporate Constituency Statutes, 70 Tex. L. Rev. 579, at 601 (1992); Marjorie Kelly, The Divine Right of Capital (2001), at 52–53.

be, maximizing shareholder wealth. *Dodge v. Ford* is a mistake, a judicial "sport," a doctrinal oddity largely irrelevant to corporate law and corporate practice. What's more, courts and legislatures alike *treat* it as irrelevant. In the past 30 years the Delaware courts have cited *Dodge v. Ford* as authority in only one unpublished case—and then not on the subject of corporate purpose, but on another legal question entirely.

Only laypersons and (more disturbingly) many law professors continue to rely on *Dodge v. Ford*. This Essay argues we should mend our collective ways. Legal instructors and scholars should stop teaching and citing *Dodge v. Ford*. At least, they should stop teaching and citing *Dodge v. Ford* as anything more than an example of how courts can go seriously astray.

C. *DODGE v. FORD* AS WEAK PRECEDENT ON CORPORATE PURPOSE

Let us begin with some of the more obvious reasons why legal experts should hesitate before placing much weight on *Dodge v. Ford*. First, the case is approaching its 100th anniversary. Henry Ford, John Dodge, and Horace Dodge have long since died and turned to dust, along with the members of the Michigan Supreme Court who heard their dispute. In fact, *Dodge v. Ford* is the oldest corporate law case selected as an object for study in this volume. This observation should provoke concern, for case law is a bit like wine: a certain amount of aging is desirable, but after too many years it goes bad, and it is a rare vintage that is still drinkable after a century. Why rely on a case that is nearly 100 years old if there is more modern authority available?

A second odd feature of *Dodge v. Ford* is the court that decided it. The state of Delaware—not Michigan—is far and away the most respected and influential source of corporate case law, a fact that reflects both Delaware's status as the preferred state of incorporation for the nation's largest public companies and the widely-recognized expertise of the judges on the Delaware Supreme Court and in the Delaware Chancery. California and New York have produced their share of influential corporate law cases, as has Massachusetts with regard to close corporations. Michigan, however, is a distant also-ran in the race between and among the states for influence in corporate law.[7]

Finally, a third limiting aspect of *Dodge v. Ford* as a source of legal authority on the question of corporate purpose is the important fact, noted earlier, that the Michigan Supreme Court's statements on the topic were *dicta*. The actual holding in the case—that Henry Ford had breached his fiduciary duty to the Dodge brothers and the company should pay a special dividend—was justified on entirely different and far narrower legal grounds. Those grounds were that Henry Ford, as a

---

7. Guhan Subramanian, The Influence of Antitakeover Statutes on Incorporation Choice: Evidence on the "Race" Debate and Antitakeover Overreaching, 150 U. Pa. L. Rev. 1795 (2002).

controlling shareholder, had breached his fiduciary duty of good faith to his minority investors.[8]

As the majority shareholder in the Ford Motor Company, Henry Ford stood to reap a much greater economic benefit from any dividends the company paid than John and Horace Dodge did. Ford had other economic interests, however, directly at odds with the Dodge brothers. First, because the Dodge brothers wished to set up their own car company to compete with Ford (as they eventually did), Ford wanted to deprive them of liquid funds for investment.[9] Second, Ford wanted to buy out the Dodge brothers' interest in the Ford Motor Company (as he eventually did) at the lowest price possible. Withholding dividends from the Dodge brothers was an excellent, if underhanded, strategy for accomplishing both objectives.[10]

Thus *Dodge v. Ford* is best viewed as a case that deals not with directors' duties to maximize shareholder wealth, but with controlling shareholders' duties not to oppress minority shareholders. The one Delaware opinion that has cited *Dodge v. Ford* in the last 30 years, *Blackwell v. Nixon*,[11] cites it for just this proposition.

Finally, not only is the Michigan Supreme Court's statement on corporate purpose in *Dodge v. Ford dicta*, it is much more mealy-mouthed *dicta* than is generally appreciated. As Professor Einer Elhauge has emphasized, the Michigan Supreme Court described profit-seeking in *Dodge v. Ford* as the "primary"—but not the exclusive—corporate goal. Indeed, elsewhere in the opinion the Court noted that corporate directors retain "implied powers to carry on with humanitarian motives such charitable works as are incidental to the main business of the corporation."[12]

D. THE LACK OF AUTHORITY FOR *DODGE v. FORD*'S POSITIVE VISION OF CORPORATE PURPOSE

Dodge v. Ford accordingly suffers from several deficiencies as a source of legal precedent on the question of corporate purpose. The case is old; it hails from a state court that plays only a marginal role in the corporate law arena; and it involves a controlling shareholder/minority shareholder conflict that independently justifies the holding in the case while rendering the opinion's discourse on corporate purpose judicial *dicta*. Nevertheless, one might still defend the continued teaching and

---

8. Einer Elhauge, Sacrificing Corporate Profits in the Public Interest, 80 N.Y.U. L. Rev. 733 (2005); Nathan Oman, Corporations and Autonomy Theories of Contract: A Critique of the New *Lex Mercatoria*, 83 Denver U. L. Rev. 101 (2005); D. Gordon Smith, The Shareholder Primacy Norm, 23 J. Corp. L. 277 (1998).

9. Nathan Oman, Corporations and Autonomy Theories of Contract: A Critique of

the New *Lex Mercatoria*, 83 Denver U. L. Rev. 101, at 135 (2005).

10. Einer Elhauge, Sacrificing Corporate Profits in the Public Interest, 80 N.Y.U. L. Rev. 733, at 774 (2005).

11. Blackwell v. Nixon, 1991 WL 194725 (Del. Ch. September 26, 1991).

12. Einer Elhauge, Sacrificing Corporate Profits in the Public Interest, 80 N.Y.U. L. Rev. 733, at 773 (2005).

citing of *Dodge v. Ford* if the discussion of corporate purpose found in the case was an elegant early statement of a modern legal principle.

Here we run into a second problem: shareholder wealth maximization is *not* a modern legal principle. To understand this point, it is important not to rely on the unsupported assertions of journalists, reformers, and even the occasional law professor as sources of legal authority, but instead to look at the actual provisions of corporate law. "Corporate law" can itself be broken down into three rough categories: (1) "internal" corporate law (the requirements set out in individual corporations' charters and by-laws); (2) state corporate codes, and (3) corporate case law.

Let us first examine internal corporate law, especially the statements of corporate purpose typically found in corporate charters (also called "articles of incorporation"). Most state codes permit, or even require, incorporators to include a statement in the corporate charter that defines and limits the purpose for which the corporation is being formed. If the corporation's founders so desire, they can easily include in the corporate charter a recitation of the *Dodge v. Ford* view that the corporation in question "is organized and carried on primarily for the profit of the stockholders." Real corporate charters virtually never contain this sort of language. Instead, the typical corporate charter defines the corporate purpose as anything "lawful."[13]

What about state corporation codes? Do they perhaps limit the corporate purpose to shareholder wealth maximization? To employ the common saying, the answer is "not just no but hell no." A large majority of state codes contain so-called other-constituency provisions that explicitly authorize corporate boards to consider the interests of not just shareholders, but also employees, customers, creditors, and the community, in making business decisions.[14] The Delaware corporate code does not have an explicit other-constituency provision, but it also does not define the corporate purpose as shareholder wealth maximization. Rather, Section 101 of the General Corporation Law of Delaware simply provides that corporations can be formed "to conduct or promote any lawful business or purposes."

Which leaves case law as the last remaining hope of a *Dodge v. Ford* supporter who wants to argue that, as a positive matter, modern legal authority requires corporate directors to maximize shareholder wealth. And on first inspection, corporate case law does provide at least a little hope. Contemporary judges do not cite *Dodge v. Ford*, but some modern cases contain *dicta* that echo its sentiments. Consider, for example, the Delaware Chancery's statement in the 1986 case of *Katz v. Oak Indus-*

13. Jeffrey D. Bauman, Alan R. Palmiter, and Frank Partnoy, Corporations: Law and Policy (6th ed. 2007) at 171.

14. Lawrence E. Mitchell, A Theoretical and Practical Framework for Enforcing Corporate Constituency Statutes, 70 Tex. L. Rev. 579 (1992); Guhan Subramanian, The Influence of Antitakeover Statutes on Incorporation Choice: Evidence on the "Race" Debate and Antitakeover Overreaching, 150 U. Pa. L. Rev. 1795 (2002).

tries[15] that "it is the obligation for directors to attempt within the law to maximize the long-run interests of the corporation's stockholders."[16]

This statement is about as *Dodge v. Ford*-like a description of corporate purpose as one can hope to find in contemporary case law. Many other modern cases, however, contain contrary *dicta* indicating that directors owe duties beyond those owed to shareholders. For example, just a year before the Delaware Chancery decided *Katz*, the Delaware Supreme Court handed down its famed decision in *Unocal Corp. v. Mesa Petroleum Co.*[17] In *Unocal*, the Court opined that the corporate board had "a fundamental duty and obligation to protect the corporate enterprise, which includes stockholders"—a formulation that clearly implies the two are not identical—and then went on to state that in evaluating the interests of "the corporate enterprise" directors could consider "the impact on 'constituencies' other than shareholders (i.e., creditors, customers, employees, and perhaps even the community generally.)"[18]

As important, even shareholder-oriented *dicta* on corporate purpose of the *Katz* sort does not actually impose any legal obligation on directors to maximize shareholder wealth. The key to understanding this is the qualifying phrases "attempt" and "long-run." As a number of corporate scholars have pointed out, courts regularly allow corporate directors to make business decisions that harm shareholders in order to benefit other corporate constituencies.[19] In the rare event such a decision is challenged on the grounds the directors failed to look after shareholder interests, courts shield directors from liability under the "business judgment rule" so long as any plausible connection can be made between the directors' decision and some possible future benefit, however intangible and unlikely, to shareholders. If the directors lack the imagination to offer such a "long-run" rationalization for their decision, courts will invent one.

A classic example of this judicial eagerness to protect directors from the claim that they failed to maximize shareholder wealth can be found in the oft-cited case of *Shlensky v. Wrigley*.[20] In *Shlensky*, minority investors sued the directors of the corporation that owned the Chicago Cubs for refusing to install lights that would allow night baseball games to be played at Wrigley Field. The minority claimed that offering night games would make the Cubs more profitable. The corporation's directors refused to hold night games, not because they disagreed with this economic assessment, but because they believed night games would harm the quality of life of residents in the neighborhoods surrounding

---

15. Katz v. Oak Industries, Inc., 508 A.2d 873, 879 (Del. Ch. 1986).

16. Quoted in Stephen M. Bainbridge, Director Primacy: The Means and Ends of Corporate Governance, 97 N.W. L. Rev. 547, at 575 (2003).

17. Unocal Corp. v. Mesa Petroleum Co., 493 A.2d 946 (Del. 1985).

18. Id. at 955.

19. See e.g. Margaret M. Blair & Lynn A. Stout, A Team Production Theory of Corporate Law, 85 Va. L. Rev. 247, at 303

(1999); Robert C. Clark, Corporate Law (1986) at 681–84; Einer Elhauge, Sacrificing Corporate Profits in the Public Interest, 80 N.Y.U. L. Rev. 733, at 763–776 (2005); Lisa M. Fairfax, Doing Well While Doing Good: Reassessing the Scope of Directors' Fiduciary Obligations in For–Profit Corporations with Non–Shareholder Beneficiaries, 59 Wash. & Lee L. Rev. 409, at 437–439 (2002).

20. Shlensky v. Wrigley, 237 N.E.2d 776 (Ill. App. Ct. 1968).

Wrigley Field. The court upheld the directors' decision, reasoning—*as the directors themselves had not*—that a decline in the quality of life in the local neighborhoods might in the long run hurt property values around Wrigley Field, harming shareholders' economic interests.

Shlensky illustrates how judges routinely refuse to impose any legal obligation on corporate directors to maximize shareholder wealth. Although *dicta* in some cases suggests directors ought to attempt this (in the "long run," of course), *dicta* in other cases takes a broader view of corporate purpose, and courts never actually sanction directors for failing to maximize shareholder wealth.

There is only one exception in case law to this rule: the 1985 Delaware Supreme Court decision in *Revlon, Inc. v. MacAndrews & Forbes Holdings, Inc.*[21] *Revlon* is a puzzling decision, not least because the Delaware Supreme Court decided the case the same year it handed down its apparently contradictory decision in *Unocal*. In *Revlon*, the board of a public company had decided to take the firm "private" by selling all its shares to a controlling shareholder. In choosing between potential bidders, the board considered, along with shareholders' interests, the interests of certain noteholders in the firm. This was a mistake, the Delaware Supreme Court announced—where the company was being "broken up" and shareholders were being forced to sell their interests in the firm to a private buyer, the board had a duty to maximize shareholder wealth by getting the highest possible price for the shares.

Revlon appears, on first inspection, to affirm the notion that maximizing shareholder wealth is the corporation's proper purpose. In the years following the *Revlon* decision, however, the Delaware Court has systematically cut back on the situations in which *Revlon* supposedly applies, to the point where any board that wants to avoid being subject to *Revlon* duties now can easily arrange this. The case has become nearly a dead letter. Accordingly, while the Delaware Supreme Court has not explicitly repudiated *Revlon* (at least not yet), for practical purposes the case is largely irrelevant to modern corporate law and practice.[22]

In sum, whether gauged by corporate charters, state corporation codes, or corporate case law, the notion that corporate law as a positive matter "requires" companies to maximize shareholder wealth turns out to be spurious. The offhand remarks on corporate purpose offered by the Michigan Supreme court in *Dodge v. Ford* lack any foundation in actual corporate law.

E. THE LACK OF AUTHORITY FOR *DODGE v. FORD*'S NORMATIVE VISION OF CORPORATE PURPOSE

Dodge v. Ford usually plays the role of Exhibit No. 1 for commentators seeking to argue that American law imposes on corporate directors

21. Revlon, Inc. v. MacAndrews & Forbes Holdings, Inc., 506 A.2d 173 (Del. 1985).

22. Lynn A. Stout, Bad and Not–So–Bad Arguments for Shareholder Primacy, 75 S. Cal. L. Rev. 1189, at 1204 (2002).

the legal obligation to maximize profits for shareholders.[23] It is important to recognize, however, that many experts teach and cite *Dodge v. Ford* in a more subtle, and less obviously erroneous, fashion. To these experts, *Dodge v. Ford* is not evidence that corporate law actually requires directors to maximize shareholder wealth. Rather, it is evidence that many observers believe corporate directors *ought* to maximize shareholder wealth. In other words, many legal instructors teach *Dodge v. Ford* not as a positive description of what corporate law actually is, but as a normative discourse on what many believe the proper purpose of a well-functioning corporation should be.

This is a far more defensible position. Nevertheless, the switch from using *Dodge v. Ford* as a source of positive legal authority to using *Dodge v. Ford* as a source of normative guidance carries its own hazards. Most obviously, it begs the fundamental question of what the proper purpose of the corporation should, in fact, be.

It is not enough to state that *Dodge v. Ford* represents an important perspective on corporate purpose because many people believe it represents an important perspective on corporate purpose. This argument borders on tautology (*"Dodge v. Ford* is influential because people think *Dodge v. Ford* is influential."*) Perhaps many people do share the Michigan's Supreme Court's view that it is desirable for corporations to pursue only profits for shareholders. But *why* do they believe this is desirable?

At least until fairly recently, many corporate experts found the answer to this question in economic theory. Not too long ago, it was conventional economic wisdom that the shareholders in a corporation were the sole residual claimants in the firm, meaning shareholders were entitled to all the "residual" profits left over after the firm had met its fixed contractual obligations to employees, customers, and creditors. This assumption suggested that corporations were run best when they were run for shareholders' benefit alone, because if other corporate stakeholders' interests were fixed by their contracts, maximizing the shareholders' residual meant maximizing the total social value of the firm.[24]

Time has been unkind to this perspective. Advances in economic thinking have made clear that shareholders generally are not—and probably cannot be—sole residual claimants in firms. For example, modern options theory teaches that business risk that increases the expected value of the equity interest in a corporation must simultaneously reduce the supposedly "fixed" value of creditors' interests.[25] Another branch of the economic literature focuses on the contracting problems

23. Jeffrey D. Bauman, Alan R. Palmiter, and Frank Partnoy, Corporations: Law and Policy (6th ed. 2007) at 87.

24. Lynn A. Stout, Bad and Not-So-Bad Arguments for Shareholder Primacy, 75 S. Cal. L. Rev. 1189 at 1192–95 (2002).

25. Margaret M. Blair & Lynn A. Stout, Director Accountability and the Mediating Role of the Corporate Board, 19 Wash. U. L. Q. 403, at 411–14 (2001); Thomas A. Smith, The Efficient Norm for Corporate Law: A Neotraditional Interpretation of Fiduciary Duty, 98 Mich. L. Rev. 214 (1999).

that surround specific investment in "team production," and suggests
how a legal rule requiring corporate directors to maximize shareholder
wealth ex post might well have the perverse effect of reducing shareholder wealth over time by discouraging nonshareholder groups from making
specific investments in corporations ex ante.[26] Yet a third economic
concept that undermines the wisdom of shareholder wealth maximization is the idea of externalities: when the pursuit of shareholder profits
imposes greater costs on third parties (customers, employees, the environment) that are not fully constrained by law, shareholder wealth
maximization becomes, at least from a social perspective, undesirable.[27]

Finally, it is becoming increasingly well-understood that when a
firm has more than one shareholder, the very idea of "shareholder
wealth" becomes incoherent.[28] Different shareholders have different time
frames, different tax concerns, different attitudes toward firm-level risk
due to different levels of diversification, different interests in other
investments that might be affected by corporate activities, and different
views about the extent to which they are willing to sacrifice corporate
profits to promote broader social interests, like a clean environment or
good wages for workers. These and other schisms ensure that there is no
single, uniform measure of shareholder "wealth" to be "maximized."

Most contemporary experts accordingly understand that economic
theory, alone, does not permit us to safely assume that corporations are
run best when they are run according to the principle of shareholder
wealth maximization. Not only is *Dodge v. Ford* bad law from a positive
perspective, it is bad law from a normative perspective as well. Which
gives rise to the question: what explains *Dodge v. Ford*'s enduring
popularity?

F. ON THE PUZZLING SURVIVAL OF *DODGE v. FORD*

Simple inertia may to some extent provide an answer. Corporate law
casebooks have included excerpts from *Dodge v. Ford* for generations,
and it would take a certain degree of boldness to depart from the
tradition. But there is more going on here than inertia. Casebooks
change, but *Dodge v. Ford* remains. This suggests *Dodge v. Ford* has
achieved a privileged position in the legal cannon not because it accurately captures the law (as we seen, it does not) or because it provides
good normative guidance (again, we have seen it does not) but *because it
serves law professors' needs.*

In particular, *Dodge v. Ford* serves professors' pressing need for a
simple answer to the question "What do corporations do?" Their desire

26. Margaret M. Blair & Lynn A. Stout,
A Team Production Theory of Corporate
Law, 85 Va. L. Rev. 247 (1999); Margaret
M. Blair & Lynn A. Stout, Specific Invest-
ment and Corporate Law, 7 Euro. Bus. Org.
L. Rev. 473 (2006).

27. Einer Elhauge, Sacrificing Corporate Profits in the Public Interest, 80
N.Y.U. L. Rev. 733, at 738–756 (2005).

28. Iman Anabtawi, Some Skepticism
About Increasing Shareholder Power, 53
UCLA L. Rev. 561 (2006).

for a simple answer to this question can be analogized to that of a parent confronted by a young son or daughter who innocently asks "Where do babies come from?" The true answer to where babies come from is difficult and complex, and can lead to further questions about details of the process that may lie beyond the parent's knowledge and comfort level. It is easy to understand why, faced with this situation, many parents squirm uncomfortably and default to charming fables of cabbages and storks. Similarly, professors are regularly confronted by eager law students who innocently ask, "What do corporations do?" It is easy to understand why professors are tempted to default to *Dodge v. Ford* and its charming and easily-understood fable of shareholder wealth maximization.

After all, the true answer to the question "What do corporations do?" is even more difficult, complex, and uncertain than the true answer to the question "Where do babies come from?" From a positive perspective, public corporations are extraordinarily intricate institutions that pursue complex, large-scale projects over periods of years or even decades. They have several directors, dozens of executives, hundreds or thousands of employees, thousands or hundreds of thousands of shareholders, and possibly millions of customers. Corporations resemble political nation-states with multiple constituencies that have different and conflicting interests, responsibilities, obligations and powers. Indeed, the very largest corporations—think WalMart, Exxon–Mobil, or Microsoft—have greater economic power than many nation-states do. These are not institutions whose behavior can be accurately captured in a sound bite.

The problem of explaining proper corporate purpose is just as off-putting from a normative perspective. Even the apparently-simple directive "maximize shareholder wealth" becomes far less simple, and perhaps incoherent, in a public firm with many shareholders with different investment time horizons, tax concerns, outside investments, levels of diversification, and attitudes toward corporate social responsibility. The normative question "what ought corporations to do" becomes even more daunting when the answer involves discussions of avoiding externalities, maximizing the value of returns to multiple residual claimants, and encouraging specific investment in team production.

Faced with this reality, it is entirely understandable why a legal instructor or legal scholar called upon to discuss the question of corporate purpose might be tempted to teach or cite *Dodge v. Ford* in answer. Despite its infirmities, *Dodge v. Ford* at least offers an answer to the question of corporate purpose that is simple, easy to understand, and capable of being communicated in less than ten minutes or ten pages. It is this simplicity that has allowed *Dodge v. Ford* to survive over the decades and to keep a place, however undeserved, in the canon of corporate law.

G. CONCLUSION

But simplicity is not always a virtue. In particular, simplicity is not a virtue when it leads to misunderstanding and mistake.

It might be perfectly fine for a Midwestern farmer to believe the world is flat. Although this simple model of the world is inaccurate, it is easy to understand and apply and its inaccuracy is of no consequence for someone who travels only rarely and short distances. But a simple model of a flat world might prove catastrophically inaccurate for a ship captain attempting to navigate a voyage from one continent to another. For the ship captain, a more-complicated model that acknowledges the globe's spherical shape is essential to avoid disaster.

When it comes to corporations, lawyers are ship captains. Corporations are purely legal creatures, without flesh, blood, or bone. Their existence and their behavior is determined by a web of legal rules found in corporate charters and by-laws, in state corporate case law and statutes, in private contracts, and in a host of federal and state regulations. For lawyers, an accurate and detailed understanding of the corporate entity and its purpose is just as essential to success as an accurate understanding of geography and navigation is to a ship captain, or an accurate and detailed understanding of brain anatomy and function is to a neurosurgeon.

This is why lawyers, including especially law professors, should resist the siren song of *Dodge v. Ford*. We are not in the business of imparting fables, however charming. We are in the business of instructing clients and students in the realities of the corporate form. Corporations seek profits for shareholders, but they seek others things as well, including specific investment, stakeholder benefits, and their own continued existence. Teaching *Dodge v. Ford* as anything but an example of judicial mistake obstructs understanding of this reality.

Chapter 2

A GLIMPSE OF SOCIETY VIA A CASE AND CARDOZO: *MEINHARD v. SALMON*

By
*Geoffrey P. Miller**

A. INTRODUCTION

In New York City, a year or two after the turn of the last century, two ambitious men met to discuss a matter of mutual interest. The subject was commerce. One wanted to lease and develop a piece of commercial real estate but lacked the financing to do so; the other had funds to invest but lacked knowledge of the real estate market. The deal, once struck, turned out well for both: within twenty years the property in question had become one of the most valuable parcels of real estate in the world, and in the interim had generated spectacular profits. But too much success, perhaps more than too little, can lead to disputes and litigation. Upon the expiration of the lease the parties fought over their continuing rights. Eventually their conflict reached the highest court of the State of New York, generating one of the enduring cases in the history of American law. This chapter tells the story of that case, *Meinhard v. Salmon*, and in the process explores changing patterns of land use and social status in America's premier city during the last part of the nineteenth and first part of the twentieth century.

B. BACKGROUND

Prior to 1845 the northwest corner of 42nd Street and Fifth Avenue belonged to the City of New York.[1] It appears to have been

* Stuyvesant P. Comfort Professor of Law, New York University. For excellent research assistance I thank my student David J. Carey and Jeanne Rehberg of the NYU Law Library. Sarah Gordon, Daniel Hulseboch, Stephanie Hunter McMahon, Jonathan Macey, William Nelson, Larry Ribstein and Jay Weiser provided helpful comments as this chapter was in preparation, as did participants at the NYU Law School Legal History Colloquium.

1. Abstract of Title, 3 West 42nd Street.

undeveloped. In that year the city sold the property to Garrit Storm, a well-heeled New York merchant,[2] who used the site for a home, stable, and orchard.[3] Storm also appears to have allowed part of the property to be used for a tavern.[4] Storm's holdings passed by will to Glovinia Rossell Hoffman and Louisa Matilda Livingston as tenants in common.[5] In 1852 the heirs partitioned their inheritance, with Glovinia and her husband Samuel Ver Plank Hoffman deeding the fee interest in the northwest corner of 42nd Street to Louisa Matilda Livingston.[6]

Louisa and her husband Robert Livingston were members of New York's elite society.[7] Robert's ancestors included Robert Livingston (1654–1728), the first lord of Livingston Manor, a 160,000 acre tract in Dutchess and Columbia Counties,[8] and Robert R. Livingston (1746–1813),[9] Chancellor of New York State, Ambassador to France, negotiator of the Louisiana Purchase, and holder (with Robert Fulton) of the purported exclusive rights to steam navigation in New York adjudicated in *Gibbons v. Ogden*.[10] Louisa's ancestors included Morgan Lewis (1754–1844), Attorney General, Chief Justice, and Governor of the State of New York.[11]

Sometime between 1852 and 1862 the Livingstons constructed a four-story townhouse on the property.[12] The neighborhood enjoyed no special distinction at that time. Many in old New York society still lived near Washington Square at the foot of Fifth Avenue, while the newly rich lived in the neighborhood anchored by the Astor compound on 34th Street and Fifth.[13] But high-class housing was moving north.[14] The

---

2. Abstract of Title, 3 West 42nd Street (deed to Storm). Storm was one of 130 New Yorkers who purchased $10,000 or more in government bonds during the 1813 subscription to fund the War of 1812. See When New York Aided War Loans of 1812, New York Times, June 10, 1917.

3. See On Ave. of the Americas, the Lull is Ending, New York Times, May 4, 1980.

4. See Arthur Bartlett Maurice, Fifth Avenue (1918) (reporting that the lot had once been used as a tavern).

5. See Abstract of Title, 3 West 42nd Street; Florence Van Rensselaer, The Livingston Family in America and Its Scottish Origins 336 (1949); William B. Aitken, Distinguished Families in America, Descended from Wilhelmus Beekman and Jan Thomasse Van Dyke 184 (1949).

6. Abstract of Title, 3 West 42nd Street.

7. For background on the Livingston clan, see Cynthia A. Kierner, Traders and Gentlefolk: The Livingstons of New York, 1675–1790 (1992); David Maldwyn Ellis, Landlords and Farmers in the Hudson–Mohawk Region, 1790–1850 (1946); Sung Bok Kim, Landlord and Tenant in Colonial New York: Manorial Society, 1664–1775 (1978);

Claire Brandt, An American Aristocracy: The Livingstons (1986).

8. See Robert Livingston, 11 Dictionary of American Biography 318 (1933); George Dangerfield, Chancellor Robert R. Livingston of New York 1746–1813 (1960).

9. See Robert R. Livingston, see 11 Dictionary of American Biography 320–25 (1933); James Brown Scott, Robert R. Livingston, 1 Great American Lawyers 435–472 (William Draper Lewis, ed. 1907).

10. 22 U.S. (9 Wheat.) 1 (1824).

11. See II History of the Bench and Bar of New York 171–73 (David McAdam et al. eds. 1897).

12. See Edwin L. Dunbaugh and William duBarry Thomas, William H. Webb, Shipbuilder 129 (1989).

13. See Robert A.M. Stern, Gregory Gilmartin and John Montague Massengale, Metropolitan Architecture and Urbanism 1890–1915 307 (1983); Tom Shachtman, Skyscraper Dreams 41 (1991).

14. Edwin G. Burrows & Mike Wallace, Gotham: A History of New York City to 1898 715–16 (1999); Tom Shachtman, Skyscraper Dreams 41 (1991).

opening of a cleared Central Park in the 1860s exerted an attractive force, while virtually insatiable demands for office and retail space were displacing houses further south.[15] During the late Nineteenth Century several prominent figures built homes on or near the corner of 42nd Street and Fifth Avenue, including Levi Morton, Vice President of the United States under William Henry Harrison, Boss Tweed of Tammany Hall fame, and railroad financier Russell Sage.[16]

In October 1862 Robert and Louisa Livingston leased their property to William H. Webb (1816–1899),[17] a prominent shipbuilder and naval architect.[18] Webb had amassed a fortune building luxury yachts and packet ships in the 1840s,[19] clipper ships in the 1850s,[20] and warships in the 1860s.[21] Webb also established passenger and mail lines to the Pacific Coast and from San Francisco to Australia and New Zealand.[22] He apparently acquired the Livingston property as a home for himself and his wife, or possibly as a residence for his son.[23] However, no member of the Webb family ever lived there.[24]

The New York shipbuilding industry collapsed after the end of the Civil War.[25] One of Webb's last major commissions was the 5,000 ton ram *Dunderburg*, the largest ironclad yet built[26] and, in the view of

15. See Robert A.M. Stern, Gregory Gilmartin and John Montague Massengale, Metropolitan Architecture and Urbanism 1890–1915 307–08 (1983).

16. Arthur Bartlett Maurice, Fifth Avenue (1918); Another Bomb for Russell Sage, New York Times, December 30, 1893.

17. See Edwin L. Dunbaugh and William duBarry Thomas, William H. Webb, Shipbuilder (1989); William H. Webb Dead, New York Times, October 31, 1899. Webb's father was also a New York shipbuilder with a connection with the Livingston family, having built the steamboat *Chancellor Livingston* for Robert Fulton. William H. Webb, New York Times, July 11, 1897.

18. William Henry Webb, New York Times, July 11, 1897; Edwin L. Dunbaugh and William duBarry Thomas, William H. Webb, Shipbuilder (1989).

19. See The New–York Yacht Club; Dinner to Commodore Stevens, New York Times, October 3, 1851.

20. See The Days of the Clipper: Fast Ships that Engaged in the California Trade, New York Times, September 7, 1890.

21. The frigate *Grand Admiral*, which Webb built for the Russian Navy in 1858, was then the fastest steam frigate ever built. Fred Irving Dayton, Steamboat Days (1925). In the 1860s Webb built two ironclad frigates for the Italian Navy, the *Re D'italia* and the *Portogallo*. See The Italian Iron–Clad Re D'italia: The Vessel Ashore At Long Branch, New York Times, December 30, 1863; Soiree on Board the Italian Frigate Re d'Italia, New York Times, December 3, 1863; The Italian Navy: The Broadside Iron-clad Frigate Portogallo Delivered to Her Owners, New York Times, July 23, 1864.

22. The New Steam-ship Line to Australia—An Enterprising Citizen of New–York, New York Times, August 28, 1870.

23. Edwin L. Dunbaugh and William duBarry Thomas, William H. Webb, Shipbuilder 130 (1989).

24. Edwin L. Dunbaugh and William duBarry Thomas, William H. Webb, Shipbuilder 130 (1989).

25. Reasons for the collapse included the glut of military vessels returning to civilian service, increased costs of materials, lack of skilled workers, competition from foreign yards, and the unsuitability of New York shipyards for steel hull construction. See Our Ship-Yards; Present Condition of the Ship–Building Trade in New–York, Brooklyn and Jersey City, New York Times, January 29, 1867; Joseph Cuneo, Who Was William Webb? (speech given on April 7, 2006 and available at http://www.webb-institute.edu/about_webb/williamwebb.php) (visited August 12, 2007).

26. Fred Irving Dayton, Steamboat Days (1925); New York Times, General News, July 23, 1865.

some, a factor hastening the end of the Civil War.[27] But the Navy lost interest in the project after the war and Webb sold the vessel (rechristened the *Rochambeau*) to France.[28] Webb closed his shipyard in 1870.[29] His passenger steamship business also failed, due in part to the construction of the transcontinental railroad (completed in 1869).[30] By 1872 Webb had retired from maritime-related activities.

With time on his hands Webb developed the property at the corner of 42nd Street and Fifth Avenue. He leased an adjoining lot from the Livingstons and incorporated the existing townhouse into a much larger structure, the 8–story Bristol Hotel, completed in 1875.[31] The project made eminent sense. The elevated railways which had entered service beginning in 1870 had enhanced the northward movement of commerce and housing. The elevator (introduced in New York during the 1853 Crystal Palace Exhibition) permitted developers to construct larger hotels and apartment buildings.[32] Webb understood that the days of single residences in midtown Manhattan were numbered and that the property in question could generate a good income if configured for multi-family use.

The Bristol was not a hotel in the modern sense. It was more in the nature of a high-class rooming house with long-term tenants who, for whatever reason, did not wish or could not afford to own their own residences but who desired a first-class address.[33] Webb entrusted the management to Captain James H. Corey, a domineering figure whose efforts to suppress scandals more than once landed him in trouble.[34] Under Corey's direction the hotel hosted society weddings[35] and maintained a reputation as one of the best and most exclusive hosteries in New York City,[36] although its prestige was later eclipsed by grander institutions such as the Waldorf–Astoria, the Holland House, and the Savoy.[37] Aside from dealing with demanding guests,[38] its biggest chal-

---

27. Fred Irving Dayton, Steamboat Days (1925).

28. Local Intelligence, The Dunderberg Visitors, New York Times, July 3, 1867.

29. Edwin L. Dunbaugh and William duBarry Thomas, William H. Webb, Shipbuilder 117 (1989).

30. Edwin L. Dunbaugh and William duBarry Thomas, William H. Webb, Shipbuilder 116–25 (1989).

31. See Edwin L. Dunbaugh and William duBarry Thomas, William H. Webb, Shipbuilder 130 (1989). Good images of the hotel can be found on the New York Public Library's website. See, e.g., http://digital gallery.nypl.org/nypldigital/dgkeysearch detail.cfm?trg=1strucID=692557image ID=805253word=hotel20bristols=1 notword=d=c=169,160,161,203,151,164, 176,167,168,175,208,186,179,166,187,219, 190,189,193,199,243,211,482f=lWord=l Field=sScope=sLevel=sLabel=Cities 202620Buildingstotal=11num=0imgs=12p Num=pos=1#.

32. See Edwin G. Burrows & Mike Wallace, Gotham: A History of New York City to 1898 670 (1999) (elevator); Robert A.M. Stern, Gregory Gilmartin and John Montague Massengale, Metropolitan Architecture and Urbanism 1890–1915 (1983).

33. See Family Troubles in Hotel Bristol, New York Times, December 8, 1929.

34. See, e.g., Mr. Corey Gets a Verdict, New York Times, April 20, 1883.

35. Events in the Metropolis, New York Times, December 14, 1882.

36. Preparing to Raze Old Bristol Hotel, New York Times, December 1, 1929.

37. See Robert A.M. Stern, Gregory Gilmartin and John Montague Massengale, Metropolitan Architecture and Urbanism 1890–1915 253–72 (1983).

38. See Family Troubles in Hotel Bristol, New York Times, December 8, 1929.

lenge in the early days was filling rooms during the summer months when well-to-do people fled New York for Newport or the 1,000 Islands.[39] Notwithstanding these problems, the hotel proved to be a lucrative investment for Webb, yielding approximately $40,000 in annual income.[40]

Webb's deal with the Livingstons was a ground lease for 18½ years at an annual rent of $1,065 with an option to renew for an additional 21 years.[41] The lease renewal proved contentious. The Livingstons sought a greatly increased rent. Webb refused to meet their demands. Unable to settle the matter privately, the parties appointed arbitrators pursuant to the terms of the lease. But the arbitrators could not agree either–and then could not agree on the choice of a neutral arbitrator to break the deadlock. Eventually the matter wound up in court, much to the amusement of newspapers observing bickering among the elite.[42]

C. THE PLAYERS

Representing the Livingstons in this lawsuit was Elbridge T. Gerry (1837–1927),[43] a lawyer of considerable ability, impeccable connections, strong social conscience, and a distinct personal interest in the property in question, being also the husband of Louisa Matilda Livingston (1836–1920), Robert and Louisa Livingston's only child. Gerry's family was, if anything, even more distinguished than that of his in-laws: his ancestors included iron merchant Peter P. Goelet (1764–1828)[44] and Elbridge Gerry (1744–1814), a signer of the Declaration of Independence, member of the Constitutional Convention, Governor of Massachusetts, Vice President of the United States—and eponym for the term gerrymander.

Through his law practice and personal connections Elbridge T. Gerry would also have known William H. Webb, his clients' adversary. Gerry had served as General Counsel of the Society for Prevention of Cruelty to Animals, an organization Webb co-founded in 1866. Gerry would have also been familiar with Webb's shipbuilding activities by virtue of his involvement in the city's yachting community (Gerry served as Commodore of the New York Yacht Club from 1885–1893).[45] Given

39. In 1878 some of the yearly tenants staged a rent strike intended to avoid paying summer rents, claiming that the food in the restaurant had deteriorated. Life in the Hotel Bristol, New York Times, September 25, 1878. By 1879 Corey was putting out the word that the Bristol was one of the coolest hotels in the city and that rooms were available in the summer at greatly reduced rates. Hotel Bristol, New York Times, June 10, 1879.

40. Edwin L. Dunbaugh and William duBarry Thomas, William H. Webb, Shipbuilder 130 (1989).

41. In Need of an Umpire: A Long and Futile Attempt at Arbitration, New York Times, August 16 1883.

42. See In Need of an Umpire: A Long and Futile Attempt at Arbitration, New York Times, August 16, 1883.

43. See II History of the Bench and Bar of New York 171–73 (David McAdam et al. eds 1897); Tom Shachtman, Skyscraper Dreams 38 (1991).

44. See Joseph Alfred Scoville, The Old Merchants of New York City 348–49 (1864); II History of the Bench and Bar of New York 171–73 (David McAdam et al. eds 1897); Sydney H. Coleman, Humane Society Leaders in America 65–88 (1924).

45. II History of the Bench and Bar of New York 171–73 (David McAdam et al. eds 1897).

these connections with both sides of the dispute, Gerry was probably relieved when the parties agreed (at his suggestion) to resolve the matter by drawing the name of a neutral arbitrator out of a hat.[46]

Although the crisis surrounding the renewal of the leasehold was resolved, the Bristol Hotel faced another and ultimately fatal threat: the impetuous growth of mid-town Manhattan. Between 1877 and 1881 Webb fought a successful battle against a horse-railroad which would have passed in front of the hotel along 42nd Street.[47] Later he obtained an injunction against the demolition of the Croton Reservoir,[48] a popular strolling place which occupied the blocks between 40th and 42nd Streets on Fifth Avenue.[49] But Webb's struggle to preserve the ambiance of the neighborhood was doomed. Even without the convenience of a horse railway, commerce along 42nd Street was burgeoning. Webb recognized this fact, writing in 1887 that much of the property in the vicinity of 42nd Street and Fifth Avenue had already passed from use as residences to that for business, and more is rapidly being converted for like purposes.[50]

As the leasehold approached its termination, midtown Manhattan was enjoying an astonishing boom in property values.[51] In 1900 the Fifth Avenue Hotel, at 23rd Street, sold at auction for the then-astounding sum of $4,225,000.[52] A corner lot at Fifth Avenue and 38th Street sold for $4,000,000 in 1901.[53] It was obvious that the site at 42nd Street and Fifth Avenue was no longer serving its highest and best use as a residential hotel. Elbridge and Louisa Gerry, who had succeeded as owners of the fee, needed a new partner to develop the property.[54]

46. See Quibbling Lawyers: Judge Potter Decides a Point With The Aid of a Hat, New York Times, August 17, 1883.

47. The Forty–Second–St. Job, New York Times, October 19, 1878; Restraining a New Horse Car Road, New York Times, September 11, 1880; Street Railroad Work Stopped, New York Times, September 15, 1880; Miscellaneous City News: A Railroad Company Beaten, New York Times, February 2, 1881.

48. See Aldermanic Proceedings: The Forty–Second–Street Reservoir, New York Times, October 5, 1881; The Removal of the Reservoir: Mr. Webb's Suit and The Powers of the Corporation Counsel, New York Times, June 23, 1882, Fifth–Avenue Reservoir, New York Times, February 24, 1887. For background on the reservoir see Edwin Burrows and Mike Wallace, Gotham: A History of New York City to 1898 627 (1999).

49. See http://www.nypl.org/pr/history.cfm (visited August 28, 2007). Webb opposed the demolition for technical reasons and also because he thought the project would be a source of Tammany Hall graft. Edwin L. Dunbaugh and William duBarry

Thomas, William H. Webb, Shipbuilder 131 (1989). The effect of the project on his hotel would have been mixed: the demolition would have disrupted the hotel's business but the park that was planned to replace it would have been an amenity over the long term. In the event, Webb was only able to delay the project: the reservoir was eventually demolished and replaced by the New York Public Library, completed in 1902. Arthur Bartlett Maurice, Fifth Avenue (1918).

50. Fifth-Avenue Reservoir, New York Times, February 24, 1887.

51. Large Deals in the Last Week of a Remarkable Year, New York Times, December 29, 1901.

52. Fifth Avenue Hotel Sold for $4,225,000, New York Times, April 27, 1900.

53. Large Deals in the Last Week of a Remarkable Year, New York Times, December 29, 1901.

54. Louisa Gerry was the legal owner at this time, having succeeded to the fee in 1891. City of New York v. Gerry, 100 Misc. 297, 165 N.Y.S. 659 (N.Y.Sup. 1917). The

The Gerrys identified an up-and-coming real estate developer, Walter J. Salmon (d. 1953) as a likely candidate for the leasehold. The evidence suggests that Salmon was an Episcopalian with family roots in England.[55] Salmon began as a young man to focus his considerable acumen and energy on the consolidation and development of commercial real estate in mid-town Manhattan. His strategy was to seek out the owners of the properties (often descendants of old and aristocratic families such as the Gerrys), and to acquire long-term net leases of the fee interests.[56] Salmon and the Gerrys agreed to a 20–year lease at an annual rental of $45,000, together with an agreement covering the alteration of the building from a residential hotel to a commercial building at an anticipated cost of $220,000.

But Salmon had a problem: he lacked funds to improve the premises. His resources were already stretched by another building he was renovating at the corner of 6th Avenue and 42nd Street.[57] His father had guaranteed the lease but apparently could not fund the renovation.[58] The Gerrys helped by advancing $100,000 to be repaid at $10,000 per year over 20 years (implying an interest rate of approximately 4%),[59] and about $16,000 could be obtained from rentals. But this left a shortfall of $104,000. Salmon needed money, and fast.

It is here that Morton H. Meinhard (1873–1931) enters the drama. Meinhard's ancestors were Jews from Franconia–Bavaria in South Germany.[60] His father, Henry Meinhard, emigrated with his parents and four siblings to the United States sometime around 1850 and settled in Savannah, where the clan became well established (Meinhard Road is a still a major thoroughfare there). Henry and his brother Isaac went into a wholesale dry goods business and owned sixteen slaves.[61] Sometime after the Civil War, Henry left for New York and there set up a business where Morton, his only son, started to work as a teenager.[62] Morton founded his own business in 1898. Although described in *Meinhard v. Salmon* as a merchant in woolen products, Meinhard's real occupation was finance. Morton Meinhard & Co. was a factoring concern; it lent

Gerrys chose to live north of 42nd Street, in an impressive mansion on 61st Street. See Robert A.M. Stern, Gregory Gilmartin and John Montague Massengale, Metropolitan Architecture and Urbanism 1890–1915 316 (1983).

55. The family name Salmon is typically traced to English or French origins, and Salmon's wife, Elizabeth Davy, appears to have been of English extraction. After Salmon's death she remarried in the Episcopal Church. Mrs. Salmon Wed to Francis Gillet, New York Times, March 4, 1956.

56. Saw 42nd St. Value Thirty Years Ago: Many Choice Properties are Now Controlled by Walter J. Salmon, New York Times, October 26, 1930.

57. In the Real Estate Field, New York Times, April 18, 1902.

58. See Brief for Appellants, *Meinhard v. Salmon* 4.

59. Brief for Appellants, Meinhard v. Salmon, at 5.

60. Private communication from Yehuda Meinhardt, August 4, 2007.

61. Marc I. Greenburg, Becoming Southern: The Jews of Savannah, Georgia, 1830–70, 86 American Jewish History 55–75 (1998).

62. Executive's Estate Contributes Million for Columbia Gym, New York Times, October 9, 1963; Simple Funeral for M.H. Meinhard, New York Times, May 14, 1931.

money to clothing manufacturers in the booming New York garment industry.[63]

By 1902 Morton Meinhard had cash on hand. Salmon needed money. A profitable business arrangement was to be had, and both men recognized it. How Meinhard and Salmon met is not clear. They did not travel in the same religious or business circles. Nonetheless the two had something in common: each was an ambitious young man eager to make a mark on New York City. In some fashion they met and developed a trust between them. Salmon's brief to the Court of Appeals refers to Meinhard as a friend,[64] and there is no reason to doubt that they enjoyed cordial relations.

D. THE DEAL

The deal between Salmon and Meinhard, which closed on May 19, 1902, was ostensibly separate from the lease between Salmon and the Gerrys. The lease made no reference to Meinhard and gave the Gerrys no control over how Salmon was to raise the renovation funds. Nevertheless the Gerrys had an interest in knowing that Salmon would find the money, and they probably were informed about Salmon's plans. It is also likely that Salmon and Meinhard had worked out the essential terms of their deal in advance—an inference supported by the referee's finding that Meinhard gave Salmon $5,000 on April 7, three days before the leasehold closing.[65]

The Salmon–Meinhard contract had the following terms. Meinhard would contribute half of the funds necessary to renovate the property; in return Salmon would pay Meinhard forty percent of the net profits for five years and fifty percent thereafter. The parties would share equally in losses. Salmon was given full authority to manage the property.

The deal turned out to be a spectacular success. As Salmon predicted, mid-town Manhattan prospered, and with it came demand for commercial office space. The Bristol commanded good rents from the start and increased in profitability over the years. A tax case involving Meinhard reported that the enterprise lost money only in the first year and showed ever-increasing profits thereafter.[66] In *Meinhard v. Salmon* Cardozo states that the enterprise lost money for a few years before turning a profit. Regardless, the venture prospered. Over the life of the

---

63. For discussion of the importance of the garment industry in the Nineteenth Century New York economy, see Edwin G. Burrows & Mike Wallace, Gotham: A History of New York City to 1898 664–66 (1999). In the 1890s New York supplied almost two thirds by value of ready-to-wear women's clothing and more than a quarter of the men's market. Factoring Firms Bought Out by Merger, New York Times, November 13, 1931; Norma M. Rantisi, The Ascendance of New York Fashion, International Journal of Urban and Regional Research 86, 89–92 (2004).

64. Brief for Appellant, Meinhard v. Salmon, p.9.

65. Brief for Appellants, Meinhard v. Salmon, at 5.

66. Appeal of Meinhard, 3 B.T.A. 612, 1926 WL 783 (B.T.A. 1926).

lease Meinhard and Salmon each received over $550,000 on their investments of slightly more than $52,000.

E. THE FALLOUT

All this felicity did not extend to relations between Meinhard and Salmon. Meinhard questioned charges that Salmon was making for expenses and complained that Salmon was not informing him about management decisions. The parties resolved the issues in 1908: Salmon indicated that he would be very glad to discuss fully with you at any and all times any of the affairs of the building. Meinhard agreed to allow Salmon a fixed charge of 6% of the rentals for management expenses.[67] But this compromise didn't heal the wounds. Relations between Meinhard and Salmon deteriorated to the point that they had essentially no contact after 1917.[68]

By the time the Bristol Hotel lease came up for renewal in 1922 the property was one of the most valuable pieces of real estate in the world.[69] In anticipation of the ending of the lease Elbridge T. Gerry and his son Robert Livingston Gerry (who managed the family properties after 1910),[70] had astutely purchased adjoining properties with a view towards future consolidation.[71] Despite Salmon's success with the Bristol Hotel the Gerrys shopped around for developers.[72] Eventually they settled on Salmon, executing a lease in January 1922, three months before the expiration of the old one. The new lease encompassed not only the Bristol Hotel site but also the adjoining lots owned by the Gerrys. The agreement called for demolition of the existing buildings and erection of a 25–story tower on the consolidated parcel.[73] The lease was for an initial term of 20 years (with options to renew) with annual rentals beginning at $350,000 and raising to $475,000 after ten years.

Salmon did not inform Meinhard of these negotiations. Meinhard's response, on learning of the new lease, was to sue. The trial court held for Meinhard, finding that he had established an entitlement to an equitable share in the Bristol Hotel portion of the new leasehold. The Appellate Division agreed that Meinhard was entitled to a share of the lease, but held that his share was half the entire new lease, not just half the portion attributable to the Bristol Hotel.[74]

67. Brief for Appellants, Meinhard v. Salmon, at 13–14.

68. Brief for Appellants, Meinhard v. Salmon, at 23.

69. See Bristol Building Coming Down: Tenants to Vacate Nov. 30, New York Times, November 21, 1929. By 1929 the property had the second-highest per-front foot tax value in Manhattan. Skyscraper to Rise in 5th Av. at 42d St., New York Times, July 15, 1929.

70. See Peter G. Gerry, Ex–Senator, Dies Hours Before His Brother Robert, New York Times, November 1, 1967.

71. Brief for Appellant, Meinhard v. Salmon, pp. 21–22.

72. Brief for Appellant, Meinhard v. Salmon, p. 22.

73. See Meinhard v. Salmon, 223 A.D. 663, 229 N.Y.S. 345 (App. Div. 1928).

74. Meinhard v. Salmon, 223 A.D. 663, 229 N.Y.S. 345 (App. Div. 1928). Two of the five judges dissented on the ground that Meinhard should have received a smaller share.

F. THE NEW YORK COURT OF APPEALS AND CARDOZO

In this posture the case came to the New York Court of Appeals. Here we meet the last major personage in the drama, Benjamin Cardozo, the author of the celebrated opinion.[75] Cardozo's ancestors were Sephardic Jews who had immigrated to the United States from Portugal before the Revolutionary War. Albert Cardozo, Benjamin's father, had been a judge of the New York Supreme Court (the court of general jurisdiction) but resigned to avoid impeachment amid accusations of favors done for Tammany politicians. Notwithstanding, Benjamin chose a career in law and joined his father's law firm, becoming a successful trial and appellate lawyer before his appointment as Chief Judge of the New York Court of Appeals.[76]

Writing for a divided court,[77] Cardozo upheld the Appellate Division's judgment in favor of Meinhard subject to a modification that allowed Salmon to control the operation and management of the enterprise.[78] The basis for the holding was that Salmon had breached the fiduciary duty that one co-adventurer owes another.[79] The holding is perhaps questionable. The lower court judges had felt obligated to rule for Meinhard in light of an earlier decision presenting similar facts.[80] But Cardozo was not so constrained (a dissection of the precedents, he remarked, would generate little profit.)[81] In the absence of precedent, a number of reasons favored Salmon over Meinhard:

1. The contract between Meinhard and Salmon contemplated an arrangement limited by the term of the original lease.

2. It is unlikely that the parties would have required Salmon to share a new lease with Meinhard had they bargained over the issue. All Meinhard brought to the table was money, and Salmon had good reason

---

75. The leading biographical treatment is Andrew L. Kaufman, Cardozo (1998). For a study of Cardozo's influence, see Richard A. Posner, Cardozo: A Study in Reputation (1990).

76. See Richard A. Posner, Cardozo: A Study in Reputation 2 (1990).

77. Three judges joined Cardozo's majority opinion, and two joined Judge Andrews' dissent.

78. For discussion of Cardozo's opinion, see William E. Nelson, The Legalist Reformation: Law, Politics, and Ideology in New York 1920–1980 60–61 (2001); Andrew Kaufman, Cardozo, 238–42 (1998).

79. Both the majority and dissenting opinions declined to characterize Meinhard and Salmon as partners. This reticence appears odd at first. Certainly their agreement of 1902 satisfied the traditional definition of a partnership, as an association of two or more persons to carry on as co-

owners a business for profit. Uniform Partnership Act § 6(a) (1914). This answer to this puzzle is that Meinhard had assigned his rights under the Salmon–Meinhard agreement to his wife in 1917 for tax planning reasons (her income would have been taxed at a lower bracket). Appeal of Meinhard, 3 B.T.A. 612, 1926 WL 783 (B.T.A. 1926). Meinhard's counsel had also provided a written opinion concluding that, for tax purposes, the agreement between Meinhard and Salmon was not a partnership. Salmon's counsel attempted to use these facts to demonstrate that the agreement with Meinhard was not a partnership and therefore not subject to the fiduciary duties attendant on the partnership relationship. Cardozo's refusal to characterize the Meinhard–Salmon relationship as a partnership was nothing more than a means for avoiding this technical issue.

80. Mitchell v. Reed, 61 N.Y. 123 (1874).

81. 249 N.Y. at 466.

to expect that he would have alternative sources of financing twenty years down the line.

3. Meinhard was not tricked. He knew that the lease was due to expire and must have understood that Salmon was a natural candidate for the new project. Salmon had agreed in 1908 to brief Meinhard about developments, but Meinhard did not ask.[82]

4. Salmons negotiations with the Gerrys were undertaken in good faith with no intent to mislead.[83]

5. Meinhard had no experience in the design, construction, or management of commercial real estate. Salmon, in contrast, had been in the business for more than 20 years, had successfully operated the Bristol Hotel, and had constructed and managed other buildings. The Gerrys had already considered and rejected other candidates with substantial real estate experience. By the time they turned to Salmon there were only four months left in the lease. It is ludicrous to suppose that Meinhard, in that time frame, could have persuaded the Gerrys to entrust him with the crown jewel of their real estate holdings.

6. The 500 Fifth Avenue project was separate and distinct from the Bristol Hotel venture. The old lease was to expire in 1922. The Bristol Hotel was to be demolished and all its tenants evicted. The new building was to be on a substantially larger plot and was, even as initially contemplated, to be three times taller than the old building.

7. Meinhard, as Cardozo recognized, had already been richly rewarded for his initial investment, substantially due to Salmon's capable management. Meinhard had done nothing other than cash checks. It hardly seems equitable, in those circumstances, to impose an unwanted partner on Salmon, on the same terms, for a period of up to eighty years.

On the other hand, Cardozo's judgment might perhaps be justified on the theory that the transactions costs of bargaining around the rule are low. In the future, after *Meinhard v. Salmon*, parties entering into real estate partnerships can prevent the imposition of continuing duties after the expiration of the leasehold by explicitly providing as much in their contracts.[84] Indeed, it appears that such disclaimers are now routinely found in real estate transactional documents.[85] It was perhaps more important to settle the issue than to settle it in the most efficient way; and by retaining the existing rule Cardozo arguably preserved settled expectations of parties, even though a different rule might have been more efficient if he were writing from scratch.

82. Jonathan Macey argues, in comments on this paper, that such a limitation on Salmon's obligation to keep Meinhard informed would have been unenforceable under then-prevailing law.

83. 249 N.Y. at 467–68 ([w]We have no thought to hold that Salmon was guilty of a conscious purpose to defraud. Very likely he assumed in all good faith that with the approaching end of the venture he might ignore his coadventurer and take the extension for himself.)

84. William Nelson made this point in oral comments on this paper.

85. I thank Jay Weiser for this observation.

But the opinion is remembered much more for its rhetoric than for its holding on the continuing duties of partners in real estate leases.[86] Cardozo, a virtuoso stylist, outdid himself in *Meinhard v. Salmon*, serving up a spicy bouillabaisse of metaphor and allusion to describe the nature of the fiduciary duties of a managing co-adventurer hyperbolic phrases that are etched today in the memories of countless attorneys who encountered the case in law school. Judge Posner–himself no mean judicial craftsman–remarked that [n]o judge seems ever to have come up with a better formula with which to express the concept of fiduciary duty.[87]

Although the opinion's enduring importance lies in its language, there is a connection between Cardozo's rhetoric and the facts. Had this been an easier case, had Meinhard not seemed, in a sense, so undeserving of the bounty being bestowed on him, Cardozo would not have needed to reach so deeply into his reserves of eloquence. But given the facts, it would not have been wholly satisfying if Cardozo had justified a judgment for Meinhard with the language that Judge Posner suggests as a more informative statement of a partner's duty: while normally a party to a contract is entitled, with certain exceptions, to take advantage of the other party's ignorance, a fiduciary is not; he must treat the other party's interests as if they were his own.[88] Cardozo's words get the blood flowing and evoke in the reader a visceral sense that, notwithstanding Meinhard's apparent overreaching, the judgment should still go in his favor.

A close analysis reveals the care with which Cardozo constructed the opinion. Interwoven in the text are metaphors drawn from distinct realms of human culture. Take the dictum that [n]ot honesty alone, but the punctilio of an honor the most sensitive, is then the standard of behavior. Punctilio connotes a fine point of exactness in conduct, ceremony, or procedure. It has roots in the Italian renaissance, and in concepts of chivalry and honor. Cardozo reinforces the metaphor by referring to "a tradition ... unbending and inveterate"[89] and to behavior higher than that trodden by the crowd. The allusion is to the high nobility of a bygone era whose standard of conduct was more exacting than that demanded of common folk. Co-adventurers, Cardozo suggests, should behave with similar refinement and courtesy in their mutual affairs.

Cardozo enlists a second metaphor in describing the consequences of allowing persons in Salmon's place to negotiate deals behind their partners' backs: [h]e might steal a march on his comrade under cover of the darkness, and then hold the captured ground. Loyalty and comrade-

---

86. On Cardozo's rhetorical style, see Richard A. Posner, Cardozo: A Study in Reputation (1990); Francis Bergen, The History of the New York Court of Appeals, 1847–1932 (1985).

87. Richard A. Posner, Cardozo: A Study in Reputation 104 (1990).

88. Richard A. Posner, Cardozo: A Study in Reputation 104 (1990).

89. 249 N.Y. at 464.

ship are not so easily abjured.[90] Here the image is one of military operations and warfare. Cardozo suggests that co-adventurers, like soldiers, must sacrifice for one another and not take advantage of a comrade's trust.

Elsewhere Cardozo remarks that Salmon had put himself in a position in which thought of self was to be renounced, however hard the abnegation.[91] The rule of undivided loyalty imposed in such a situation is relentless and supreme. Conduct short of that standard, Cardozo observes, would not receive from equity a healing benediction.[92] The image is one of religion, transcendence and mysticism. The connotation is that when it comes to dealings with co-partners, a person must behave with monastic purity, placing always the other's interests above his own.

Each of these metaphors has the common feature that the protagonist–a knight on a chivalric quest, a soldier behind enemy lines, a monk devoting himself to prayer and contemplation–is called, by virtue of his role, to suppress his own selfish interests in favor of some greater good. The images have a powerful resonance. They evoke a pronounced (if somewhat misty) sense that duties partners owe to one another really are important.

These images also have subtle ethnic connotations. They relate more to Christians than Jews: the latter were not involved in chivalry, did not enter monasteries, and were often exempt from military service. But the opinion does contain language pertinent to Jews. There might be, Cardozo says, something grasping about Meinhard's behavior.[93] The image of the grasping Jew is a classic ethnic stereotype. In juxtaposing the Christian duties that devolved on the Episcopalian Salmon against the grasping demands of the Jewish Meinhard, Cardozo paints a tableau reminiscent of the *Merchant of Venice*. Cardozo's reasons for evoking these stereotypes are hard to fathom but may perhaps have been a product (possibly unconscious) of complex feelings about his own religious heritage.[94]

G.   POST–DECISION

The years held different fates for the participants in this drama. William H. Webb, in addition to building the Bristol Hotel, invested in real estate and securities,[95] collected contemporary art, [96]and spearhead-

90.   249 N.Y. at 466.

91.   249 N.Y. at 468.

92.   249 N.Y. at 468.

93.   249 U.S. at 268.

94.   The adult Cardozo rarely attended religious services but kept a kosher home, maintained a family pew at Shearith Israel, accepted appointments with Jewish civic organizations and served many Jewish clients. See American Jewish Historical Society, Justice Cardozo, Sephardic Jew, at http:// ajhs.org/publications (visited June 6, 2007);

Richard A. Posner, Cardozo: A Study in Reputation 2 (1990); Andrew L. Kaufman, Cardozo 69–70 (1998); Richard Polenberg, The World of Benjamin Cardozo (Cambridge, MA: Harvard University Press, 1997).

95.   See Edwin L. Dunbaugh and William duBarry Thomas, William H. Webb, Shipbuilder 127–132 (1989).

96.   Webb's collection included works by Jan David Col (Belgian), Carl Becker (German), Emmanuel Leutze (American), Jehan

ed political opposition to Tammany Hall.[97] Webb was also active in the Society for the Prevention of Cruelty to Animals, an organization he co-founded in 1866.[98] His family life held disappointments: his older son was an invalid confined to the home and his younger son died of pneumonia at age 43 without leaving an heir.[99] Webb gave most of his money to a school for shipbuilders and home for retired shipyard workers which he established in 1890.[100] Webb died in 1899. But his legacy lives on in the Webb Institute, now located in Glen Cove, Long Island, which, consistent with Webb's original plan, still offers tuition-free undergraduate degrees in naval architecture and marine engineering.[101]

Elbridge T. Gerry died in 1927 at the age of 90, eulogized for his service as founder and president of the New York Society for the Prevention of Cruelty to Children[102] and his work on capital punishment reform.[103] His mansion on 5th Avenue and 61st Street was demolished and replaced by the Pierre Hotel.[104] One of his children, Peter Goelet Gerry (1879–1957), married a Vanderbilt heiress and became a United States Senator from Rhode Island.[105] His other son Robert Livingston Gerry (1877–1957) married the daughter of railroad tycoon E.H. Harriman and managed the Gerry real estate holdings.[106] Robert Livingston Gerry's son, Elbridge T. Gerry (1908–1999), who also lived to 90, was a polo star, an investment banker at Brown Brothers Harriman, and for 63 years a trustee for the New York Society for the Prevention of Cruelty to Children which his grandfather founded in 1875.[107] In 1955

Georges Vibert (French), and Ignacio de Leon Escosura (Spanish). Sales of Paintings: The Webb Collection to be Sold Today, New York Times, March 29, 1876.

97. See, e.g., The Costigan Bill, New York Times, February 9, 1875; Opposition To Tammany Hall, New York Times, October 27, 1876; The Taxpayers Movement, New York Times, October 13, 1877; Trying to Reduce the Estimates, New York Times, December 28, 1877; The East River Bridge: Will It Be Legal, Useful, Practicable, Or Safe? Why Its Erection Is Opposed By The Council Of Political Reform, New York Times, October 20, 1878 (letter to the editor from William H. Webb); The Washington Market Bill: Protest Against Its Passage By The Council of Political Reform and Others, New York Times, April 20, 1880; Constitutional Amendment: Work of The Committee of The Council of Reform, New York Times, November 22, 1884; Edwin G. Burrows & Mike Wallace, Gotham: A History of New York City to 1898 830 (1999). Webb repeatedly refused entreaties to run for mayor. William Henry Webb, New York Times, July 11, 1897.

98. American Society for the Prevention of Cruelty to Animals, New York Times, April 24, 1866.

99. Edwin L. Dunbaugh and William duBarry Thomas, William H. Webb, Shipbuilder 129–132 (1989).

100. See Editorial, New York Times, July 17, 1890; Good Use for His Wealth: William H. Webb's Academy and Home for Shipbuilders, New York Times, July 17, 1890. The original facility was built on 13 acres overlooking the Harlem River on Sedgewick Avenue in the Bronx.

101. See http://www.webb-institute.edu/about_webb/williamwebb.php (visited August 12, 2007).

102. See Sydney H. Coleman, Humane Society Leaders in America 65–88 (1924).

103. Elbridge T. Gerry Dies in 90th Year, New York Times, February 19, 1927.

104. See Robert A.M. Stern, Gregory Gilmartin and Thomas Mellins, New York 1930: Architecture and Urbanism between the Two World Wars 217 (1987).

105. http://politicalgraveyard.com/bio/gerry.html#R9M0IXWHE.

106. See Peter G. Gerry, Ex–Senator, Dies Hours Before His Brother Robert, New York Times, November 1, 1967.

107. Elbridge T. Gerry, 90, Polo Star and Banker who Bred Trotters, New York

the Gerry family sold the property on 42nd Street and Fifth Avenue to the Metropolitan Life Insurance Company, which still owns the fee.[108]

Walter Salmon continued to acquire properties at the intersection of 42nd Street and Fifth Avenue. He eventually obtained 858 feet along 42nd Street and substantial frontage along Fifth Avenue.[109] Many estates of Gilded Age elites passed under his control, including, in addition to the Gerry holdings, those of Levi Morton, Russell Sage, and John Watts de Peyster.[110] In 1927 Salmon built the 32–story Salmon Tower just west of the Bristol,[111] and in 1931 he completed a much larger building at 500 Fifth Avenue that included the Bristol Hotel plot. Salmon and his wife were active in New York society[112] and established themselves as breeders and owners of race horses, with entries under their salmon-pink silks winning the Preakness Stakes in 1926 and 1929.[113] The Depression, however, brought significant challenges. With a glut of office space on the market, including the Empire State and Chrysler buildings as well as Salmon's buildings at 42nd Street and Fifth Avenue, the drop-off of business activity spelled vacancies and cash flow problems. Salmon's building at 500 Fifth Avenue weathered the storm, although it incurred significant losses. Ironically, it appears to have been saved by cash contributions from Meinhard mandated as a result of the Court of Appeals' decision (Salmon reportedly sent Cardozo a bouquet of flowers on each anniversary of the opinion).[114] Salmon's other big project was not so fortunate. The Salmon Tower at 11 West 42nd Street failed and went through reorganization.[115] Salmon never again developed a major building. He died in 1953 as a respected figure in New York real estate circles, succeeded in business by his son (also named Walter Salmon).[116]

Morton Meinhard built his business into one of the major garment factors in the country. He married the spirited Carrie Wormser, a member of one of New York's richest Jewish families.[117] The Meinhards

Times, March 6, 1999; *O'Reilly v. Gerry*, 249 A.D. 850, 292 N.Y.S. 533 (A.D. 2 Dept. 1937).

108. See Abstract of Title, 3 West 42nd Street.

109. Saw 42nd St. Value Thirty Years Ago: Many Choice Properties are Now Controlled by Walter J. Salmon, New York Times, October 26, 1930.

110. Saw 42nd St. Value Thirty Years Ago: Many Choice Properties are Now Controlled by Walter J. Salmon, New York Times, October 26, 1930.

111. See Salmon Tower, http://www.emporis.com (visited June 6, 2007).

112. See, e.g., Coming Charity Events, New York Times, March 10, 1929; Benefit for the Navy Club, New York Times, February 4, 1929.

113. Display Captures Preakness Stakes, New York Times, May 11, 1926; Walter J. Salmon, Realty Man, Dies, New York Times, December 26, 1953.

114. See Nicholas L. Georgakopoulos, *Meinhard v. Salmon* and the Economics of Honor, 1999 Columbia Business Law Review 137, 144 n.11 (1999) (quoting private correspondence with C. Robert Morris, Professor of Law at Minnesota Law School, Feb. 2, 1998).

115. Asks Interest Rate Cut: Salmon Appeals to Bondholders on 11 West Forty-second St., New York Times, June 12, 1934; Fight Reorganizing Plan, New York Times, October 28, 1938.

116. See Space Deal Made at 500 Fifth Ave., New York Times, April 16, 1960; Lights Improved at Bryant Park, New York Times, June 19, 1962; Walter Salmon, Jr., Horseman and Real–Estate Executive, New York Times, January 29, 1986.

117. See Miss Wormser Attacks A Burglar In Her Room; Was Scared Till She Found He Wasn't a Mouse. Saved Valuable Property But the Thief Got Away with $5,000 In Jewels—Then Mr. Wormser Shot

collected Renaissance art[118] and were major donors to Jewish charities.[119] But Meinhard did not have much time to savor his victory in the Bristol Hotel case. He died childless in 1931 at age 58 of pernicious anemia while on an ocean tour in the Sea of Japan.[120] By then the stock market crash had wiped out much of his wealth.[121] His firm, Morton H. Meinhard & Co., was sold to C.I.T. Financial Corp.—undoubtedly for less than it could have commanded a few years before.[122] His victory in *Meinhard v. Salmon* proved pyrrhic as well. By 1934 his estate owed $845,000 on the 500 Fifth Avenue property and could not satisfy its charitable bequests.[123] Walter J. Salmon bought out the estate's interest at a bargain price.[124] But Meinhard enjoyed a posthumous redemption or sorts: thirty-two years after his death his estate made the single largest gift—$1,000,000—towards the construction of Columbia University's new gym.[125]

Benjamin Cardozo went on to the Supreme Court of the United States, where he served with distinction and renown from 1932 until his death in 1938. He enjoys today one of the best reputations of any American judge, due in no small measure to the capacities for eloquence displayed in such fulsome measure in *Meinhard v. Salmon*.[126]

H. CONCLUSION

What about the property over which the parties had fought such a battle? In 1929 Salmon negotiated a new lease with the Gerry Estates (successor to Elbridge T. Gerry).[127] In July 1929 Salmon announced plans for an impressive office tower with stores on the street level, banking facilities at the second level and office floors above.[128] By October 1929 he had filed plans for an art deco building, costing $2,350,000, designed by Shreve, Lamb & Harmon Associates. Tenants were evicted in November

at the Milkman, New York Times, February 8, 1906.

118. See, e.g., A Hitherto Unknown Panel by Simone Martini, 102 Burlingame Magazine 66–68 (1960); Photographic Evidence, 60 Burlingame Magazine 289 (1932).

119. Simple Funeral for M.H. Meinhard, New York Times, May 14, 1931; M.H. Meinhard Honored: Dinner of Settlement Board is Tribute to His 25 Years' Work, New York Times, May 3, 1928 (reporting that Meinhard gave more than $1 million to charitable causes in his lifetime).

120. Simple Funeral for M.H. Meinhard, New York Times, May 14, 1931.

121. M.H. Meinhard Left $1,678,798 Estate; Debts Reduce it from $3,172,420–Inadequate to Provide 124 Bequests in Will, New York Times, July 3, 1934.

122. C.I.T. Financial Corp.–Company History, available at http://quincy.hbs.edu: 8080/lehman/company_histories/c/company History.html.

123. M.H. Meinhard Left $1,678,798 Estate; Debts Reduce it from $3,172,420–Inadequate to Provide 124 Bequests in Will, New York Times, July 3, 1934.

124. See Nicholas L. Georgakopoulos, *Meinhard v. Salmon* and the Economics of Honor, 1999 Columbia Business Law Review 137, 144 n.11 (1999) (quoting private correspondence with C. Robert Morris, Professor of Law at Minnesota Law School, Feb. 2, 1998).

125. Executive's Estate Contributes Million for Columbia Gym, New York Times, October 9, 1963.

126. See generally Richard A. Posner, Benjamin Cardozo: A Study in Reputation (1990).

127. Skyscraper to Rise in 5th Av. at 42d St., New York Times, July 15, 1929.

128. Skyscraper to Rise in 5th Av. at 42d St., New York Times, July 15, 1929.

and by December wreckers were demolishing the building, Salmon himself knocking the first hole.[129] Twenty-two hundred workers were employed in the construction.[130] The new tower, rising 60 stories, opened with great ceremony in March 1931. The building, however, never quite lived up to expectations. Its prestige was overshadowed by the 102–story Empire State Building, also designed by Shreve, Lamb and Harmon and opened in 1931. Like other commercial properties, 500 Fifth Avenue faced a challenging rental environment during the Depression. The building remains a feature of the midtown landscape today.

Lastly, what about the case? Cardozo himself rarely mentioned the opinion; there appears to be no reference to it in the Cardozo papers at Columbia University. His only recorded comment is in a letter to Felix Frankfurter noting that *"Meinhard v. Salmon* is one of the cases in which some of my colleagues think that my poetry is better than my law."* I think its law is better than its poetry (which, indeed I cannot discover).[131] But if Cardozo would not celebrate the opinion, others did. *Meinhard v. Salmon* became and remains today a fruitful source for citations in judicial opinions. By the summer of 2007, according to WestlawTRADE, the case had been cited 1,021 times, including 296 New York cases, 120 cases in the Second Circuit, 591 decisions from other federal and state courts, and 14 international cases. The case also achieved recognition in the legal academy. It was excerpted in contemporary casebooks including Clark and Douglas's *Cases on the Law of Partnership* and Mecham's *Cases on the Law of Partnerships*.[132] Today virtually every casebook on corporations or business organizations contains an excerpt.[133] Yet even *Meinhard v. Salmon* has not survived untarnished. Its demanding standard of fiduciary duty does not, in fact, govern many cases. Citations to the punctilio are usually no more than perfunctory bows to authority. The current version of the Uniform Partnership Act defines a partner's duty to co-adventurers in modest and limited terms distinctly unlike the gaudy prose of Cardozo's opinion.[134]

---

129. Razing Bristol Building, New York Times, December 3, 1929.

130. New Skyscraper Opened by Salmon, New York Times, March 3, 1931.

131. Letter from Cardozo to Felix Frankfurter, Feb. 23, 1929, quoted in Andrew L. Kaufman, Cardozo 241.

132. Charles E. Clark & William O. Douglas, Cases on the Law of Partnerships: Joint Stock Associations, Business Trusts, and Other Noncorporate Business Associations 504–14 (1932); Floyd R. Mechem, Cases on the Law of Partnership 479–88 (1935).

133. For a sampling, see William T. Allen, Reinier Kraakman & Guhan Subramanian, Commentaries and Cases on the Law of Business Organizations, 2d ed. 45 (2007);

Jesse H. Choper, John C. Coffee, Jr. & Ronald J. Gilson, Cases and Materials on Corporations 731 (6th ed. 2004); Melvin Aron Eisenberg, Corporations and Other Business Organizations 71 (9th ed. 2005); William A. Klein, J. Mark Ramseyer & Stephen M. Bainbridge, Agency, Partnerships, and Limited Liability Entities: Unincorporated Business Associations 202 (2nd Ed. 2007); William A. Klein, J. Mark Ramseyer & Stephen M. Bainbridge, Business Associations: Agency, Partnerships, and Corporations: Cases and Materials 109 (6th ed. 2006); Robert W. Hamilton and Jonathan R. Macey, Cases and Materials on Corporations including Partnerships and Limited Liability Companies 67–71 (9th ed. 2005).

134. See Uniform Partnership Act § 404 (1997).

Nevertheless *Meinhard v. Salmon* stands as a monument that is likely to survive even after the brick, mortar and steel of 500 Fifth Avenue have been reduced to rubble. Through the opinion and the facts surrounding it we gain a fascinating glimpse of New York's changing ethnic, social, and economic environment—the rise and fall of industries, the booms and busts of business conditions, the dispersal and commercialization of landed estates, the influence of immigrants, the role of yachting, horse racing, art collecting and charitable work in establishing social standing, the importance of family and heritage, and the enduring constancy of a plot of land that provided a commodious stage for all the sound and fury that went on above.

Chapter 3

HOPE AND DESPAIR IN THE MAGIC KINGDOM: *IN RE WALT DISNEY COMPANY DERIVATIVE LITIGATION*

By
James D. Cox*
Eric Talley**

Depending on one's perspective, executive compensation represents either agency cost's most grotesque symptom or the key to its spiritual salvation. The divide between those who own a firm and those who manage it—and the costs associated with remedying that gulf—are by now well understood. Simply put, managers and owner/shareholders concur that profit maximization is the appropriate aspiration for corporate endeavors, but their non-symmetric economic stakes cause them to disagree as to both the means for doing so, and the party(ies) whose profits are to count in that maximization process.

The task of aligning interests of managers and owners is therefore a vital one for organizational and legal design. In concept (if not practice), the burden has historically been shouldered by a quasi-"portfolio" of legal proscriptions, corporate governance structures, and executive pay arrangements, all working simultaneously. Under this view, a well crafted pay package, governance device, or fiduciary obligation would preferably work to complement other components of the portfolio, augmenting their benefits and/or dampening their shortcomings. Consequentially, then, our collective optimism about conquering agency cost problems transcends compensation packages alone, embracing instead a belief that courts are keenly able to mediate the mutual interaction of these incentive devices, whether shareholders attempt to do so explicitly or not.

* Brainerd Currie Professor of Law, Duke University.

** Professor of Law, University of California at Berkeley.

The recent Delaware Supreme Court case of *In re Walt Disney Company Derivative Litigation*[1] presented a prime—and somewhat historic—opportunity for corporate law to embrace its idyllic role as an incentives mediator, and to do so in an explicit way. As we shall illustrate in the pages below, the opinion at the very least casts a dark shadow over such functional romanticism, and more likely pushes the conversation regarding enforcement of executive compensation in another (possibly unexpected) direction. Despite this ill foreboding, *Disney* nonetheless deserves its iconic moniker, for at least two reasons. First, as developed below, *Disney* minimally documents the virtually insurmountable challenge that courts face in addressing intractable agency costs issues through their executive compensation jurisprudence.[2] Perhaps more constructively, however, *Disney* might be understood as an early harbinger of a new template (still embryonic) for understanding and applying fiduciary obligations for directors and officers. If the latter proves to be the case (and mitosis is still underway), it would most definitely push *Disney* into the realm of corporate law stardom.

A.   THE PAYCHECK IN THE COURTROOM

Lawyers, young and old, are well-advised not to base their livelihood exclusively on fees from challenging executive compensation in public companies. To do so is a recipe for ignominious starvation. Despite the abundance of seemingly worthy targets for such challenges, the pre-*Disney* jurisprudence around compensation had grown steadily and consistently deferential towards executive pay. Descriptively, at least, one can trace this evolution across three dimensions.

1.   The Slow Defeat of Substance by Process

Perhaps more than anything else, Delaware courts lost their appetite for reining in executive compensation because they failed to develop a durable template for benchmarking and judging the appropriateness of specific compensation packages. If anything, while navigating their wayward tact, courts have likely contributed to the overall insularity of the compensation setting process, possibly even making the problem worse, not better. A review of the history of the courts' interface with executive compensation reveals that exorbitant pay levels have long been fodder for public debate, but one that increasingly played out beyond the courtroom walls.

That hasn't always been the case. During the Great Depression there were numerous legal attacks on executive compensation—many of them successful—focusing on bonus and incentive compensation arrangements. The policy import of these suits and compensation-related abuses was ably captured in both press accounts and in extensive

---

1. 906 A.2d 27 (2006).

2. Executive compensation is by no means the only area of the courts' difficulties in dealing with agency costs. Courts have not earned high marks in their treatments of management-owner conflicts in several other areas, such as going private transactions and defensive maneuvers.

congressional hearings leading up the enactment of the federal securities laws. In fact, prior to *Disney*, the most famous well known attack on executive compensation came precisely from that era. *Rogers v. Hill*[3] involved a shareholder suit surrounding bonuses awarded to executives and directors of the American Tobacco Company between 1929 and 1931. The CEO of American Tobacco, who already earned an annual salary in excess of $1 million (around $14 million in today's dollars), was granted the option to purchase immediately shares for an amount $1,169,000 below their current market value (approximately $16 million in current dollars). As part of their approval of the option arrangement, the directors awarded themselves handsome options as well. The case ended triumphantly for the plaintiff in the U.S. Supreme Court. The Court concluded that even though the arrangement had been approved by the stockholders and was therefore "supported by the presumption of regularity" that presumption nevertheless would not justify payments of sums as salaries so large as in substance and effect to amount to spoliation or waste of corporate property.

> ... *If a bonus payment has no relation to the value of services for which it is given, it is in reality a gift in part, and the majority stockholders have no power to give away corporate property against the protest of the minority....* The facts alleged by the plaintiff are sufficient to require the District Court, upon consideration of all the relevant facts brought forward by the parties, determine whether and to what extent payments to individual defendants under the by-laws constitute misuse and waste of the money of the corporation.[4]

The substantive reasonableness inquiry reflected in *Rogers* would undoubtedly strike today's corporate law practitioners and scholars as both quaint and anachronistic; for it has been steadily abandoned over the last half century, displaced entirely (or nearly so) by a gradual elevation of process over substance. Signs of the sea change were first manifest in the context of the Delaware Supreme Court's treatment of executive stock options some 30 years later. Given the dominance that Delaware by then enjoyed in incorporations, it is not surprising that the state took the lead in defining the first governing standards for evaluating bonus and profit-sharing (e.g., stock option) arrangements for executives. It did so, evidently, in an admirably self aware fashion, first feigning allegiance to substantive standards that would putatively guide its review. In the leading case, *Beard v. Elster*,[5] the Court set forth the following litmus test for evaluating stock options:

> All stock option plans must be tested against the requirements that they contain conditions, or that surrounding circumstances are such, that the corporation may reasonably expect to receive the contemplated benefit from the grant of the options. Furthermore, there

---

3. 289 U.S. 582 (1933).

4. Rogers v. Hill, 289 U.S. 582, 591–92 (1933)(quoting in part J. Swan's dissenting opinion in the Second Circuit's decision dismissing the suit)(emphasis added).

5. 160 A. 2d 731 (Del. 1960).

must be a reasonable relationship between the value of the benefits passing to the corporation and the value of the options granted.[6]

This language tended to echo prior precedents, in which the Court had (*inter alia*) struck down stock options granted to executives because the options could be exercised up to six months *after* their holder had resigned.[7] In contrast, *Beard* upheld an option grant that required executives to be employees when they exercised their options. Although the Court noted this factual distinction to justify its holding, it also emphasized another important (though unrelated) observation: that the option plan had been expressly approved by independent directors—a theme that would begin to take a more prominent position on stage in future cases.

Curiously, the *Beard* opinion spends little time exploring its articulated substantive standard: that there must exist a reasonable relationship between the gains the employee reaps by exercising the option and the value the corporation receives from the executive's continued service. Perhaps one reason for this neglect is the fundamental indeterminacy and, hence, non-administrability of such a standard in practice. As is well understood, an option's ultimate payoff is the difference between its strike price and the underlying security's market value at the time of exercise, a gap that reflects (or at least supposed to reflect) the change in the security's value since the date the option was granted the executive. The realized profit could be due to multiple factors, many of which, if not most, defy easy attribution either directly or indirectly to the option holder's contribution. Yet a substantive reasonability test requires a court to make just such an attribution. In the shadow of this indeterminacy, it is perhaps understandable why the *Beard* Court ultimately placed great faith on a more familiar and accessible indicator: the conceptualization of outside directors as unbiased monitors, exercising their business judgment within the protective shell of organizational independence.[8] Notwithstanding whether this account is more myth than

---

6. Id. at 737.

7. *See* Kerbs v. California Eastern Airways, 90 A.2d 652, 656 (Del. 1952); Gottlieb v. Heyden Chemical Corp., 90 A.2d 660, 664 (Del. 1952).

8. Another and more important consequence of the courts' emphasis on process is that there is no legal standard by which compensation decisions might be judged. To be sure, compensation is to be "fair" and not "wasteful." But these are merely code words for "deliberate," "thoughtful," and "reasonably examined." These are expressions of process devoid of substance. In analogous areas where the courts are called on to assess the fairness of transactions because they involve obvious self dealing on the part of officers or even directors, their inquiry is more substantive. Thus, whether a building rented from a company controlled by the lessee's CEO is fair to the lessee is determined by comparing the lease's terms with leases of comparable properties. See e.g., Lewis v. S.L. & E., Inc., 629 F.2d 764 (2d Cir. 1980)(fairness of related-party transaction judged by whether rents were substantially below prevailing market rents). This approach works poorly for CEO compensation. It entails the risk of the same mischief presented by the compensation committee's encounter with their consultants. And compensation practices within an industry or across many referent industries may be so out of line that the resulting reference is untrustworthy. But the greatest concern simply is that CEOs are not like apples or even prime real estate among which crisp comparisons can be made. When challenging an executive's compensation the issue is confused by the unique endowments of the executive as well as the equally unique challenges that con-

description in practice,[9] judicial comfort with the concept of the independent director (or shareholder) approval steadily began to displace the substantive judicial scrutiny of executive compensation that had theretofore been the norm.[10]

2. Demand Requirements and the Alchemy of Layered Process

Not only have process concerns provided ballast to the tenets of corporate law as applied in the boardroom, but such focal concerns were soon to colonize courtroom procedure as well. Today, the single greatest barrier that a shareholder-plaintiff faces in challenging executive compensation claims is a thoroughgoing procedural hurdle: satisfying the so-called "demand requirement." A suit challenging executive compensation is almost certain to be classified as a derivative suit: the shareholder sues in equity to force the corporation to assert its rights against another (often a corporate fiduciary). Under Delaware law, a shareholder may not commence most derivative suits before first making a demand on the board, which can refer the matter to a committee of disinterested and independent directors that is empowered to dismiss the suit as harmful to the corporation's best interests. The demand requirement is excused, however, if the shareholder can allege facts establishing a reasonable doubt either that the directors were disinterested and independent or that the action challenged was facially harmful to the corporation.

A leading Delaware case, *Aronson v. Lewis*,[11] reflects how high a hurdle the demand requirement places in the path of the derivative suit

front the firm. Third party reference points may prove helpful, but only as a starting point. In the end, the courts are likely to defer to the compensation committee's judgment regarding just how a host of intangible variables are to be weighed in setting executive compensation.

9. Although many of the reforms promulgated during the Sarbanes Oxley place great emphasis on board and committee independence, the evidence is relatively weak that such independence infatuations have a significant effect on the advent or severity of corporate scandals. Stephen P. Ferris, and Xuemin (Sterling) Yana, "Do independent directors and chairmen matter? The role of boards of directors in mutual fund governance," Journal of Corporate Finance Volume 13, Issues 2–3, June 2007, Pages 392–420.

10. 160 A.2d at 737. The result of the shift from substance to process is that suits against executive compensation have their highest chance for success in close corporations and much lower level of success in public corporations. This is because process is more likely overlooked in close corporations whereas process is most always present in public corporations due to

their ability to retain talented and compulsive counsel. Consider that, in their study of all litigated compensation disputes between 1912 and 2000, Professors Thomas and Martin report that plaintiffs' success is about fifty percent greater in close corporations than it is in public corporation when the complaint is not process but substantively based and twice as high when the complaint focuses on process. Because the Thomas and Martin study does not reveal the 124 cases captured in their study it is likely that the public company cases are skewed toward the earlier time period of their study and do not therefore reflect the more contemporary emphasis on process over substance. If their data is so skewed, which this author believes is highly likely, then, even though their data reflect slim odds of successes enjoyed by plaintiffs attacking compensation decisions in public companies, even those slim odds are even slimmer today when the emphasis on process produces even greater insularity for compensation decision making. See Randall S. Thomas & Kenneth J. Martin, Litigating Challenges To Executive Pay: An Exercise In Futility, 79 Wash.U.L. Q. 569, Tbls. 4 & 8 at 608 & 610 (2001).

11. 473 A.2d 805 (Del. 1984).

plaintiff when the focus is executive compensation. *Aronson* involved a challenge to the employment contract awarded to Leo Fink, the owner of 47 percent of the firm's voting stock. When Fink was 75 years old, the firm granted him an employment contract that would pay him $150,000 a year (plus 5 percent of the firm's pre-tax profits above $2.4 million). Fink could terminate the contract at any time and would receive a six figure consulting payment for the remainder of his life; the payments would be made even if he became incapacitated. The board also approved interest free loans to Fink that totaled $225,000. Announcing that the suit could proceed without the approval by Fink's hand-picked board only if the plaintiff's complaint alleged facts that created "reasonable doubt" regarding either the board's independence or that the compensation arrangement was excessive, the Delaware Supreme Court dismissed the action. Neither Fink's dominant ownership stake nor a facially one-sided employment/loan agreement was deemed sufficient to raise a reasonable doubt as to either the compensation package's reasonability or that it was the product of an independent judgment by the directors approving the compensation.[12]

Post *Aronson* decisions largely confirm the view that the decision was not aberrational.[13] One observable impact of *Aronson* is the greater prominence that the demand requirement plays in Delaware after *Aronson*. Prior to *Aronson*, defendants made motions to dismiss the derivative suit challenging executive compensation for failure to make a demand on the board in roughly the same percentage of cases in Delaware (14 percent) as outside of Delaware (18 percent); after *Aronson*, however, such motions in executive compensation decisions proliferated, and are now made in seventy-five percent of Delaware cases compared with only

---

12. Lewis was allowed to amend his complaint and as amended withstood the defendants' motion to dismiss. *See* Lewis v. Aronson, 1985 WL 11553, 11 Del. J. Corp. L. 243 (Del. Ch. May 1, 1985). However, even this subsequent opinion held that demand was not excused by allegation that Fink controlled a *majority* of the shares, that the board nominees were his nominees, or that a majority of the directors served in subservient officer positions that could be terminated as a result of Fink's financial interests in various firms. What permitted the complaint to withstand a motion to dismiss was the allegation that the compensation arrangement was a means of addressing Fink's concern that, in a multifaceted stock sale and purchase arrangement involving companies that seven of the Meyer's directors were themselves officers or directors, that Fink had received too low a price for the shares he sold. Thus, the complaint alleged the consulting contract with Fink was a ruse, being merely a means to use the assets of Meyers to compensate Fink for his sale of shares to companies in which seven of the Meyers directors were

officers or directors. So alleged, the court believed that a demand on the board could be excused since a majority of the Meyers directors were interested in the outcome of the suit. The court also believed reasonable doubt was raised in the amended complaint whether the contract with Fink was the product of a reasonable business judgment. The amended complaint alleged that Fink lived in Florida but Meyers' operations were in New York and states other than Florida. Moreover, the amended complaint also alleged that through a contract Meyers had with a second corporation and that corporation's contract with Fink that Fink was already bound to provide managerial services to Meyers. The court said this additional fact raised a reasonable doubt whether the services Fink would provide are so grossly inadequate that no sound business judgment would deem it worth what the Meyers was called upon to pay for those services.

13. *See e.g.,* Levine v. Smith, 591 A.2d 194 (Del. 1991)(requiring demand because at least 12 of 21 directors of General Motors were believed to be independent).

fourteen percent for non-Delaware cases during the same post-*Aronson* period.[14]

And, if the demand requirement is insufficiently imposing in its own right for plaintiffs, lurking in the shadows is the reality of its stubborn persistence and reappearance at later procedural junctures. Thus, when the directors of Zapata Corporation agreed in 1977 to accelerate the exercise date for stock options for senior officers to just before the company announced a self-tender for its shares at substantial premium over the market price,[15] the plaintiff, eyeing a clear case for excusing the demand, filed suit on behalf of Zapata. However, four years later, the corporation creatively resurrected the demand requirement by appointing two new directors to its board of directors, assigning them to a newly created special litigation committee, and charging the committee with the responsibility for assessing whether the suit was in the corporation's best interest. The Delaware Supreme Court's landmark decision, *Maldonado v. Zapata Corporation*,[16] specifically approved the use of such a committee to insulate a company from what would otherwise be a demand-excused shareholder suit, essentially reintroducing judicial deference to "independent" directors at yet another juncture (with some caveats).[17] By so doing, the case cast additional doubt on the efficacy of derivative litigation for policing compensation practices.

3. The State Competition Dimension

A third dimension of the judiciary's apparent reluctance to scrutinize executive compensation decisions can also be understood in the context of state competition for the provision of corporate law. Under most such accounts, states seek to project themselves as attractive jurisdictions for incorporation, offering (depending on whose account one believes) either the most "efficient" combination of statutes and corporate jurisprudence, or the most protective havens for managers to wallow in perquisites, value extraction and private benefits of control. Regardless of which interpretation one ultimately subscribes to, it has become clear in recent years that significant network effects have enabled Delaware to enjoy a secure (and likely unerodable) advantage over other states in attracting and retaining public incorporations. Within such a protected market environment, Delaware's jurisprudence and statutory structure is unlikely to be penalized even if it were to take on an excessively lax and permissive posture, minimizing the airing of dirty corporate laundry, emphasizing process over substance, and generally going along to get along. Although it is extremely challenging to test

---

14. Randall S. Thomas & Kenneth J. Martin, Litigating Challenges to Executive Pay: An Exercise in Futility?, 79 Wash. U.L.Q. 569, 579 (2001).

15. The apparent rationale for this move was to permit executives to avoid serious tax consequences, though so doing caused the corporation to lose the concomitant tax deduction.

16. 430 A.2d 779 (Del. 1981).

17. In particular, the *Zapata* court held that in addition to requiring that the special committee be independent and fully informed, the court would exercise its own business judgment in deciding whether the suit should go forward. *Id.*

whether Delaware has drifted into such a territory,[18] the notable lack of substantive skepticism that Delaware has traditionally accorded executive compensation and the corresponding procedural hurdles to those challenging executive pay is at the very least highly suggestive.

More recently, it has been posited that if Delaware remains wary of any competing jurisdiction, it is not sister states but rather federal jurisprudence that represents the greatest threat. For example, Mark Roe has examined interesting correlations between Delaware decisions and poaching on Delaware's turf by federal regulatory developments.[19] The thesis is that the Delaware judiciary finds its spine to resist managerial appropriation of shareholder wealth only in instances when needed to moderate or deflect entirely further federal incursions on state corporate law. Thus, judicial laxity toward managerial excesses, particularly in Delaware, may occasionally be accompanied by outlier decisions, instrumentally calculated to stave off subsequent federal regulatory intrusions.

B. *DISNEY* AS A CULMINATING EVENT

The *Disney* case embodied each of the above maladies associated with corporate law's treatment of executive pay. Initially, many observers marked the litigation as signaling an important move towards closer judicial scrutiny of executive compensation decisions. Its ultimate resolution, however, along with events since, suggest that its effects have likely been smaller than (or at least very different from) those a *priori* expectations.

The case initially arose from the Disney board's approval of an executive compensation contract with Michael Ovitz and its implied approval of a no-fault termination of Ovitz resulting in his receipt of a sum in excess of $140 million after barely one year of employment. The Chancery Court held, based on facts set forth in a complaint that could not be more egregious, that the plaintiff's complaint withstood the defendant's motion to dismiss. Among the facts alleged was that Ovitz was hired pursuant to pressure from Disney's CEO, Michael Eisner; that Eisner and Ovitz had been close friends for 25 years; that Ovitz had never been an executive for a publicly owned entertainment company; that internal documents had warned that Ovitz was unqualified; that a member of the compensation committee received a $250,000 fee to secure Ovitz's employment with Disney; that neither the compensation committee nor the board had received, or had an opportunity to review, either the draft or final employment contract with Ovitz; that the compensation committee and the board had devoted hardly any time at their meetings to reviewing and approving the employment of Ovitz; that the compensation committee and the board had delegated the details of the transaction to Eisner; that the board did not condition it becoming

---

18. Some, however, have certainly tried. See, e.g., Guhan Subramanian, The Disappearing Delaware Effect, 20 J. L. Econ. & Org. 32–59 (2004).

19. *See* Marc J. Roe, Delaware's Competition, 117 Harv. L. Rev. 588 (2003); Marc J. Roe, Delaware's Politics, 118 Harv. L. Rev. 2491 (2005).

effective upon their final review or approval; that the final version of the employment contract varied significantly from the drafts earlier summarized for the compensation committee;[20] that from the outset of his employment Ovitz performed poorly; that no experts were consulted at any time in either the employment or termination of Ovitz; that the terms for Ovitz's departure were entered into without express committee or board approval; and, finally, that the severance agreement entered into by Eisner, acting for Disney, awarded Ovitz $140 million for being fired, and did so far more quickly than if he had worked through the entire term of his contract for Disney.

1. The Judicial Windup

These are, no doubt, provocative facts in their own right. But what made the Disney litigation even more interesting was the recidivist relationship it had cultivated over time with the Delaware judiciary. In 2000, the Delaware Supreme Court took a first pass at the Ovitz compensation dispute, in *Brehm v. Eisner*,[21] affirming a prior dismissal by the Chancery Court for failure to state a claim. In so doing, however, the *Brehm* left the courtroom door partly ajar, allowing the plaintiffs the opportunity to re-plead their case. In fact, the Court provided a veritable "how-to" manual on demonstrating that the board, notwithstanding its disinterestedness and reliance on outside experts and subcommittees (both facially permitted under DGCL 141(e)),[22] might have breached its duties approving the original contract and the non-fault termination:

> To survive a Rule 23.1 motion to dismiss in a due care case where an expert has advised the board in its decisionmaking process, the complaint must allege particularized facts (not conclusions) that, if proved, would show, for example, that: (a) the directors did not in fact rely on the expert; (b) their reliance was not in good faith; (c) they did not reasonably believe that the expert's advice was within the expert's professional competence; (d) the expert was not selected with reasonable care by or on behalf of the corporation, and the faulty selection process was attributable to the directors; (e) the subject matter (in this case the cost calculation) that was material and reasonably available was so obvious that the board's failure to consider it was grossly negligent regardless of the expert's advice or

20. For example, the drafts summarized for the compensation committee provided that Ovitz could invoke the non-fault termination clause (that resulted in substantial financial awards) if he was *wrongfully* terminated, died or became disabled. The final version allowed any departure to trigger the clause unless he was terminated for gross negligence or malfeasance.

21. 746 A.2d 244 (Del. Sup. Ct. 2000) (en banc).

22. Section 141(e) reads:

A member of the board of directors, or a member of any committee designated by the board of directors, shall, in the performance of such member's duties, be fully protected in relying in good faith upon the records of the corporation and upon such information, opinions, reports or statements presented to the corporation by any of the corporation's officers or employees, or committees of the board of directors, or by any other person as to matters the member reasonably believes are within such other person's professional or expert competence and who has been selected with reasonable care by or on behalf of the corporation. 8 Del. C. § 141(e).

lack of advice; or (f) that the decision of the Board was so unconscionable as to constitute waste or fraud.[23]

The second significant intersection that Delaware courts had with the *Disney* litigation came in 2003, when the plaintiffs re-pled their complaint, this time following—almost to the letter—the recipe provided three years before in *Brehm*.[24]Once again, Disney moved to dismiss the complaint, this time arguing that the complaint dealt solely with duty of care issues, and that Disney had an "exculpatory" provision in its charter, authorized under Section 102(b)(7) of the Delaware Code, allowing it to shield directors from all monetary liability associated with a breached duty of care.

Chancellor Chandler, however, refused to grant the motion, noting that by its text, § 102(b)(7) provisions do not "eliminate or limit the liability of a director: (i) [f]or any breach of the director's duty of loyalty to the corporation or its stockholders; (ii) for acts or omissions not in good faith or which involve intentional misconduct or a knowing violation of the law ... or (iv) for any transaction from which the director derived an improper personal benefit."[25]

Focusing on the second exclusion above, Chandler ruled that since the plaintiff had alleged that the Disney board acted without taking into account the welfare of the company, they were essentially making a pleading that fell within one of the exceptions to § 102(b)(7). In denying Disney's demurer and excusing demand, the Chancellor observed:

> These facts, if true, do more than portray directors who, in a negligent or grossly negligent manner, merely failed to inform themselves or to deliberate adequately about an issue of material importance to their corporation. Instead, the facts ... suggest that the defendant directors consciously and intentionally disregarded their responsibilities, adopting a "we don't care about the risks" attitude concerning a material corporate decision. Knowing or deliberate indifference by a director to his or her duty to act faithfully and with appropriate care is conduct, in my opinion, that may not have been taken honestly and in good faith to advance the best interests of the company. Put differently, all of the alleged facts, if true, imply that the defendant directors knew that they were making material decisions without adequate information and without adequate deliberation, and that they simply did not care if the decisions caused the corporation and its stockholders to suffer injury or loss. Viewed in this light ... [the] complaint alleges a breach of the directors' obligation to act honestly and in good faith in the corporation's best interests for a Court to conclude, if the facts are true, that the defendant directors' conduct fell outside the protection of the business judgment rule.[26]

---

23. Brehm, at 261.

24. In re Walt Disney Co. Derivative Litigation, 825 A.2d 275 (Del. Ch. 2003).

25. *Id.*

26. *Id.* at 289.

To be sure, the underlying complaint had remained faithful to its evolved Delaware rhetorical heritage, focusing on process rather than the substantive reasonableness of compensation itself. However, Chandler's assessment of possible procedural inadequacies hinted strongly that the need for attentiveness among outside directors could critically hinge—at least in part—on the magnitude of Ovitz' compensation package.

But perhaps more compelling, this linkage bore directly on another important consideration posed to the Delaware courts in *Disney*, namely the existence and content of a theretofore unexplored third rail in fiduciary duty law: the duty to act in good faith. Then–Chancellor William Allen's 1991 *Caremark* opinion[27] had laid some of the initial groundwork for good faith jurisprudence, holding that a board (and/or individual members) did not act in good faith if there was a "sustained and systematic" failure of director oversight. That opinion pushed an already well established linkage between the monitoring role of directors and good faith, suggesting the possibility that woefully bad governance constituted bad faith, and was therefore actionable.

Allen's *Caremark* opinion, however, left two important questions largely unresolved. The first was whether a "sustained and systematic failure of oversight" was anything more than a simple duty of care violation by means of nonfeasance rather than misfeasance–a question that Chandler's 2003 opinion had provisionally (but not conclusively) answered in the affirmative. Second, just how extreme a departure from "good governance" would such a failure of oversight have to be in order to be actionable? For this answer, we had to wait (and in many ways we are still waiting).

After a protracted trial, Chancellor Chandler released his opinion in *Disney* in the late summer of 2005.[28] Perhaps most notably, Chandler largely reaffirmed his earlier sentiment (albeit hedging his bets all the while) that a failure to act in good faith was, in principal, an alternative means for breaching one's fiduciary duties:

> Upon long and careful consideration, I am of the opinion that the concept of intentional dereliction of duty, a conscious disregard for one's responsibilities, is an appropriate (although not the only) standard for determining whether fiduciaries have acted in good faith. Deliberate indifference and inaction in the face of a duty to act is, in my mind, conduct that is clearly disloyal to the corporation. It is the epitome of faithless conduct.

In applying this standard, Chancellor Chandler did something that many observers had found surprising (at least in light of his prior holdings in the case): he held that the Disney defendants would still receive protection from the Business Judgment Rule—that is, they would enjoy a strong presumption that they acted with appropriate care and good faith when acting for the corporation. In applying this standard,

---

27. Caremark Int'l Inc. Derivative Litig., 698 A.2d 959 (Del.Ch.1996).

28. In re Walt Disney Co. Derivative Litigation, 907 A.2d 693 (Del.Ch. 2005).

Chandler found that while Disney's senior executives, board and compensation committee were far from exemplar paragons of corporate governance best practices, the plaintiffs had not overcome the business judgment rule and demonstrated a dereliction of duties meeting the "deliberate indifference and inaction" standard. In fact, in at least some specific aspects of the case (such as the allegation involving the board's decision to grant Ovitz a non-fault termination), Chandler held that any alternative decision by the board was legally unsupportable and would have been subject to a legitimate legal claim by Ovitz for damages.

2. The Supreme Court Opinion

Almost a year after the Chancery Court issued its decision on the merits, a unanimous Supreme Court of Delaware affirmed.[29] Compared to Chandler's 84 page tome,[30] the Supreme Court's analysis appears veritably svelte at 47 pages. Its looks are deceiving, however; for much of the opinion incorporated the Chancery Court opinion either by reference or verbatim.

In addressing the issue of good faith, the Court found (as did Chandler) that such a doctrine was independently actionable and distinct from the duty of care. Specifically approving the lower court's formulation of bad faith as stemming from "intentional indifference and inaction" in the face of a duty to act, the Supreme Court added a visual metaphor of a *spectrum of scienter* to animate its conception of bad faith. On one extreme end of this spectrum resides deliberate and subjective motivation to do harm to the corporation and its shareholders. The opinion does not delve far into this matter, and indeed the pled facts did not allege subjective bad faith; but it would seem self evident that such conduct both should be actionable and would be on many grounds outside good faith (e.g., waste and *ultra vires*).

On the other end of the spectrum, the Court explored grossly negligent conduct, which historically would have triggered duty of care liability. Although Chandler had not definitively answered whether such conduct would also trigger good faith liability, the Supreme Court answered this with an unambiguous "no." In order to violate one's duty to act in good faith, the majority held, one had to do more than breach a duty of care. Much (though not all) of the Court's reasoning was through statutory construction: significant portions of Delaware's statutory scheme (such as §§ 102(b)(7) and 145) single out good faith distinctly, differentiating it explicitly from due care.

This left a final, Goldiloxian category, involving interstitial motivations along the lines of the Chancery Court's formulation of bad faith. Here, the Court found numerous grounds for supporting Chandler's formulation; not only would many hypothetical situations involving subjective intent to harm shareholders fall into this category, but (as noted above) notable portions of Delaware's statutory canvas were

29. In re Walt Disney Co. Derivative Litigation, 906 A.2d 27 (Del. 2006).   **30.** 907 A.2d 693 (Del.Ch. 2005).

already painted with the colors of good faith. In a very real sense, possibly motivated good faith's longstanding but largely uninterrogated statutory presence, the Court seemed compelled to find that good faith should mean *something*, and here was an appropriate way to fill in the gap. After its discussion of good faith as a general matter, Justice Jacobs specifically approved of Chandler's "deliberate indifference and inaction" metric for bad faith; and moreover, the Court concluded that such a formulation was possibly under-inclusive still:

> [W]e uphold the Court of Chancery's definition as a legally appropriate, although not the exclusive, definition of fiduciary bad faith. We need go no further. To engage in an effort to craft (in the Court's words) "a definitive and categorical definition of the universe of acts that would constitute bad faith" would be unwise and is unnecessary to dispose of the issues presented on this appeal.[31]

Significantly, the Court also upheld Chandler's utilization of the business judgment rule presumption when scrutinizing defendants' alleged bad faith. Although we can surely speculate as to whether the case would have come out differently in the absence of such deference, the applicability of the business judgment rule within good faith cases may suggest something even more: it may imply, for example, that prospective defendants can attempt to address liability risk under the good faith doctrine by papering their decisions with additional layers of process.

3. The Aftermath

Relative to many of the other cases discussed in this volume, the *Disney* case is of a very young and still-ripening vintage. Its text, subtext, and reach are likely to be debated and remain unsettled for some time to come. However, since *Disney*, the Supreme Court has had at least one occasion to revisit the good faith doctrine, issuing an opinion that warrants mention here.

In November 2006, the court decided *Stone v. Ritter*,[32] a case in which shareholders had brought suit against AmSouth bank in connection with a $40 million deferred prosecution settlement it reached with federal banking authorities, settling charges that it had failed to take appropriate investigative/reporting steps upon receiving credible evidence of material wrongdoing involving a money laundering and Ponzi scheme conducted by one of its account holders.

In *Ritter,* the Chancery Court had dismissed the shareholder action, holding that the plaintiffs had not adequately plead pursuant to *Caremark* that the fine was a result of a "systematic and sustained failure of director oversight." In its opinion, the Supreme Court affirmed, and in so doing specifically linked the *Caremark* doctrine to the good faith doctrine established in *Disney*. More significantly, the Court proceeded also to render an opinion once again on whether a "bad faith" action

---

31. *Id.* at 67.

32. Stone ex rel. AmSouth Bancorporation v. Ritter, 911 A.2d 362 (Del. 2006).

constitutes a separately actionable claim from other claims involving breached fiduciary duties:

> It is important, in this context, to clarify a doctrinal issue that is critical to understanding fiduciary liability under Caremark as we construe that case. The phraseology used in Caremark and that we employ here—describing the lack of good faith as a "necessary condition to liability"—is deliberate. The purpose of that formulation is to communicate that a failure to act in good faith is not conduct that results, ipso facto, in the direct imposition of fiduciary liability. The failure to act in good faith may result in liability because the requirement to act in good faith "is a subsidiary element[,]" i.e., a condition, "of the fundamental duty of loyalty." [citing Guttman v. Huang, 823 A.2d 492, 506 n. 34 (Del.Ch.2003).] It follows that because a showing of bad faith conduct, in the sense described in Disney and Caremark, is essential to establish director oversight liability, the fiduciary duty violated by that conduct is the duty of loyalty.

This is somewhat of a curious place to end up, particularly in light of the fact that (a) none of the Disney cases had explicitly identified good faith with loyalty; and (b) Chancellor Allen in his *Caremark* opinion specifically noted that the case was one he identified as a duty of care case, and not a duty of loyalty case.[33] Be that as it may, the immediate post-Disney interpretation of the good faith doctrine—for both executive compensation and other arenas of corporate behavior—is that the doctrine of good faith resides as a wholly owned subsidiary of the duty of loyalty.

C. DOES *DISNEY* MARK A SEA CHANGE FOR FI-DUCIARY LAW?

The *Disney* opinion and its immediate progeny have placed the debate around executive compensation, as well as the emerging doctrine of good faith, in an especially murky territory. Although it now seems possible to challenge executive pay decisions on the grounds that they were made in bad faith, the task of doing so is complicated in at least three ways. First, defendants retain the protection of the business judgment rule, which effectively precludes all but the strongest cases from going forward. Second, because of the business judgment rule's focus on process, it is likely that corporate defendants may feel invited to erect additional procedural measures to insulate them from future liability claims. And finally, at least recent interpretations of Disney have characterized the good faith doctrine, somewhat curiously, as a flavor of the duty of loyalty.

In varying degrees, each of these aspects of *Disney* supports our earlier concern: that there is no *there* with respect to substantive standards by which courts can mediate claims of excessive executive compensation. Moreover, as a matter of doctrine, *Disney* seems to provide a type of mixed message. It embraces a fiduciary obligation to act

---

33. *In re* Caremark, 698 A.2d at 967.

in good faith, but moves it more toward the intentional spectrum of misconduct than many before *Disney* believed was its rightful location. Given this mixed message, it is not entirely clear whether *Disney* will ultimately be seen to mark a sea change for the historical judicial deference accorded executive pay decisions (at least within Delaware).

To be sure, the *Disney* plaintiffs got their day in court, so the demand requirement did not prove insuperable. But even here, *Disney* permits larger themes to be considered. Thus, taking the cynical view, we might cast the earlier Delaware *Disney* decisions grappling with the demand requirement as analogous to the cat playing with a mouse (no allusions to Mickey here intended) before swallowing it whole. *Brehm* provided a path for the plaintiff to escape the talons of the demand requirement and following the prescribed template the amended complaint ultimately survived a motion. This provided just enough hope that Delaware can clean the corporate stables so that federal encroachment was not necessary. Indeed, the Disney wars took place soon after Congress had already done some significant poaching on state law terrain by enacting the Sarbanes–Oxley Act of 2002. In hindsight, the Delaware Supreme Court may have merely been involved in an elaborate doctrinal gesticulation which did enough—but only enough—to keep Washington regulators and lawmakers convinced that Delaware's courts remain vigilant about compensation-borne agency costs.

Viewed in this light, the Delaware Supreme Court may have squandered an opportunity to be creative and innovative in fields of governance, compensation, and managerial accountability. Whether they did so rightly or wrongly is subject to considerable argument; but regardless of one's side in this debate, the sound and fury of the good faith rhetoric that ultimately produces meandering and flaccid substantive intervention is at the very least annoying to many commentators.

Nevertheless, our opinion is that it is still too early to write off *Disney*'s possible wake in at least two respects. First, the opinion still has a number of loose ends that have yet to be tied up. It is clear that the doctrine of good faith—while showing few signs of kinetic energy—has considerable potential force. It is incompletely theorized, and subject to additional refinement, alteration, and growth. It is quite possible that the Delaware courts will utilize this largely blank canvass to craft an image of the good faith duty that is rigorous and coherent.

Second, and more abstractly, the current disorganized state of fiduciary law after the *Disney* and *Ritter* decisions may provide an interesting opportunity for the emergence of a transcendental "über-duty" that envelops and swallows the other conventional duties more holistically and parsimoniously. Indeed, the traditional substantive and doctrinal distinctions between the duties of care and loyalty have always seemed a bit artificial and difficult to defend—at least to us. To be sure, the standard distinction between them is well-worn territory: the duty of care focuses on acts of managerial negligence or shirking, while the duty of loyalty focuses on conflicts of interest or stealing. Nevertheless, at their economic core, both duties are essentially legal constructs that endeavor to achieve the same result: minimizing the incidence and effects of managerial "moral hazard." It is difficult—and in many ways troubling—to understand why two legal duties with largely coterminous goals tend to go about effectuating those goals in such distinct ways.[34] Although some legal scholars have argued that perhaps care and loyalty are regulated differently because they involve different stakes or different psychological frames for the participants,[35] the evidence for such clams seems to be somewhat unimpressive.[36]

The addition of the duty to act in good faith (with its contorted doctrinal contours) may, much like chemical clarification, cleanse these doctrinal waters by muddying them even further. Indeed, the sorts of facts that would typically establish such an allegation tend to reflect extreme managerial inattentiveness, very much akin to that described by William Allen in the *Caremark* case, and which was, until very recently, perceived as a flavor of the duty of care (pertaining to nonfeasance). Nevertheless, as *Ritter* apparently concludes, such violations are now to be categorized (curiously) as breached duties of loyalty. At the same time, while conventional duty of loyalty cases involving uncleansed conflicts of interest do not invoke the business judgment rule, the duty to act in good faith apparently does receive the rule's presumptive protection. Future decisions inevitably must grapple with locating actionable neglectfulness within this new—and confusing—terrain. Nevertheless, the end result of this doctrinal maelstrom is that the boundaries between care, loyalty, and good faith are likely to become irretrievably intertwined. And that ultimately may be a good thing, if what emerges is a more holistic fiduciary duty that blends elements of care, loyalty and good faith, into an all things considered standard for managerial comportment. Rather than cubby holing behavior into one category or another, courts may develop a jurisprudential standard whose commands can be summarized simply: Do not engage in unreasonable amounts of moral hazard.

At minimum, the *Disney* opinion has placed a new bottle on the scales of justice; it is a bottle that is still sufficiently empty that subsequent judicial applications may fill it not with the stale bromides of the past, but rather a rich blend of substantive reference points that will guide future mediations of disputes regarding executive compensation. We believe this is possible by wisely addressing—on a case-by-case basis—the issues inherent in executive pay, which include the relative independence of the compensation process, demanding strong links between pay and performance, and evidence that the corporate and not the executive's interest pervades the compensation package. If appropriately developed, such a doctrine may well plant the seeds for what could become, perhaps ironically, a less deferential, less procedurally fixated, more finely tailored, more efficient, and ultimately more sensible legal landscape, to the benefit of shareholders and managers alike.

---

34. For example, the business judgment rule historically does not apply to "uncleansed" duty of loyalty cases, while it provides strong protection to any duty of care case.

35. Cooter & Friedman 66 N.Y.U. L. Rev. 1045 (1991).

36. Arlen, Spitzer & Talley, 31 J. Legal. Stud. 1 (2002).

Chapter 4

THE TRANSAMERICA CASE

By
*Jill E. Fisch**

It may seem odd for a book entitled *Iconic Cases in Corporate Law* to include a chapter about the Transamerica decision.[1] Transamerica, after all, is a decision by a federal court, interpreting the proxy rules adopted by the United States Securities and Exchange Commission pursuant to its authority under the federal securities laws. Characterizing Transamerica as a building block of U.S. corporate law appears to run counter to the traditional distinction between state corporate law and the securities laws which, in contrast to corporate law are mandatory, adopted by Congress and, through its delegated rule-making authority, the SEC, and focused on securities transactions rather than the internal affairs of the corporation. Concededly the distinction between corporate law and securities law is neither clear nor absolute. The subject of shareholder voting perhaps best illustrates the uncertain boundary between the two. Of the issues regulated by the federal securities law, the proxy rules reflect the most extensive intrusion law into the internal affairs of the corporation. This intrusion was not apparent at the time that Congress enacted the federal securities laws, nor is it obvious from the text of the federal statutes themselves. Nonetheless, the SEC, through the adoption and enforcement of the federal proxy rules, has taken substantial—some might say primary—responsibility for delineating the scope of shareholder voting rights. Through its regulation of shareholder voting, the SEC has played a critical role in determining the extent to which shareholders, through the exercise of voting rights, can exercise power over corporate management.

Although at the time, the Transamerica decision represented a watershed event in support of shareholder voting power, the SEC almost immediately began to retreat from its role as shareholder advocate.

---

* T.J. Maloney Professor of Business Law, Fordham University.

1. SEC v. Transamerica Corp., 163 F.2d 511 (3d Cir. 1947).

Through its repeated amendments to the federal proxy rules and the positions it adopted in subsequent litigation over those rules, the SEC has placed increasing limits on shareholder access to the proxy. More significantly, the SEC's active efforts to determine the appropriate limits on shareholder voting power have put it, and not state courts or legislatures, in the primary position of determining the subjects that are proper for a shareholder vote, the extent to which shareholders can increase their role in corporate governance by amending the corporate bylaws and the appropriate role of shareholders in the nomination of directors.

There are reasons to question the limits imposed by the SEC on shareholder voting.[2] Although the SEC has traditionally portrayed itself as the "investor's advocate,"[3] some critics argue that the SEC has been unduly influenced by corporate management, a concern perhaps most visible in its recent amendments concerning shareholder power to nominate directors.[4] Independent of the substantive merits of the SEC's position, however, there are reasons to question the SEC's decision to federalize shareholder voting rights and to impose universal standards rather than allowing individual state or issuer experimentation and regulation. The Transamerica decision reveals the origins of this process.

A.   BACKGROUND TO THE TRANSAMERICA CASE

The background to the Transamerica decision was the SEC's promulgation of rules governing the solicitation of proxies. By the mid 1800s, dispersed ownership of publicly traded stock had made it difficult for shareholders to attend annual meetings in person. Some shareholders sought to appoint a representative or proxy to vote their shares at the meeting. At the same time, issuers began to have difficulty meeting quorum requirements and began to seek proxy voting authority from shareholders in conjunction with providing notice of the annual meeting.

The permissibility of proxy voting was unclear under state law. State courts generally agreed that shareholders had no common law right to vote their stock by proxy, and held that such a right had to be conferred either by statute or in the corporation's charter or by-laws.[5] A

2. One of the better known advocates for increased shareholder voting power is Lucian Bebchuk. See, e.g, Lucian A. Bebchuk, The Myth of the Shareholder Franchise, 93 Va. L. Rev. 675 (2007) (advocating increased shareholder voting power including ballot access and reimbursement of costs).

3. Securities & Exchange Commission, The Investor's Advocate: How the SEC Protects Investors, Maintains Market Integrity, and Facilitates Capital Formation, avail. at http://www.sec.gov/about/whatwedo.shtml (Nov. 19, 2007).

4. See, e.g., Kara Scannell, Cox, in Denying Proxy Access, Puts His SEC Legacy on Line, Wall. St. J., Nov. 29, 2007, at C1 (describing SEC's adoption of proxy rule amendments as re-opening concern that Chairman Cox would "roll back shareholder rights in favor of business interests.")

5. See, e.g., Market S. R. Co. v. Hellman, 109 Cal. 571 (1895) ("At common law a stockholder has no right to cast his vote by proxy"), quoting Cook on Stock and Stockholders § 610; Leonard H. Axe, Corporate Proxies, 41 Mich. L. Rev. 38 (1942) (explaining that, at common law, proxy voting required "special authorization," typically in the form of a charter or by-law provision).

few courts went further and held that shareholder voting was a personal obligation of the shareholder and could not be delegated—even where permitted by a corporation's charter—absent explicit statutory authority.[6] State legislatures responded to these decisions, first with permissive statutes that authorized proxy voting and subsequently by affirmatively granting shareholders the right to vote by proxy.[7]

By the early 1900s, it had become common for corporations to solicit shareholder proxies for the annual meeting. These proxies generally authorized a management representative, typically the corporate secretary, to vote the shareholder's stock on his or her behalf. It was usual for proxies to be broadly worded, allowing the representative to exercise all rights that the shareholder would have had, if he or she had been present at the annual meeting, including the right to exercise the proxy's own discretion in voting on matters that were not specifically mentioned in the annual meeting notice.[8]

Management at some companies misused this proxy authority, however. Some shareholders were forced or deceived into granting proxy authority.[9] Reports surfaced of corporations issuing dividend checks which provided that the shareholder, by endorsing the check, designated a corporate officer as his or her proxy.[10] It was also "an accepted corporate practice" for management to submit to the shareholders for their approval, all acts and transactions by the corporation's officers and directors during the prior year, and the standard corporate proxy authorized this so-called "ratification" of the acts of management.[11] Through these measures, management was able to obtain shareholder approval of management self-dealing transactions, substantial executive compensation and other abusive transactions.

In the early 1930s, Congress heard testimony concerning these abuses, and when it passed the Securities Exchange Act of 1934, it granted the Commission authority to make rules governing the solicitation of proxies, subject to the proviso that the rules be "necessary or appropriate in the public interest or for the protection of investors."[12] The SEC initially focused its rulemaking on disclosure and the prohibi-

---

6. See, e.g., Taylor v. Griswold, 14 N.J.L. 222 (1834) (holding that corporation lacks the power to adopt a by-law permitting shareholders to vote by proxy absent legislative authorization).

7. See, e.g., Arthur H. Dean, Non–Compliance with Proxy Regulations: Effect on Ability of Corporation to Hold Valid Meeting, 24 Cornell L. Q. 483, 488 n.11 (1939) (quoting various state statutes granting shareholders the right to vote by proxy).

8. See Dean, supra note 7 at 490 (describing solicitation of proxies prior to the adoption of the Securities Exchange Act of 1934).

9. See, e.g., Rice & Hutchins, Inc. v. Triplex Shoe Co., 16 Del. Ch. 298, 309

(1929) (invalidating effort of management to vote shareholder proxies to ratify self-dealing transactions without advising the stockholders of their intentions).

10. Indeed, this practice seemingly continued after the adoption of the Securities Exchange Act at unlisted corporations that were not subject to the federal proxy rules. See David M. Friedman, SEC Regulation of Corporate Proxies, 63 Harv. L. Rev. 796, 816 n.77 (1950) (citing case described in connection with proposed legislation to extend Regulation 14(a) to unlisted companies).

11. Dean, supra note 11 at 490.

12. Securities Exchange Act of 1934, 15 U.S.C. § 78n(a).

tion of fraud. Specifically, in response to the abuses described above, the SEC required management to provide shareholders with adequate information about the issues on which the proxy was to be voted, as well as any personal interest of the proxy.[13]

In 1939, however, shareholders John and Lewis Gilbert locked horns with Bethlehem Steel.[14] Prior to the annual meeting, the Gilberts had informed management that they intended to move to amend the bylaws to provide for shareholder election of the auditors. When management sent out to shareholders the notice of the annual meeting and the proxy form, it did not mention the Gilbert motion. The management solicitation did not seek general proxy authorization however; it sought voting authority only for the election of directors. Management seemingly assumed that the Gilbert motion would not pass if only those shareholders physically present at the meeting were able to vote on it.

The Gilberts complained to the SEC, and the SEC advised Bethlehem Steel that, in its opinion, the failure to inform shareholders about the motion rendered its proxy solicitation false and misleading. The Commission suggested that the company adjourn the meeting and notify shareholders about the motion. Bethlehem Steel did adjourn the meeting, and wrote to shareholders informing them about the Gilbert motion. Management did not, however, seek voting authority with respect to the Gilbert's motion and, at the annual meeting, the motion was defeated by those shareholders physically present.

The Commission responded the next year by amending the federal proxy rules. As it explained: "The Commission has been seriously concerned regarding the responsibility of corporate management to communicate to security holders information with respect to matters which minority groups have indicated will be brought up for action at a proposed meeting."[15] As a result, it amended Rule X–14A–9(I), renumbered as Rule X–14A–8, to require that, if proxies were to be used to vote at an annual meeting or to provide a quorum, that the proxy solicitation provide notice to shareholders of any matter expected to be raised at the annual meeting, and that the form of proxy provide shareholders with the opportunity to specify their desired action with respect to each such matter.

Just two years later, the Commission went further, adopting its initial version of the shareholder proposal rule. As amended in December 1942, federal proxy rules required that shareholder proposals be included in the company's proxy statement, and that "Stockholders making proposals for action which are opposed by management must be given not more than 100 words in the proxy in which to state their position,

---

13. Rules LA 1–7, Sec. Exch. Act Rel. No. 378 (Class A), (Sept. 24, 1935).

14. Dean, supra note 7 at 503; John Bainbridge, Profiles, The Talking Stock-holder—II, The New Yorker, Dec. 18, 1948 at 33.

15. Sec. Exch. Act Rel. No. 2376, 1999 WL 955899 (Jan. 12, 1940).

provided the security holder gives the management reasonable notice of his intention."[16]

Who were the Gilbert brothers, whose actions at Bethlehem Steel and other companies spurred the Commission's rulemaking efforts? John and Lewis Gilbert were perhaps the best known shareholder activists of all time.[17] The Gilberts were men of independent means, who acquired, largely by inheritance, shares in several hundred corporations. Beginning in the 1930s, the Gilberts embarked on a lifelong crusade to increase shareholder participation in corporate governance. As part of this crusade, the Gilberts regularly attended annual meetings, speaking from the floor and introducing shareholder proposals on a wide variety of corporate governance issues. In the 1940s, the Gilberts typically focused on issues such as proper auditing, the provision of post-meeting reports to shareholders, and convenient location of shareholder meetings. The Gilberts were also long time advocates of enhancing director accountability through the elimination of staggered boards, director ownership of stock, and limits on executive compensation. Over the years following the adoption of the federal proxy rules, the Gilberts would introduce hundreds of shareholder proposals, and studies show that they were responsible for over half of all proposals introduced by retail investors. Their activism, including regular attendance at annual meetings, continued for almost seventy years until John Gilbert's death in 2002.[18]

B. THE TRANSAMERICA DECISION

The Transamerica case[19] resulted from a classic example of the Gilberts' shareholder activism. John Gilbert owned seventeen shares of Transamerica stock. Prior to the annual meeting, Gilbert advised Transamerica, as per the SEC rules, that he intended to introduce four proposals at the 1946 annual meeting: 1) to change the location of the annual meeting;[20] 2) to have independent public auditors of the company, to be elected by the shareholders; 3) to eliminate an existing bylaw, bylaw 47; and 4) to require that a report of the proceedings of the annual meeting be sent to all shareholders. These proposals were comparable to those introduced by the Gilbert brothers at many companies during this time period.

Transamerica's Bylaw 47, the subject of one of Gilbert's proposals, appeared to present an obstacle to Gilbert's plan. Bylaw 47 required notice of any bylaw amendments to be contained in the notice of the annual meeting—a document that was prepared and distributed by management. Transamerica argued that the board of directors had the

---

16. Sec. Exch. Act. Rel No. 3347, 1949 WL 35734 (Dec. 18, 1942).

17. See John Bainbridge, Profiles, The Talking Stockholder—I, The New Yorker, Dec. 11, 1948 at 40 (profiling Lewis Gilbert and describing his brother John).

18. See Davis Global Advisors, Inc., In Memory, Global Proxywatch, Volume 6, p.

2, July 26, 2002, http://web.management. mcgill.ca/Art.Durnev/proxy.pdf (reporting John Gilbert's death).

19. SEC v. Transamerica Corp., 163 F.2d 511 (3d Cir. 1947).

20. This proposal became moot prior to the litigation. Id. at 513, n 1.

discretion to decide what was contained in the notice of the annual meeting and that the board could therefore exclude Gilbert's proposals from that notice. Since Gilbert's proposals did not comply with Bylaw 47, they were not, according to Transamerica, permissible subjects for a shareholder vote under Delaware law.

The SEC advised Transamerica that it was required to include Gilbert's proposals in its proxy statement; when Transamerica refused, the SEC brought suit. The district court largely agreed with Transamerica.[21] The court determined that Transamerica was entitled to exclude Gilbert's proposals if they were not proper subjects for a shareholder vote, and that state law—in this case Delaware law—governed the issue of what constituted a proper subject for a shareholder vote. With respect to the annual meeting report, the court found that Gilbert's proposal was barred by Delaware law, which gives the directors authority over the business and operations of the corporation; the court concluded that the decision to provide such a report was therefore within the directors' discretion.

Turning to Bylaw 47, the court stated that the bylaw was valid and that Delaware law authorized the directors to act as gatekeepers with respect to issues to be considered at the annual meeting. The court explicitly found that, under Delaware law, the shareholders did not possess an absolute right to amend the bylaws. The court then rejected the SEC's argument that such a bylaw improperly deprived shareholders of their state law power to amend the bylaws, holding that this power was adequately preserved through an alternative mechanism consistent with Delaware law—a special meeting which the corporation was required to hold upon the request of a majority of the shareholders.

Finally, the district court concluded that Gilbert's resolution regarding the shareholder election of auditors was not barred by Bylaw 47 because it had not been explicitly framed as a bylaw amendment. As a resolution, the proposal was, according to the court, a proper subject for a shareholder vote, both because it did not conflict with any provision in Transamerica's bylaws or charters, and because the Delaware statute did not reserve the selection of the auditors to the directors. Moreover, as the court explained: "The matter of independent auditors is therefore of such fundamental importance that it should be considered and passed upon by stockholders themselves at a meeting and is not such a matter which it may be said the stockholders have already delegated to others."[22]

Both sides appealed to the Third Circuit Court of Appeals. Unlike the district court, the Third Circuit gave almost no consideration to the scope of shareholder voting rights under Delaware state law beyond recognizing the fact that shareholders had the power to amend corporate bylaws. The Court of Appeals did not even consider the possibility that the board's statutory authority over corporate operations could limit the

---

21. SEC v. Transamerica Corp., 67 F. Supp. 326 (D. Del. 1946).

22. 67 F. Supp. at 335.

permissible scope of shareholder voting power. Rather, in determining what constituted a proper subject for shareholder action under Rule X–14A–7, the court appeared to apply federal, rather than state law.

Not only did the court find that subjects of the Gilbert proposals to be proper, it also concluded that any issuer-specific limitations on the shareholder voting power conferred by that rule were improper.[23] The court's rationale was that such limitations would interfere with the intent of Congress to require fair corporate suffrage. In particular, the court concluded Congress intended shareholder voting rights to operate as a check on the abuse of power by corporate management, and that SEC rule X–14A–7 was consistent with that intention. As the court stated: "The power conferred upon the Commission by Congress cannot be frustrated by a corporate by-law."[24]

Importantly, the Transamerica decision is not based on state law authority about the allocation of power between shareholders and directors. Shareholder voting rights are, after all, the product of state law. State corporation statutes determine shareholder voting rights in the first instance, but typically they expressly require a shareholder vote only on a few critical issues such as the election of directors, mergers, charter amendments and dissolution. The statutes do not prohibit shareholders from voting on other issues, but neither do they explicitly permit it. Indeed, state law does not expressly give shareholders the right to introduce and vote on a shareholder resolution. In addition, shareholder voting rights are state-specific. In Delaware, for example, shareholder have the power to amend the bylaws, and that power cannot be eliminated.[25] In Indiana and Oklahoma, in contrast, only the board of directors has the power to amend the bylaws unless the charter confers that power on the shareholders.[26]

In addition, the statutes expressly contemplate issuer-specific tailoring of shareholder voting rights through the corporation's internal documents: the charter and bylaws. Nothing in state corporation statutes precludes corporations from adopting procedural rules concerning the exercise of shareholder voting rights—notice requirements, required holding periods or minimum holdings for the exercise of particular rights. Similarly, state law authorizes issuer-specific rules governing shareholder voting power. Delaware law, for example, authorizes corporations to adopt supermajority voting requirements,[27] to provide for the election of directors either by plurality or majority voting,[28] and to

---

23. In particular, as the court noted, Transamerica subsequently amended Bylaw 47 to require notice of shareholder-proposed bylaw amendments submitted by holders of 1% of the outstanding stock. The court concluded that this requirement was unduly onerous because it would have required approximately 1500 average shareholders to band together to request a vote on a bylaw amendment. 163 F.2d at 513 n.2. The court cited no state law authority for this conclusion.

24. 163 F.2d at 518.

25. 8 Del. C. § 109(a).

26. Indiana: 23–1–39–1; Oklahoma: § 1013.

27. 8 Del. C. § 102(b)(4).

28. 8 Del. C. §§ 141, 216 (amended 2006).

dispense with an annual meeting by electing directors by written consents.[29]

Nor is the Transamerica decision based on state decisional law. Concededly several recent Delaware decisions have emphasized the importance of shareholder voting and subjected board interference with the shareholder franchise to a higher level of judicial scrutiny.[30] However, the Transamerica decision predates these cases by many years. More importantly, the decision explicitly references congressional rather than state policy regarding the importance of shareholder voting.

The court's decision in Transamerica thus staked out the role of federal law in determining the scope of shareholder voting rights and the role of the federal government in enforcing those rights. The court stated that congressional intent in regulating proxy solicitation was not limited to disclosure: "It was the intent of Congress to require fair opportunity for the operation of corporate suffrage."[31] Moreover, the Transamerica decision established the authority of the SEC, both in dictating mechanisms to protect shareholder voting rights and in imposing its view of fair corporate suffrage upon issuers.

Importantly, the Transamerica decision also had the effect of partially displacing state courts in the lawmaking process. In the Transamerica case specifically, Bylaw 47 limited shareholder's statutory power to amend the bylaws. The validity of Bylaw 47 was based upon the extent to which this limitation was permissible, but that question was a matter of Delaware law. One would expect this type of question to be decided, in the first instance, by the Delaware Chancery court. Even if the Transamerica bylaw inappropriately thwarted shareholders' voting rights, one obvious alternative to the Third Circuit's federalization of this question was for Gilbert to challenge the validity of the bylaw in state court.

C. FURTHER DEVELOPMENT OF THE FEDERAL PROXY RULES

The Transamerica decision represented the high point in SEC protection of shareholder voting. Rule X–14A–7 afforded shareholders the broadest power with respect to the introduction of shareholder proposals; it imposed no qualification requirements, limits on the number of proposals allowed, or subject matter limits. Within a few years, however, the SEC began to limit the scope of the shareholder proposal rule. In addition, Transamerica is the only case in which the SEC brought suit to compel an issuer to include a shareholder proposal.[32]

29. 8 Del. C. § 228.

30. See, e.g., Blasius Indus., Inc. v. Atlas Corp., 564 A.2d 651, 660–62 (Del. Ch. 1988); see also Schnell v. Chris–Craft Indus., Inc., 285 A.2d 437, 439 (Del. 1971).

31. 163 F.2d at 518.

32. Indeed, the SEC gradually moved from a defender of shareholder voting rights to a defender of issuer efforts to exclude shareholder proposals. See Medical Comm. for Human Rights v. SEC, 432 F.2d 659 (D.C. Cir. 1970), vacated as moot, 404 U.S. 403 (1972), (in which the SEC issued a

Subsequent to the Transamerica case, the SEC gradually began to retreat from its expansive view of the appropriate scope of shareholder voting power.

Following the Transamerica decision, use of the shareholder proposal rule slowly but gradually increased. Published statistics showed that shareholder proposals were introduced at large and well-known companies, yet their use was relatively rare in the 1940s and 50s. One study reported that during the period 1945–57 (pre-Transamerica), 1.4% of proxy statements submitted to the SEC contained shareholder proposals.[33] By 1955 that number had risen to 3.1%.[34] The Gilbert brothers were responsible for approximately half the shareholder proposals submitted during this time period; in 1955, they submitted 65% of all proposals.[35] The shareholder proposals dealt primarily with corporate governance issues. Cumulative voting, selection of auditors, elimination of staggered boards and executive compensation were the most popular issues.[36]

In addition, the SEC began the process of refining the shareholder proposal rule, a process that has continued to the present day. Through half a dozen amendments to the federal proxy rules, the SEC introduced advance notice requirements, limits on the number of words and the number of proposals, qualification requirements for proposing shareholders, and limitations on resubmission of previously-submitted proposals. In addition, in response to uses of shareholder proposal that it viewed as inappropriate, the SEC moved from the broad concept of proper subject matter it had advocated in the Transamerica decision to a rule that articulated a growing number of bases on which management was permitted to exclude a shareholder proposal as improper. These bases included proposals made "primarily for the purpose of promoting general economic, political, racial, religious, social or similar causes," proposals that addressed the "conduct of the ordinary business operations of the issuer," proposals relating to director elections and proposals concerning specific amounts of dividend payments.

In 1976, the SEC also formally created the so-called precatory proposal.[37] Having determined that shareholder proposals which took the form of a directive or mandate could create a tension with state statutes giving boards exclusive authority over corporate decision-making,[38] the SEC decided that this problem could generally be addressed by framing

---

no-action letter permitting issuer to exclude shareholder proposal).

33. Frank D. Emerson & Franklin C. Latcham, The Sec Proxy Proposal Rule: The Corporate Gadfly, 19 U. Chi. L. Rev. 807, 812 (1951–1952).

34. Frank D. Emerson, Some Sociological and Legal Aspects of Institutional and Individual Participation Under the SEC's Shareholder Proposal Rule, 34 U. Det. L.J. 518, 537 (1957).

35. Id. at 542.

36. Id. (describing statistical breakdown of shareholder proposals by subject matter).

37. Adoption of Amendments Relating to Proposals by Security Holders, Sec. Exch. Act Rel. No. 12999, 1955 WL 5976 (Nov. 22, 1976).

38. Indeed, such a provision in the Delaware statute had led the district court in Transamerica to conclude that the request for an annual meeting report was not a proper subject for shareholder action. Transamerica, 67 F.Supp. at 330.

the proposal as a request or recommendation rather than a mandate. Concededly there was state law authority that shareholders lacked the power to interfere with certain types of corporate decisions.[39] It is not clear, however, that this authority operated as a limitation on shareholder voting power—conceivably shareholders were free to pass resolutions or bylaw amendments subject to a subsequent judicial determination as to the validity of those resolutions or the extent to which management was required to comply with them. Nonetheless, the SEC reasoned that it would be illogical to allow shareholders to vote on actions that they lacked the power to take. Accordingly, it added a note to the rule stating that, "A proposal that may be improper under the applicable state law when framed as a mandate or directive may be proper when framed as a recommendation or request."[40] Interestingly, and somewhat ironically, there is no explicit authority in state law empowering shareholders to vote on precatory resolutions. Thus, in the guise of ensuring that shareholder voting did not conflict with state law, the SEC granted shareholders voting rights that arguably extended beyond those afforded by state law, although the significance of the rights was somewhat limited.

The bases for exclusion were interpreted and applied by the SEC staff through the no-action process.[41] The no-action process is an informal and non-binding adjudication that results from the requirement in Rule 14a–8 that issuers notify the SEC if they intend to exclude a shareholder proposal. An issuer that seeks to exclude a proposal submits to the staff an explanation of the bases upon which exclusion can be justified and requests that the SEC take no enforcement action against it if the proposal is excluded. The staff responds by advising the issuer whether it agrees. If the staff agrees, the proposal is excluded. If the staff states that, in its opinion, the proposal cannot be excluded, the issuer generally acquiesces.

Staff decisions are not binding upon the courts, which may compel that a proposal be included despite the staff position. In addition, the letters have no precedential value. Nonetheless, as the D.C. Circuit recognized in *Medical Committee for Human Rights*,[42] shareholders rarely pursue litigation if the staff issues a no action letter, as a result, the SEC staff position essentially becomes the law unless or until the Commission itself overturns it or announces a formal change in policy. From time to time the SEC does issue a more formal interpretation of

---

39. See, e.g., Charlestown Boot & Shoe Co. v. Dunsmore, 60 N.H. 85(1880) (rejecting efforts by shareholders to control directors' exercise of their power to run the corporation).

40. See Adoption of Amendments, 1976 WL 160347 (explaining rationale for addition of this note).

41. See Statement of Informal Procedures for the Rendering of Staff Advice with Respect to Shareholder Proposals, Sec.

Exch. Act Rel. No. 12599, 1976 WL 160411 (July 7, 1976) (describing evolution of no-action process with respect to shareholder proposals).

42. See Medical Comm. for Human Rights, 432 F.2d at 672 ("For the small investor, personal recourse to the Commission's proxy procedures without benefit of counsel may well be the only practicable method of contesting a management decision to exclude his proxy proposal").

the rules in the form of an interpretive release, which is designed to provide broader guidance than the no-action process. Some of the SEC's releases with respect to Rule 14a–8 are discussed in more detail below.

The no-action process has, from time to time, produced some controversy on the question of what constitutes a proper subject for shareholder action. One example is the exclusion for social, religious, political and similar proposals. In 1969, the Medical Committee for Human Rights, owner of five shares of Dow Chemical stock, submitted a shareholder proposal that requested Dow to take steps to restrict the manufacture and sale of napalm. Dow refused to include the proposal, arguing that it was excludable both as "primarily for the purpose of promoting general economic, political, racial, religious, social or similar causes"[43] and as "relating to the conduct of the ordinary business operations of the issuer."[44] The SEC staff, which had shifted its approach to shareholder proposals substantially from the bastion of shareholder sovereignty reflected in the Transamerica litigation, issued a no-action letter advising Dow that it could exclude the proposal. The Medical Committee appealed to the SEC, which affirmed the staff decision.[45]

The Medical Committee then challenged the SEC's determination in the Court of Appeals, which held that the SEC's decision lacked an adequate basis and remanded, stating that the SEC's interpretation of its rule was inconsistent with the congressional intent behind section 14(a). The court stated that: "Our own examination of the issue raises substantial questions as to whether an interpretation of Rule 14a–8(c)(2) which permitted omission of this proposal as one motivated primarily by general political or social concerns would conflict with the congressional intent underlying Section 14(a) of the Act."[46] The court noted that the manufacture of napalm was economically significant to the company and had also subjected Dow to controversy.[47] In addition, the court explicitly distinguished the proposal at issue from questions of general social policy that are beyond management's control: "the proposal relates solely to a matter that is completely within the accepted sphere of corporate activity and control."[48]

At roughly the same time, the Project on Corporate Responsibility, a shareholder group, was waging a proxy contest at General Motors called Campaign GM.[49] The shareholders introduced nine proposals on a variety of issues, including the appointment of public interest directors to the board, and proposals to address air pollution and employee safety. The

43. The SEC adopted this exclusion following an unsuccessful effort by a shareholder to raise the issue of segregated seating through a shareholder proposal at Greyhound. Medical Committee for Human Rights, 432 F.2d at 678. See Peck v. Greyhound Corp., 97 F. Supp. 679 (S.D.N.Y. 1951) (deferring to the SEC's decision that the proposal could be excluded).

44. Medical Committee for Human Rights, 432 F.2d at 676, 679.

45. See SEC v. Medical Committee for Human Rights, 404 U.S. 403, 404 (1972) (describing procedural history).

46. Id. at 680.

47. Id. at 681.

48. Id.

49. See Jill E. Fisch, From Legitimacy to Logic: Reconstructing Proxy Regulation, 46 Vand. L. Rev. 1129, 1154 (1993) (describing Campaign GM).

SEC required General Motors to include two of these proposals in its proxy statement, but allowed the company to exclude the others with little explanation.

Congress considered a legislative response. In 1970, Senator Edmund Muskie introduced the Corporate Participation Bill.[50] The bill was designed to overrule SEC restrictions on social policy proposals by allowing shareholders to introduce proposals aimed at advancing "the general welfare." When the Supreme Court dismissed the Medical Committee for Human Rights case as moot, because Dow had included the proposal and it failed to command the 3% vote necessary for resubmission, Justice Douglas wrote in dissent that Senator Muskie's bill reflected "substantial sentiment" for a more liberal approach to the use of shareholder proposals.[51] Shortly thereafter, the SEC amended rule 14a–8 to provide that social policy proposals could only be excluded if they were "not significantly related to the business of the issuer or is not within the control of the issuer." Although at first blush this amendment appeared to increase the issuer's power to exclude social policy proposals[52] (See Douglas opinion at 410 n.6), staff interpretations (perhaps influenced by the statements by the Second Circuit and members of Congress) came to reflect an increasingly liberal approach to social policy proposals. As a result, in the following years, shareholder proposals on social, religious and political issues became commonplace, and religious and political groups came to dominate the shareholder proposal process.

Another issue concerned the use of shareholder proposals to address executive compensation. Starting in the late 1970s, executive compensation, and CEO pay in particular, began to escalate.[53] The process increased in the 1980s, presumably in response to substantial cuts in the maximum income tax rate. Pay increased in absolute terms, as a multiple of average worker pay, and in comparison to executive compensation in other countries. Companies developed new forms of compensation such as guaranteed bonuses, golden parachutes, and compensation to cover tax liabilities.

The increases generated substantial controversy. Congress responded through a variety of efforts, largely unsuccessful, to create tax penalties for excessive executive compensation.[54] The SEC responded by increasing required disclosure of executive compensation. Shareholder activists called for limits on pay and greater ties to performance. Despite legislative, regulatory and media attention, however, the SEC staff took the position that shareholder proposals relating to executive compensa-

---

50. S. 4003, § 2, 91st Cong., 2d Sess.

51. SEC v. Medical Committee for Human Rights, 404 U.S. 403, 410 (1972) (Douglas, J., dissenting).

52. See id. at 410 n.6 (stating that the SEC's proposed rules "might strengthen Dow's hand").

53. See generally Lucian Bebchuk & Jesse Fried, PAY WITHOUT PERFORMANCE: THE UNFULFILLED PROMISE OF EXECUTIVE COMPENSA-

TION (2004) (describing growth in executive compensation and development of various compensation forms).

54. "The Bill Agee Bill," adopted in 1984, imposed a special tax on golden parachutes. Internal Revenue Code section 162(m), adopted in 1993, limited the deductibility of non-performance based executive compensation of over $1 million/year.

tion dealt with ordinary business issues and could therefore be excluded under Rule 14a–8(c)(7).[55] As Senator Levin explained, "The policies of the SEC place a major roadblock in the way of stockholders having a say in how CEO pay is set within their own corporation."[56] The SEC did not reverse this position until 1992.[57] As the staff explained: "In view of the widespread public debate concerning executive and director compensation policies and practices, and the increasing recognition that these issues raise significant policy issues, it is the Division's view that proposals relating to senior executive compensation no longer can be considered matters relating to a registrant's ordinary business."[58]

The SEC's change in policy addressed compensation, but not the broader question of employment related policies. The staff continued to permit the exclusion of many proposals dealing with employment as relating to ordinary business operations, adopting a case-by-case approach in which it attempted to evaluate the extent to which the proposal raised significant social policy concerns. In 1992, New York City Employees' Retirement System (NYCERS), an institutional investor, submitted a proposal to Cracker Barrel requesting that the board implement hiring policies that barred discrimination on the basis of sexual orientation.[59] Not only did the staff permit Cracker Barrel to exclude the proposal, it announced a new blanket prohibition on employment related proposals. Explaining that "the line between includable and excludable employment-related proposals based on social policy considerations has become increasingly difficult to draw," the staff stated that henceforth, social policy concerns would not have the effect of removing the proposal

55. See, e.g., Transamerica Corp., SEC No–Action Letter, 1990 WL 285806 (Jan. 10, 1990) (stating that "the Division's existing position regarding proposals dealing with compensation arrangements is that such matters relate to the conduct of a registrant's ordinary business operations and may be excluded pursuant to rule 14a–8(c)(7)"). The SEC had taken this position since it added the exclusion for proposals relating to ordinary business operations in 1954. Solicitation of Proxies, Exchange Act Release No. 4979 (Jan. 5, 1954). The SEC immediately interpreted this provision to allow exclusion of shareholder proposals dealing with employment compensation. See Edward Aranow & Herbert Einhorn, Proxy Contests for Corporate Control 293 (2d ed. 1968) (observing that SEC permitted ATT to exclude shareholder proposal regarding employee benefits as "ordinary business operations."); see also Curtin v. American Tel. & Tel. Co., 124 F. Supp. 197, 198 (S.D.N.Y. 1954) (deferring to the SEC's determination that pensions are "matters that primarily are the responsibility and concern of the corporate management and its directors rather than that of its stockholders"). Ironically, the SEC originally took the position that shareholder proposals regarding executive compensation were proper, and early shareholder activists like the Gilberts frequently introduced such proposals. See Emerson & Latcham, supra note 33, 19 U. Chi. L. Rev. at 821–25 (describing shareholder proposals on executive compensation during the 1948–51 proxy seasons).

56. Runaway Executive Pay, 138 Cong Rec § 214 (1992).

57. See Executive Compensation Disclosure, Exchange Act Release No. 30,851, 1992 WL 151039 (June 23, 1992) (describing the SEC's reversal in position and listing companies for which the SEC required inclusion of proposals on executive compensation).

58. Reebok Int'l Ltd., SEC No–Action Letter, 1992 WL 55815 (Mar. 16, 1992).

59. Cracker Barrel Old Country Store, Inc., 1992 WL 289095 (Oct. 13, 1992). The proposal requested the Cracker Barrel board to "1) implement nondiscriminatory policies related to sexual orientation, and 2) add explicit prohibitions against such discrimination to the Company employment policy statement." Letter Inquiry dated July 13, 1992, Fed. Sec. L. Rep. at 77,285.

from the realm of ordinary business operations. "Rather, determinations with respect to any such proposals are properly governed by the employment-based nature of the proposal." The SEC affirmed the staff position. NYCERS challenged the SEC's decision in court, arguing that the SEC's change in position violated the Administrative Procedure Act, but the Second Circuit refused to issue an injunction, concluding that the no-action letter was simply "interpretive and non-binding" and therefore was not subject to the procedural requirements of a formal legislative rule.

The SEC's change generated extensive public outcry. One reason, as demonstrated in the Cracker Barrel dispute itself, was that institutional investors had become a growing force in corporate governance and the shareholder proposal process. Institutions–public pension funds, union funds, mutual funds, insurance companies, university endowments, foundations and others–owned an increasing percentage of the market and had begun to make active use of rule 14a–8. Institutional presence significantly affected the shareholder proposal process. Indeed, virtually no shareholder proposals had ever received majority approval until 1988,[60] when a CalPERS sponsored proposal at Gillette to prohibit greenmail[61] received 53% approval.[62] There were several reasons for this lack of success. First, although rule 14a–8 reduces the cost of submitting a shareholder proposal, since the proposal is distributed as part of the company's proxy materials, the costs of any proxy solicitation are borne personally by the sponsoring shareholder. These costs can be substantial–the average cost of a proxy contest ranges from $250,000 to $1 million.[63] Few investors have the type of financial or other interest in a shareholder proposal to justify this expenditure. Second, shareholder voting suffers from a collective action problem. Dispersed investors with relatively small stakes have little financial incentive to pay attention to the voting process, or even to vote. Third, the collective action problem is enhanced by the relative unimportance of shareholder voting. As indicated above, the economic significance of most shareholder proposals is reduced by their precatory nature, and as described in further detail below, very few director elections involve an election contest. As a result, shareholders can rationally conclude that, in the vast majority of cases, their votes do not matter.

60. See, e.g., George W. Dent, Jr., SEC Rule 14a–8: A Study in Regulatory Failure, 30 N.Y.L. SCH. L. REV. 1,7 (1985) (stating that "no shareholder proposal opposed by management has ever come close to receiving approval of a shareholder majority"); but see Susan W. Liebeler, A Proposal to Rescind the Shareholder Proposal Rule, 18 GA. L. REV. 425, 426 (1984) (stating that, according to the SEC staff, as of 1981 only two shareholder-sponsored proposals had been approved).

61. "The term 'greenmail' refers to the practice of buying out a takeover bidder's

stock at a premium that is not available to other shareholders in order to prevent the takeover." Unocal Corp. v. Mesa Petroleum Co., 493 A.2d 946, 956 n.13 (Del. 1985).

62. CALIF-PUBLIC–EMP; California Public Employees' Retirement System wins approval of Gillette Co. shareholder proposal Business Wire May 3, 1988.

63. William W. Bratton, Hedge Funds and Governance Targets, working paper at 30 (2006), Georgetown Law and Economics Research Paper No. 928689, available at: http://ssrn.com/abstract=928689.

By the early 1990s, institutional investors, particularly pension funds and unions, had begun to sponsor shareholder proposals regularly. Empirical studies showed that shareholder proposals sponsored by institutional investors, which tended to focus on corporate governance, received greater shareholder support than other proposals and were more likely to be approved.[64] Institutional activism was also leading institutional investors to pay greater attention to their voting rights, which contributed to the new success of shareholder proposals.[65]

Employment related proposals were of particular interest to public pension funds and union funds. Fearing the impact of the Cracker Barrel rule, a number of high-profile institutional investors petitioned the SEC to overturn its decision.[66] Institutional pressure was supplemented by congressional pressure. As part of the National Securities Markets Improvement Act of 1996, Congress required the SEC to conduct a comprehensive study of the shareholder proposal process to determine whether shareholders had adequate access to proxy statements and whether such access had been "impaired by recent statutory, judicial, or regulatory changes."[67] The SEC responded by soliciting input from issuers, shareholders and other market participants and was flooded with responses critical of the existing application of the shareholder proposal rule.[68]

Finally, in 1998, as part of another set of revisions to the proxy rules, the Commission reversed its decision in Cracker Barrel.[69] The SEC's release indicated that the SEC was returning to its prior approach of evaluating employment related proposals on a case by case basis. In addition, the SEC explicitly reinstated its prior position that employment-related issues are proper subjects for shareholder proposals so long as they raise "substantial policy or other considerations."[70]

More recently, the SEC has struggled with shareholder voting over poison pills. Institutional investors have generally opposed the adoption of poison pills, staggered boards, and other antitakeover devices that allow management to resist a tender offer despite shareholder opposi-

---

64. Stuart L. Gillan & Laura T. Starks, 1998, Corporate Governance Proposals and Shareholder Activism: The Role of Institutional Investors, 57 J. Fin. Econ. 275 (2000).

65. Institutional attention to the voting process was enhanced by the SEC's adoption of Investment Company Act Rule 30b1–4 2003, requiring required mutual funds to disclose their proxy voting policies and voting records. See SEC Press Release, Securities and Exchange Commission Requires Proxy Voting Policies, Disclosure by Investment Companies and Investment Advisers, Jan. 23, 2003, available at http://www.sec.gov/news/press/2003–12.htm (describing disclosure requirement).

66. 1997 Proposed Amendments, supra note 55, at 50,683 n.15 (stating that a num-

ber of institutional investors including the Interfaith Center on Corporate Responsibility, the Calvert Group Ltd., and the Comptroller of the City of New York requested that Cracker Barrel be overturned).

67. National Securities Markets Improvement Act of 1996, Pub. L. No. 104–290, 510(b)(1), 110 Stat. 3416, 3450.

68. See Amendments to Rules on Shareholder Proposals, Exchange Act Release No. 39,093, 62 Fed. Reg. 50,682 (Sept. 26, 1997) (describing the SEC's efforts to obtain information from market participants and resulting comments).

69. Amendments to Rules on Shareholder Proposals, Exchange Act Release No. 34–40018, 63 Fed. Reg. 29,107 (1998).

70. 63 Fed. Reg. at 29108.

tion. Beginning in the late 1980s, institutional investors began to introduce shareholder proposals seeking to limit director authority to adopt or maintain poison pills. Initially many of these proposals were precatory and simply requested that the board take action such as repealing the company's poison pill.[71] The SEC generally required issuers to include these proposals. Many corporate boards, however, simply ignored the proposals, even when they received majority approval.[72] As a result, by the late 1990s, shareholders had begun to submit binding proposals to eliminate poison pills, typically in the form of proposed bylaw amendments.[73]

Poison pill bylaws raise the broader question about the permissible scope of shareholder-adopted bylaws and the extent to which shareholders, through bylaw provisions, can limit director discretion. As many commentators have noted, such proposals create a conflict between the shareholders' statutory power to amend the bylaws and the boards' statutory authority to run the corporation.[74] The conflict has not been fully resolved by the state courts which have not been called upon to determine the permissible scope of the shareholders' power to limit director authority through the bylaws. In part, judicial resolution of this question has been frustrated by the SEC's preference for precatory proposals because, in the view of the Delaware courts, unless and until a binding proposal in the form of a bylaw amendment is submitted, voted upon and approved by a majority of the shareholders, a judicial determination of its validity is not ripe.[75]

The most extensive consideration of poison pill bylaws took place in Oklahoma. The Teamsters submitted a precatory shareholder proposal to the Fleming Companies in 1996, requesting that the board redeem the company's poison pill.[76] The proposal was approved by a majority of the shareholders, but the board ignored it and failed to redeem the pill. The following year, the Teamsters resubmitted its proposal, this time in the form of a binding bylaw amendment providing that the company could not adopt or maintain a poison pill without approval by a majority of the shareholders. Fleming refused to include the proposal in its 1997 proxy statement, arguing that the proposal was not a proper subject for a

---

71. See, e.g., Dale Arthur Oesterle, Revisiting the Anti–Takeover Fervor of the '80s through the Letters of Warren Buffet: Current Acquisition Practice is Clogged by Legal Flotsam from the Decade, 19 Cardozo L. Rev. 565, 603 (1997) (reporting substantial number of precatory shareholder proposals recommending that board redeem a poison pill received majority support).

72. Id.

73. See Brett H. McDonnell, Shareholder Bylaws, Shareholder Nominations, and Poison Pills, 3 Berkeley Bus. L.J. 205, 254 (2005) (describing how "the weak effect of precatory proposals" led to shareholder ef-

forts to introduce poison pill bylaw amendments).

74. See, e.g., id.; Lawrence A. Hamermesh, Corporate Democracy and Stockholder–Adopted By–Laws: Taking Back the Street?, 73 Tul. L. Rev. 409 (1998).

75. See, e.g., General Datacomm Industries, Inc. v. State of Wisconsin Investment Board, 731 A.2d 818, 818 (Del. Ch. 1999) (refusing to decide validity of proposed bylaw because the issues were "not yet ripe for judicial resolution ").

76. International Bhd. of Teamsters Gen. Fund v. Fleming Cos., 1999 OK 3, 975 P.2d 907, 914 (Ok. Sup. 1999).

shareholder vote under Oklahoma law. The Teamsters then brought suit, in federal district court, to compel Fleming to include the proposal.[77]

The district court summarily issued an order ordering Fleming to include the Teamsters proposal, and Fleming did so. The proposal was included in Fleming's 1997 proxy statement and received the approval of approximately 60% of the shareholders. Fleming appealed to the Tenth Circuit, which certified to the Oklahoma Supreme Court the question of whether the Teamsters' bylaw was valid. The Oklahoma court held that it was, finding nothing in the Oklahoma statute that "indicates the shareholder rights plan is somehow exempt from shareholder adopted bylaws."[78]

Although, it lost in court, ultimately Fleming prevailed. In 2001, the Oklahoma legislature amended the corporation statute, in response to the Fleming decision, to eliminate shareholder power to amend the bylaws.[79] Oklahoma is now one of a small majority of states in which the directors have the exclusive authority to amend the bylaws. Thus the Fleming case is notable not simply for its narrow ruling on the permissibility of poison pills bylaws, but also for its revelations about the respective roles of the states and the federal government in the protection of shareholder voting rights. The Fleming case is virtually unique in allowing a state court to make the determination of whether a shareholder proposal constituted a proper subject for a shareholder vote. At the same time, the Oklahoma legislature's response—eliminating the judicially recognized shareholder voting power—offers some support for the Transamerica court's view that a broad recognition of federally protected voting rights is necessary to achieve congressional intent under section 14(a), and that Congress's intent to ensure fair corporate suffrage should not be frustrated even by means that are permissible under state law.

As the foregoing examples illustrate, the determination, for purposes of rule 14a–8, of what constitutes a proper subject for shareholder action, has been difficult. In the vast majority of these cases, the determination has been made by the SEC staff. Although the staff's determination can been reviewed and overturned, either by the Commission itself or by the courts, such review is rare. Moreover, the structure of the no-action process has the effect of largely preventing state courts from having the opportunity to consider the question of what constitutes a proper subject for shareholder voting, despite the fact that the answer to this question is based in state corporation law, not the federal proxy rules. The recent Fleming case, although exceptional in allowing this role to the state

77. International Bhd. of Teamsters Gen. Fund v. Fleming Cos., No. Civ. 96–1650–A, 1997 U.S. Dist. LEXIS 2980, at *1 (W.D. Okla. Jan. 24, 1997). Fleming asked the SEC for a no-action letter, but the SEC refused to take a position in light of the pending litigation. Fleming Companies, Inc., 1996 WL 34432841 (Dec. 3, 1996).

78. International Bhd. of Teamsters Gen. Fund v. Fleming Cos., 1999 OK 3, 22, 975 P.2d 907, 914 (Ok. Sup. 1999).

79. Gary W. Derrick, New Developments in Oklahoma Business Entity Law, 56 Okla. L. Rev. 259, 265–67 (2003) (describing legislative response to Fleming decision).

court, highlights the importance both of better determining shareholders' state law voting rights and of directly confronting the question of whether federal law authorizes the SEC to expand or contract those rights.

D. THE FEDERALLY DELINEATED SHAREHOLDER RULE IN DIRECTOR ELECTIONS

The shareholder role in director elections has also been determined largely by federal law. Although state statutes empower shareholders to elect the directors, they are silent on shareholder rights with respect to the nomination process. Moreover, management control of the proxy machinery creates an uneven playing field. Although a dissident shareholder can nominate his or her own slate of directors and solicit proxies in favor of that slate, the costs of mounting a proxy contest are so large as to make an election challenge unavailable to the vast majority of shareholders.[80]

A federal rule, equivalent to the shareholder proposal rule, enabling shareholders to nominate candidates who would be included in the company's proxy statement would help to counteract management control. The SEC initially considered allowing shareholders to use the shareholder proposal rule to nominate directors. In 1942, the SEC solicited comments on a staff proposal that would have provided that "minority stockholders be given an opportunity to use the management's proxy material in support of their own nominees for directorships."[81] The proposal was not adopted.[82] According to some commentators, the decision was based on unfavorable congressional and public reaction.[83]

Shortly thereafter, the SEC staff began issuing interpretations that shareholders could not use rule 14a–8 to nominate director candidates. Subsequently, the SEC formally amended the text of the Rule to exclude proposals relating to director elections.[84] Initially, the staff interpreted this exclusion somewhat narrowly, concluding that while shareholders could not nominate directors or oppose management candidates through

---

80. See generally Lucian A. Bebchuk & Marcel Kahan, A Framework for Analyzing Legal Policy Toward Proxy Contests, 78 Cal. L. Rev. 1071 (1990) (advocating state law changes that would address this problem).

81. See Division of Corporation Finance, Staff Report: Review of the Proxy Process Regarding the Nomination and Election of Directors, July 15, 2003, available at http://www.sec.gov/news/studies/proxyreport.pdf (describing history of direct nomination proposal).

82. In the 1942 proxy rule amendments, the Commission stated, without explanation, that it was not adopting the proposal. Exch. Act. Rel No. 3347, 1942 WL 34864 (Dec. 18, 1942).

83. See Security and Exchange Commission Proxy Rules: Hearings on H.R. 1493, H.R. 1821, and H.R. 2019 Before the House Comm. on Interstate and Foreign Commerce, 78th Cong., 1st Sess. (1943) (recounting SEC decision).

84. See Adoption of Revised Proxy Rules, Exchange Act Release No. 4037, 1947 WL 24687 (Dec. 17, 1947). Rule X–14A–8(a) included the sentence "This rule does not apply, however, to elections to office." See Amendment of Proxy Rules, Sec. Exch. Act Rel. No. 4775, 1952 WL 5254 (Dec. 11, 1952) (setting forth text of Rule X–14A–8(a)).

the shareholder proposal process, the exclusion did not bar proposals relating to the election process itself, such as proposals for cumulative voting or seeking to implement general qualifications for directors.[85] This position was clarified when the SEC adopted the current version of the exclusion in 1976, which provides an issuer can exclude a proposal that "relates to an election for office."[86] The SEC adhered to the narrow interpretation of the election exclusion for approximately sixteen years.[87] The SEC revisited the subject of shareholder nominations during this time period; it conducted an extensive study in 1977, which was followed by hearings in four cities.[88] The hearings focused specifically on a proposed rule change that would have enabled shareholders to nominate director candidates directly. The subject proved extremely controversial and, faced with strong opposition from corporations and managers, the SEC failed to amend its rule, deferring to increased issuer use of nominating committees.[89]

In 1990, however, the staff began to interpret the election provision more broadly and began to allow issuers to exclude proposals that "might result in contested elections.[90] By 1998, the SEC was consistently excluding shareholder proposals that "might result in contested elections."[91] This had the effect of barring proposals that sought to impose director qualifications such as independence as well as preventing shareholders from amending corporate bylaws to provide for shareholder nominations.[92]

Institutional investors, who were becoming increasingly activist in the 1990s, were frustrated with the limitations imposed on shareholder voting power through the federal proxy rules.[93] In response to institutional pressure, the SEC conducted an extensive three year review of the

---

85. Adoption of Amendments Relating to Proposals by Security Holders, Exchange Act Release No. 12,999, 1976 WL 160347 (Nov. 22, 1976) (explaining that Commission had previously held that proposals dealing with matters such as qualifications for directors and cumulative voting were not excludable on the basis that they related to an election for office).

86. Id. The adopting release specifically explained that the language of the exclusion was intended to clarify the SEC's continued adherence to its previous position that proposals dealing with matters such as cumulative voting rights, general qualifications for directors, and political contributions by the issuer" were not excludable.

87. AFSCME v. Am. Int'l Group, Inc., 462 F.3d 121, 128 (2d Cir. 2006).

88. SEC, Staff Report on Corporate Accountability: A Re-examination of Rules Relating to Shareholder Communications, Shareholder Participation in the Corporate Electoral Process and Corporate Governance Generally, Senate Comm. on Banking, Hous. & Urban Affairs, 96th Cong., 2d Sess. 98–127 (Comm. Print 1980).

89. Id.

90. AFSCME,, 462 F.3d at 128.

91. AFSCME, 462 F.3d at 128, n.7

92. See, e.g., Amoco Corp., SEC No–Action Letter, 1990 WL 286092 (Feb. 14, 1990) (allowing exclusion under Rule 14a–8(c) of a proposal to allow large shareholders to nominate director candidates on a common ballot with management).

93. See, e.g., Letter from Richard H. Koppes, CalPERS General Counsel, to Linda C. Quinn, Director, Division of Corporation Finance, Securities and Exchange Commission (Nov. 3, 1989); Coffee, 15 Cardozo L. Rev. 837, 907 n.9 (describing rulemaking petitions filed by United Shareholders Association and Fidelity Management & Research Co. in 1990 asking SEC to amend the federal proxy rules to remove these limitations).

federal proxy rules.[94] Following this review, the SEC amended the proxy rules in 1992 to remove some constraints on institutional activism as well as to permit investors to run short slate election contests.[95] The amendments did not, however, require issuers to include shareholder nominees on the company's proxy statement.

Shareholders' concerns about their limited input into the composition of corporate boards was heightened by the corporate misconduct scandals of the late 1990s. In 2002, the American Federation of State County and Municipal Employees ("AFSCME") developed a proposal by which shareholders owning at least 3% of a company's stock could nominate a short slate of directors. The proposal was submitted at six issuers in connection with their 2002 annual meetings, but the SEC permitted issuers to exclude the proposal on the grounds that it related to an election for office, and the SEC declined to review the staff's decisions.[96]

In response, the AFL–CIO petitioned the SEC to adopt a rule that would allow shareholder-nominated directors to appear on a company's proxy ballot.[97] The Commission directed the staff to review the federal proxy rules and, on October 23, 2003, the Commission proposed a direct access rule, largely modeled on the AFSCME proposal, that would enable shareholders, under limited circumstances, to have a minority slate of nominees included in the issuer's proxy statement.[98] As proposed, the SEC's rule would have allowed shareholders owning at least 5% of the company to nominate a minority slate of up to three director candidates upon the occurrence of a triggering condition. The triggering conditions were either a withhold vote of at least 35% for one of management's director candidates or shareholder approval of a proxy access proposal submitted by shareholders owning 1% of the company. The SEC indicated that it was also considering a third trigger–the refusal of the issuer to implement a shareholder proposal that had received approval by a majority of the shareholders. Because of the requirement of a triggering event, shareholder access at a particular company would require at least two years. The SEC held hearings and received letters of comment from 690 individuals and organizations.[99] The SEC did not adopt the rule, and

---

94. Regulation of Communications Among Shareholders, Exchange Act Release No. 31,326, 1992 WL 301258 (Oct. 16, 1992).

95. Id.

96. SEC Division of Corporation Finance, Staff Report: Review of the Proxy Process Regarding the Nomination and Election of Directors, July 15, 2003, at 1, available at http://www.sec.gov/news/studies/proxyreport.pdf.

97. AFL-CIO, Request for Rulemaking to Permit Shareholder–Nominated Director Candidates to Appear in Corporate Proxy Statements and Proxy Cards (May 15, 2003), at http://www.sec.gov/rules/petitions/

petn4–491.htm (petitioning for "comprehensive new rules that will give shareholders equal access to the proxy for their director nominees").

98. Security Holder Direct Nominations, Exchange Act Release No. 48,626, 2003 WL 22350515 (Oct. 14, 2003).

99. Summary of Comments In Response to the Commission's Solicitation of Public Views Regarding Possible Changes to the Proxy Rules, Exchange Act Release No. 34–47778, Division of Corporation Finance Staff Report, Appendix A at 21, July 15, 2003, avail. at http://www.sec.gov/news/studies/proxycomsum.pdf.

media reports and commentators attributed the proposal's failure to political pressure and opposition by corporate representatives including the Business Roundtable and the Chamber of Commerce.[100]

In light of the SEC's failure to adopt a direct access rule, AFSCME resumed its efforts to modify the nomination process through a shareholder-adopted bylaw. In 2004, AFSCME submitted its director nomination bylaw to AIG for inclusion in the company's 2005 proxy statement. AIG sought a no-action letter from the SEC, which issued the requested letter advising AIG that the proposal could be excluded on the grounds that it related to an election.[101] AFSCME then brought suit in federal court seeking to compel AIG to include the proposal despite the SEC's position.[102] The district court agreed that the proposal could be excluded and AFSCME appealed. The SEC submitted an amicus brief, arguing that the proposal was properly excluded.[103] As with the Medical Committee for Human Rights case, once again, the SEC took a position in litigation supporting limits on shareholder voting rights, in an odd turnabout from its position in Transamerica. The Second Circuit rejected the SEC's argument, finding that the SEC's current characterization of the exclusion for proposals that relate to an election was inconsistent with the SEC's narrower 1976 interpretation of the rule. The court therefore ordered AIG to include the proposal.[104]

In May 2007, the SEC held a series of three roundtable discussions on shareholder voting rights and the federal proxy rules.[105] Although the subject of direct nomination was not formally on the agenda, Chairman Cox announced that the SEC was in the process of developing a proposal that would allow shareholder nominees to be included in the issuer's proxy statement.[106] On July 25, 2007, the SEC approved two alternative rulemaking proposals. The first alternative proposed overruling the AFSCME decision and codifying the SEC's interpretation that proxy access proposals are excludable under Rule 14a–8.[107] The alternative proposed permitting proxy access proposals under limited circumstances.[108] In order to qualify, a proposing shareholder or shareholder group would have to own at least 5% of the company's stock for at least a year and have filed a schedule 13G, and the proposal would have to take the form of a binding amendment to the company's bylaws. The proposed rule also required increased disclosure about the proponent and

100. See, e.g., Ron Orol, Daily Deal/The Deal July 2, 2004 (attributing SEC's failure to adopt rule to opposition by Chamber of Commerce and Business Roundtable).

101. SEC No–Action Letter 2005 WL 372266 (Feb. 14, 2005).

102. AFSCME v. Am. Int'l Group, Inc., 361 F. Supp. 2d 344 (S.D.N.Y. 2005).

103. See AFSCME, 462 F.3d at 126 n.5 (describing filing by SEC of amicus brief).

104. AFSCME v. Am. Int'l Group, Inc., 462 F.3d 121 (2d Cir. 2006).

105. SEC Announces Roundtable Discussions Regarding Proxy Process, Press Release, Apr. 24, 2007, avail. at http://www.sec.gov/news/press/2007/2007–71.htm.

106. Roy Harris, Letting Investors Play the Proxy Game CFO.com May 8, 2007.

107. Shareholder Proposals Relating to the Election of Directors, Sec. Exch. Act Rel. No. 56161, 2007 WL 4442681 (July 27, 2007).

108. Shareholder Proposals, Sec. Exch. Act Rel. No. 56160, 2007 WL 2175940 (July 27, 2007).

any previous dealings with the company.[109] Unlike the 2003 proxy access rules, the 2007 proposal did not seek to dictate the terms of proxy access.

On November 28, 2007, the SEC, by a 3–1 vote, adopted the first proposal, overturning the AFSCME decision and prohibiting the use of Rule 14a–8 for proxy access proposals.[110] Chairman Cox explained the decision as preserving the status quo and preventing "an easy end run around the Commission's required disclosures and our antifraud rules in proxy contests."[111] He stated that the SEC would continue to study proxy access and revisit the issue.[112] There are reasons to question the Chairman's stated justification for the rule, especially because the proxy rules do not compel disclosure for issuers that voluntarily adopt proxy access bylaws. A variety of institutional investor groups, including the Council for Institutional Investors ("CII"), criticized the SEC's decision as obstructing the rights of shareholders.[113] Former SEC Commissioner Harvey Goldschmid termed the decision a "tragic mistake."[114]

At least two issuers have adopted shareholder access provisions voluntarily. In 2003, Apria Healthcare adopted a provision allowing shareholders owned at least 5% of the company to submit up to two nominees for inclusion in the company's proxy statement.[115] In 2007, Comverse Technology, adopted a proxy access bylaw, allowing shareholders who have owned at least 5% of the company for at least two years to submit one nominee for inclusion in the proxy statement.[116]

E. RECENT DEVELOPMENTS IN SHAREHOLDER VOTING RIGHTS

Although the SEC has not adopted a direct access rule, shareholder activism has affected the scope of shareholder voting rights. One significant development is majority voting. Historically directors in the United States are elected by a plurality vote. Contested elections are rare, in part because of the barriers to shareholder nomination of directors, as detailed above.[117] As a result, the vast majority of elections in publicly-

---

109. Id., 2007 WL 2175940.

110. Shareholder Proposals Relating to the Election of Directors, Sec. Exch. Act Rel. No. 56914, 2007 WL 4442610 (Dec. 7, 2007). See Greg Farrell, SEC limits investors' proxy power; Vote described as "tragic," "appalling" and "a sad day for shareowners", USA Today, Nov. 29, 2007, at 1B (describing the rule's adoption).

111. Chairman Christopher Cox, Speech by SEC Chairman: Electronic Shareholder Forum Rules; Codification of Interpretation of Rule 14(a)(8)(i)(8), SEC Open Meeting, Nov. 28, 2007, avail. at http://www.sec.gov/news/speech/2007/spch112807cc.htm.

112. Id.

113. Farrell, supra note 110.

114. Id.

115. Policy Regarding Alternative Director Nominations by Stockholders, Exhibit A to Apria Healthcare Group Inc., Def. 14A dated March 23, 2004, avail. at http://sec.edgar-online.com/2004/03/23/0000892569–04–000370/Section18.asp.

116. Ted Allen, Comverse Adopts Access Bylaw, ISS Corporate Governance Blog, Apr. 27, 2007, avail. at http://blog.issproxy.com/2007/04/comverse_adopts_access_bylawsu.html. The adoption of the bylaw appears to be part of an attempt by Comverse to address investor concerns following its involvement in stock-options backdating that led to the criminal prosecution of three company executives. Id.

117. Lucian Bebchuk reports that contested elections involving a rival team of directors seeking to run the company numbered approximately 12 per year between

traded companies involve a single slate of directors—those directors chosen by management or the company's board of directors In an uncontested election, shareholders lack the ability to vote "against" this incumbent slate; the shareholders' choice is limited to voting for the slate of directors or withholding voting authority.[118] Withhold votes have little legal significance and, as a practical matter, a director can be elected on the basis of as little as a single share voted in his or her favor.[119]

Despite the fact that withhold votes do not prevent a director from being elected, institutional investors in the 1980s began to "vote no" as a way of communicating their lack of satisfaction with an issuer. Institutions withheld votes from director candidates when they were dissatisfied with individual directors or to protest a board's lack of responsiveness to a particular shareholder concern such as a poison pill.[120] In some cases, activist institutions hired proxy solicitation firms to encourage shareholders to withhold their votes, creating a type of contested election despite the presence of a single slate of candidates.[121] Some commentators endorsed "vote no," arguing that it provided a valuable yet minimalist outlet for shareholder activism.[122] Withhold campaigns gradually increased in popularity, reaching a high point when 45% of shareholders withheld their votes from CEO and Chairman Michael Eisner at the 2004 Disney annual meeting.[123] During the 2004 proxy season, 12 directors received withhold votes of more than 50%.[124]

Despite the relatively low cost and accessibility of vote no campaigns, the Disney vote illustrated their limited effectiveness. In *Disney*, the board promptly voted a statement of confidence in Michael Eisner. The board eventually replaced Eisner as CEO, but it took a full year to

1996 and 2005. Of these, only 25%, or approximately 3 per year involved companies with a market capitalization exceeding $200 million at the time of the challenge. Lucian Bebchuk, The Myth of the Shareholder Franchise, 93 Va. L. Rev. 675, 686–87 (2007).

118. As Joseph Grundfest explains, "SEC regulations in effect since 1967 require that the 'form of proxy which provides for the election of directors . . . provide . . . means for security holders to withhold authority to vote for each nominee,' even when a board stands unopposed for reelection." Joseph A. Grundfest, Just Vote No: A Minimalist Strategy for Dealing with Barbarians Inside the Gates, 45 Stan. L. Rev. 857, 903 (1993).

119. The Delaware Chancery Court has determined that proxies that withhold authority on the issue of electing directors are present for purposes of the quorum requirement of the annual meeting. North Fork Bancorporation, Inc. v. Toal, 825 A.2d 860, 869 (Del. Ch. 2000). Moreover, withhold

votes can be significant, as indicated below, if an issuer uses majority voting rather than plurality voting. See id.

120. See Joann S. Lublin, Lubrizol and TIAA–CREF Fund Duel Over "Dead–Hand" Takeover Defense, WALL ST.J., Mar. 23, 1999, at A4.

121. See, e.g., id. (describing TIAA–CREF's hiring of proxy solicitation firm in withhold campaign at Lubrizol 1999 annual meeting).

122. See Grundfest, supra note 118, at 857 (advocating "vote no" campaigns).

123. Ronald Grover & Tom Lowry, Now It's Time to Say Goodbye: How Disney's Board Can Move Beyond the Eisner Era, Business Week, March 15, 2004, at 30.

124. The ISS Institute for Corporate Governance, Majority Voting in Director Elections

From the Symbolic to the Democratic (2005), available at http://www.issproxy.com /pdf/MVwhitepaper.pdf.

do so.[125] Withhold votes might communicate shareholder dissatisfaction but, like precatory proposals, it appears that they do not reflect a meaningful exercise of shareholder power.

The next step was majority voting. As indicated above, the vast majority of U.S. corporations elect directors by plurality voting. Plurality voting is not the only option, however. In every state except Nevada (which requires plurality voting), corporations can utilize majority voting instead, and historically a handful of corporations have done so.[126] In January 2005, Business Week reporter Louis Lavelle published an article advocating majority voting.[127] The idea was promptly embraced by institutional investors and endorsed by the CII and the International Corporate Governance Network ("ICGN"), Others took majority voting seriously as well. The American Bar Association formed a task force on majority voting. Even the Business Roundtable conceded that majority voting "provides for enhanced accountability of board members to shareholders."[128]

By February 2007, a study revealed that 52% of Fortune 500 companies had adopted a policy, bylaw or charter provision providing for some type of majority voting.[129] Delaware amended its corporation statute to facilitate majority voting and to make it clear that director resignations in connection with majority voting policies were valid and binding. Legislation was introduced in California, that would have required majority voting.[130] California adopted the legislation in an amended form, similar to the Delaware statute, that facilitated rather than mandated majority voting.[131]

It is important to keep in mind that the effectiveness of majority voting depends critically on the issuer's holdover policy. The failure of a director to win a majority vote does not automatically lead to his or her removal. Rather, the director will typically remain as a holdover director until he or she resigns or is replaced. Many issuers have addressed the holdover problem by requiring a director who receives a withhold vote to

125. Id.

126. Id. (listing Fortune 500 companies with majority voting); see also North Fork Bancorp., 825 A.2d at 860, 864 (describing requirement that Dime directors be elected by an affirmative vote of a majority of shares present).

127. Louis Lavelle, "Commentary: A Simple Way to Make Boards Behave," BusinessWeek, Jan. 31, 2005.

128. Testimony of John J. Castellani, President, the Business Roundtable, before the House Committee on Financial Services, Mar. 8, 2007, avail. at http://www.house.gov/apps/list/hearing/financialsvcs_dem/htcastellani030807.pdf.

129. Claudia H. Allen, Study of Majority Voting in Director Elections, Feb. 5, 2007, at 1, available at http://www.ngelaw.com/files/upload/majority_callen_020707.pdf.

130. Senate Floor Analyses, Senate Bill 1207, May 16, 2006, available at http://info.sen.ca.gov/pub/05–06/bill/sen/sb_1201–1250/sb_1207_cfa_20060516_095323_sen_floor.html (describing bill).

131. See Senate Bill No. 1207, approved by the Governor on Sept. 30, 2006, avail. at http://www.corp.ca.gov/pol/leginfo/sb_1207.pdf (amending section 708 of the California corporation code to authorize California corporations to adopt majority voting); Cydney Posner, California Majority Vote Bill, In the News, Cooley, Godward, Kronish LLP, July 25, 2006, available at http://www.cooley.com/news/inthenews.aspx?id=39809420 (describing reformulation of the legislation from requiring to facilitating majority voting).

submit his or her resignation.[132] The resignation is reviewed by the board's Corporate Governance Committee, typically within a 90 day period, which then makes a recommendation to the board on whether to accept or reject the resignation.[133] Significantly, the board has the authority to determine whether or not the director will actually be required to resign. Additionally, should the board accept the director's resignation, it, rather than the shareholders, generally has the statutory authority to replace the removed director. Shareholders do not even have the right to approve the replacement director until the next annual meeting.

Because majority voting policies are quite new, their effectiveness has not yet been tested. Unless and until shareholders refuse to elect a director—a decision that is likely to occur much less frequently than the somewhat symbolic withhold votes—it remains unclear whether majority voting will increase board responsiveness or accountability.

Majority voting is the most recent development in the context of director elections, but shareholder voting is also receiving attention with respect to another critical corporate governance issue—executive compensation. As indicated above, executive compensation has been a controversial topic, and a subject of shareholder activism, since the time of the Transamerica case. John and Lewis Gilbert, for example, frequently sponsored shareholder proposals seeking to limit executive compensation, although the proposals never received majority approval.[134] Executive compensation has also been the focus of extensive SEC rule-making, as the SEC has continually expanded and refined the disclosure requirements applicable to an issuer's top executives.[135] Recent SRO rule-making has sought to improve the process of setting executive pay by requiring the use of compensation committees composed of independent directors.[136] Investors, however, particularly institutions, have continued

---

132. The carefully crafted amendments to the Model Business Corporation Act, adopted by the ABA Committee on Corporate Laws in 2006, provide that a director who fails to receive a majority vote will continue to serve for no more than 90 days with no right to hold over. See The Committee on Corporate Laws, ABA Section of Business Law, Changes in the Model Business Corporation Act—Amendments to Chapter 7 and Related Provisions Relating to Shareholder Action Without a Meeting, Chapters 8 and 10 Relating to Shareholder Voting for the Election of Directors, and Chapter 13 Relating to Appraisal and Other Remedies for Fundamental Transactions, 61 Bus. Law. 1427 (Aug. 2006) (describing the amendments).

133. See, e.g., Pfizer Corporate Governance Principles, available at http://www.stoel.com/webfiles/CorpCounselRoundtable Pfizer–Nike–Intel–ProgressEnergy.pdf. (providing that a director who receives a majority withheld votes shall promptly tender his or her resignation, which will be

considered by the Corporate Governance committee and then acted on by the board).

134. See, e.,g., Bainbridge, Talking Stockholder Part I, supra note 17 at 54 (describing Lewis Gilbert's proposals to limit executive compensation at American Tobacco); Emerson, supra note 33 at 540–41 (describing proposals submitted by the Gilberts dealing with executive compensation).

135. The SEC's initial requirements, which have subsequently been refined, are contained in Executive Compensation Disclosure, Sec. Exch. Act. Rel. No. 31327, 57 Fed. Reg. 48126 (Oct. 21, 1992). See generally Jennifer S. Martin, The House of Mouse and Beyond: Assessing the SEC's Efforts to Regulate Executive Compensation, 32 Del. J. Corp. L. 481 (2007) (describing SEC's regulatory efforts including revisions to its disclosure requirements).

136. See, e.g., New York Stock Exchange Listed Company Manual § 303A.05(a) (requiring listed companies to

to express concern both about overall levels of compensation and, more importantly, about the extent to which compensation is unrelated to performance.

Investors have sought to raise these concerns through the shareholder proposal process. As indicated above, shareholder proposals relating to executive compensation have had a mixed reception from the SEC staff, which has permitted issuers to exclude many such proposals as relating to the issuer's ordinary business operations. Since approximately 1992, however, the staff has generally permitted proposals concerning compensation of senior executives.[137]

The latest such proposals seek to have issuers adopt advisory votes on executive compensation, a so-called "say on pay."[138] The concept is modeled upon the process adopted by England in 2002, and subsequently adopted in several other countries, in which shareholders engage in a non-binding vote to ratify executive remuneration.[139] Say on pay proposals first appeared on proxies in 2006. In 2007, they have been introduced at dozens of companies and, at some, have received majority approval.[140] Legislation is currently under consideration in Congress that would mandate say on pay for U.S. issuers.[141] Recently Aflac became the first U.S. company to provide say on pay, announcing that it had voluntarily instituted a non-binding shareholder vote that would begin with its 2009 annual meeting.[142]

Extended scope of permissible shareholder proposals, increased shareholder access to the director nomination process, majority voting, and say on pay are all developments that are likely to increase shareholder voting power. As such, they represent a potentially critical change in the importance of the shareholder franchise. The shareholder franchise has also become more significant as certain shareholders have sought to harness shareholder voting power in order to effect more

---

have a compensation committee composed entirely of independent directors).

137. See Eastman Kodak Company (publicly available Feb. 13, 1992) ("[I]t is the Division's view that proposals relating to senior executive compensation no longer can be considered matters relating to a registrant's ordinary business."). See also Staff Legal Bulletin No. 14A (July 12, 2002) (modifying staff position on executive compensation proposals), available at http://www.sec.gov/interps/legal/cfslb14a.htm.

138. See, e.g., Affiliated Computer Services, Inc. No Action Letter, 2007 WL 945176 (March 27, 2007) (describing "say on pay" proposal submitted by AFSCME and rejecting effort by Affiliated Computer Services to exclude the proposal).

139. See Paul Hodgson, "Having a Say on Pay: A Brief History of Shareholder Voting on Executive Compensation" (Jan. 16, 2007) (available at www.thecorporate

library.com (describing history of "say on pay")).

140. See L. Reed Walton, Motorola: Third Majority for "Say on Pay", ISS Corporate Governance Blog, May 31, 2007, available at http://blog.issproxy.com/2007/05/motorola_third_majority_for_sa_1.html (reporting majority approvals at Motorola, Verizon and Blockbuster).

141. See Marlene Kennedy, Getting a say on pay for execs, timesunion.com, Apr. 20, 2007, available at http://timesunion.com/AspStories/story.asp?storyID=582473 & category=BUSINESS & newsdate =4/20/2007 (describing progress of H.R. 1257, sponsored by Barney Frank, in Congress).

142. See Allan Sloan, Aflac Looks Smart on Pay, Wash. Post, May 29. 2007, at D1 (describing Aflac's voluntary adoption of "say on pay").

significant changes in corporate control and operations. Most prominent among such shareholders are hedge funds. Activist hedge funds, in particular, have begun to use short slate proxy contests in order to accomplish their objectives.

Hedge funds are lightly regulated investment funds that charge a performance fee and are sold to high net worth accredited investors. The term is used to distinguish hedge funds from regulated investment funds that are marked to retail investors, but the terminology also comes from the investment strategy of many hedge funds, which is designed to produce a return that is hedged against market risk. The hedge fund industry has grown tremendously in the last decade; currently an estimated 9000 hedge funds control assets of $1.4 trillion.[143] Hedge fund strategies vary enormously, but a number of hedge funds are activist investors, seeking to obtain board representation on their portfolio companies in hopes of encouraging structural or operation changes to improve performance.[144]

Unlike other institutions or retail investors, hedge funds hold large, concentrated stakes in their portfolio companies–the typical activist hedge fund may hold only 12–20 positions at any given time. This enables the hedge fund to overcome the collective action and free-rider problems associated with proxy contests.[145] As a result, proxy contests are on the rise.[146] Activist hedge funds have threatened proxy contests at dozens of companies in the past several years. Although many of the contests are settled before they go to a shareholder vote—often with management agreeing to nominate a couple of hedge fund representatives to the board[147]—Bill Bratton found 28 cases in which the contest went to a shareholder vote during the 2003–2006 time period. These cases represent real contests, with economic significance, in which shareholder voting matters. Hedge funds have been able to command the support of their fellow investors—winning proxy contests with surprising frequency. Of the contests that were resolved at the time of Bratton's study, hedge funds were successful 79% of the time. Significantly, Alon Brav, et al., report that hedge fund activism also has a positive impact on issuer performance and stock returns, and that this impact is not limited to the short window following the initial announcement of the fund's intended activism.[148]

---

143. Tomoeh Murakami Tse, Pension funds raise risk, dive into hedge funds, Wash. Post, July 25, 2007.

144. See William W. Bratton, Hedge Funds and Governance Targets, 95 Geo. L.J. 1375 (2007) (describing hedge fund activism and evaluating its impact on firm performance).

145. See, id. at 1381 (stating that "the activist funds have employed the proxy system, widely thought to be moribund, with remarkable, perhaps unprecedented, success.").

146. See Ellen Rosen, Hedge Funds' Activism Creates New Wealth for Law Firms, N.Y. Times, Apr. 20, 2007 (describing increase in proxy contests due to hedge fund activism).

147. Alon Brav and his co-authors describe an example in Pirate Capital's activism at James River Coal Co. See Alon Brav, et al., Hedge Fund Activism, Corporate Governance, and Firm Performance, working paper dated Aug. 30, 2007, at 13–14, avail. at http://papers.ssrn.com/sol3/papers.cfm?abstract_id=948907.

148. Id.

F. THE MECHANICS OF THE VOTING PROCESS

As shareholder voting becomes potentially more significant, it is worth considering the mechanics of the voting process, which has received relatively little attention. Because most stock is held in street name, issuers do not mail proxy statements and other solicitation material directly to investors.[149] Instead, the majority of solicitation material is delivered to banks and brokers, who are then obligated by SEC rules to deliver the information to the ultimate beneficial owners of the stock. Banks and brokers outsource the mechanical process of delivering proxy materials to an intermediary—generally American Data Processing ("ADP").[150] The costs for ADP's services are borne by issuers. ADP also collects and tabulates shareholder voting instructions and provides a vote count to issuers. In recent years, ADP has developed mechanisms to enable shareholders to vote by mail, by telephone and over the internet.[151]

The process of collecting and tabulating votes has not kept pace with the market. One problem occurs when the beneficial owner fails to submit voting instructions. For many years, the NYSE handled this by allowing the brokers, who were, after all, the record holders, to vote stock for which no instructions had been received. This procedure is known as discretionary voting.[152]

NYSE Rule 452 provides that, if the beneficial owner of shares held in street name has not indicated how those shares should be voted, the broker may vote the shares in its discretion.[153] NASD Rule 2260(c)(2) piggybacks onto Rule 452 by providing that, if discretionary voting is permitted under Rule 452, the broker is also allowed to vote for Nasdaq listed companies.[154] Brokers have typically exercised that discretion to support management, including voting in favor of the company's recommended slate of directors. Thus discretionary voting historically provided incumbent management with a strong base of support. Broker voting offers a partial explanation of the low rates at which shareholder proposals are adopted. Discretionary voting is not permitted with respect to non-routine matters, such as mergers and election contests. The NYSE determines whether a matter is routine; it has set out in Rule 452

149. According to the SEC, "It has been estimated that as much as 85% of exchange-traded securities are held in street name." SEC, Roundtable on Proxy Voting Mechanics, May 23, 2007, available at http://ftp.sec.gov/spotlight/proxyprocess/proxyvotingbrief.htm.

150. ADP Investor Communications is now Broadridge Financial Solutions, Inc. See https://myservice.broadridge.com/public_site/default.asp (reporting name change). Since 1999 ADP, now Bridgeridge, has handled over 90% of all investor communications distributions in the United States to beneficial owners by banks and brokers. Broadridge Investor Relations, History, available at http://www.broadridge-ir.com/main/history.htm.

151. See Stephen Choi & Jill E. Fisch, How to Fix Wall Street: A Voucher Financing Proposal for Securities Intermediaries, 113 Yale L. J. 269, 301–04 (2003) (describing ADP's services).

152. See Roundtable on Proxy Voting Mechanics, supra note 149 (describing broker voting).

153. NYSE Rule 452, Giving Proxies by Member Organization.

154. NASD Rule 2260(c)(2).

a list of non-routine matters.[155] This determination has been criticized, particularly in light of the NYSE's decision that vote no campaigns in which there is no opposing director slate are routine matters.[156] Responding to these concerns as well as the challenged posed by majority voting, the NYSE recently submitted a proposed change to Rule 452 which, if approved by the SEC, would prevent brokers from engaging in discretionary voting in uncontested director elections.[157]

Another problem arises from the fact that ADP is responsible for deciding which votes to count. The process generally involves ADP cross-checking the number of votes received from beneficial owners against the broker's total holdings of record. So long as broker has not submitted votes for more shares than it holds, ADP will count the votes. In cases of an over-vote, ADP will generally go back to the broker for a reconciliation. Individual brokers use different processes to determine which votes to count, and that determination is not regulated.[158] The process of determining which votes are valid is not transparent either to issuers or shareholders. Moreover, the intermediation prevents shareholders from ascertaining that their votes have been properly received and counted.[159] It is worth noting that ADP is hired by brokerage firms, but its fees are borne by the issuer. This structure creates an agency problem in which ADP cannot easily be held accountable by issuers or shareholders.

A third problem with the vote-counting process can arise from short selling. When shares are shorted, they are borrowed from one owner, in order to be sold to a second owner. In theory, both owners have a claim to the voting rights associated with those shares.[160] Yet, if both owners vote, the shares will be voted twice.[161] ADP's procedures do not provide a mechanism to track potential over-voting, and such voting is only likely to trigger attention if it leads to the submission of more votes by a broker's customers than shares held. In rare cases, however, over-voting can skew the results of an election. As Ed Rock and Marcel Kahan explain, for example, the margin of victory in the controversial MONY/ AXA deal was only 1.7 million shares out of 50.1 million, yet at the time

---

155. See Press Release, New York Stock Exch., NYSE Adopts Proxy Working Group Recommendation to Eliminate Broker Voting In 2008 (Oct. 24, 2006), available at http://www.nyse.com/press/1161166307645. html?sa   campaign=/rss/newsreleases /NYSE.comRuleProposalsNewsReleases (describing NYSE process of classifying proposals as "routine" or "non-routine").

156. See Roundtable on Proxy Voting Mechanics, supra note 149 (identifying NYSE position that vote no campaigns are routine matters for purposes of NYSE Rule 452).

157. See Press Release, supra note 155.

158. Roundtable on Proxy Voting Mechanics, supra note 149.

159. See, e.g., Choi & Fisch, supra note 151 at 303 n. 159 (recounting examples of shareholder disputes with ADP's recording of their votes).

160. See Shaun Martin & Frank Partnoy, Encumbered Shares, 2005 U. Ill. L. Rev. 775, 779–80 (2005) (describing challenge of determining appropriate voting rights when stock is loaned).

161. See Marcel Kahan & Edward B. Rock, Hedge Funds in Corporate Governance and Corporate Control, 155 U. Pa. L. Rev. 1021, 1079–82 (2007) (describing the over-voting problem).

of the vote, approximately 6.2 million shares had been shorted.[162] If voting rights were allocated improperly with respect to the shorted shares, an adjustment could easily have led to the opposite result.

The technical problem of determining how to count votes in the presence of short selling is the tip of a more significant problem—the question of whether a shareholder who limits his or her economic interest in a stock should retain the right to vote that stock. Shareholder voting rights are based on an ownership conception of the shareholder. Growth in derivatives and other financial innovations, as well as increased liquidity in the securities markets, have challenged this ownership conception. It is now possible to separate out legal title from economic interest by creating hedged positions in which a shareholder lacks an economic interest in stock but retains voting rights. Bernard Black and Henry Hu call this empty voting.[163] Derivatives also enable shareholders to acquire voting rights without acquiring the economic risk associated with ownership. Black and Hu term these rights "morphable voting rights."[164]

Whether shareholders should continue to retain voting rights if they partially or completely hedge their economic risk is an open question. Traditionally voting rights were based on legal title. At the same time, shareholders who lack an economic interest may exercise their voting rights in a way that is inconsistent with the interests of their fellow shareholders and the corporation. Some commentators have identified this as a particular concern with respect to hedge funds. Perhaps the most highly publicized example of this kind of behavior involves the proposed merger between Mylan Laboratories and King Pharmaceuticals.[165] The two companies entered into a merger agreement which was subject to shareholder approval. Based on market reaction, the merger was attractive for King, but not for Mylan. Perry, a hedge fund, owned approximately 7 million shares in King, and wanted the merger to be approved. Accordingly, prior to the vote on the merger, Perry purchased 9.9% of Mylan stock. Perry then entered into equity swaps that had the effect of fully hedging its position in Mylan. Accordingly, Perry obtained the power to vote 9.9% of Mylan stock with no economic interest in Mylan, freeing it to vote that stock in favor of the merger which would enhance the value of its King holdings. Although the merger fell through for other reasons, Perry's actions were widely criticized as empty voting or vote buying. Perry's actions were challenged in federal court by Carl Icahn,[166] but the failure of the merger mooted the question of whether Perry could be legally precluded from voting the Mylan stock before the court could consider it.[167]

162. Id. at 1081.

163. Henry T. C. Hu & Bernard Black, The New Vote Buying: Empty Voting and Hidden (Morphable) Ownership, 79 Cal. L. Rev. 811 (2006).

164. Id.

165. See Rock & Kahan, supra note 161 (describing this transaction in detail).

166. See Jesse Eisinger, Long & Short: Icahn Cries Foul at Perry's No–Risk Play in Takeover Fight, Wall St. J., Dec. 15, 2004, at C1 (reporting on the litigation).

167. See Icahn Drops Mylan Labs Suit, Wall St. J., July 26, 2005, at C4 (reporting termination of litigation).

Interestingly, empty voting is not a recent innovation. In a 1911 New Jersey case, the management of a corporation reportedly borrowed stock and transferred it into the names of persons who were friendly to management.[168] After those persons gave management proxies to vote the stock, the company closed its books for the purposes of recording transfers. Thereafter, the loaned stock was returned to its true owners. Other stockholders challenged the right of management to use these proxies to vote the stock in their own interests rather than in the interests of the true owners. Although the court found that the challenged proxies were insufficient to affect the outcome of the election and therefore refused to grant any relief, the court observed in dicta that the proxy relationship was based on agency principles and that the true owner of the shares at the time of the meeting had the right to have those shares voted in his economic interest.

Whether state courts will respond to challenges such as empty voting remains unclear. On the one hand, state common law prohibits vote selling,[169] and state courts presumably have the power to invalidate votes cast by those who have purchased the right to vote divorced of any economic interest in the stock. On the other hand, the wide range of derivatives means that a substantial number of shareholders have hedged their economic interest in whole or in part. Courts currently lack easy mechanisms both for identifying the extent of such hedging and determining the circumstances under which it should deprive a stockholder of voting power. For example, a shareholder who owns both a share of stock and a put option entitling that shareholder to sell the stock on a future date at a preset price has reduced or eliminated his exposure to changes in market price. A shareholder who owns a share and simultaneously sells a share short has eliminated his economic interest in the stock but retains the right to vote the stock. Similar examples are relatively commonplace, and it is difficult to believe that all such shareholders can or should be disenfranchised.

G. THE LONG TERM IMPLICATIONS OF TRANS-AMERICA

In the Transamerica case, the combined efforts of the SEC and the Third Circuit had the effect of largely federalizing the subject of shareholder voting. The SEC, through its adoption and implementation of the federal proxy rules, has been simultaneously both the dominant source of and the major constraint on shareholder voting power. Problematically, as the SEC's views on the appropriate allocation of authority between shareholders and corporate management have shifted, so have shareholder voting rights. Although the SEC has continually paid lip service to the proposition that its determinations are subject to the limits imposed by state law, both the no-action process and the decisions of the SEC and its staff when engaged in that process limit the opportunity for

---

168. Bache v. Central Leather Co., 78 N.J. Eq. 484 (1911).

169. See, e.g., Schreiber v. Carney, 447 A.2d 17 (Del. Ch. 1982).

state law to develop to address the relevant issues. Concededly there are exceptional cases in which state courts have had the opportunity to determine the appropriate scope of shareholder voting power–the Fleming case is one example. But it is far more common for the SEC's decisions to preclude state court action. As a result, shareholders' substantive voting rights have been largely determined by federal law. SEC rules and no-action determinations have limited shareholder power to nominate directors and otherwise to control the election process. SEC rulings have forced many shareholder resolutions into the form of non-binding precatory proposals instead of bylaw amendments, despite state corporation laws granting shareholders authority to amend the bylaws. And SEC interpretations have favored shareholder voting on social policy issues while limiting shareholder voice on poison pills, executive compensation and other governance issues.

Ironically, the strongest defense of this federalization of shareholder voting is also its biggest weakness. There is substantial evidence in the legislative history of the Securities Exchange Act of 1934 of management misuse of the proxy solicitation process to limit its accountability to shareholders.[170] Congress intended to address this problem by empowering the SEC to adopt rules that would protect the shareholder franchise. Both the SEC and the federal courts recognized and acted to further that congressional objective in the Transamerica decision–the SEC by acting to enforce John Gilbert's right to submit his proposals for a shareholder vote, and the court by refusing to allow Transamerica to circumvent the effect of the shareholder proposal rule through a bylaw provision.

Yet many critics claim that the SEC has largely abandoned its role as advocate of shareholder rights.[171] At times, the SEC appears to consider itself some type of corporate governance czar, charged with the task of evaluating the wisdom, in policy terms, of shareholder nominations, binding bylaw proposals, and say on pay. Problematically, the SEC's policy perspective has been strongly influenced by corporate management. As the history of the shareholder proposal rule demonstrates, the SEC has moved away from the position it espoused in Transamerica, increasingly toward restricting shareholder voting power. Both the SEC's imposition of ever-greater substantive limits on the scope of a permissible shareholder proposal and its increasing limitations in terms of shareholder qualifications, and number and length of proposals, reflect an agency perception that shareholder voting rights under rule 14a–8 are potentially abusive and must be narrowly constrained. It is difficult to find compelling evidence of such abuse in the history of proxy voting. Even the Gilberts, who pioneered the use of the shareholder proposal rule, and who were responsible for the majority of shareholder proposals in the years predating institutional activism, introduced proposals that, by modern standards, appear to be at the core of an

170. See Jill E. Fisch, From Legitimacy to Logic: Reconstructing Proxy Regulation, 46 Vand. L. Rev. 1129 (1993) (reviewing this evidence).

171. Farrell, supra note 110.

investor's legitimate interests–the appointment of auditors, reports of annual meetings, executive compensation and the like.

One solution would be for the SEC to get out of the business of refereeing shareholder voting. A shareholder proposal rule that provided shareholder access to the proxy, without subject matter limitations, subject to minimal procedural requirements, would return questions about the approximate scope of shareholder voting power to state courts.[172] A likely and beneficial result would be the development of a body of case law that addressed the extent to which the board's statutory authority to run the corporation constrains shareholder voting power. In addition, state courts would have the opportunity to address the ability of management to use procedural restrictions such as advance notice requirements to limit shareholder voting rights. In the end, the state legislatures and courts could make a determination about appropriate scope of management authority and the utility of shareholder voting in ensuring management accountability.

This solution might lead to a concern that, without SEC intervention, state courts and legislatures will restrict shareholder voting rights. The Delaware chancery court, for example, might have determined that Transamerica's bylaw operated as a valid limit on shareholders' statutory authority to amend the bylaws. An initial answer to this concern is that states already have the power to determine the scope of shareholder voting rights–the SEC rules do not permit shareholder proposals, nominations or proxy access beyond the rights granted by state law. If a state, such as Oklahoma, does not permit shareholders to amend the bylaws, a shareholder cannot introduce a bylaw amendment under rule 14a–8. A second answer is that state experimentation and variation with respect to shareholder voting is no different from the variation found in other areas of corporate law. Corporate scholars have largely defended regulatory competition and most believe that market forces will lead to the dominance of efficient legal rules.[173] In other words, under state regulation, the policy questions with which the SEC has struggled will be subject to the discipline of market forces. Should those market forces fail, as some believe they did in the 1920s, Congress can intervene and subject the shareholder voting process to minimum federal standards.

---

172. The SEC could, of course, enforce a requirement that the shareholder proposal and supporting statement comply with rule 14a–9–full and accurate disclosure is at the core of the SEC's competence.

173. Representative scholarship arguing that state regulatory competition produces efficient corporate law includes Ralph K. Winter, Jr., State Law, Shareholder Protection, and the Theory of the Corporation, 6 J. Legal Stud. 251 (1977) and Roberta Romano, The Genius of American Corporate Law (1993). See also Jill E. Fisch, The Peculiar Role of the Delaware Courts in the Competition for Corporate Charters, 68 U. Cin. L. Rev. 1061 (2000)(evaluating regulatory competition and competing scholarly explanations for Delaware's dominance).

Chapter 5

MAPPING JUDICIAL REVIEW:
SINCLAIR v. LEVIEN

By
Robert B. Thompson *

The intensity of judicial review of corporate decisions is the central issue of corporate law. *Sinclair Oil Corp. v. Levien,*[1] a foundational decision in Delaware corporate jurisprudence from 1971, defines the space within which judicial review occurs with a format that still guides courts today. Along one boundary is deference by judges to decisions of business managers that is reflected in the business judgment rule. Along the other boundary is an intrusive judicial involvement by which the court asks the corporation or other defendant to prove the intrinsic fairness of the transaction. Since *Sinclair,* the Delaware courts have filled in the space defined within those boundaries with a host of other decision points and varying degrees of judicial review, but it was *Sinclair* that provided the landscape.

The case remains in wide use today in classrooms (and courtrooms) because it presents an attractive pedagogical package.[2] Three challenged actions were before the court; for two of those actions the court adopted deference and for the other, intrinsic fairness. Hence, the outcome provides a structure that directs students to address the differences between the two standards. At the same time, the case raises the difficult policy question of how far a parent corporation can go in directing the actions of the subsidiary for the parent's own purposes. The *Sinclair* court takes a rather narrow definition of self-dealing, requiring that the parent get something at the expense of the subsidiary before a court will interfere with the directors' decision.

* New York Alumni Chancellor's Chair in Law and Professor of Management, Vanderbilt University. I am grateful for the research help provided by Cynthia Kutka from the Walker library of the Owen Graduate School of Management and the comments of Robert Payson, one of the lawyers in the case.

1. 280 A.2d 717 (Del. 1971).

2. *Sinclair* remains a principal case in most corporations casebooks, a rare feat for a case of its age.

This story unfolds in three parts. Section A introduces the parties and frames the issues presented in the case. Section B develops, with a graphic aid, the judicial space defined by the *Sinclair* court and filled in by judges over the ensuing decades. Section C analyzes the fiduciary duty of controlling shareholders (as opposed to duties of directors and managers without share control.) *Sinclair* provides room for "selfish" ownership for a majority shareholder, so long as the minority shareholders receive a proportional benefit, a standard that at the time seemed to expand the discretion for majority shareholders. Viewed from a point decades later, this part of *Sinclair* has not proved to be a template for broader applications and other doctrines have developed to constrain the actions of majority shareholders.

A. THE PARTIES AND THE CASE

Sinclair Oil Corporation ("Sinclair"), one of the country's twenty or thirty largest companies in the years before this case, owned 97% of a separate company, Sinclair Venezuelan Oil Company ("Sinven"), through which it engaged in petroleum operations in Venezuela for more than three decades.[3] A Sinven minority shareholder brought a derivative suit challenging allegedly selfish action by the parent Sinclair in operating Sinven.

Sinclair's founder, Harry Sinclair, began acquiring crude oil in the American plains states in the early 20th century while still in his 20s.[4] In 1916 he organized Sinclair Oil, a $50 million oil producing and refining firm to operate in the mid-continent oil fields through Kansas and Oklahoma in competition with the long dominant Standard Oil.[5] The company's search for new oil fields led it across the Caribbean in the late 1920s when it acquired a majority interest in an existing company in Venezuela that became Sinven.[6] This ownership interest increased to 86% by 1952[7] and to 96% by later in that decade.[8]

There was no doubt that Sinclair, the parent, completely controlled Sinven, the subsidiary. Sinclair named every Sinven board member. Almost without exception, every Sinven board member was a director,

---

3. See Fortune 500 available at http://money.com/magazines/fortune/fortune500_archive_snapshots/1955/3533.html (last visited August 30, 2007) (describing Sinclair as 21st in revenue for 1955. That ranking generally fell though the 20s, 30s and 40s thought the 1950s and 1960s until Sinclair's acquisition by Atlantic Richfield during the pendency of this case.)

4. Sinclair, A Great Name in Oil at 16 (1956) (hereinafter "Great Name").

5. Great Name, supra note at 17.

6. Oil Merger Approved, N.Y. Times December 18, 1928. By that time, the company had been listed on the American Stock Exchange for several years. See New Stocks on the Curb, N.Y. Times October 10, 1924

(describing Venezuelan Petroleum Company admitted to trading on the New York Curb Market Association).

7. See Sidelights on the Financial and Business Developments of the Day, November 19, 1952 (describing minority shareholder efforts to pressure Sinclair to acquire their interests; Sinclair at the time owned 86% of the shares).

8. Sidelights on the Financial and Business Developments of the Day, Feb. 7, 1958 (describing name change of Venezuelan Petroleum Company to Sinclair Venezuelan Oil Company, and Sinclair's ownership of more than 96% of the stock.)

officer or other employee of a company in the Sinclair group.[9] The Chancellor, in writing the opinion for the lower court, found that these individuals "were not in a position to make judgments as to what was in [Sinven's] best interest, alone, without regard to Sinclair's other operations, and it would be surprising if they were. I say this because [Sinven] was regarded as part of an integrated company, according to the testimony of [Sinclair's CEO]."[10]

This litigation was brought as a derivative suit, as was true for most cases in this time period alleging breach of fiduciary duty in publicly held corporations.[11] As such, the suit was formally in the name of Sinven, and any recovery would normally go to the corporate treasury. Unlike most corporate actions and lawsuits that are brought by the board on behalf of the corporation, derivative suits are brought by an individual shareholder arguing that the directors' self-interest will prevent them from bringing suit on behalf of the corporation. The United States Supreme Court in 1949 observed that derivative suits have long been "the chief regulator of corporate mismanagement."[12] Yet at the same time, there was widespread concern about these claims serving as strike suits brought to obtain attorneys' fees rather than to rectify the harm to the corporation.[13]

Francis S. Levien was not the typical derivative suit plaintiff, usually portrayed at the time as owning only a few shares of stock and open to a quick settlement that would benefit the lawyers more than the corporation.[14] Levien owned a substantial block of the stock, having purchased 3000 shares, (about two and a half percent of the non-Sinclair owned Sinven shares traded on the American Stock Exchange), for approximately $135,000 in April 1960, several years before the litigation was brought.[15] Nor was he a professional plaintiff. As a lawyer, he had

9. 280 A.2d at 719. The Chancellor, in writing the opinion after the trial in this case, found that these individuals "were not in a position to make judgments as to what was in [Sinven's] best interest, alone, without regard to Sinclair's other operations, and it would be surprising if they were. I say this because [Sinven] was regarded as part of an integrated company, according to the testimony of [Sinclair's CEO]." Levien v. Sinclair Oil Corp., 261 A.2d 911, 914 (Del. Ch. 1969) rev'd in part Sinclair Oil Corp. v. Levien, 280 A.2d 717 (Del. 1971).

10. Levien v. Sinclair Oil Corp., 261 A.2d 911, 914 (Del. Ch. 1969) rev'd in part Sinclair Oil Corp. v. Levien, 280 A.2d 717 (Del. 1971).

11. In the time between then and now, class actions alleging breach of duties owed to individual shareholders as in a merger, supplanted derivative suits as the most common vehicle for seeking to enforce fiduciary duties. See Robert B. Thompson & Randall S. Thomas, The New Look of Shareholder Litigation: Acquisition–Oriented Class Actions, 57 Vand. L. Rev. 133, 167 (2004) (class actions outnumber derivative suits by 8–1 among fiduciary duty claims in Delaware over a two year period).

12. Cohen v. Beneficial Indus. Loan Corp., 337 U.S. 541, 548 (1949).

13. See e.g. Franklin S. Wood, Survey and Report Regarding Stockholders Derivative Suits (1944) (commenting that derivative suits in the 1930s and 1940s were largely frivolous).

14. See e.g. Franklin S. Wood, Survey and Report Regarding Stockholders Derivative Suits (1944); Roberta Romano, The Shareholder Suit: Litigation without Foundation, 7 J. L. Econ. & Org. 55 (1991).

15. See Brief of Sinclair Oil Corporation, in the Supreme Court of Delaware, #34, 1974 at 2 (noting that Levien had received dividends of $90,700 by the time of his testimony in this action, at which time the stock was selling at the same price that he paid for it).

participated three decades before in the landmark Delaware Supreme Court fiduciary duty litigation in *Guth v. Loft, Inc.*[16] As an investor he had done well in that case and in business and later he became something of an activist shareholder.[17] The Columbia University gymnasium today bears his name.

His lawyers, too, were not the usual plaintiff's lawyers. Potter, Anderson & Carroon, one of the leading firms in Delaware and usually counsel for corporations, had joined the case after the well-known New York City litigator Milton Pollack had withdrawn to become a federal judge in New York.[18] Clarence Southerland, long-time managing partner of the firm prior to becoming the first chief justice of the revived Delaware Supreme Court, had argued the case for the Levien team in Guth v. Loth, Inc.

Plaintiff's lawsuit complained of three actions by Sinclair in its running of Sinven. First, Sinclair had caused Sinven to pay out $108 million in dividends over a six-year period in the 1960s, $38 million more than Sinven's earnings during the same period in what was, in effect, a partial liquidation. Second, Sinclair itself was growing elsewhere in the Americas and in Africa, and plaintiffs complained of Sinven not being included in those opportunities. Third, Sinclair had caused Sinven to enter into a contract with a wholly owned Sinclair subsidiary, Sinclair International, and International breached the contract in two respects. It failed to pay for the oil on time as required in the contract, running an average uncollected daily balance of about $2.8 million[19] and International failed to purchase the minimum quantity specified in the contract, a result sometimes termed "underlifting."[20]

In the liability phrase of the trial, Chancellor Duffy found for the plaintiff on all three claims. The Delaware Supreme Court, after ac-

---

16.   5 A.2d 503 (Del. 1939).

17.   See for example Time Magazine, December 23, 1957 describing his part in gaining control of the New York, New Haven & Hartford Railroad in 1954. http://www.time.com/time/magazine/article/0,9171,936802,00.html?promoid=googlep.

18.   Telephone conversation with Robert Payson, August 21, 2007. J. Lincoln Morris and Edward S. Cowen also represented Mr. Levien in the Chancery Court. Leroy A. Brill joined the team for the appearance in the Supreme Court. Other lawyers of the Potter Anderson & Carroon firm represented the parent in the *Getty* case infra note , joining Henry Canby of Richards Layton & Finger, who argued opposite the firm in the *Sinclair* case. The Potter firm was also involved on the parent side in Singer v. Creole Petroleum Corp., 297 A.2d 440 (Ch. Ct. 1972) modified by 311 A.2d 859 (Del. 1973), a derivative suit against Standard Oil of New Jersey for claims relating to its 95% owned Venezuelan subsidiary. For lawyers it was a small town and as lawyers

elsewhere, they could make alternative legal arguments in distinct cases. Delaware, for a long period called on its judges to be able to shift roles as well. Until 1951 all appeals were heard by the state's remaining trial judges excepting the jurist who had decided the case below. The result was that these judges sitting as the appellate court were expected "to overrule a fellow trial judge and to expect the possibility of being overruled themselves in another case, perhaps argued the same day." See Maurice A. Hartnett, Delaware Courts' Progression in Delaware Supreme Court Golden Anniversary at 16 (Randy J. Holland and Helen L. Winslow Eds 2001).

19.   261 A.2d at 924.

20.   280 A.2d at 719. A claim as to the consolidated tax return, an issue addressed in the Getty case being litigated at this same time, was not pursued in the trial below. 261 A.2d at 927.

knowledging that parent shareholders owe fiduciary duties to the minority shareholders of a subsidiary, announced a split decision, affirming the contract breach claim but reversing the other two. The Supreme Court declared that the more intrusive intrinsic fairness test turns on self-dealing, defined in this case as when a parent receives something to the exclusion of the subsidiary.[21] Since the minority in this case had received a proportionate share of the money paid out, the exclusion element was absent. Thus, business judgment review was appropriate for the dividends claim and plaintiff could prevail only upon showing improper motive or conduct amounting to waste.[22]

In contrast, the Court agreed with the Chancellor that intrinsic fairness was appropriate for the contract claim. This claim fit within the traditional self-dealing claim in which a conflicted director or shareholder was on both sides, but held a different proportion of the claims on each side so as to tilt its incentives. Thus in the International/Sinven contract in which Sinclair owned all of International and 97% of Sinven, Sinclair would receive 100 cents of every dollar directed toward International but only 97 cents of every dollar directed to Sinven. If it were negotiating on behalf of both, an outside observer would expect that Sinclair would prefer a contract favoring the side where it would receive 100% of the benefit.

The third claim, relating to Sinclair's alleged taking of a corporate opportunity, adds little but confusion to the holdings already considered. In response to plaintiff's assertion that new Sinclair ventures in Alaska, Canada, Paraguay, Algeria, Somalia and other places around the world should be shared with Sinven, the Chancellor assessment was that the argument on these facts was "out of the mainstream of the corporate opportunity cases."[23] Nevertheless, the Chancellor believed the opportunity claim to be a companion piece to plaintiff's attack upon dividends. He concluded that the extraordinary dividends and the absence of any serious effort to expand or develop Sinven did not amount to fair dealing toward the minority shareholders in managing the corporation's business.[24] The Chancellor noted the vigor with which management implemented a company-wide expansion program that was absent from the "lone subsidiary with minority stockholders."[25]

When the Supreme Court got to this part of the case, it treated this claim more like a corporate opportunity claim, ruling that the plaintiff

---

21. 280 A. 2d at 720. The Court used intrinsic fairness here as it did in Guth v. Loft. In other cases, such as Sterling v. Mayflower Hotel Corp., 93 A. 2d 107 (Del. 1952) and Keenan v. Eshleman, 2 A.2d 904 (1938), a contemporary decision of *Guth*, the court used entire fairness. In later years, the courts have viewed these terms as interchangeable. See e.g. Tanzer v. International Gen. Indus. Inc. 402 A.2d 382, 386 (Del. Ch. 1979) ("The words 'entire fair-

ness' are synonymous with the words 'intrinsic fairness' ".)

22. 280 A.2d at 722.

23. 261 A.2d at 919.

24. The complaint included a separate claim raising corporate opportunity claims relating to investments in Columbia which the Chancellor dismissed because the plaintiff lacked standing. 261 A.2d at 923.

25. 261 A.2d at 920.

could point to no opportunities that came to Sinven.[26] Without further explanation, the Court quickly shifted back to the self-dealing test of there being no exclusion of and detriment to Sinven's minority shareholders and applied the business judgment rule. This part of the case is best viewed in tandem with the law expounded in the dividends portion of the opinion. It adds little of value concerning the law of corporate opportunity.

The damages portion of the case produced several more years of litigation, focused mostly on whether Sinclair could claim various setoffs under the contract, particularly because the contract terms set a price above the then current world market price (but at a discount to the posted prices that the Venezuelan government insisted be used.) Apparently the contract was one way that Sinclair was able to persuade the government to accept a discount off of its posted price and move the transfer price at least some of the way toward the world market price in a market where there was a glut of oil. The Chancellor's basic approach, (by then he had moved to the supreme court and was sitting by designation) was that Sinclair made the contract and he had no problem holding them to it. He was, however, only willing to award interest for the slow payment, but not the underlifting.[27] The Supreme Court affirmed.[28] Venezuela's continued efforts to pull as much revenue as it could from its ground led to one more round of the litigation. The parent (now Arco after its takeover of Sinclair) sought to pay the minority shareholders their 3% directly since paying the entire multi-million dollar judgment into the Sinven corporate treasury would see more than half of that amount disappear to a Venezuelan tax. Arco lost that claim before Vice–Chancellor Brown,[29] but the case is said to have thereafter settled on similar terms. The $5.6 million judgment suggests this suit should not fairly be considered as a strike suit, although the 3% that was the actual benefit to the minority ($167,000) is not as impressive a number.[30]

B. MAPPING THE SPACE FOR JUDICIAL DECISIONS AND CHARTING THE PATH THAT COURTS WILL TAKE IN A FIDUCIARY DUTY CASE

Sinclair provides the bookends that identify the space within which judicial review of corporate actions occurs. At one end is the business judgment rule, a presumption by the court that the decision of the board of directors should stand free of judicial interference unless there is a showing of fraud or gross overreaching. At the other end is the intrinsic fairness standard which differs in two important ways. First, the burden

---

26. 280 A.2d at 722.

27. Levien v. Sinclair Oil Corp. 314 A.2d 216 (Del. Ch. 1973).

28. Sinclair Oil Corp. v. Levien, 332 A. 2d 139 (Del. 1975) (per curiam).

29. Levien v. Sinclair Oil Corp., 1975 WL 1952 (Del. Ch.) 1 Del. J. Corp. L. 230.

30. 314 A.2d at 223. The amount attributable to the plaintiff's shares would have been less than $5000.

of proof is on the party with the fiduciary duty and second, the applicable standard requires that the substance of the transaction, its intrinsic fairness, be "subject to careful judicial scrutiny."[31]

These bookends were not new to Delaware law in 1971. The business judgment rule had long been expressed as a corollary to the core principle of the Delaware statute in Section 141 bestowing all corporate powers on the board of directors.[32] Similarly, Delaware already had a rich heritage of imposing duties of loyalty, care and good faith on corporate fiduciaries. The 1939 case of *Guth v. Loth, Inc.* is a classic illustration.[33] It arose in the same era as *Meinhard v. Salmon*, the New York case containing Judge Cardozo's oft-quoted language defining the duty owed as "the punctilio of an honor the most sensitive" and imposing standards stricter than the morals of the marketplace.[34] The Delaware opinion takes a similar view portraying the rule as "inveterate and uncompromising in its rigidity" and resting on "a broader foundation of wise public policy that, for the purpose of removing all temptation, extinguishes all possibility or profit flowing from a breach of the fiduciary relations."[35] It found that Guth, as president of Loft, Inc. could not take for himself the opportunity to acquire the Pepsi–Cola trademark, secret formula, goodwill and business. The transaction occurred at a time when Guth had become incensed by Coca Cola's refusal to discount the price of its syrup to Loft's chain of candy stores and soda fountains and had set about looking for a replacement cola. As it happened, Pepsi–Cola had been adjudicated a bankrupt at about the same time. Guth, in alliance with a key Pepsi manager, formed a new corporation to acquire the Pepsi assets using Loft capital, facilities and other assets in the effort. The new venture, in turn, sold Pepsi syrup back to Loft, its chief customer.

In ruling that there was a breach of fiduciary duty, the Court addressed the core elements of corporate opportunity that continue to frame the debate today: Did the opportunity come to him as an officer of Loft? Was it closely associated with the existing business as to throw the corporate officer into competition with the company? Would the corporation have been able to finance the project? Was it within Loft's line of business? Did Loft have an interest or expectancy? In answering these questions affirmatively the Court framed the issue as not to be decided on narrow or technical grounds, "but upon broad considerations of corporate duty and loyalty."[36]

Sinclair took these core principles of board authority and judicial review and put them in a structure that if presented linearly would

31. 280 A.2d at 720.

32. Del Code Ann. tit. 8 § 141. See Smith v. Van Gorkom, 488 A.2d 858 (Del. 1985) ("the business judgment rule is the offspring of the fundamental principle, codified in 8 Del.C. § 141(a), that the business and affairs of a Delaware corporation are managed by or under its board of directors.")

33. 5 A.2d 503 (1939).

34. 249 N.Y. 458, 164 N.E. 545, 546 (NY 1928).

35. *Guth v. Loft, Inc.* 5 A.2d 503, 510 (1939).

36. *Guth v. Loft, Inc.* 5 A.2d 503, 511 (1939)

define space something like what appears in Figure 1. The figure is best understood if approached from the starting point at the top middle. The case soon gets to a decision point, termed here the "Sinclair point," where the court has to decide whether the case is to be judged by the business judgment rule as represented by the left downward sloping line or the intrinsic fairness standard, as represented by the right downward sloping line. The *Sinclair* substantive holding was that self-dealing in the form of receiving a benefit at the expense of the minority is what determines which path the court takes.

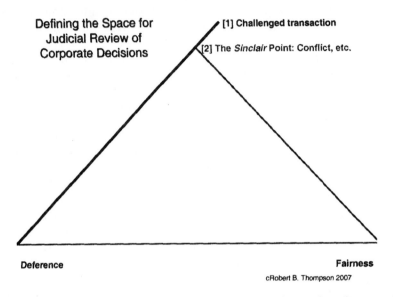

Defining the Space for
Judicial Review of
Corporate Decisions

[1] Challenged transaction

[2] The *Sinclair* Point: Conflict, etc.

Deference

Fairness

cRobert B. Thompson 2007

Subsequent cases make clear, as represented by this figure, that each fiduciary duty case has a starting point and it is the business judgment rule. It is as if every time a judge gets a case with a fiduciary duty allegation in it, he or she goes immediately to a spot on the floor marked with an X (or in the figure above a [1]). That point says that the judge will begin with deference. If nothing is shown by the plaintiff to push the court off of that position, the inevitable result is deference to the board's action and no judicial interference absent fraud or over-reaching or waste or gift. What can divert a fiduciary duty case to the other line? *Sinclair* makes clear that is self-dealing as representing a conflict of interest and a breach of the duty of loyalty. Other cases make clear that a breach of a duty of care (absent statutory exculpation) could also serve the same purpose.[37] Absent the plaintiff showing either one of these elements or something like it, the case moves inextricably toward deference, as if it were pulled by gravity.

With this space so defined, the way was open for a richer, more layered response making greater use of the territory defined by defer-ence and intrinsic fairness. The Chancellor, for example, noted that

37. See e.g. Smith v. Van Gorkom, 488   A.2d 858 (Del. 1985).

Sinclair could have installed a truly independent board and speculated that change of fact might have invoked the business judgment test.[38] Delaware Section 144, passed in 1967, addressed this possibility.[39] If there is a director or officer conflict, a reason that would move the court off of the business judgment rule deference path, a decision by independent directors after full disclosure can cleanse the transaction of its voidability. The statute itself does not specify if business judgment deference is the result but more recent case law suggests that it is.[40]

Alternatively the statute provides for cleansing by action of the shareholders, an alternative that can divert the case from its path toward intrinsic fairness and reset the case back in the direction toward deference. The subsection of the Delaware statute dealing with shareholder cleansing, unlike parallel provisions of the Model Business Corporation Act,[41] does not require that the shareholder action be by *disinterested* shareholders, thus omitting the word clearly inserted in the prior subsection relating to directors.[42] Earlier courts, worried about the possible misuse of shareholder cleansing by majority shareholders, tweaked the applicable judicial review in such a situation so that it did not go all the way back to deference.[43] More recently, Delaware case law has in effect read "disinterested" into the statute with the consequence a level of judicial review after such cleansing that seems indistinguishable from the deference and waste standard that would occur under the default application of the business judgment rule.[44]

Perhaps the biggest change since *Sinclair* in the relative space occupied by deference and by the more intrusive judicial review has been the insertion of the *Aronson* requirement that demand be made on directors by the shareholder seeking to bring a derivative suit unless the demand is excused.[45] Demand is required, the Supreme Court said in *Aronson,* unless the plaintiff presents particularized facts creating a

38. 261 A.2d at 919 (To meet its fiduciary duty, Sinclair "could have installed a truly independent board and had it done so the business judgment test might have been dispositive of most of this case.")

39. Del. Code Ann. tit. 8 § 144.

40. See e.g. Oberly v. Kirby, 592 A.2d 445, 466 (Del. 1991) ("section 144 allows a committee of disinterested directors to approve a transaction and bring it within the scope of the business judgment rule.")

41. Mod. Bus. Corp. Act § 8.63.

42. Compare Del. Code Ann. tit 8 § 144(a)(1) to 144(a)(2).

43. See e.g. Fliegler v. Lawrence, 361 A.2d 218, 221 (Del. 1976) (where majority of shares voted in favor of a self-dealing transaction were cast by defendants in their capacity as shareholders, court "cannot say that 'the entire atmosphere has been freshened' and that departure form the objective fairness test is permissible."); Gottlieb v.

Heyden Chemical Corp., 91 A.2d 57 (1952) (where formal approval by majority of independent, fully informed shareholders, burden of proof shifts to objecting shareholder to demonstrate the terms are so unequal as to amount to a gift or waste of corporate assets); Remillard Brick Co. v. Remillard–Dandini Co., 109 Cal App. 2d 405, 241 P. 2d 66 (1952) (even though the requirements of the statutory conflicting interest provision were technically met, transactions that are unfair and unreasonable to the corporation may be avoided.)

44. Marciano v. Nakash, 535 A.2d 400, 405 n.3 (Del. 1987) ("approval by fully-informed disinterested directors under 144(a)(1) or disinterested shareholders under 144(a)(2) permits invocation of the business judgment rule and limits judicial review to issues of gift or waste with the burden of proof on the party attacking the transaction.").

45. Aronson v. Lewis, 473 A.2d 805 (Del. 1984).

reasonable doubt that a majority of the board is not independent and not disinterested.[46] The effect is an "Aronson point" in the litigation, parallel to the Sinclair point discussed above. If a court determines that the facts merit that a demand be made, the case turns onto a path to judicial deference, parallel to what it would do if court were to find no self-dealing under *Sinclair*. However, *Aronson* revised the *Sinclair* decision point in a material way. The question asked by the court is not whether there was self-dealing at the time of the original transaction such that intrinsic fairness rather than the business judgment deference standard of review should apply, but whether the directors' *later* decision not to bring a suit will be respected by the court.

Defendants will often benefit from moving the court's focus to this later decision point. In a case like Sinclair, such a move would force the court to address the decision of the board not to file a suit in response to the shareholder's demand. It will often be easier to refute any breach of the duty of loyalty or care as to this later decision than the initial action. Thus the board could decide that a suit, even if likely meritorious, would be too disruptive of the business of the company and distracting to its executives such that going forward was not warranted. If this second decision is made by directors who are not conflicted and who have met their duty of care, the court will defer as it would to any board decision. After the *Aronson* decision, the Delaware court made plaintiff's choice especially stark by holding that the mere act of making demand would be the plaintiff's concession that there was no conflict of the board, thus virtually assuring the second decision would gain deferential business judgment review.[47] The Court backed away from the breadth of that holding in a subsequent decision and said that a board could appear disinterested, but still act conflicted in ways to lose the deference.[48]

For defendants, the practical choice is between having a court look at the conflicted interest transaction, making the defendant prove the intrinsic fairness to a judge, or taking advantage of an internal corporate governance alternative and having the case reviewed by directors, ostensibly disinterested, but nevertheless picked by the same process as the other directors and likely to be decision-makers more sympathetic to business realities. The result was to open up a second alternative to obtaining something like the deferential review of Sinclair's initial bookend even when self-dealing exists.

Of course, obtaining this deferential review requires a majority of independent and disinterested directors. Some corporations, such as

---

46. Aronson's holding is broader in that it also permits demand to be excused if plaintiff presents particularized facts creating a reasonable doubt that "the transaction was otherwise a valid exercise of business judgment."

47. Spiegel v. Buntrock, 571 A.2d 767, 776 (Del. 1990) ("stockholders who, like Spiegel, make a demand which is refused, subject the board's decision to judicial re-view according to the traditional business judgment rule.")

48. Scattered Corp. v. Chicago Stock Exchange, Inc. 701 A.2d 70 (Del. 1997) (a board that appears independent ex ante may not necessarily act independently ex post in rejecting a demand; failure of an otherwise independent-appearing board to act independently could constitute wrongful refusal.)

Sinclair, were not willing to incur the perceived costs of such a structural change and until the stock exchange listing standard reforms that followed Enron were not required to do so. The result would appear to doom this group of possible defendants to intrusive intrinsic fairness review when a fiduciary duty claim alleging self-dealing is brought. However, Delaware has provided yet another point where defendants can move the case back to the path toward deference. In the decade after *Sinclair*, starting with federal cases arising after Watergate and allegations of foreign bribery, corporations without any independent directors began to expand their board to add a couple of independent directors. Those new directors became a committee to review the litigation and exercise the default power of directors to run the corporation, including the authority to dismiss a derivative suit. In *Zapata Corp. v. Maldonado*, the Delaware Supreme Court reversed a Chancery Court opinion that had blocked such action and held that the actions of such a committee could at least divert the course of the litigation from the intrinsic fairness review and channel it toward a less intrusive judicial review.[49] The Court, however, did not redirect the judicial review completely toward deference. Instead it applied the "Zapata two-step." First the corporation, not the plaintiff, has the burden of proving the disinterestedness and independence of the directors and their process. Second, even if the committee satisfied this standard, the court could still impose its own independent business judgment, clearly more intrusive that ordinary deference.[50]

Clearly a plaintiff would rather be at *Zapata* than at the other alternatives, but defendants also know this and strategize to block the *Zapata* path. In chronological terms, *Aronson* actually came three years after *Zapata* and had the practical effect of blocking plaintiffs' access to this more intrusive judicial review so long as the companies had done sufficient advance planning and provided enough independent directors to require demand on directors under *Aronson*. Case law has not yet made clear the extent to which planners could cleanse a conflict by sending a case to a committee of independent directors after a suit is brought but before resolution of a demand hearing.

The decision tree so far just presents Delaware law. If other states are included, new choices are presented. For example, the Model Business Corporation Act requires universal demand in every case.[51] The result is to move the focus of judicial review further down the litigation process. Once demand is made, there will then be action by a board or a committee, most often not to proceed. The crucial question will be the intensity of judicial review of a challenge to such board action not to proceed. The Model Act provides two alternative levels of review depend-

49. 430 A.2d 779 (Del. 1981) reversing Maldonado v. Flynn, 413 A.2d 1251 (Del. Ch. 1980).

50. 430 A.2d at 789 ("Court should, when appropriate, give special consider-ation to matters of law and public policy in addition to the corporation's best interests.")

51. Mod. Bus. Corp. Act § 7.42.

ing upon who appoints the decision-maker.[52] If the decision-making group is appointed by a board with a disinterested majority, the burden of proof is on the plaintiff. If the committee is appointed by a board whose majority is not disinterested, the burden of proof shifts to the defendant.[53] Thus, depending on the outcome of this factual inquiry, the judicial review will be at different places in the decision-space.

If these alternatives are added to the decision tree presented as Figure 1 above, the revised figure would now look something like Figure 2, with the planner in Delaware being able to insert at least three additional points between the original transaction and the court's Sinclair point of decision, any of which can keep the case from moving down the path to intrinsic fairness review.

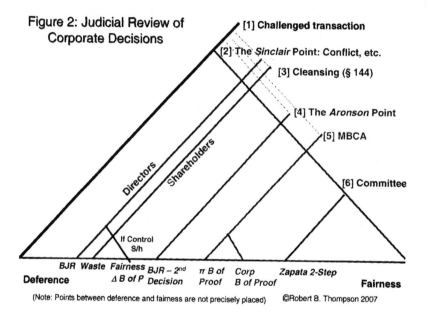

Figure 2: Judicial Review of Corporate Decisions

[1] Challenged transaction
[2] The *Sinclair* Point: Conflict, etc.
[3] Cleansing (§ 144)
[4] The *Aronson* Point
[5] MBCA
[6] Committee

Directors
Shareholders
If Control S/h

Deference — BJR   Waste   Fairness   Δ B of P   BJR – 2nd Decision   π B of Proof   Corp B of Proof   Zapata 2-Step — **Fairness**

(Note: Points between deference and fairness are not precisely placed)   ©Robert B. Thompson 2007

The intermediate level of review that Delaware has imposed in a takeover context in *Unocal*[54] and *Revlon*[55] also occupies space in the middle of the triangle's bottom line. Many corporate planners will be able to avoid *Revlon* by structuring the acquisition as a share for share merger that has been held not to trigger *Revlon's* duty.[56] Further,

52. Mod. Bus. Corp. Act § 7.44(d).

53. Mod. Bus. Corp. Act § 7.44(d). The burden of proof is for the requirements specified in subsection (a): whether the decision-making group has determined "in good faith, after conducting a reasonable inquiry upon which its conclusions are based, that the maintenance of the derivative proceeding is not in the best interests of the corporation."

54. Unocal Corp. v. Mesa Petroleum Co. 493 A.2d 946 (Del. 1985) (because of omnipresent specter of board self-interest in taking defensive action, enhanced judicial re-

view where directors must show they had reasonable grounds of believing a danger to corporate policy and effectiveness existed and that the defensive tactic was reasonable in relation to the threat posed).

55. Revlon, Inc. v. MacAndrews & Forbes Holdings, Inc. 506 A.2d 173 (Del. 1986) (when break-up of company inevitable, duty of directors changes to getting the best price for stockholders).

56. Paramount Communications, Inc. v. Time Inc., 571 A.2d 1140 (Del. 1990).

Unocal has not often been used by the Delaware Supreme Court to invalidate defensive tactics.[57]

All of this complexity follows from the space defined by *Sinclair* and the possibility, acknowledged by the Chancellor, that planners can themselves affect the level of judicial review they get by their own internal corporate structures. Not surprisingly, lawyers work to mold their case to fit within the alternative governance devices available to shape judicial review. Thus, process and substance are necessarily intertwined and affect the outcome of any fiduciary duty case. Section C addresses remaining question of substance in the parent-subsidiary context.

C. HOW FAR SHOULD PARENT SHAREHOLDERS BE ABLE TO GO IN CONTROLLING THEIR SUBSIDIARY CORPORATIONS FOR SELFISH INTERESTS?

Apart from defining the space within which judicial review of corporate actions occurs, *Sinclair* also addressed how far parent companies might go in controlling subsidiaries without triggering intrusive judicial review. Those who control a corporation (beginning here with directors who don't also own a majority of shares) by law have a very broad authority to direct the operation of the business.[58] They can appoint its officers, buy and sell assets, determine its business plan, and anything else in the control and management of the firm. At the same time, the courts regularly have applied fiduciary duties so that "corporate officers and directors are not permitted to use their position of trust and confidence to further their private interest."[59] This was most often developed in conflict of interest transactions where a fiduciary was on both sides of the transaction as in the classic case of *Globe Woolen Co.*[60] or in corporate opportunity cases such as *Guth* where fiduciaries were said to have taken an opportunity belonging to the corporation.

When those in control of the board are also the majority shareholders, the same kinds of conflict of interest can also exist. In cash-out mergers, for example, the majority shareholder is able to establish the terms of a merger by which the minority shareholders will be forced to exit the enterprise, in a context where the majority is clearly on both sides of the transaction. The same judicial checks arising from entire

57. Robert B. Thompson & D. Gordon Smith, Toward a New Theory of the Shareholder Role: Sacred Space in Corporate Takeovers, 80 Tex. L. Rev.261, 284 (2000) (survey of Delaware cases between 1985 and 2000 applying Unocal found that no defensive tactic failed the Unocal test). Cf. Omnicare, Inc. v. NCS Healthcare, Inc., 818 A. 2d 914 (Del. 2003) (finding lack of fiduciary out clause in a merger agreement to be preclusive and coercive and a violation of Unocal where two shareholders who controlled more than 50% of the vote and con-

tractually obligated themselves to vote for the merger).

58. Del. Code Ann. tit 8 § 141(a).

59. Guth v. Loft, Inc. 5 A.2d 503, 510 (Del. 1939).

60. Globe Woolen Co. v. Utica Gas & Elec. Co., 224 N.Y. 483, 121 N.E. 378 (1918) (director of a corporation presided at a board meeting where board approved a contract with a corporation of which he was chief shareholder).

fairness are seen here. There is, however, an extra dimension, not present when the controllers are merely directors but not major shareholders. The majority shareholder likely has paid a premium to acquire a controlling block. Such a block can command a premium because it can reduce the uncertainty to the shareholder as to the direction of the enterprise. There is what a Massachusetts court would later term the majority's right of "selfish ownership."[61] As applied in *Sinclair*, this right of selfish ownership included the parent's power to direct the payment of dividends when it needs the money so long as the minority share holders receive their proportionate share of the amount paid out.

Courts have struggled regularly with the balance between a majority shareholder's rights of selfish ownership and the majority shareholders' fiduciary duty to other shareholders in the context of sales of a control block for a premium. Courts outside of Delaware have sometimes extended fiduciary duty to a majority's misuse of their power of control to benefit themselves in selling their own shares.[62] Delaware law "has acknowledged, albeit in a guarded and complex way, the legitimacy of the acceptance by controlling shareholders of a control premium."[63] The Chancellor's opinion in *Sinclair* confronts the asserted fiduciary duty of a majority shareholder acting not in the sale of the shareholder's property, but in doing what directors and officers normally do in directing the use of the corporation's assets. The Chancellor characterized this behavior as the controlling shareholder preferring its own interest in "drying up" the subsidiary; it was a failure "to apply the corporation's assets for the benefit of all stockholders" and a breach of duty.[64] The Supreme Court's holding clearly puts limits on such a broad duty.

When should a parent corporation be able to direct the operation of the subsidiary to protect its rights of selfish ownership? Based on economic principles, it would be possible to argue that so long as all shareholders are at least as well off as they were before the transaction, a transaction that produces gains to the majority maximizes aggregate gains.[65] It would be possible to go further and argue that transactions should be permitted even if some shareholders are worse off, so long as the gain to the others exceeds the loss to the first group and if investor by ex ante diversification can mitigates this harm and maximize total gain.[66] These arguments, would seem to fit clearly within an entire

61. Wilkes v. Springside Nursing Home, Inc., 370 Mass. 842, 353 N.E.2d 657, 663 (1976). Wilkes does not provide deference in that situation, but a level of review that is between deference and intrinsic fairness.

62. Jones v. H. F. Ahmanson & Co. 1 Cal 3d 93, 460 P.2d 464, 81 Cal. Rptr. 592 (Cal. 1969); See also Perlman v. Feldmann, 219 F.2d 173 (2d Cir, 1954).

63. Mendel v. Carroll, 651 A2d 297, 305 (Del. Ch. 1994) (board not authorized to deploy corporate power against the majority

shareholder in the absence of a threatened serious breach of fiduciary duty by the controlling stock).

64. 261 A.2d at 921.

65. Frank Easterbrook & Daniel Fischel, Corporate Control Transactions, 91 Yale L. J. 698 (1982).

66. A diversified shareholder would have to have the equal ability to invest in firms who are controlling shareholders of other firms for this protection to exist.

fairness analysis and don't by themselves resolve the issue of whether judicial review should be cut off prior to such consideration by a judge.

The *Sinclair* case followed closely on a similar Delaware case raising the issue as to whether a parent must share the benefits of an oil import quota with its subsidiary.[67] A few years earlier another Delaware case raised the issue of allocation of benefits between parent and subsidiary derived from filing a consolidated tax return.[68] In both of the prior cases, the subsidiary was no worse off than if would have been as a free-standing corporation outside of a group and the court deferred to the decision of the board in allocating the benefit. All three cases could support a pareto optimal efficiency standard for excluding corporate action from judicial review, but each added an additional requirement to the core pareto optimal standard.

In the *Getty* case addressing the oil import allocation, the government regulations provided that that controlling corporation and its subsidiaries would be regarded as one for purposes of entitlement to an oil import quota.[69] In the particular facts, the parent was entitled to a quota based on its historical imports, but the subsidiary, being an inland refinery, had not historically participated in such a program. How should a court review such an allocation? The Supreme Court in *Getty* rejected intrinsic fairness for business judgment review "where the terms of a parent-subsidiary transaction are not set by the parent but by a third party, usually the State or Federal government."[70] Such a holding would also take in a consolidated tax return as in *Meyerson* where a profit-making parent and its loss-sustaining subsidiary qualified under the Internal Revenue Code to file a consolidated tax return that would reduce the total amount of taxes by permitting the parent to set off the subsidiary's losses against the parent's income.[71]

In deciding *Sinclair*, a year after *Getty,* the Supreme Court extended its prior reasoning to settings where the benefit came not from a third party, but from the individual needs of the majority shareholder. Proportional sharing became an alternative condition that would permit corporate action to go forward with no intrusive judicial review. The space for selfish behavior had widened.

Is proportional sharing enough of a check for the court to let go of intrusive judicial review? *Sinclair* occurred at a time when there was great concern about the deterioration of standards of director responsibility. A famous 1974 article by Columbia professor William Cary lamented the relaxation of fiduciary standards in Delaware and suggested

67. Getty Oil Co. v. Skelly Oil Co., 267 A.2d 883 (Del. 1970).

68. Meyerson v. El Paso Natural Gas Co. 246 A.2d 789 (Del. Ch. 1967).

69. In *Getty*, as in *Sinclair*, it was the Supreme Court reversing a broad ruling by the Chancellor. Getty Oil Co. v. Skelly Oil Co., 267 A.2d 883 (Del. 1970) (reversing 255 A.2d 717 (Del. Ch. 1969)). Thus, the time-line of the decisions was the Chancellor's opinion in *Getty* followed his opinion in *Sinclair,* both of which preceded the Supreme Court's reversal in *Getty* and its subsequent reversal of *Sinclair.*

70. 267 A.2d at 887.

71. Meyerson v. El Paso Natural Gas Co. 246 A.2d 789 (Del. Ch. 1967).

the need for a federal role.[72] The series of cases he offered to show Delaware's lax reputation was deserved included *Sinclair;* indeed *Sinclair* gets more ink than any of the other examples.[73]

Outside of *Sinclair,* Professor Cary's main focus was on directors when there is no majority shareholder. When there is a majority shareholder, the proportional sharing rules have not provided a basis to govern related cases and instead other legal doctrines have developed to control such actions. For example, perhaps the greatest extension of majority shareholder power in the period prior to Professor Cary's article was granting to majority shareholders the authority to rearrange the ownership of the venture by exercise of an eminent domain type power by which it could take the minority's interest in the business simply by paying a statutorily determined fair value. After the Delaware legislature had amended its merger statute to permit cash as consideration for mergers, adventuresome planners used the new flexibility to push through deals with disparate payment terms for the majority and minority interest; the majority got shares in the continuing venture and the minority were forced to accept cash or to litigate for fair value under appraisal. Just days before the Supreme Court's decision in *Sinclair,* Vice–Chancellor Marvel had relegated dissatisfied plaintiffs to appraisal, absent fraud or blatant overreaching,[74] even though appraisal had real deficiencies for plaintiffs.[75]

Six years later, in *Singer v, Magnavox,* the Supreme Court reversed this prior Delaware law and subjected cash-out mergers to an entire fairness test.[76] After another six years, the Court cut back on *Singer.* It abandoned a business purpose requirement and sought to funnel disputes to an appraisal process dramatically modified to "bring our law current," but still with entire fairness as the standard for self-dealing.[77] Since then the Court has paid particular attention to parent subsidiary

---

72. William L. Cary, Federalism and Corporate Law: Reflections upon Delaware, 83 Yale L. J. 663 (1974).

73. 83 Yale at 679. The other examples in Cary's list were purchase of minority interest without full disclosure, proxy contests and defensive tactics, misleading proxy statements, destruction of accrued dividends, de facto mergers, and directors' duty of care.

74. David J. Greene & Co. v. Schenley Indus., Inc., 281 A.2d 30 (Del. Ch. 1971).

75. Weinberger v. UOP, Inc., 457 A.2d 701 (Del. 1983). Until that time Delaware courts used a very bureaucratic "Delaware block" method of valuation. The appraisal statute required plaintiff to take several steps to perfect the appraisal claim, where non-compliance with any step forced the shareholder to accept the amount specified in the merger plan by the majority, often a low-ball amount. Attorneys fees and other costs were borne by the plaintiff. No vehicle

for class action or sharing of expenses was provided and the plaintiff got nothing until the case was over. For many years Delaware awarded only simple interest for a process that could take years to litigate.

76. Singer v. Magnavox Co., 380 A.2d 969, 980 (Del. 1977) (merger for the sole purpose of freezing out minority stockholders is an abuse of the corporate process; even if proof of freeze-out purpose not made, court will scrutinize transaction for compliance with entire fairness.) Earlier in the opinion, the court said that limiting plaintiff solely to appraisal "does not square with the duty stated so eloquently and so forcefully by Chief Justice Layton in Guth." 380 A. 2d at 978. The opinion, written, by now Justice Duffy, echoes some of the opinions of then Chancellor Duffy in the Singer and Getty cases at the trial court level.

77. Weinberger v. UOP, Inc., 457 A.2d 701 (Del. 1983).

transactions, requiring entire fairness review even if there has been approval by disinterested directors or ratification by minority shareholders.[78]

Nor has the permissiveness accorded to directors in paying what may be excessive dividends extended to the much more common setting when majorities fail to pay dividends for selfish reasons. In case law that has mostly occurred outside of Delaware and has involved closely held corporations, courts have regularly invoked non-payment of dividends as a prime indicia of oppression of minority shareholders. This has led to judicial relief under statutes permitting dissolution or other remedies or under common law fiduciary duties, often enhanced because of the illiquidity and intimacy that characteristics the close corporation setting.[79] Often, the nonpayment of dividends that is found actionable is accompanied by corporate actions with an explicitly disproportionate effect. For example, the majority may fire the minority shareholder from a job as a manager in a corporation where salaries but no dividends are paid so that only the majority is receiving monetary return from the corporation.

Majority conduct that in isolation may not appear disproportionate may seem more fair and appropriate when the viewed from a broader perspective. In *Chiles v. Robertson*, for example, the challenged behavior was the majority acting for the corporation to agree to the transfer of a lease where a related corporation of the majority shareholder was the tenant.[80] This occurred in a series of corporations and most of the leases provided that the consent could not be unreasonably withheld. The landlord corporation, in which the minority shareholder had an interest, received no additional compensation for this consent. As a result of a larger leveraged buyout restructuring, the lease was reworked to provide for an "upcharge" that helped finance the transaction. As an extension of the Sinclair/Getty/Meyerson pareto optimal argument above, the court might have argued that the lack of benefit to the minority was due to the long-standing contract terms so that the majority got nothing at the expense of the minority. Instead the Oregon court said the majority had to use the power of control in a way that would benefit all shareholders proportionately.[81]

---

78. Citron v. E.I. DuPont de Nemours & Co., 584 A.2d 490, 502 (Del. Ch.1990) ("The controlling shareholder relationship has the inherent potential to influence, however subtly, the vote.... no court could be certain whether the transaction terms fully approximate what truly independent parties would have achieved.... Given that uncertainty, a court might well conclude that even minority shareholders who have ratified a parent/subsidiary merger need procedural protections..." as provided by an entire fairness review.); Kahn v. Lynch Communication Systems, Inc. 638 A.2d 1110, 1116–1117 (Del. 1994) (entire fairness is exclusive standard for cash out by a con-

trolling shareholder, but approval of transaction by independent directors or informed vote of majority of minority shareholders shifts the burden of proof on the issue of fairness to the challenging shareholder.)

79. See F. Hodge O'Neal & Robert B. Thompson, O'Neal & Thompson's Oppression of Minority Shareholders and LLC Members §§ 3.4, 7.13 (tracking development of oppression cases).

80. Chiles v. Robertson, 767 P.2d 903 (Or. App. 1989).

81. 767 P.2d at 923.

As a result, the Sinclair/Getty/Meyerson trilogy no longer stands out as a guide to the substantive parent/subsidiary relationship. Nor is the trilogy as essential as it was then to defendants. At the time, *Sinclair* was phrased as something of a threshold decision between business judgment rule deference and intrinsic fairness review, but it was often seen as outcome determinative; without being on the right side of the Sinclair decision point, defendants would lose.[82] But a series of high profile Delaware Supreme Court cases finding that defendants met the fairness standard shows that there remains a real chance for defendants to win even when the court rules that the intrinsic fairness standard is appropriate.[83] The results, however, may be asymmetrical as there does seem to have been a shift in courts' willingness to overturn director's action after deciding the business judgment rule is appropriate.

D. CONCLUSION

Sinclair defined the space for judicial review of corporate decisions. The bookends illustrated so clearly in Sinclair remain the most observable features in defining judicial review. In the decades since, courts have created a more complex multilayered process so that the same broad issues may now reappear at multiple places in the litigation of shareholder suits. That, in turn, has expanded the room for lawyers' strategic choices to influence how the cases are presented to judges. For law students, the challenge is to understand both the basic similarity of the issues that are being decided in a variety of different settings,[84] and how framing the issue in one of the settings versus another can have a dramatic impact on how the case is presented.

Secondly, Sinclair's resolution of the substantive question as to how far controlling shareholders can go in directing the operations of the subsidiary has had little impact over the succeeding decades. *Sinclair* took a specific set of controlling shareholder transactions out of the area for intrusive judicial review. Controlling shareholders can direct a dividend policy that meets their own cash flow needs so long as they share proportionately with the minority. But that ends up being a small subset of decisions that directors and controlling shareholders make and the benefit/detriment rule has not proven to have broad application in other circumstances. Other doctrines have grown up to regulate controlling

---

82. James D. Cox and Thomas Hazen, Corporations § 11.11 at 254 (extremely rare that controlling shareholders could establish intrinsic fairness after self-dealing found so more appropriate to view Sinclair as a test of who prevails in a suit.)

83. See Cinerama, Inc. v. Technicolor, Inc. 663 A.2d 1156 (Del. 1995) (evidence sustained chancery court's determination that merger satisfied entire fairness); Nixon v. Blackwell 626 A.2d 1366 (Del. 1993) (defendants met the burden of establishing entire fairness as to use of an ESOP and key man life insurance); Kahn v. Lynch Communication Sys., Inc., 1995 WL 301403

(Del. Ch. 1995) aff'd 669 A.2d 79 (Del. 1995) (merger satisfied entire fairness).

84. See e.g. Aronson v. Lewis, 473 A.2d 805, 812 (Del. 1984) (business judgment rule comes into play in several places in a derivative action—in addressing a demand, in determination of demand futility, in efforts of independent disinterested directors to dismiss the action, and as a defense to the merits of this suit. "However, in each of these circumstances there are certain common principles governing the application and operation of the rule.")

shareholder transactions, including another of the court's decisions of 1971, *Schnell v. Chris Craft*,[85] where the Court blocked management from advancing the date of the annual meeting, declaring that, "inequitable action does not become permissible simply because it is legally possible."[86] Judicial review of controlling shareholder action remains more vibrant than might have been anticipated in the wake of *Sinclair*. At the same time, the mapping of judicial review provided in this opinion continues to accurately present the path of judicial review in fiduciary duty cases.

85. Schnell v. Chris–Craft Indus., Inc., 285 A.2d 437 (Del. 1971).

86. Schnell v. Chris–Craft Indus. Inc., 285 A.2d 437, 439 (Del. 1971).

Chapter 6

PROTECTION OF MINORITY SHAREHOLDERS IN CLOSELY–HELD CORPORATIONS: *DONAHUE v. RODD ELECTROTYPE CO.*

By
Douglas K. Moll*

A. INTRODUCTION

For many years, the law's regulation of internal disputes in closely held corporations was no different from the law's regulation of such disputes in corporations generally. Due in no small part to seminal decisions like *Donahue v. Rodd Electrotype Co.*,[1] however, most jurisdictions have gradually come to recognize that closely held corporations and their publicly held counterparts, as well as the expectations of the shareholders in those ventures, are sufficiently distinct to warrant a different legal treatment. Before the impact of the *Donahue* opinion can be appreciated, some background on the position of the minority shareholder in the closely held corporation is needed.

In a publicly held corporation, a shareholder is typically a passive investor who neither contributes labor to the corporation nor takes part in management responsibilities. A shareholder in a publicly held corporation simply invests money and hopes to receive a return on that money through capital appreciation and/or dividend payments.[2] By contrast, in a closely held corporation a shareholder typically expects an active participatory role in the company, usually through employment and a meaning-

---

* Beirne, Maynard & Parsons, L.L.P. Professor of Law, University of Houston Law Center.

1.   328 N.E.2d 505 (Mass. 1975).

2.   *See, e.g., Exadaktilos v. Cinnaminson Realty Co.*, 400 A.2d 554, 560 (N.J. Super. Ct. Law Div. 1979) ("Large corporations are usually formed as a means of attracting capital through the sale of stock to investors, with no expectation of participation in corporate management or employment. Profit is expected through the payment of dividends or sale of stock at an appreciated value.").

ful role in management.[3] A shareholder in a closely held corporation also invests money in the venture and, like all shareholders, hopes to receive a return on that money. Because there is no active market for the company's shares,[4] however, any financial return is normally provided by employment compensation and dividends rather than by sales of stock at an appreciated value.

Conventional corporate law norms of majority rule and centralized control can lead to serious problems for a minority investor in a closely held corporation. Traditionally, most corporate power is centralized in the hands of a board of directors. The directors set policy, elect officers, and supervise the normal operation of the corporation. Because directors are elected by shareholder vote, the board of a closely held corporation is typically controlled by the shareholder (or shareholders) holding a majority of the voting power. Through this control of the board, a majority shareholder (or majority group) has the ability to take unjustified actions that are harmful to a minority shareholder's interests. Such actions are usually designed to restrict (or deny all together) the minority's financial and participatory rights, and they are often referred to as "freeze-out" or "squeeze-out" techniques that oppress a minority shareholder in a closely held corporation. Common freeze-out techniques include the termination of a minority shareholder's employment, the removal of a minority shareholder from the board of directors, the refusal to declare dividends, the denial of access to information, and the siphoning off of corporate earnings to the majority shareholder.[5]

Quite often, these tactics are used in combination. For example, rather than declaring dividends, closely held corporations often distribute their earnings to shareholders in the form of salary and other employment-related compensation.[6] (Reasonable employment compensation is tax deductible to a corporation as a business expense, while dividend payments are not). In a closely held corporation where dividends are not paid, therefore, a minority shareholder who is discharged from employment and removed from the board of directors is effectively denied any return on his investment as well as any input into the management of the business.[7] Such conduct often culminates with a

---

3. *See, e.g., id.* at 561 ("Unlike their counterparts in large corporations, [minority shareholders in closely held corporations] may expect to participate in management or to influence operations, directly or indirectly, formally or informally. Furthermore, there generally is an expectation on the part of some participants that their interest is to be recognized in the form of a salary derived from employment with the corporation.") (citation omitted).

4. *See infra* note 11 and accompanying text.

5. *See, e.g., Donahue,* 328 N.E.2d at 513 (noting some of the possible freeze-out techniques).

6. *See, e.g., Landorf v. Glottstein,* 500 N.Y.S.2d 494, 499 (Sup. Ct. 1986) (stating that, in a closely held corporation, "dividends are often provided by means of salaries to shareholders"); *Hirschkorn v. Severson,* 319 N.W.2d 475, 477 (N.D. 1982) ("[T]he corporation paid no dividends.... Rather, the corporate directors distributed the profits via salary increases, bonuses, and benefits....").

7. *See, e.g., Balvik v. Sylvester,* 411 N.W.2d 383, 388 (N.D. 1987) ("Balvik was ultimately fired as an employee of the corporation, thus destroying the primary mode of return on his investment. Any slim hope of gaining a return on his investment and remaining involved in the operation of the

majority proposal to purchase the shares of the minority owner at an unfairly low price. In short, this denial of financial and participatory rights is at the core of many lawsuits alleging that the majority shareholder used his control in an abusive or "oppressive" fashion against a minority shareholder.

Under traditional corporate law principles, the basic components of a freeze-out scheme are generally legal. Terminating an employee or removing a director, for example, rarely invokes corporate law scrutiny, in part because such conduct is not normally considered to affect the rights of a shareholder.[8] Further, the business judgment rule typically protects internal corporate decisions, such as employment, management, and dividend matters.[9] As a result, traditional corporate law largely permits the conduct that tends to form the basis of a classic freeze-out.

In a publicly held corporation, a minority shareholder can escape abusive conduct of the majority shareholder by selling his shares into the market and by correspondingly recovering the value of his investment. This ability to liquidate provides some protection to investors in publicly held corporations from potential abusive conduct by those in control.[10] In a closely held corporation, however, the minority shareholder's investment is effectively trapped, as there is no ready market for the stock of a closely held corporation.[11] In fact, often the only potential purchaser of a minority shareholder's shares is the oppressive majority shareholder himself or the corporation controlled by the oppressive majority. As

---

business was dashed when Sylvester removed Balvik as a director and officer of the corporation.").

8. *See infra* notes 32–34 and accompanying text.

9. *See infra* notes 40–41 and accompanying text.

10. In a publicly held corporation, the presence of a well-functioning market also exerts some discipline on those in control:

> Market restraints are most visible and workable in the case of publicly held corporations. If management is inefficient, indulges its own preferences, or otherwise acts contrary to shareholder interests, dissatisfied shareholders will sell their shares and move to more attractive investment opportunities. As more shareholders express their dissatisfaction by selling, the market price of the company's shares will decline to the point where existing management is exposed to the risk of being displaced through a corporate takeover.... The mere threat of displacement, whether or not realized, is a powerful incentive for managers of publicly held corporations to promote their shareholders' interests so as to keep the price of the company's shares as high and their own positions as secure as possible.

J.A.C. Hetherington & Michael P. Dooley, *Illiquidity and Exploitation: A Proposed Statutory Solution to the Remaining Close Corporation Problem*, 63 VA. L. REV. 1, 39–40 (1977) (footnote omitted); *see, e.g., Rosenfield v. Metals Selling Corp.*, 643 A.2d 1253, 1262 n.18 (Conn. 1994) ("The market for corporate control serves to constrain managers' conduct that does not maximize shareholder wealth. It therefore serves to align the interests of managers more closely with the interests of shareholders in publicly traded corporations. The market for corporate control does not affect, however, the incentives of managers of closely held corporations.").

11. *See, e.g., Donahue v. Rodd Electrotype*, 328 N.E.2d 505, 514 (Mass. 1975) ("In a large public corporation, the oppressed or dissident minority stockholder could sell his stock in order to extricate some of his invested capital. By definition, this market is not available for shares in the close corporation."); *Brenner v. Berkowitz*, 634 A.2d 1019, 1027 (N.J. 1993) ("[U]nlike shareholders in larger corporations, minority shareholders in a close corporation cannot readily sell their shares when they become dissatisfied with the management of the corporation.").

mentioned, these parties will usually offer an amount that is significantly below the fair value of the minority's shares—if they choose to make an offer at all.

A market is, of course, only one way to cash out of a company. Even without a market for a company's shares, a minority shareholder could still recover the value of his investment if he could force the corporation (or the majority shareholder) to purchase his shares on demand. No state's corporation law, however, provides such a right. Without an explicit buyout provision in a stockholders' agreement or a company's organizational documents, corporate shareholders have no right to compel redemption of their holdings.[12]

Dissolution of a company can also provide liquidity to business owners by requiring the sale of the company and by allocating to each owner his proportionate share of the company's sale value. If a minority shareholder in a closely held corporation had the right to compel dissolution, a mechanism for recovering the value of the invested capital would exist. In the closely held corporation setting, however, a minority shareholder has no default right to dissolve a corporation by "express will" (i.e., voluntary dissolution usually requires the assent of at least a majority of the outstanding voting stock of a corporation).[13] For an oppressed minority shareholder, therefore, voluntary dissolution rights are largely unhelpful.

In summary, when a majority shareholder in a closely held corporation exercises his control in an oppressive fashion against a minority shareholder, the minority is in a vulnerable position. Prospects for judicial relief under traditional corporate law principles are slim, and there is little ability to exit the situation. It is this vulnerable position that spurred the *Donahue* court's analysis and the legal framework that it created.

B. THE *DONAHUE* DECISION

Harry Rodd was a director, officer, and controlling shareholder of Rodd Electrotype Company of New England, Inc. ("Rodd Electrotype"), a Massachusetts closely held corporation. Throughout his time at the corporation, Rodd actively participated in the company's management.[14] Joseph Donahue was a minority shareholder of Rodd Electrotype. Upon Joseph's death, his wife, Euphemia Donahue, inherited his shares.[15]

The lawsuit in *Donahue* involved a dispute over the corporation's purchase of Rodd's stock. At the time of the purchase, Rodd was seventy-seven years old, not in the best of health, and was looking to retire from

---

12. *See, e.g., Goode v. Ryan,* 489 N.E.2d 1001, 1004 (Mass. 1986) ("In the absence of an agreement among shareholders or between the corporation and the shareholder, or a provision in the corporation's articles of organization or by-laws, neither the corporation nor a majority of shareholders is under any obligation to purchase the shares of minority shareholders when minority shareholders wish to dispose of their interest in the corporation.").

13. *See, e.g.,* DEL. CODE ANN. tit. 8, § 275(b) (2006).

14. *Donahue,* 328 N.E.2d at 508–09.

15. *Id.* at 509–10 & n.8.

the business. The corporation (whose board included Rodd's two sons, Charles Rodd and Frederick Rodd, and the clerk of the corporation, Harold Magnuson) purchased Rodd's holdings for $36,000 (45 shares at $800/share). At approximately the same time as the purchase, Rodd resigned from his director and officer positions with the company.[16]

Euphemia Donahue demanded that her shares be purchased at the same price, but the corporation refused.[17] She sued Rodd, the three members of the board of directors, and the corporation itself. Donahue sought to rescind the company's purchase of Rodd's shares and to compel Rodd to repay the $36,000 purchase price to the corporation.[18] She alleged "the defendants caused the corporation to purchase [Rodd's] shares in violation of their fiduciary duty to her, a minority stockholder of Rodd Electrotype."[19] Specifically, Donahue argued that the corporation's purchase of Rodd's shares was an "unlawful distribution of corporate assets to controlling stockholders," which allegedly constituted a breach of duty to her "because the Rodds failed to accord her an equal opportunity to sell her shares to the corporation."[20]

The trial judge dismissed the plaintiff's complaint on the merits. He determined that "the purchase was without prejudice to the plaintiff and implicitly found that the transaction had been carried out in good faith and with inherent fairness."[21] The Appeals Court affirmed.[22]

The Massachusetts Supreme Judicial Court began its analysis by referencing "the distinctive nature of the close corporation" and by defining such a venture as "typified by ... (1) a small number of stockholders; (2) no ready market for the corporate stock; and (3) substantial majority stockholder participation in the management, direction and operations of the corporation."[23] The court then observed that, "[a]s thus defined, the close corporation bears striking resemblance to a partnership," and it stated that "[c]ommentators and courts have noted that the close corporation is often little more than an 'incorporated' or 'chartered' partnership."[24]

Significantly, the court then turned its attention to a lengthy discussion of the freeze-out dangers faced by minority shareholders in closely held corporations, as well as the obstacles that such shareholders encounter in challenging oppressive conduct under traditional corporate law:

> Although the corporate form provides the above-mentioned advantages for the stockholders (limited liability, perpetuity, and so forth), it also supplies an opportunity for the majority stockholders to oppress or disadvantage minority stockholders. The minority is

16. *Id.* at 510.

17. *Id.* at 511. In prior years, the corporation had offered to purchase Donahue's shares for between $40 and $200 a share. All of these offers had been rejected. *Id.* at 511 n.10.

18. *Id.* at 508.

19. *Id.*

20. *Id.* at 511.

21. *Id.* at 508 (footnote omitted).

22. *See id.*

23. *Id.* at 511.

24. *Id.* at 512.

vulnerable to a variety of oppressive devices, termed 'freeze-outs,' which the majority may employ. An authoritative study of such 'freeze-outs' enumerates some of the possibilities: 'The squeezers (those who employ the freeze-out techniques) may refuse to declare dividends; they may drain off the corporation's earnings in the form of exorbitant salaries and bonuses to the majority shareholder-officers and perhaps to their relatives, or in the form of high rent by the corporation for property leased from majority shareholders ...; they may deprive minority shareholders of corporate offices and of employment by the company; they may cause the corporation to sell its assets at an inadequate price to the majority shareholders....' In particular, the power of the board of directors, controlled by the majority, to declare or withhold dividends and to deny the minority employment is easily converted to a device to disadvantage minority stockholders.

The minority can, of course, initiate suit against the majority and their directors. Self-serving conduct by directors is proscribed by the director's fiduciary obligation to the corporation. However, in practice, the plaintiff will find difficulty in challenging dividend or employment policies. Such policies are considered to be within the judgment of the directors.... [G]enerally, plaintiffs who seek judicial assistance against corporate dividend or employment policies do not prevail.

Thus, when these types of 'freeze-outs' are attempted by the majority stockholders, the minority stockholders, cut off from all corporation-related revenues, must either suffer their losses or seek a buyer for their shares.... [They] must liquidate [their] investment in the close corporation in order to reinvest the funds in income-producing enterprises.

At this point, the true plight of the minority stockholder in a close corporation becomes manifest. He cannot easily reclaim his capital. In a large public corporation, the oppressed or dissident minority stockholder could sell his stock in order to extricate some of his invested capital. By definition, this market is not available for shares in the close corporation....

Thus, in a close corporation, the minority stockholders may be trapped in a disadvantageous situation. No outsider would knowingly assume the position of the disadvantaged minority. The outsider would have the same difficulties. To cut losses, the minority stockholder may be compelled to deal with the majority. This is the capstone of the majority plan. Majority 'freeze-out' schemes which withhold dividends are designed to compel the minority to relinquish stock at inadequate prices. When the minority stockholder agrees to sell out at less than fair value, the majority has won.[25]

25. *Id.* at 513–15 (citations omitted) (footnotes omitted).

To protect against this potential for abuse, the *Donahue* court imposed a fiduciary duty of "utmost good faith and loyalty" between shareholders in closely held corporations:

> Because of the fundamental resemblance of the close corporation to the partnership, the trust and confidence which are essential to this scale and manner of enterprise, and the inherent danger to minority interests in the close corporation, we hold that stockholders in the close corporation owe one another substantially the same fiduciary duty in the operation of the enterprise that partners owe to one another. In our previous decisions, we have defined the standard of duty owed by partners to one another as the 'utmost good faith and loyalty.' Stockholders in close corporations must discharge their management and stockholder responsibilities in conformity with this strict good faith standard. They may not act out of avarice, expediency or self-interest in derogation of their duty of loyalty to the other stockholders and to the corporation.[26]

In applying this fiduciary duty of utmost good faith and loyalty to the facts of the dispute, the *Donahue* court announced an accompanying "equal opportunity" rule:

> [I]f the stockholder whose shares were purchased was a member of the controlling group, the controlling stockholders must cause the corporation to offer each stockholder an equal opportunity to sell a ratable number of his shares to the corporation at an identical price. Purchase by the corporation confers substantial benefits on the members of the controlling group whose shares were purchased. These benefits are not available to the minority stockholders if the corporation does not also offer them an opportunity to sell their shares. The controlling group may not, consistent with its strict duty to the minority, utilize its control of the corporation to obtain special advantages and disproportionate benefit from its share ownership.[27]

Because "[t]he plaintiff and her son were not offered an equal opportunity to sell their shares to the corporation," the court concluded that, "[o]n its face . . . the purchase of Harry Rodd's shares by the corporation is a breach of the duty which the controlling stockholders, the Rodds, owed to the minority stockholders, the plaintiff and her son."[28] The court ordered the lower court to rescind the purchase of Rodd's shares or to require the corporation to purchase Donahue's shares for the same $36,000 sum that Rodd received.[29]

C. ANALYSIS AND DISCUSSION

The legacy of the *Donahue* decision lies in its recognition of the plight of minority shareholders in closely held corporations and in its

---

26. *Id.* at 515 (citations omitted) (footnotes omitted).

27. *Id.* at 518 (footnote omitted).

28. *Id.* at 520.

29. *Id.* at 521.

efforts to craft common-law protections in response. Although the validity of the equal opportunity rule and the usefulness of the partnership analogy can be questioned, the significance of the *Donahue* decision lies less in its detail and more in its overall push for enhanced minority shareholder rights.

1. Recognition of the Minority Shareholder's Plight

As mentioned, the *Donahue* decision acknowledged the unique dangers that minority shareholders face in closely held corporations. The *Donahue* court recognized that seemingly garden-variety decisions to, for example, terminate a shareholder's employment, remove a shareholder from management, or deny the declaration of dividends can actually be components of a premeditated freeze-out—an intentional effort to harm a minority shareholder's investment by stripping the shareholder of all financial and participatory rights in the venture. Without a market for the company's stock or other ability to liquidate the shares, the minority shareholder has no ability to escape the oppressive situation by recovering the value of his investment.[26] The mere recognition of this freeze-out problem in the closely held setting was significant, as it highlighted the need to consider additional common-law protections.

2. The *Donahue* Doctrine

The *Donahue* court, of course, went beyond mere recognition of the freeze-out problem. The court crafted a judicial doctrine in response—i.e., a shareholder-to-shareholder fiduciary duty with an accompanying equal opportunity rule. It is helpful to examine each aspect of the doctrine individually.

a. The Shareholder-to-Shareholder Fiduciary Duty

To grasp the significance of the shareholder-centered fiduciary duty imposed by the *Donahue* court, it is important to understand how the duty altered existing legal principles affecting minority shareholder rights. Under traditional corporate law principles, shareholders challenging employment, management, or dividend decisions—decisions that form the grist of most shareholder oppression disputes—are hamstrung by several legal obstacles.

First, fiduciary duties are conventionally viewed as running to the corporation (or to the shareholders collectively), but not to an individual shareholder.[28] As a consequence, a minority shareholder can have diffi-

---

26. *See id.* at 513–15.

28. *See, e.g., Schautteet v. Chester State Bank*, 707 F. Supp. 885, 888 (E.D. Tex. 1988) ("Officers and directors owe fiduciary duties only to the corporation. Therefore, [a minority shareholder] has no individual fiduciary right to enforce against any officer or director of [the company]." (citations omitted)); *id.* at 889 (noting that "most abuses of majority control constitute breaches of the fiduciary duties the majori-

ty owes to the corporation, just as officers and directors owe fiduciary duties solely to the corporation"); *see also* Hetherington & Dooley, *supra* note 10, at 12 & n.30 (mentioning the traditional view that duties run "solely between the majority and the corporation," and observing that "[t]he notion that the fiduciary obligations of management run only to the corporation provides the minority in close corporations virtually

culty challenging, for example, a termination of employment or a removal from management on traditional fiduciary duty grounds, as a court usually requires that harm to the corporation be shown, rather than harm merely to the minority shareholder.[29] By holding that shareholders in a closely held corporation "owe one another" a fiduciary duty, the *Donahue* court changed the principal focus of a fiduciary duty analysis to an individual shareholder.[30] Indeed, the court found that the shareholder-to-shareholder fiduciary duty was breached, even though the court did not disagree with the trial court's finding that the stock repurchase was fair to the corporation.[31]

Second, even if a fiduciary duty analysis focuses on an individual shareholder, that analysis is implicated only when majority conduct affects *shareholder* rights.[32] Employment and management positions with a corporation, however, are not traditionally viewed as part of one's rights as a shareholder. In fact, stock ownership and employment/management benefits are largely viewed as unrelated in the publicly held setting.[33] This helps to explain why terminations of employment and

no protection against oppression and exploitation by the control group").

It should be noted that the assertion that fiduciary duties do not conventionally run to an individual shareholder is somewhat of a debatable proposition. In the controlling shareholder context, a number of judicial decisions speak of a duty owed by the majority to the minority. *See, e.g., Southern Pac. Co. v. Bogert*, 250 U.S. 483, 487–88 (1919) (noting that "[t]he majority has the right to control; but when it does so, it occupies a fiduciary relation toward the minority"); *Riblet Prods. Corp. v. Nagy*, 683 A.2d 37, 40 (Del. 1996) ("To be sure, the Majority Stockholders may well owe fiduciary duties to Nagy [a single shareholder] as a minority stockholder.").

29. *See, e.g.*, Hetherington & Dooley, *supra* note 10, at 12 ("[C]ourts undoubtedly ... have been influenced by traditional common law attitudes emphasizing ... proof of harm to the corporation as distinguished from the interests of individual shareholders."); *see also Donahue*, 328 N.E.2d at 513 & n.14 (noting, while discussing traditional fiduciary duty principles, that "in practice, the plaintiff will find difficulty in challenging dividend or employment policies," and observing that "[i]t would be difficult for the plaintiff in the instant case to establish breach of a fiduciary duty *owed to the corporation*, as indicated by the finding of the trial judge").

30. *See Donahue*, 328 N.E.2d at 515.

31. *See id.* at 519 ("Although the purchase price for the controlling stockholder's shares may seem fair to the corporation and other stockholders ... the controlling stockholder whose stock has been pur-

chased has still received a relative advantage over his fellow stockholders, inconsistent with his strict fiduciary duty....").

32. *See, e.g., Nagy*, 683 A.2d at 40 ("This is not a case of breach of fiduciary duty to Nagy [a minority shareholder] *qua* stockholder.... Nagy does not allege that his termination amounted to a wrongful freeze out of his stock interest in [the corporation], nor does he contend that he was harmed as a stockholder by being terminated.").

33. As one commentator observed:

From the standpoint of an employee in a publicly held corporation ... the economic interest in stock ownership and the economic interest in employment are largely separate. As a stockholder, the employee's interest is the same as all other stockholders. The employee-stockholder seeks an expected return on his investment that adequately compensates for the risk of investing in the enterprise....

Such an employee's interest in his job, by contrast, is some function of the personal satisfaction that the job brings and the level of monetary compensation and other benefits that the job provides. If the employee is satisfied with his job, but comes to believe that the stock in his employer is a bad investment, the employee can simply sell the stock. If the employee desires to change jobs or is fired, but continues to believe that the stock is a good investment, the employee may continue to hold stock in his former employer. The act of changing jobs does nothing

removals from management positions—two primary components of a classic freeze-out—rarely invoke corporate law scrutiny in publicly held corporations. Simply put, such actions are not viewed as affecting shareholder rights.[34]

In a closely held corporation, however, most terminations of employment and removals from management positions do affect shareholder rights, as employment and management benefits are typically a substantial part of a shareholder's return on investment. Many closely held corporations distribute much, if not all, of their earnings as salaries and other employment compensation.[35] As a consequence, one needs to maintain a job to receive a financial return on investment. Moreover, the financial and other benefits of employment and management positions in a closely held corporation help to offset the high risk of failure associated with investing in small businesses. Without these benefits, in other words, an investment in a closely held corporation often makes little economic sense.[36] In the closely held setting, therefore, majority conduct

to alter the risk-return calculation that makes the stock in the employer either a good or a bad investment.

Robert A. Ragazzo, *Toward a Delaware Common Law of Closely Held Corporations*, 77 WASH. U. L.Q. 1099, 1107–08 (1999).

34. *Cf. id.* at 1108 ("Because these employee and stockholder interests are largely separate in a publicly held corporation, it is entirely proper that the general corporate rule provides the employee-stockholder with no special protection against discharge.")

35. *See supra* note 6 and accompanying text.

36. As one commentator observed:

In a closely held corporation, a shareholder-employee has interests in his job and stock that are often economically intertwined. Holding stock in a closely held corporation, viewed purely as an investment decision, seems almost irrational from an economic perspective. Small businesses are exceedingly risky enterprises with high failure rates. To compensate fairly for this level of risk, the expected return would also have to be disproportionately large. Moreover, many investors in small businesses invest a significant portion of their life savings in the business. This practice defeats their ability to diversify their investment portfolios and exposes them to company-and industry-specific risk. As a result, investors in closely held corporations would seem well advised to trust their capital to diversified mutual funds rather than a small corporation.

If investors in closely held corporations are economically rational, it can only be because such investments have compen-

sating benefits not available to investors in publicly held corporations. In many cases, a shareholder in a closely held corporation expects to receive such compensating benefits through employment. The shareholder may invest for the purpose of having a job that produces higher compensation than could be garnered through employment by third parties. Even if the employee-shareholder's compensation is no higher than his next best alternative, an investment in a closely held corporation may still be justified because the ability to keep his job may be more stable and certain. Additionally, the employee may simply derive satisfaction from working in a business that he himself takes a substantial part in managing.

* * *

Thus, a shareholder in a closely held corporation often has a significant investment interest in his job. He often invests for the purpose of having a job, and the salary and other benefits he receives are conceived to be part of the return on his investment.... After discharge, the minority is relegated to the corporation's expected returns to justify the risk of its investment capital. As discussed above, these returns are unlikely to be satisfactory on their own.

Ragazzo, *supra* note 33, at 1109–10 (footnotes omitted); *see also* Douglas K. Moll, *Shareholder Oppression v. Employment at Will in the Close Corporation: The Investment Model Solution*, 1999 U. ILL. L. REV. 517, 548–50 (1999) (discussing the benefits of employment and management positions in a closely held corporation, such as relatively higher compensation, the prestige as-

that negatively affects employment or management positions can be viewed as harming shareholder rights, as the conduct often impacts a shareholder's expected return.[37] As a result, such action should typically invoke a fiduciary duty analysis. By citing terminations of employment and removals from management positions as examples of freeze-out conduct, and by suggesting that the shareholder-centered fiduciary duty was meant to protect against such conduct,[38] the *Donahue* court demonstrated that it appreciated these points. Indeed, only one year after the *Donahue* decision, the Massachusetts Supreme Judicial Court found a breach of the *Donahue* fiduciary duty when the controlling group unjustifiably terminated the employment of a minority shareholder and removed him from the board of directors.[39]

Third, even if a fiduciary duty analysis is implicated, it is still difficult to challenge internal matters (such as employment, management, or dividend decisions) under traditional corporate law principles because of the deference of the business judgment rule. The business judgment rule operates to shield a manager from liability so long as the manager's decision was made "on an informed basis, in good faith, and in the honest belief that the action taken was in the best interests of the company."[40] Under the rule, courts review the substantive business decisions of those in control with considerable deference and with a correspondingly minimal amount of scrutiny.[41]

The *Donahue* doctrine, however, significantly curtails the effects of the business judgment rule. By specifically noting that employment, management, dividend, and other internal decisions can be part of a majority-directed freeze-out, and by explicitly mentioning the business judgment rule as a traditional impediment to challenging such decisions,[42] the *Donahue* court strongly suggested that the shareholder-to-shareholder fiduciary duty framework was meant to displace the traditional deference of the business judgment rule. In fact, in the subsequent decision of *Wilkes v. Springside Nursing Home, Inc.*,[43] the business judgment rule did not prevent the Massachusetts Supreme Judicial Court from finding a breach of the *Donahue* fiduciary duty when a minority shareholder was unjustifiably terminated from employment and

sociated with officer and director positions, and other intangible benefits stemming from working for oneself).

37. *See, e.g.*, Moll, *supra* note 36, at 550 ("Because close corporation employment provides these additional aspects of value, the retention of a particular close corporation job may be a vital component of a shareholder-employee's return on investment.").

38. *See Donahue v. Rodd Electrotype Co.*, 328 N.E.2d 505, 513, 515 (Mass. 1975).

39. *Wilkes v. Springside Nursing Home, Inc.*, 353 N.E.2d 657, 663–64 (Mass. 1976).

40. *Aronson v. Lewis*, 473 A.2d 805, 812 (Del. 1984).

41. *See, e.g.*, Frank H. Easterbrook & Daniel R. Fischel, The Economic Structure of Corporate Law 93 (1991) ("Statements of the [business judgment] rule vary; its terms are far less important than the fact that there is a specially deferential approach."); *see also Wilkes*, 353 N.E.2d at 662 ("[C]ourts fairly consistently have been disinclined to interfere in those facets of internal corporate operations, such as the selection and retention or dismissal of officers, directors or employees, which essentially involve management decisions subject to the principle of majority control.").

42. *Donahue*, 328 N.E.2d at 513–14.

43. 353 N.E.2d 657 (Mass. 1976).

removed from the board of directors in a closely held corporation that did not pay dividends.[44]

Put differently, the *Donahue* court recognized, at least implicitly, that conflicts of interest—the presence of which bar application of the business judgment rule[45]—can be more subtle in the closely held setting. As a result, the court understood that a broader view of such conflicts was needed. For example, because employment is often the vehicle for

44. *Id.* at 663–64. In *Wilkes*, the court acknowledged majority prerogatives and altered the *Donahue* framework as a result:

[W]e are concerned that untempered application of the strict good faith standard enunciated in *Donahue* to cases such as the one before us will result in the imposition of limitations on legitimate action by the controlling group in a close corporation which will unduly hamper its effectiveness in managing the corporation in the best interests of all concerned. The majority, concededly, have certain rights to what has been termed 'selfish ownership' in the corporation which should be balanced against the concept of their fiduciary obligation to the minority....

Therefore, when minority stockholders in a close corporation bring suit against the majority alleging a breach of the strict good faith duty owed to them by the majority, we must carefully analyze the action taken by the controlling stockholders in the individual case. It must be asked whether the controlling group can demonstrate a legitimate business purpose for its action. In asking this question, we acknowledge the fact that the controlling group in a close corporation must have some room to maneuver in establishing the business policy of the corporation. It must have a large measure of discretion, for example, in declaring or withholding dividends, deciding whether to merge or consolidate, establishing the salaries of corporate officers, dismissing directors with or without cause, and hiring and firing corporate employees.

When an asserted business purpose for their action is advanced by the majority, however, we think it is open to minority stockholders to demonstrate that the same legitimate objective could have been achieved through an alternative course of action less harmful to the minority's interest. If called on to settle a dispute, our courts must weigh the legitimate business purpose, if any, against the practicability of a less harmful alternative.

Id. at 663 (citations omitted).

Despite this acknowledgement of majority prerogatives, subjecting the majority's conduct to a legitimate business purpose/less

harmful alternative analysis indicates that the business judgment rule has largely been displaced, as the court is doing more than simply asking whether a decision by the controlling group can be attributed to a rational business purpose. *See, e.g., Sinclair Oil Corp. v. Levien*, 280 A.2d 717, 720 (Del. 1971) (observing that decisions are protected under the business judgment rule "if they can be attributed to any rational business purpose."). Indeed, the *Wilkes* framework requires proof of a legitimate business purpose for the majority's conduct–not simply an attribution by the court. *See, e.g.,* Stephen M. Bainbridge, *The Business Judgment Rule as Abstention Doctrine*, 57 Vand. L. Rev. 83, 100 (2004) ("[T]he reference to a rational business purpose requires only the possibility that the decision was actuated by a legitimate business reason, not that directors must prove the existence of such a reason."). In addition, even with proof of a legitimate business purpose, the *Wilkes* analysis will still find liability if there are alternatives that are less harmful to the minority. Thus, the *Wilkes* framework is quite different from a classic business judgment rule approach, as the framework calls for close scrutiny of the majority's decisions. *See* Terry A. O'Neill, *Self-Interest and Concern for Others in the Owner–Managed Firm: A Suggested Approach to Dissolution and Fiduciary Obligation in Close Corporations*, 22 Seton Hall L. Rev. 646, 692 (1992) ("The burden-shifting scheme devised in *Wilkes* effectively deprives majority shareholders of the protection of the business judgment rule by requiring close judicial scrutiny of the majority's action whenever the minority is harmed.").

45. *See, e.g., Brehm v. Eisner*, 746 A.2d 244, 264 n.66 (Del. 2000) ("The business judgment rule has been well formulated by ... other cases. Thus, directors' decisions will be respected by courts unless *the directors are interested or lack independence relative to the decision*, do not act in good faith, act in a manner that cannot be attributed to a rational business purpose or reach their decision by a grossly negligent process that includes the failure to consider all material facts reasonably available.") (emphasis added).

distributing profits in a closely held corporation,[46] the termination of a minority shareholder's employment can be a mechanism for the majority to appropriate a disproportionate share of the company's income stream to itself.[47] In a publicly held corporation, a termination does not have a similar effect, as the profits of a corporation are typically captured by stock appreciation and/or dividends rather than employment. Similarly, whereas a majority-directed decision to withhold dividends may affect all shares in the same manner,[48] the decision in a closely held corporation may be motivated by an effort to coerce a minority shareholder to sell out to the majority at an unfairly low price.[49] Once again, in a publicly held corporation, the denial of dividends does not have a similar effect, as a company's retention of profits simply boosts the market value of its shares–a value that an investor can capture at any time by selling into the market.[50] Thus, by suggesting that internal management decisions should be subject to real scrutiny, the *Donahue* opinion signaled that traditional business judgment rule deference was less appropriate in the closely held setting.[51]

46. *See supra* note 6 and accompanying text.

47. *See, e.g., Nagy v. Riblet Prods. Corp.*, 79 F.3d 572, 577 (7th Cir. 1996) ("Many closely held firms endeavor to show no profits (to minimize their taxes) and to distribute the real economic returns of the business to the investors as salary. When firms are organized in this way, firing an employee is little different from canceling his shares.").

48. *See* Douglas K. Moll, *Shareholder Oppression & Dividend Policy in the Close Corporation*, 60 WASH. & LEE L. REV. 841, 858–59 & n.64 (2003) (discussing the dividend "irrelevance proposition" and noting that "[i]f a dividend of one dollar per share is paid, a . . . shareholder is enriched by one dollar per share," while "[i]f that same amount is instead retained in the company, the company's value increases by one dollar per share and, correspondingly, the value of the . . . stock increases by one dollar per share").

49. *See, e.g., Litle v. Waters*, Civ. A. No. 12155, 1992 WL 25758, at *8 (Del. Ch. Feb. 11, 1992) (describing the plaintiff's allegation "that the company was rich with cash and that the only reason that the company did not make dividends was to aid [the majority] to buy [the minority] out for less than fair value"); *see also Wilkes*, 353 N.E.2d at 664 ("[W]e may infer that a design to pressure Wilkes into selling his shares to the corporation at a price below their value well may have been at the heart of the majority's plan.").

50. *See supra* text accompanying note 10; *supra* note 48.

51. Several post-*Donahue* courts have explicitly acknowledged that majority shareholder decisions in closely held corporations call for more judicial scrutiny than conventional business judgment rule deference. *See, e.g., Smith v. Atlantic Props., Inc.*, 422 N.E.2d 798, 801, 804 (Mass. App. Ct. 1981) (stating, in a closely held corporation dispute, that "[t]he judgment . . . necessarily disregards the general judicial reluctance to interfere with a corporation's dividend policy ordinarily based upon the business judgment of its directors"); *Fox v. 7L Bar Ranch Co.*, 645 P.2d 929, 935 (Mont. 1982) ("When it is also considered that in close corporations dividend withholding may be used by controlling shareholders to force out minority shareholders, the traditional judicial restraint in interfering with corporate dividend policy cannot be justified." (internal quotation omitted)); *Exadaktilos v. Cinnaminson Realty Co.*, 400 A.2d 554, 561 (N.J. Super. Ct. Law Div. 1979) ("[T]he statutory language embodies a legislative determination that freeze-out maneuvers in close corporations constitute an abuse of corporate power. Traditional principles of corporate law, such as the business judgment rule, have failed to curb this abuse. Consequently, actions of close corporations that conform with these principles cannot be immune from scrutiny."); *see also* Frank H. Easterbrook & Daniel R. Fischel, *Close Corporations and Agency Costs*, 38 STAN. L. REV. 271, 293 (1986) ("It makes sense, therefore, to have greater judicial review of terminations of managerial (or investing) employees in closely held corporations than would be consistent with the business judgment rule. The same approach

In short, the shareholder-to-shareholder fiduciary duty imposed by the *Donahue* court improved the legal protections available to minority shareholders in closely held corporations. Several courts outside of Massachusetts have followed this aspect of the *Donahue* holding.[52]

b. The Equal Opportunity Rule

The "equal opportunity" aspect of the *Donahue* decision has been harshly criticized, and largely for good reason. After all, while it is possible that a corporation is purchasing its stock simply to make a preferential distribution of corporate assets to its controlling shareholder, it is also possible that the purchase is motivated by legitimate business reasons. For example, stock may be repurchased to facilitate the retirement of a less productive employee (as was arguably the case in *Donahue* itself),[53] or to prevent competitors from having access to corporate information. When such legitimate grounds are present, compelling the corporation to also purchase the shares of the remaining investors may strain the corporation's finances–so much so that all of the transactions must be abandoned.[54]

could be used with salary, dividend, and employment decisions in closely held corporations where the risks of conflicts of interest are greater."). In addition, because the managerial constraints provided by a market are absent in a closely held corporation, the judicial deference embodied in the business judgment rule makes even less sense. *See supra* note 10.

When courts suggest that a rejection of business judgment rule deference is warranted, they are presumably contemplating majority decisions that impact the rights of individual shareholders. For more general decisions, such as the choice of one business opportunity over another, courts should typically defer to the majority's prerogatives. *Cf.* James D. Cox, *Equal Treatment for Shareholders: An Essay*, 19 CARDOZO L. REV. 615, 631 (1997) ("Though great flexibility should be accorded managers on matters related to the conduct of the corporation's business, this is not necessarily the case regarding decisions that impact the relative rights of owners' interests in the firm. The former is more clearly the type of business activity which is best lodged with the firm's managers; the latter is not.") (footnote omitted).

52. *See, e.g., Guy v. Duff & Phelps, Inc.*, 672 F. Supp. 1086, 1090 (N.D. Ill. 1987); *Orchard v. Covelli*, 590 F. Supp. 1548, 1556–59 (W.D. Pa. 1984); *W & W Equip. Co. v. Mink*, 568 N.E.2d 564, 574 (Ind. Ct. App. 1991); *Evans v. Blesi*, 345 N.W.2d 775, 779 (Minn. Ct. App. 1984); *Fought v. Morris*, 543 So. 2d 167, 170–71 (Miss. 1989); *Daniels v. Thomas, Dean & Hoskins, Inc.*, 804 P.2d 359, 366 (Mont. 1990); *Crosby v. Beam*, 548 N.E.2d 217, 220 (Ohio

1989); *A. Teixeira & Co. v. Teixeira*, 699 A.2d 1383, 1386–87 (R.I. 1997); *Jorgensen v. Water Works, Inc.*, 582 N.W.2d 98, 104–06 (Wis. Ct. App. 1998); *see also Hoggett v. Brown*, 971 S.W.2d 472, 488 n.13 (Tex. App. 1997) (noting that "a majority shareholder's fiduciary duty ordinarily runs to the corporation," but "in certain limited circumstances, a majority shareholder who dominates control over the business may owe such a duty to the minority shareholder.").

53. *See* Easterbrook & Fischel, *supra* note 51, at 294–95 ("Buy-out arrangements on contingencies such as retirement are common in closely held corporations. Such agreements provide some liquidity and ensure that the identity of the managers and the investors remains the same, reducing agency problems.... The terms of the purchase in *Donahue* were not extraordinary. The trial court found them fair. The purchase appears to have been nothing more than an attempt to facilitate the retirement of a manager who, by virtue of advancing age and poor health, could no longer contribute. The firm doubtless was the better for his retirement.").

54. *Cf. id.* at 298–99 ("The court that decided *Donahue* ... never considered the possibility that its rule of equal opportunity might be inconsistent with the observed behavior of participants in both partnerships and closely held corporations. Both types of firms must provide some mechanism for dealing with retirements or terminations in situations where the firm will continue to exist. Most firms could not sur-

The scope of the equal opportunity rule is also problematic, as it is not entirely clear that the *Donahue* court intended to limit its equal opportunity rule to the stock repurchase context. Admittedly, on the facts of *Donahue*, the equal opportunity rule was applied in the context of a repurchase of the controlling owner's shares. Moreover, in part of its discussion, the court referred to the rule as "[t]he rule of equal opportunity in stock purchases by close corporations."[55] Some of the court's language, however, suggests that the rule was intended to have a broader application. In one passage, the court noted generally that "[t]he controlling group may not, consistent with its strict duty to the minority, utilize its control of the corporation to obtain special advantages and disproportionate benefit from its share ownership."[56] Further, the concurring judge distanced himself from "any implication . . . that the rule concerning a close corporation's purchase of a controlling stockholder's shares applies to all operations of the corporation as they affect minority stockholders"[57]—suggesting that the court's opinion created such a broader implication. Finally, the court seemed to hold out the equal opportunity rule as a way of satisfying the partnership-like fiduciary duty that the court imposed on shareholders of closely held corporations.[58] Under this view, equal opportunity would seem to be relevant whenever the fiduciary duty is implicated—no matter what the setting. Thus, there is some question as to whether the *Donahue* court intended to limit the equal opportunity rule to stock repurchase disputes.

Of course, giving an expansive scope to the equal opportunity rule is likely to unduly restrict the management and operation of a corporation. For example, if a controlling shareholder receives a salary increase for an outstanding job performance, must an equivalent increase be offered to other shareholders? If a controlling shareholder receives an officer position, must a minority shareholder be offered the same? Simply put, there may be legitimate business reasons for treating investors unequally, such as vastly different skills, experience, and ability. If equivalence is required for every internal business decision, it may be impossible for the corporation to operate effectively.[59]

Further, one could argue that the equal opportunity rule is sensible, if at all, only for investors who were intended to be similarly situated. Harry Rodd and Joseph Donahue,[60] however, may not have been in the same boat. Indeed, the *Donahue* court noted that Harry Rodd was always

---

vive if the purchase of the interest of a retiring member required that everyone else be given the opportunity to sell out at the same price.").

55. *Donahue v. Rodd Electrotype Co.*, 328 N.E.2d 505, 519 (Mass. 1975).

56. *Id.* at 518.

57. *Id.* at 521 (Wilkins, J., concurring).

58. *See id.* at 518–19.

59. *See* Easterbrook & Fischel, *supra* note 51, at 295 ("It is hard to imagine, for example, how closely held corporations could function under a requirement that all shareholders have an 'equal opportunity' to receive salary increases and continue in office regardless of their conduct. Yet this is the logical implication of *Donahue*, which holds that the business justifications for unequal treatment are irrelevant.").

60. Recall that the plaintiff, Euphemia Donahue, had inherited her shares from her deceased husband, Joseph Donahue. *See supra* text accompanying note 15.

an active manager of the business, while Joseph Donahue never participated in management.[61] One could argue, therefore, that Rodd's expectations were that ownership and management would always go hand-in-hand—*i.e.*, he would never have one without the other. The same cannot be said for Donahue. Stated differently, Rodd never expected to be a substantial shareholder in a company that he was not actively managing, but Donahue did invest with such an expectation. Thus, while leaving Donahue as a non-managing shareholder was arguably consistent with his expectations over the years, doing the same to Rodd would not have been. The equal opportunity rule makes little sense when the investors were not similarly situated to begin with.[62]

In light of these issues, it is not surprising that the equal opportunity aspect of *Donahue* has been rejected by a number of courts.[63] Significantly, even Massachusetts has effectively abandoned the equal opportunity rule. In *Wilkes v. Springside Nursing Home, Inc.*,[64] the Massachusetts Supreme Judicial Court reaffirmed the *Donahue* fiduciary duty but scaled back the accompanying equal opportunity rule. In its place, the court articulated an oppression framework that effectively permits unequal treatment between controlling and minority shareholders so long as: (1) a legitimate business purpose exists for such unequal treatment and (2) there is no alternative course of action less harmful to the minority's interest.[65]

3. The Partnership Analogy

The *Donahue* court emphasized the similarities between the closely held corporation and the partnership as part of its rationale for imposing a shareholder-to-shareholder fiduciary duty. The court's argument proceeded, at least in part, in the following manner: (1) closely held corporations and partnerships are similar; (2) because of their similarities, partnership principles should apply in the closely held corporation context; and (3) just as partnership law imposes a fiduciary duty between

---

61. *See Donahue*, 328 N.E.2d at 509.

62. *See, e.g.*, Ragazzo, *supra* note 33, at 1127–28 & n.145 ("Moreover, the equal opportunity rule is of questionable legitimacy. It is facially in accord with Aristotle's first principle of justice: similarly situated people should be treated similarly.... [But there is also] Aristotle's second principle of justice: dissimilarly situated people should be treated dissimilarly. [T]he retiring founder [Harry Rodd] might be seen as occupying a different position than the passive minority shareholders. The retiring founder never contemplated owning stock in a corporation he was not active in managing.").

63. *See, e.g.*, *Toner v. Baltimore Envelope Co.*, 498 A.2d 642, 647–54 (Md. 1985); *Delahoussaye v. Newhard*, 785 S.W.2d 609, 611–12 (Mo. Ct. App. 1990); *see also Nixon v. Blackwell*, 626 A.2d 1366, 1376 (Del.

1993) ("It is well established in our jurisprudence that stockholders need not always be treated equally for all purposes."). The language of some opinions, however, still seems to embrace the equal opportunity framework. *See, e.g.*, *Crosby v. Beam*, 548 N.E.2d 217, 221 (Ohio 1989) ("Majority or controlling shareholders breach such fiduciary duty to minority shareholders when control of the close corporation is utilized to prevent the minority from having an equal opportunity in the corporation.").

64. 353 N.E.2d 657 (Mass. 1976).

65. *See id.* at 663; *supra* note 44 (discussing *Wilkes*); *see also* Easterbrook & Fischel, *supra* note 51, at 296 ("The court in *Wilkes* inquired into the business purpose of the conduct at issue.... Thus the court effectively repudiated the equal opportunity rule of *Donahue*....").

partners, so too should corporate law impose a fiduciary duty between shareholders in closely held corporations.[66] Each of these component steps is worthy of discussion.

First, it is certainly true that closely held corporations and partnerships typically share a number of attributes. In both structures, for example, there tends to be fewer owners (at least relative to large, publicly traded companies), the owners often participate in management, there are usually restrictions on the transferability of ownership positions,[67] and there is no active market for the firm's ownership interests.

There are, however, substantial differences between the two structures. To cite a few examples, a corporation provides limited liability to its owners, while a partnership does not. A corporation (other than an S-corporation) is subject to double taxation, while a partnership receives pass-through income tax treatment. Finally, in a closely held corporation, a shareholder has no default ability to liquidate his ownership position.[68] In a partnership, by contrast, a dissociating partner has the right to either dissolve the partnership (which provides liquidity) or to receive a buyout of his interest.[69] Thus, while closely held corporations are similar in many respects to partnerships, they are by no means identical.

Second, it is probably unfair to assert that the *Donahue* court was arguing for the wholesale application of partnership principles to the closely held corporation. The court analogized to partnerships simply to impose a partnership-like owner-to-owner fiduciary duty. Other aspects of partnership law that might have been helpful to Donahue—*e.g.*, the more liberal dissolution rules, or the granting of a right to participate in the management of the business[70]—were not imported.

Third, the actual partnership principle applied in the closely held corporation context–the owner-to-owner fiduciary duty–is a curious choice. In the partnership setting, at least one of the reasons for imposing a fiduciary duty between partners is that the misconduct of a partner can produce liability for the partnership and, due to unlimited liability, the other partners. The threat of a lawsuit for breach of fiduciary duty constrains inappropriate partner behavior that can put the assets of the other partners at risk. When limited liability is present, however, as in the corporation, this need for a fiduciary duty is less compelling, as shareholders do not face unlimited liability for the wrongs of their managers and fellow owners.

Nevertheless, if the ability of one partner to harm another partner is a justification for imposing a fiduciary duty in the partnership context, one could make the same argument in the closely held corporation

---

66. *See Donahue*, 328 N.E.2d at 512–15.

67. The restrictions are a matter of contract in the corporation and are a default statutory rule in the partnership. *See, e.g.*, DEL. CODE ANN. tit. 8, § 202 (2006); REVISED UNIF. PARTNERSHIP ACT § 503 (1997).

68. *See supra* notes 10–13 and accompanying text.

69. *See, e.g.*, REVISED UNIF. PARTNERSHIP ACT § 701 (1997).

70. *See id.* §§ 401(f), 801.

setting. While it is true that a shareholder's actions cannot harm another shareholder by exposing him to unlimited liability, a shareholder can harm another shareholder by engaging in freeze-out conduct. Thus, broadly speaking, the ability of an owner to harm another owner is a justification for imposing a fiduciary duty in both the partnership and closely held corporation settings. Viewed in this manner, the *Donahue* court's imposition of a fiduciary duty between shareholders should be understood as motivated primarily by an appreciation of the harms of oppressive conduct in closely held corporations, rather than by a generic similarity between closely held corporations and partnerships.

4.   A Contrary Approach? The *Nixon v. Blackwell* Decision

In responding to the freeze-out problem in the closely held corporation, *Donahue* is representative of a broader judicial movement to create special common-law protections for oppressed minority shareholders.[71] A discussion of *Donahue*, however, would not be complete without considering a contrary judicial approach—i.e., an explicit refusal to create special common-law rules for the protection of minority shareholders in closely held corporations. Under this approach, an oppressed investor can attempt to rely on traditional legal principles for protection (e.g., traditional corporate or contract law doctrines), but no additional common-law safeguards are provided.

Nixon v. Blackwell,[72] a Delaware Supreme Court decision, exemplifies this approach. As the *Nixon* court observed:

> We wish to address one further matter which was raised at oral argument before this Court: Whether there should be any special, judicially-created rules to "protect" minority stockholders of closely-held Delaware corporations.

> The case at bar points up the basic dilemma of minority stockholders in receiving fair value for their stock as to which there is no market and no market valuation. It is not difficult to be sympathetic, in the abstract, to a stockholder who finds himself or herself in that position. A stockholder who bargains for stock in a closely-held corporation and who pays for those shares ... can make a business judgment whether to buy into such a minority position, and if so on what terms. One could bargain for definitive provisions of self-ordering permitted to a Delaware corporation through the certificate

---

71. Indeed, most jurisdictions have developed special common-law doctrines (often aided by statutes) that are designed to protect minority shareholders in closely held corporations from oppressive majority conduct. In those jurisdictions that offer protection, the protection is doctrinally articulated either as a fiduciary duty that shareholders in closely held corporations owe to one another, *see, e.g., Donahue v. Rodd Electrotype Co.,* 328 N.E.2d 505 (Mass. 1975), or as a right to dissolution or other remedy on the grounds of oppressive conduct by those in control. *See, e.g., In re Kemp & Beatley, Inc.,* 473 N.E.2d 1173 (N.Y. 1984); *see also* F. HODGE O'NEAL & ROBERT B. THOMPSON, 2 O'NEAL AND THOMPSON'S CLOSE CORPORATIONS AND LLCS: LAW AND PRACTICE § 9.27, at 9–185 n.6 (3d ed. 1996) ("Thirty-nine states base relief on oppression, or language that would be at least as likely to provide relief to petitioning shareholders.").

72. 626 A.2d 1366 (Del. 1993).

of incorporation or by-laws by reason of the provisions in 8 *Del.C.* §§ 102, 109, and 141(a). Moreover, in addition to such mechanisms, a stockholder intending to buy into a minority position in a Delaware corporation may enter into definitive stockholder agreements, and such agreements may provide for elaborate earnings tests, buyout provisions, voting trusts, or other voting agreements.

The tools of good corporate practice are designed to give a purchasing minority stockholder the opportunity to bargain for protection before parting with consideration. It would do violence to normal corporate practice and our corporation law to fashion an ad hoc ruling which would result in a court-imposed stockholder buy-out for which the parties had not contracted.

In 1967, when the Delaware General Corporation Law was significantly revised, a new Subchapter XIV entitled "Close Corporations; Special Provisions," became a part of that law for the first time. . . . Subchapter XIV is a narrowly constructed statute which applies only to a corporation which is designated as a "close corporation" in its certificate of incorporation, and which fulfills other requirements, including a limitation to 30 on the number of stockholders, that all classes of stock have to have at least one restriction on transfer, and that there be no "public offering." 8 *Del.C.* § 342. Accordingly, subchapter XIV applies only to "close corporations," as defined in section 342. "Unless a corporation elects to become a close corporation under this subchapter in the manner prescribed in this subchapter, it shall be subject in all respects to this chapter, except this subchapter." 8 *Del.C.* § 341. The corporation before the Court in this matter, is not a "close corporation." Therefore it is not governed by the provisions of Subchapter XIV.

One cannot read into the situation presented in the case at bar any special relief for the minority stockholders in this closely-held, but not statutory "close corporation" because the provisions of Subchapter XIV relating to close corporations and other statutory schemes preempt the field in their respective areas. It would run counter to the spirit of the doctrine of independent legal significance, and would be inappropriate judicial legislation for this Court to fashion a special judicially-created rule for minority investors when the entity does not fall within those statutes, or when there are no negotiated special provisions in the certificate of incorporation, by-laws, or stockholder agreements. The entire fairness test, correctly applied and articulated, is the proper judicial approach.[73]

73. *Id.* at 1379–81 (footnotes omitted); *see Clemmer v. Cullinane*, 815 N.E.2d 651, 652–53 (Mass. App. Ct. 2004) ("That [*Nixon*] decision–in 'very forceful dicta'—declined to adopt the heightened fiduciary duty of 'utmost good faith and loyalty' our courts have found applicable to close corporations. Rather, the court declared that no special judicially-created rules would be rec-ognized to protect minority shareholders in closely held corporations.") (footnotes omitted).

Other courts have followed *Nixon. See Merner v. Merner*, 129 Fed. Appx. 342, 343 (9th Cir. 2005) (unpublished opinion); *Hunt v. Data Mgmt. Res., Inc.*, 985 P.2d 730, 732–33 (Kan. Ct. App. 1999).

As this passage indicates, the *Nixon* court declined to create a common-law shareholder oppression doctrine for two reasons: (1) minority shareholders can protect themselves via contract; and (2) the Delaware legislature has already provided protection to minority shareholders in closely held corporations through special statutory provisions. Both of these rationales can be questioned.

With regard to contractual protection, a minority shareholder who is cognizant of the risks of oppressive majority conduct can certainly seek to protect his financial and participatory rights by contract before committing his capital to the venture. As the *Nixon* court suggests, shareholder agreements, supermajority requirements, and buy-sell provisions are only some of the contractual tools that shareholders can use to strengthen their employment, dividend, exit, and other rights. If the controlling shareholder or the corporation is unwilling to enter into protective contractual arrangements, the minority shareholder can simply refuse to invest in the company.

Despite this apparent opportunity for ex ante contracting, it is widely recognized that a minority shareholder in a closely held corporation typically fails to contract for protection from abusive majority conduct.[74] Some factors contributing to this failure to contract include: (1) "overtrust" due to family or friendship ties;[75] (2) lack of sophistication; (3) an inability to appreciate the universe of potentially oppressive behavior;[76] (4) relationship-oriented concerns about harming the trust between the shareholders;[77] and (5) the level of expense associated with

74. *See generally* Douglas K. Moll, *Minority Oppression & The Limited Liability Company: Learning (or Not) From Close Corporation History*, 40 WAKE FOREST L. REV. 883, 911–16 (2005) (discussing the failure of the typical closely held corporation shareholder to contract for protection from dissension).

75. *See, e.g., Meiselman v. Meiselman*, 307 S.E.2d 551, 558 (N.C. 1983) (observing that "close corporations are often formed by friends or family members who simply may not believe that disagreements could ever arise") (internal quotation omitted); Moll, *supra* note 74, at 912 ("Because close corporation owners are frequently linked by family or other personal relationships, there is often an initial atmosphere of mutual trust that diminishes the sense that contractual protection is needed.").

76. For example, in *Davis v. Sheerin*, 754 S.W.2d 375 (Tex. App. 1988), the court found oppression based primarily on the majority's denial of the minority's status as a shareholder. *See id.* at 381. The majority shareholder maintained that the minority shareholder had previously made a gift of his 45% ownership interest to the majority. *See id.* It is hard to imagine a lawyer antici-

pating such oppressive conduct in advance and contracting for protection against it. *See, e.g.,* William Carney, *The Theory of the Firm: Investor Coordination Costs, Control Premiums and Capital Structure*, 66 WASH. U. L.Q. 1, 59–60 (1987) ("Investors in closely held enterprises are likely to be subject to conditions of bounded rationality, under which they either fail to perceive the complete set of problems that may occur later, or underestimate the probability of their occurrence."); Moll, *supra* note 74, at 913–14 ("In light of the countless ways in which oppressive conduct can occur, it is quite difficult to foresee all (if not most) of the situations that may require contractual protection. This inability to appreciate the universe of potential problems may result in incomplete contracting or, possibly, in no contracting at all.") (footnote omitted).

77. As one commentator observed:

[T]he typical decision to invest in a close corporation venture is, for all intents and purposes, a decision to engage in a long-term association with other shareholders that will involve significant personal interaction in the future. Effective contracting for protection is particularly challenging in such a setting, as the par-

effective contracting.[78] There may be legitimate reasons, therefore, for the absence of contractual safeguards in many closely held corporation disputes. As a result, there is a strong argument that a judicial "safety net" tailored to the closely held corporation setting, such as the *Donahue* doctrine, is still needed.[79]

With regard to the statutory provisions of subchapter XIV of the Delaware General Corporation Law, it is useful to observe that subchapter XIV focuses almost exclusively on facilitating ex ante contractual arrangements between the shareholders.[80] If contractual arrangements are not entered into, either due to the above-mentioned impediments to contracting or because the minority shareholders received their stock via gift or inheritance, subchapter XIV provides little aid in the event of oppressive conduct.[81] Sections 352 and 353 provide for the appointment

ties usually seek to avoid harming their relationship during the contracting process. Indeed, a minority shareholder may be hesitant to even raise the topic of dissension because of a fear that it will damage the trust between the shareholders—trust that is critical to the operation of any small business. This hesitation may result in no planning for dissension at all.

Even if the topic of dissension is broached, a similar concern exists that any "hard feelings" created by the bargaining process will hinder the parties' abilities to work together in the future. Given this concern and the related desire to preserve as much goodwill between the shareholders as possible, a minority investor at the outset of a close corporation venture is likely to feel constrained in its ability to freely exercise any bargaining advantage that it has—i.e., constrained in its ability to fully "flex" its bargaining "muscle" against the majority shareholder. When the typical familiarity between close corporation participants is factored into the analysis, the minority shareholder is likely to feel even more constrained, as the shareholder will be concerned that fair (but hard) bargaining may harm both a business *and* a family/friendship relationship. Unlike discrete, single-interaction transactions, therefore, effective contracting in the close corporation setting is frequently hindered by relationship-oriented concerns. As a result, contractual protection for the minority shareholder is often incomplete or nonexistent.

Moll, *supra* note 74, at 914–16 (footnotes omitted).

78. *See id.* at 916 n.112 ("It should also be noted that ex ante contracting is expensive, as it often requires the assistance of an attorney. In fact, effective ex ante contracting may require the services of multiple attorneys—one (or more) representing the majority's interests, and one (or more) representing the minority's interests. This level of expense may be prohibitive for many small businesses, especially at their inception.").

In addition, the ability to contract does not help shareholders who received their stock via gift or inheritance. These shareholders had no opportunity to bargain for protection before becoming stockholders.

79. Partners in a partnership and members in a limited liability company also have a broad ability to contract for protection. Despite that ability, the law provides a default owner-to-owner fiduciary duty in both organizational structures. *See* REVISED UNIF. PARTNERSHIP ACT § 404 (1997); UNIF. LTD. LIAB. CO. ACT § 409 (1996). In other contexts, therefore, the law does not view the ability to contract and the presence of an owner-to-owner fiduciary duty as mutually exclusive.

80. For example, if a minority shareholder considers the possibility of oppressive conduct in advance, the minority can contract for: (1) an agreement restricting the discretion of directors, *see* DEL. CODE ANN. tit. 8, § 350 (2006); (2) management of the corporation by the shareholders, *see id.* § 351; (3) running the corporation like a partnership, *see id.* § 354; and/or (4) an option to dissolve the corporation on specified grounds, *see id.* § 355.

81. Indeed, even the *Nixon* court stated that "[w]e do not intend to imply that, if the [c]orporation had been a close corporation under subchapter XIV, the result in this case would have been different." *Nixon v. Blackwell*, 626 A.2d 1366, 1380 n.19 (Del. 1993).

of a custodian or provisional director in certain narrow circumstances,[82] but there is no other provision for judicial intervention. Subchapter XIV, in other words, focuses on preventative planning rather than remedial relief. In a classic freeze-out case involving a denial of the minority's financial and participatory rights, as well as the absence of advance planning for dissension, subchapter XIV would provide no protection. Once again, there is a strong argument that a judicial "safety net," such as the *Donahue* doctrine, is still needed.

D. CONCLUSION

The legacy of *Donahue* stems not from its detail, but from the general thrust of the court's approach. The *Donahue* court recognized the peculiar vulnerability of minority shareholders in closely held corporations and crafted a protective common-law doctrine in response. To a large degree, this effort foreshadowed a broader judicial movement to develop special common-law protections for oppressed shareholders in closely held corporations. By understanding that the expectations and positions of shareholders in closely held and publicly held corporations are different, and, more importantly, by acting on that understanding, the *Donahue* opinion cemented its position as an iconic case in corporate law.

---

82. *See* DEL. CODE ANN. tit. 8, §§ 352–353 (2006).

Chapter 7

JUDICIAL REVIEW OF CORPORATE DECISIONS: *KAMIN v. AMERICAN EXPRESS COMPANY*

By

*Jonathan Macey**

A. INTRODUCTION

Kamin v. American Express Company[1] is an iconic case in American corporate law and corporate governance because its mere six pages contain virtually everything that one needs to know about how U.S. courts view the legal duties of directors and the nature and purpose of the famous business judgment rule.

The board action being challenged in this case was its decision to make what is known as an "in kind" dividend payment. While dividend payments more often than not come in the form of cash, corporations also can distribute other sorts of assets to their shareholders as dividends. These payments, known as "in kind" distributions, usually consist of a company's own stock but other assets also can be distributed, including warrants to buy stock at a discount, or stock in other companies.

Can directors ever be sued successfully for paying a dividend? The business judgment rule makes it extremely unlikely, even in cases in which the decision to pay a dividend is demonstrably not the best policy from the shareholders' perspective. But a close reading of this case suggests that it would not be completely impossible for such a suit to succeed. The outcome will depend on whether the directors of the company paying the dividend did enough to enable themselves to claim the benefits of the protections from liability offered by the business judgment rule.

* Deputy Dean and Sam Harris Professor of Corporate Law, Corporate Finance and Securities Law, Yale University and Professor in the Yale School of Management.

1. 383 N.Y.S. 2d 807 (Sup. Ct. 1976), aff'd on opinion below, 387 N.Y.S. 2d 993 (App. Div. 1976).

Of course, even if the only thing accomplished by the court in *Kamin* was an explanation of the legal responsibilities of boards of directors, that would have been enough to merit inclusion on this text; however the case teaches us much more than that. The case also represents a cogent example of the extent to which judges are willing to use economic analysis in reaching their legal conclusions. This chapter will explore that aspect of the New York Supreme Court's decision in *Kamin* as well.

Discussion is broken down as follows: Section B contains a recitation of the critical facts in the case. Section C explains what the business judgment rule is and why the decision made by the American Express Company's board of directors to pay a dividend qualifies for the protections of the business judgment rule. Section D builds on the analysis in the preceding section, developing a taxonomy that explains categorization of different board actions and how those actions are evaluated by courts. Finally, Section E looks at the court's economic analysis and includes concluding observations about how courts and economists tend to evaluate the decisions of directors of public companies differently.

An interesting policy question is also raised by the case. Specifically, why did the American Express board decided to distribute the shares that the company owned as a dividend to shareholders rather than simply to sell the shares and keep the proceeds?

Apparently, the decision to "dividend out" the stock was made for what might best be described as "cosmetic" reasons. Specifically, the board was worried about the way the American Express income statement would be affected if they sold the stock. The court reasoned that the $25 million loss would "have a serious effect on the market value of the publicly traded American Express stock."[2] This is a very strange assertion. As long as the American Express directors were selling the stock at its fair market value (an assumption not contested in the case), then the sale should have no effect on the share value of American Express. The stock would be sold for what it was worth, and the American Express balance sheet would not be affected: the line item where the dollar value of the American Express stock position appeared would simply be replaced by a line item showing an entry for cash in the exact same amount. The economic value of the company would not be affected by such a stock sale, and neither should the economic value of the company's stock. For this reason, the economics and financial aspects of the case deserve our attention as much as the legal aspects of the case.

B. *KAMIN v. AMERICAN EXPRESS:* FACTUAL BACKGROUND

In 1972, American Express spent $29.9 million to buy 1,954,418 shares of common stock of Donaldson, Lufken and Jenrette ("DLJ") for

---

2. 383 N.Y.S.2d at 811.

an average price of around $15.30. This turned out to be a terrible investment. Within three years the DLJ stock had declined in value by 84 percent, to about $2.05 per share, giving the 1.95 million shares a total market value of around $4.0 million.

If the American Express board of directors had simply sold the stock, they would have sustained a huge loss. Such a loss, however, at more than $25 million, would have saved American Express about $8 million in taxes as an off-set against taxable gains. Rather than sell the stock and take the loss, on July 28, 1975, the American Express board of directors voted to declare a special, one-time dividend payment of DLJ shares to all stockholders. By distributing the DLJ stock to shareholders instead of selling it, American Express gave up the ability to take this capital loss. It is alleged that on October 8, 1975 and October 16, 1975, plaintiffs demanded that the directors rescind the previously declared dividend in DLJ shares and take steps to preserve the capital loss which would result from selling the shares. This demand was rejected by the board of directors on October 17, 1975.

C. QUALIFYING FOR AND APPLYING THE BUSINESS JUDGMENT RULE

It is worth noting that, as its name implies, the business judgment rule is a rule that applies when, and only when, the board of directors actually exercises its business judgment. This seemingly obvious point masks a rather complex idea. It is not always easy to tell when a board of directors is actually exercising its business judgment. For example, if a corporation were harmed because the board of directors had failed to take prudent and necessary steps to protect the company from harm, the shareholders might be severely harmed. But such a case would not involve any exercise of business judgment on the part of the directors, and thus the business judgment rule would not be applicable, at least not directly. Along these lines, if the directors had ordered the company to act hastily without using its business judgment, the business judgment rule also would not be applicable.

Thus, before attempting to articulate and then to apply the business judgment rule, we must preliminarily check to see if the case presents a fact pattern in which the business judgment rule is applicable. This, in turn, involves a two part inquiry. First, we must determine if a business decision was made. Second, we must determine whether the directors exercised their business judgment when they made that decision.

The court in *Kamin* quickly disposed of the first issue. Recall that the decision being made in this case was the decision to pay a dividend. The court observes that "specifically, the question of whether or not a dividend is to be declared or a distribution of some kind should be made is exclusively a matter of business judgment for the board of directors."[3] In other words, paying a dividend is the type of decision—like where to

---

3. Id. at 810.

locate the company's various plants and divisions, what sort of health benefits to offer, and when and whether to make major capital expenditures—that is typically are made by a corporation's board of directors. Thus, in answering the first question, we look to ordinary commercial custom and practice, as well as the internal corporate governance documents of the company, where they speak to this issue, in order to determine whether the decision made was one that is typically reserved for the board of directors without input from the shareholders. In this case the court found that it was.

Having determined that the issue in this case (dividend payments) is one that the directors ordinarily decide, we next turn to the question of whether the board of directors exercised their business judgment when making this decision. The particular facts of this case made this an easy question for the New York court. The judge specifically found that the very "objections raised by the plaintiff to the proposed dividend action were *carefully considered* and unanimously rejected by the board at a special meeting called precisely for that purpose"[4] (emphasis supplied). In other words, the court found that the American Express board decision to distribute the company's DLJ stock as a dividend was a business decision, to which the board applied its business judgment.

So what? The American Express board was determined to have made a business judgment but what are the consequences of this determination? The consequences are this: the business judgment rule is applicable to the board's decision.

The business judgment rule is a rule that says that directors who are being sued for business judgments win because courts will not interfere with their discretion unless the plaintiffs can allege, with particularity, that the directors have acted, or are about to act, in bad faith, in their own self-interest or for a dishonest purpose. In other words, in situations such as the one that presented itself in *Kamin v. American Express*, the determination that the board decision being challenged was a business judgment is outcome determinative.

The business judgment rule reflects the simple policy that courts will not interfere with the valid business judgment of corporate boards of directors because doing so will be bad for investors. The business judgment rule reflects the idea that we live in an area of specialization in which different people have expertise in doing different things. It is appropriate to give people considerable autonomy when they are acting legitimately and within their own particular areas of expertise.

Judges specialize in judging, not in running businesses. Directors are the people that the shareholders elect to run the companies in which they have invested. As such it would be bad policy for judges to interfere with the directors' decisions about running the business unless there truly were something suspicious going on. Having found nothing suspicious in the dividend decision made by the directors—the cause for

4. Id. at 811.

litigation in *Kamin*—the court determined that it should not interfere in that decision.

In a world in which perfection is impossible, judges must make tough choices, including what sort of error bias they should make. Since a zero error rate is an unattainable goal, judges must decide whether they want to err on the side of perhaps protecting defendant directors from liability too aggressively, or to err on the side of wrongfully imposing personal liability on directors. Above all else, what *Kamin v. American Express* shows is that judges in the U.S. have determined to err more on the side of protecting directors from liability and less on the side of imposing wrongful personal liability on directors.

This is the essence of the business judgment rule: when the criteria for applicability are met by the facts of a case, the business judgment rule works to protect directors from the possibility of judicial error.

There are a number of public policy justifications for the protections provided by the business judgment rule. Paramount among the justification for the business judgment rule is the principle that we want to encourage directors to take risks. If directors feared personal liability for every honest decision they made that turned out badly, shareholders would suffer because managers would avoid taking the risks necessary to garner high rates of return for shareholders.

One way to conceptualize the theory behind the business judgment rule is as a practical response to the fact that top managers and other corporate decision-makers are self-interested. Consequently, they will not make decisions that are in the shareholders' interests if those decisions are directly contrary to their own personal interests. If there were no business judgment rules, CEOs and other top corporate officials would be out of business.

The decision illustrates a rather straightforward case in which the business judgment rule should have been applicable to the facts. Subsequent sections will consider closely whether this case was really so simple and how altering some of the facts might have changed the results.

Much of the debate in corporate law deals with the rather challenging question of where to draw the line between situations in which the business judgment rule applies and situations in which it does not. Also of interest, of course, are the consequences of a decision by courts not to apply the business judgment rule. Those are the questions addressed in the following sections of this chapter.

D. QUALIFYING FOR THE BUSINESS JUDGMENT RULE: A PLAINTIFF'S PERSPECTIVE

As indicated in the previous section, directors do not automatically qualify for the benefits of the protections afforded by the business judgment rule; they have to qualify for it.

Consistent with the general approach to the law of the business judgment rule, the court in *Kamin* made the following inquiries:

- The court asked whether the decision made was one that "is exclusively a matter of business judgment of the board of directors."[5] The judges decided that it was.

- The court looked at whether there were claims of "fraud or self dealing, bad faith or oppressive conduct." The judges noted that their "[e]xamination of the complaint reveals that there is no claim of fraud or self-dealing, and no contention that there was any bad faith or oppressive conduct."[6]

- Finally, the judges looked at the quality of the decision-making process employed by the board and concluded that it passed muster.

These three bullet points provide a convenient thumbnail sketch of the three conditions precedent to the utilization of the business judgment rule. In only those cases in which the three conditions are met do directors enjoy the benefits of the protection of this rule. But these conditions are a bit tricky and merit further explication.

1. The Requirement that the Decision be Exclusively a Matter of the Business Judgment of the Board of Directors

First, not every decision that directors make is "exclusively" theirs to make. Input from shareholders is sometimes required. Major decisions such as the sale of all assets and mergers require a shareholder vote under the law of every state. Additional shareholder votes on particular issues may be required under the laws of an individual state or in the corporate charter of a company. In such cases, it appears that courts will scrutinize directors' decisions a bit more carefully. The explanation for this is that directors should be more careful when making important "bet the company" or "once-in-a-lifetime" decisions as compared to more ordinary everyday decisions. In particular, directors have faced heightened scrutiny in the context of decisions about whether to sell their companies in merger transactions. Unfortunately, the scrutiny of directors' decisions in the context of decisions to remain independent have received less scrutiny, even where this decision is accompanied by a determination to utilize (or fail to relinquish) powerful defensive devices, such as poison pill rights plans.

By way of contrast, the decision about whether to pay a dividend, which was the decision made in *Kamin,* is within the sole discretion of corporate directors, subject only to the constraint that the dividend must be paid out of some sort of surplus. This means that no dividend may be paid by a corporation that is insolvent or that is rendered insolvent by the dividend payment.

---

5. Id. at 810.   **6.** Id.

Two other important qualifications are in order here. First, the business judgment rule does not apply to all conduct by directors, only to decisions made by directors. State law permits lawsuits against directors outside of the decision-making context for neglecting or otherwise failing to perform their duties. Chief among the responsibilities of board members that lie outside of the decision-making context is the directors' responsibility to insure that the corporation's operations are supervised adequately[7]. The protections of the business judgment rule, in other words, do not apply where one or more directors is charged with neglecting or abdicating his duties.

The business judgment rule is qualified in that it applies only in the decisional context and not in the oversight context. However, there is a qualification to this qualification. The protections of the business judgment rule can apply in the oversight context with regard to directors' *decisions* about how much oversight a particular corporation might require.[8] The point here is that it is absolutely essential that directors meet and carefully consider what sort of oversight infrastructure is most appropriate for their companies. At this meeting, the directors should consider the size and complexity of their organizations as well as any other special factors that may be unique to their business.[9]

Well-advised directors can qualify to have the business judgment rule applied to their oversight functions as well as to their decisions if they reach an unbiased, fully deliberative, and well informed decision about the sorts of monitoring and oversight arrangements that are most appropriate for their companies. Directors also should periodically review and update their oversight decisions, consulting outside experts where appropriate, to ensure that they continue to be in compliance with their oversight responsibilities.

2. The Allegation Issue: Complaints Really are Important

The court in *Kamin* opined that the business judgment rule will not apply to shield directors from liability in situations in which the *complaint* alleges that directors' decision under challenge involves claims of "fraud or self-dealing" or contentions of "bad faith or oppressive conduct." This is an odd characterization. After all the complaint filed in a lawsuit is entirely the creation of the plaintiffs. At first blush, it would appear that little could be easier than inserting allegations of fraud, self-dealing, bad faith or oppressive conduct, if such assertions were all that were required to shift the presumptions and the burden of proof in a particular lawsuit.

---

7. See discussion of the Caremark case, Ch. 14, infra.

8. See discussion of the Caremark case, Ch. 14, infra.

9. For example, some businesses are particularly susceptible to problems associated with corruption of domestic or foreign officials; other industries such as health care or military contractors have significant regulatory compliance responsibilities; certain manufacturers need to be cognizant of environmental hazards caused by their activities.

The catch is that merely making general allegations in a complaint is not enough. Instead, the complaint must allege with particularity specific facts that tend to show the requisite fraud, self-dealing, bad faith or oppressive conduct. This makes sense from the defendants' perspective. After all, if unfounded, unsubstantiated allegations could shift the burdens of proof and persuasion that lie at the heart of the business judgment rule. Then the rule would not provide very useful protection for directors.

On the other hand, the requirement that fraud, self-dealing, bad faith or oppressive conduct must be pled with particularity is a heavy burden for plaintiffs because at the complaint stage of a lawsuit, which generally takes place before the plaintiffs have the opportunity to engage in the process of evidence gathering known as "discovery," the plaintiffs often have no opportunity to collect the evidence they need to draft a complaint that pleads with particularity the conditions necessary to overcome the burdens of the business judgment rule.

The heightened pleading requirement, coupled with the lack of discovery, creates a difficult situation for plaintiffs. They are consigned to their own devices, to what is known among judges as utilizing "the tools at hands," which include public records, including the publicly filed corporate records such as the quarterly and annual reports that public companies are required to file with the Securities and Exchange Commission, documents such as shareholder lists that shareholders have the right to access, published media accounts of corporate behavior, and court documents from unrelated actions such as directors' or executives' divorce proceedings, at which information about corporate activity might be revealed.

There are, however, several factors in the plus column for plaintiffs. First, whatever specific allegations a plaintiff can manage to dredge up for the complaint will be taken as true for purposes of summary judgment motions and motions to dismiss the complaint. This is certainly an advantage for plaintiffs.

Second, it appears that judges will protect plaintiffs, at least to some extent, from their own incompetence, which, in legal jargon, generally goes under the name of "inartful pleading." The court in *Kamin*, along the way to dismissing the complaint and granting summary judgment for the defendants, wrote "nor does this appear to be a case in which a potentially valid cause of action is inartfully stated."[10] By this the court meant that even if a plaintiff neglected to allege in their complaint that the defendants conduct involved fraud, self-dealing, bad faith or oppressive conduct, but the trial judge reading the complaint nevertheless can somehow figure out that the defendants engaged in conduct that fits this description, then the judge will not dismiss the complaint. This is an interesting observation and it appears in a few other cases as well. Interestingly, while judges may be willing to help out the clients of lawyers who stupidly draft a complaint alleging that directors are guilty

10.   383 N.Y.S.2d at 811.

of making an imprudent decision, there are no recorded cases in which this has actually happened.

In *Kamin* itself, of course, the complaint was dismissed. The court could not think of a valid cause of action that was hidden inside of an inartfully stated complaint. The reason why there are no other cases in which the judges have been more successful in their creative endeavors on behalf of plaintiffs is not hard to figure out. Judges, it seems, have the same problem that plaintiffs do in these sorts of cases: they don't have any better access than the plaintiffs to information that would enable them to allege with particularity that defendants engaged in fraud, self-dealing, bad faith or oppressive conduct.

Kamin provides an important lesson about judicial involvement in the governance and operation of U.S. corporations. Judges place lawsuits, based on the complaints filed with them, into one of two categories. *Kamin* and a few other cases fit into the "duty of care" category. Cases in this category are those that allege that the defendant directors made a bad business decision. The basic lesson in *Kamin*, expressed as the application of the business judgment rule, is that judges are not in the least bit inclined to permit lawsuits to go forward, much less to impose liability on directors, where this is the only allegation that the plaintiffs can allege.

The second category of cases is comprised of those in the "duty of loyalty" category. These are cases in which the plaintiffs can allege, with particularity, bad behavior such as fraud, self-dealing, bad faith or oppressive conduct. As the court makes clear in *Kamin*, judges are willing, even eager, to side with plaintiffs in cases that present this sort of fact pattern. In sharp contrast to "duty of care" cases, in those lawsuits that are characterized as "duty of loyalty" cases, the defendant directors, rather than the plaintiffs, have the burden of proof. Moreover, what the directors have to prove is that the transaction or decision at issue was "entirely fair" to the corporation, rather than that neither the transaction nor the decision had some sort of rational basis.[11]

3.   The Decision-making Process Employed by the Board

In a critical section of the *Kamin* opinion, the court stresses the fact that the decision made by the directors was "carefully considered and unanimously rejected by the Board at a special meeting called precisely for that purpose. . . ."[12] The court suggests that there is no disagreement among the parties on this point. Indeed, the board considered the plaintiffs' assertion that the dividend payment was a bad idea because they were requested to do so by the plaintiffs.

The minutes of this special meeting showed that the defendants were fully aware that a sale rather than a distribution of the DLJ shares might result in a realization of substantial tax savings. Nevertheless, the court observes, the directors "concluded that there were countervailing

---

11.   See section below for further discussion.

12.   383 N.Y.S.2d at 811.

considerations"[13] that led them to reject the strategy that the plaintiffs thought would save the most money for the company.

It is important to focus closely on this portion of the opinion in order to precisely determine the standard for director conduct being articulated. It is confusing as to whether the court is looking at the quality of the deliberations in the boardroom or simply at whether they deliberated at all. This is a curious ambiguity in an otherwise masterful opinion.

There are two very different ways to interpret the court's opinion. It may be that the court is satisfied that the board "carefully considered" the decision. In other words, it may be the case that process is enough and the fact of the board's deliberation is all that matters.[14] On the other hand, it may be that the court is requiring more than mere deliberation. It could be that, as is sometimes suggested, the court is requiring some plausible justification by the board for its decision. Most cases stress the fact that the business judgment rule requires deliberation. In other cases, however, most notably *Shlensky v. Wrigley*,[15] the court appears to use what might be best described as a *rational basis* approach to the business judgment rule. Under the rational basis approach, instead of focusing on the quality of the board's deliberations, judges instead inquire whether the directors' decision can be attributable to any rational basis. If, so, then the decision will not be set aside under a rational basis approach, regardless of how irrational it may be.

For example, in *Shlensky v. Wrigley*, shareholders in the corporation that owned and operated the Chicago Cubs baseball team and the team's stadium, Wrigley Field, sued to compel the corporation, the Chicago National League Ball Club, Inc., to install lights at Wrigley. The plaintiffs' theory was that without lights, the Cubs had to play all of their home games during the day, which hurt attendance and revenue, especially for weekday games. The plaintiffs observed that all of the other teams in the major league[16] had lighted fields in their stadiums. The plaintiffs argued that the directors were acting for reasons unrelated to the financial interests and welfare of the corporation.

Interestingly, unlike the court in *Kamin*, the court in *Shlensky v. Wrigley* paid no attention to the quality or the quantity of board deliberations that led to the decision to decline to install lights. Indeed, there is no indication that the issue was even discussed at a board meeting. Instead, the court embarks upon its own analysis of the possible costs and benefits of installing lights at Wrigley Field, opining that *"it appears to us* that the effect on the surrounding neighborhood *might well be considered* by a director who was considering the patrons

13. Id.

14. See Smith v. Van Gorkom discussed in Ch. 12, infra.

15. 237 N.E.2d 776 (Ill. App. 1968).

16. At the time there were twenty major league baseball teams including the Cubs.

or who would or would not attend the games if the park were in a poor neighborhood."[17]

In other words, the deciding factor in the case was not whether the judges believed that the quality of the directors' deliberation had been adequate or that they had considered their decision. Rather the deciding factor in *Shlensky v. Wrigley* was whether the business decision under challenge could be justified on any rational basis; the dispositive question was whether, had the directors considered the issue, they could have rationally reached the decision that they did.

It is not clear which of these approaches is better. Clearly they yield different results in different cases. For example, if the court in *Shlensky v. Wrigley* had taken a deliberative approach, they might well have found that the question was never "*carefully considered.*" Because the court in Wrigley focused on a different question, which was whether the business transaction had a rational purpose instead of whether the business transaction was carefully considered, the defendants won.

In *Smith v. Van Gorkom*, by contrast, the defendant directors suffered a complete loss when the Delaware Supreme Court decided that the board was grossly negligent in approving a friendly takeover offer by an outside company despite the fact that there were myriad business justifications for the decision made by the board. There is no dispute that there was a perfectly rational justification for the board decision in *Smith v. Van Gorkom*. Shareholders were unambiguously better off as a result of the significant premium they garnered from the transaction. If the court in *Smith* had used the rational basis approach utilized in *Shlensky*, the result would have been entirely different because the decision in that case, to sell a publicly held company with lots of problems for substantially more cash than the highest price at which the firm's shares had ever traded, was clearly "rational."

The question to which we turn now is whether the decision in *Kamin* can be defended not only on the basis that the decision was a result of an adequate process of deliberation within the board, but also on the grounds that it can be justified as having some rational basis. To complete this inquiry, we must look at the accounting, economics and finance behind the board's decision to pay the in-kind dividend.

E. THE ACCOUNTING, ECONOMICS AND FINANCE OF KAMIN v. AMERICAN EXPRESS

The board of directors justified their decision to make an in-kind dividend payment of the DLJ stock rather than simply to sell it because they were worried that the loss realized in such a sale would look bad. Specifically, the board's explanation for their "exit strategy" from American Express's disastrous investment in DLJ was that the alternative strategy of selling the stock would have the adverse affect of causing the company to realize a loss of $25 million in net income figures on its

---

17.   237 N.E.2d 776, 779 (Ill. App. 1968).

financial statements, which, it was alleged, would have a serious negative effect on the market value of the publicly traded American Express stock.

To understand this concern we first must understand a bit about accounting. The two basic financial documents that depict the financial condition of a business are the balance sheet and the income statement. The balance sheet is the financial statement that provides a snapshot of a company's assets (what it owns), liabilities (what it owes) and shareholders' equity (what's left over after liabilities are subtracted from assets) for a company at a specific point in time. The three components of the balance sheet (assets, liabilities, and shareholders' equity) are designed to provide a financial snapshot of what the company owns (such as securities, property, buildings and equipment and cash) and owes (to banks suppliers and other creditors), as well as the amounts that represent the value of the investments made by the shareholders. Balance sheets follow this basic equation:

$$\text{Assets} = \text{Liabilities} + \text{Shareholders' Equity}$$

Cash, inventory and property are on the asset side of the balance sheet. On the liability side there are both accounts payable and long-term debt along with other liabilities of the company.

The income statement, on the other hand, is the financial statement that shows how much revenue and profit a company has generated over a certain period of time. The income statement also shows the costs and expenses that should be associated with earning that revenue. The literal "bottom line" of the statement usually shows the company's net earnings or losses for the period covered.

Income statements start off by depicting the total amount of income brought into the company from sales or provision of services made during the accounting period covered by the income statement. From this, "top line" (which is referred to as the gross revenue or gross sales line because expenses have not been deducted from it yet), many deductions are made in order to account for operating expenses and other costs associated with earning the revenue. Finally, after all relevant expenses have been deducted, one reaches the "bottom line" of the income statement at which it is possible to tell how much the company actually made or lost during the accounting period covered by the income statement.

Deductions from gross sales are taken for things like bad debts, or money that the company does not expect to collect on certain sales due to merchandise returns. Operating expenses also show up on the income statement

Moving down from the net revenue line, there are several lines that represent various kinds of operating expenses. Although these lines can be reported in various orders, the next line after net revenues typically shows the costs of the sales. This number tells you the amount of money the company spent in the direct production of the goods or services it sold during the accounting period.

The next line subtracts the costs of sales from the net revenues to arrive at a subtotal called "gross profit" or sometimes "gross margin." It's considered "gross" because there are certain expenses that haven't been deducted from it yet. Other items that operate to reduce the gross income figure to the bottom line net income figure are operating expenses, which are expenses such as salaries of administrative personnel, research and development and marketing that support the company's operations for a given period.

Depreciation is also subtracted from gross profit on the income statement in order to determine the amount of a company's net revenue. Depreciation takes into account the wear and tear on some assets, such as machinery, tools and furniture, which are used over the long term. Companies spread the cost of these assets over the periods they are used. This process of spreading these costs is called depreciation or amortization.

After all of the various operating expenses are deducted from gross profit we arrive at operating profit or "income from operations" of the business. This figure does not take into account the expenses due from the business for interest and income tax payments, but otherwise it shows the net income. Finally, interest expenses and income taxes owed are deducted to determine the proverbial bottom line: net profit or net losses.

A company's balance sheet and income statements are related to one another. The changes in assets and liabilities that you see on the balance sheet are also reflected in the revenues and expenses as they flow through to the income statement, where they affect a company's gains or losses. And here we come to the heart of *Kamin v. American Express*.

Assuming that American Express (Amex) paid cash for the DLJ stock it acquired, the acquisition would change the balance sheet less than one might at first suppose. The total assets, liabilities and shareholders' equity would stay exactly the same immediately before and after the purchase. The only change would be that the company would have $29.8 million less in cash and $29.8 million in DLJ securities. Liabilities and shareholders' equity would not change at all.

As time moved on and the value of American Express's investment in DLJ stock declined, the real economic value of American Express would, of course, decline along with it. But, that does not necessarily mean that the *accounting treatment* of the DLJ stock would change. There are a number of different ways that a balance sheet might change to reflect changing value of assets over time. The most important choice in accounting treatment is between the use of what is known as book value (or historical cost adjusted for depreciation) and market value. The SEC has long fought a losing battle against the use of market value accounting, favoring the presentation of information that is verifiable by bureaucrats and lawyers (book value) over the presentation of information that is useful to investors (market value). Nowadays, accounting rules would require a company's balance sheet to be adjusted to reflect changes in the value of assets such as publicly traded stock, for which there is an active market. But when *Kamin* was decided, the SEC required (or in this case, allowed) public companies like American Express to record the value of assets on their balance sheets at their historical cost. In this situation, the result of the accounting rules was, of course, to distort the true financial condition of American Express, because the assets of the company and the shareholders' equity would be falsely inflated after the value of the company's DLJ stock had plummeted.

Thus, when American Express distributed its DLJ shares, its assets as recorded on its balance sheet would be wiped out. Shareholders' equity would decline by the amount of the assets that was removed from the balance sheet. If the DLJ stock had been sold, the loss on the sale would flow through to the income statement, showing a corresponding charge to income in the period in which the assets were written off. By distributing the DLJ stock as a dividend to shareholders, however, American Express was able to confine the accounting impact of its bad investment to its balance sheet because dividend payments, unlike losses, don't affect the income statement.

The fact that American Express could avoid reflecting the huge losses suffered on the company's disastrous investment in DLJ stock as a drop in earnings on its income statement appears to have mattered considerably to the Amex directors. The American Express directors were said to be "fully aware" that the company would miss out on the tax advantages of selling the stock and taking the loss rather than "hiding the loss" on the books by distributing the DLJ stock as a dividend. Nevertheless, the court found that the directors were justified in distributing the stock as a dividend on the grounds that a sale of the stock, unlike a dividend, would cause the company to have to reduce its net income for the period.

The court then baldly asserts that reducing the company's net income "would have a serious effect on the market value of the publicly traded American Express stock."[18] This makes no sense from a financial or economic perspective. One of the most basic tenets of finance is that stock, like other financial assets, should be valued at the present value of the future income to investors. From an economic perspective, nothing at American Express whatsoever changed when the company's board of directors decided to distribute the DLJ stock as a dividend. After all, the DLJ stock had already plummeted in value by the time it had been distributed. Mere recognition of the losses on the company's books should not have affected the firm's share price at all. The court's blithe pronouncement that recognizing the loss for accounting purposes represents a clear rejection of what financial economists call the "Efficient Capital Markets Hypothesis" (ECMH), which is among the most widely

18. 383 N.Y.S.2d at 811.

understood and accepted ideas in modern finance, is plainly accurate. The ECMH posits that share prices react quickly to reflect all available information relevant to the valuation of the company's shares. Of course, acceptance of the ECMH in *Kamin* would imply that the effect of the losses suffered by American Express from its investment in DLJ would already be impounded in Amex's share price by the time the company adjusted its public accounting statements to reflect the share price decline.

In fact, the court's analysis appears to endorse the policy of actually misleading investors. If the court were indeed correct that adjusting the income statement to reflect the loss on the shares would have a serious effect on the market value of the publicly traded American Express stock, then clearly the company should be required to adjust its financial statements to fully and completely reflect the true financial condition of the company. Of course, the fact is, that unless the company had illegally failed to disclose its ownership of the DLJ shares, its share price would decline as the value of the DLJ shares it owned declined (adjusting also of course for other events taking place in the Company that became publicly known).

Thus, the court's assertion that the directors were correct in avoiding the realization of its loss on the net income figures in its accounting statements seems both wrong and perverse. It is wrong because it assumes that avoiding the realization of the stock loss would enable the company to avoid feeling the impact on its share prices. It is perverse because it assumes that this somehow would be acceptable.

To illustrate the point simply, imagine that ownership of a particular stock (let's call it XYZ) was Amex's only asset. Suppose further that the value of XYZ shares dropped from being worth millions of dollars to being worth zero. Amex's share prices should decline along with the value of its only asset XYZ. When XYZ's share price hit zero, Amex's share price should go to zero as well, *regardless of the accounting treatment of the company's investment in XYZ*. The financial statements of the company should reflect the company's true financial condition, and so should the company's share price. Company directors should not be permitted to prop up the company's share prices contrary to economic reality, even in situations in which they are able to do so.

My argument is incomplete up to this point. If I am correct in my assertion that the decision to distribute Amex's shares was not made in order to avoid a serious negative effect on the market value of the publicly traded stock of American Express, then I should have a theory for why the company decided to forego the favorable accounting treatment it would have received if it had simply sold the shares, taken the tax loss, and distributed the shares as a dividend instead. One possibility is that certain officers and directors of American Express received compensation based, in part, on the reported earnings of the company for accounting purposes. By distributing the DLJ stock as an in-kind dividend and avoiding showing a decline in earnings for that particular reporting period, these officers and directors would receive more "performance based" compensation from the Company. Seen from this perspective, even if the decision to make the in-kind dividend payment to shareholders made them worse off, the board did it anyway because they were more concerned with propping up the compensation for the affected officers and directors than they were with shareholder value.

If this approach to the case is correct, then the result reached in the case is more ambiguous. The problem with using this analysis is two-fold. First, only four of the twenty directors of American Express were insiders with compensation plans impacted by the dividend decision. The other sixteen directors were independent outsiders with no self-interest at stake. Second, as the court observed, every action taken by a board of directors affects earnings and therefore may affect the compensation of the officers involved in the decision. If courts were to review actively all such decisions, then judges, not officers and directors, would have the ultimate say over every decision made by public companies.

From this perspective, it appears that the strongest justification for the outcome in *Kamin* is not that the board's decision was particularly defensible or sound, but rather that judges simply are unwilling to displace directors as the key decision-makers in U.S. corporations. This is understandable, of course. Shareholders elect directors, not judges, to run the companies in which they have invested. Market forces ultimately discipline managers and directors, not judges, for making decisions that harm investors. Given a choice between two bad alternatives: (a) allowing an apparently bad board decision to withstand a lawsuit; and (b) creating a legal precedent in which courts displace directors whenever a decision is made that might affect the company's earnings, the court chose the "least worst" outcome.

F. DIGGING DEEPER: SOME QUIBBLES WITH THE U.S. APPROACH TO JUDICIAL REVIEW OF CORPORATE DECISION–MAKING

The basic teaching of the court in the iconic case *Kamin v. American Express* is that directors are shielded from legal liability from their decisions "unless it is made to appear that the acts were fraudulent or collusive"[19] and destructive of shareholder value. Directors are insulated from liability from "mere" errors in judgment.

Delving a bit more deeply, however, *Kamin* also reveals that evaluating the motivations of directors is not always as easy as it appears to be. In this case, it would be possible to argue that the directors were acting collusively to protect their incentive compensation packages.

Perhaps the most interesting aspect of *Kamin* is what the court *does not* talk about. The court makes no mention whatsoever of what, from a business perspective, is clearly the most important aspect of the case. Specifically, the court does not consider-even in passing, the question of

19. 383 N.Y.S.2d at 810, quoting Leslie
v. Lorillard, 110 N.Y. 519 (1888).

why the directors made their decision to distribute the DLJ stock as an in-kind dividend. Why didn't they sell the stock or keep it for themselves? Why return it to the shareholders? Does it make a lot of sense, or any sense at all, to require directors to deliberate without requiring them to articulate, even in the most conclusory or sketchy way?

From a plaintiffs' perspective, this lack of interest in requiring directors to articulate a reason for their actions is frustrating. From the perspective of the directors of U.S. public corporations who are potential defendants in a suit, the judicial perspective reflects the fact that judges actually are uninterested in the business justifications that directors might have for their decisions.

From a jurisprudential perspective, judges' lack of interest reflects their interest in confining their inquiries and evaluations to areas in which they have special competence and expertise. Judges feel quite competent in evaluating the *process* by which decisions are made. They feel less competent in evaluating the *substance* of those decisions but can determine whether a particular decision was *carefully* considered by the board or not. And courts do not hesitate to evaluate whether directors have carefully considered the business decisions that plaintiffs are challenging in a particular case. When looking at business decisions, however, judges uniformly and routinely decline to make even a superficial evaluation of whether the directors' decision was plausible or reasonable.

This "process" focused approach reflected in *Kamin* and followed in many other important corporate law cases[20] is not without significant flaws. First, it creates an artificial demand for lawyers. Whether this is an unintended consequence or not is anybody's guess. Directors who make business decisions, even ordinary business decisions, need lawyers to serve as the architects for the process used in reaching such decisions. Thus, the intense judicial focus on process necessarily increases the demand for the services of corporate lawyers. Virtually any business decision can be rationalized if the directors making the decision—and their lawyers–design a process that makes it appear as though the decision reached by the directors was "carefully considered."

Thus one flaw with the obsessive focus on process is that bad decisions will not be subject to challenge by shareholders so long as such decisions are surrounded by the appearance of process. This, in turn, means that as long as directors are careful to employ good lawyers, even the worst business decisions will avoid successful legal challenge.

Another problem with the dominant judicial approach to ordinary business decisions that is reflected in *Kamin* increases the cost of doing business because easy decisions that ought not be larded with process and leavened with lawyers must be in order to satisfy courts that such decisions, however obvious from a business perspective, were "carefully considered."

---

20. Including several in this book, perhaps most notably *Smith v. Van Gorkom,*   Ch. 12, infra.

In other words, the obsessive focus on process reflected in *Kamin* imposes two sorts of costs on investors. One type of cost emerges when directors make bad, albeit carefully considered, decisions. The second type of costs emerges when directors make good, albeit obvious, decisions. As for the first type of cost, the problem is that the approach to the business decisions reflected in *Kamin* allows directors to immunize themselves from bad decisions as long as those decisions are cloaked in a sufficiently lustrous patina of process.

The second sort of cost is the direct and indirect costs imposed by the judicial bureaucratization of the corporation. *Kamin* and the myriad other business judgment rule cases focusing on process shift the burden of corporate decision-making out of the hands of the directors themselves and into the hands of the corporation's lawyers. Directors are obviously interested in protecting themselves from liability from controversial or even demonstrably bad decisions. The way to do this is to permit the company's inside and outside counsel to design the process by which all important or controversial corporate decisions are made. The most obvious consequence of this approach is the increase in transaction costs associated with making a decision. Good decisions that ought to be made quickly and easily now require several meetings so that the directors can build the necessary water-tight record that their decision was carefully considered.

Another problem with the transaction costs imposed by the focus on process that characterizes the judicial approach to the business judgment rule is that it necessarily slows down the decision-making process. Judges don't inquire into whether a decision made by directors was bad. They focus only on whether the decision was made carefully. For many decisions the only consequence of this is that obvious transaction costs like fees for legal advisors and the opportunity cost of the directors' time associated with corporate decisions necessarily increase. But for other decisions, those that need to be made very quickly, the primary cost of the business judgment rule's process-oriented focus is delay. Any delay that causes a corporation to miss a valuable business opportunity can impose significant costs on the shareholders.

Here an important cautionary note is in order. The point here is not that the judicial approach to business decisions taken in *Kamin* is unambiguously bad; only that it is not unambiguously good. The virtue of the process-oriented approach to the business judgment rule in *Kamin* is that it enables directors to operate under conditions of certainty even in the litigation-crazed U.S. litigation environment. The way to achieve this certainty is to have lawyers design the process by which corporate decisions are made, and to document that the decisions are made "carefully." As long as the directors can demonstrate that their decisions were made carefully, they will avoid liability unless the plaintiffs can demonstrate that their decisions were either self-interested or fraudulent.

As *Kamin* itself illustrates, the term "self-interested" is rather narrowly defined. In order for a decision or transaction to be considered sufficiently self-interested to disqualify the directors making the decision from the protections of the business judgment rule, it appears that a tangible personal benefit is required, and even then it is not so clear. As discussed above, and as *Kamin* itself illustrates, the benefit taken must not only be tangible, it must be sufficiently odious and pervasive to suggest that the board's own decision making process was tainted.

G. CONCLUSION

Judges review the ordinary business decisions of corporate boards of directors from a "process" oriented perspective. In sharp contrast, federal judges in constitutional cases evaluate whether the statutes passed by state legislatures and Congress are constitutional by using what is known as "rational basis review." Such review, in contrast to more rigorous levels of review including intermediate scrutiny and strict scrutiny, simply asks whether the governmental action at issue is a rational means to an end that may be legitimately pursued by government.

The key point here is that rational basis review and the business judgment rule are used in exactly the same context. Both are used to evaluate the decisions made by elected decision-makers. These decision-makers are boards of directors in the corporate context and legislatures in the political context. When the relevant decision-making body (legislatures or boards of directors) is pursuing a legitimate corporate or legislative objective untainted by any suspect or illegitimate goals (such as self-interest in corporate law or the disenfranchisement of discrete and insular minorities in the political arena) courts grant them great deference. Oddly, this deference manifests itself in the form of a process-oriented review in the corporate context, but in the form of rational basis review in the legislative context.

The rational basis test is the default test for courts deciding questions of law regarding government action. The business judgment rule is the default test for courts deciding questions of law regarding corporate action.

In the context of judicial review of legislative actions, in situations in which a vulnerable group's interests are involved and that interest is strong, federal courts intervene more actively. Likewise, in the context of legislative review of actions by corporate boards of directors, where there is evidence of self-interest or self dealing by a majority of the board, courts also will intervene more actively. In the corporate context, more active review can involve courts using their own business judgment to evaluate directors' decisions.

It is not at all obvious why courts focus on process in the corporate context and rationality in the constitutional context. A strong argument can be made on policy ground that the opposite should be true. But that argument will have to wait for another day.

Chapter 8

THE ICONIC INSIDER
TRADING CASES

By
*Stephen M. Bainbridge**

The modern federal insider trading prohibition fairly can be said to have begun with the Securities and Exchange Commission's (SEC or "Commission") enforcement action in *Cady, Roberts & Co.*[1] Curtiss–Wright Corporation's board of directors decided to reduce the company's quarterly dividend. One of the directors, J. Cheever Cowdin, was also a partner of stock brokerage firm Cady, Roberts & Co. Before the news was announced, Cowdin informed one of his partners, Robert M. Gintel, of the impending dividend cut. Gintel then sold several thousand shares of Curtiss–Wright stock held in customer accounts over which he had discretionary trading authority. When the dividend cut was announced, Curtiss–Wright's stock price fell several dollars per share. Gintel's customers thus avoided substantial losses.

Cady, Roberts involved what is now known as tipping: an insider who knows confidential information does not himself trade, but rather informs—tips—someone else, who does trade. It also involved trading on an impersonal stock exchange, instead of a face-to-face transaction. As the SEC acknowledged, this made it "a case of first impression."[2] Nonetheless, the SEC held that Gintel had violated Rule 10b–5.

A.   THE INSIDER TRADING PROHIBITION EMERG-
ES

It was not immediately clear whether *Cady, Roberts* would have significant precedential value.[3] It was an administrative ruling by the

---

* William D. Warren Professor of Law, UCLA School of Law, Bainbridge@law.ucla.edu.

1. In re Cady, Roberts & Co., 40 S.E.C. 907, 1961 WL 59902 (1961).

2. *Id.* at *1.

3. See, e.g., Recent Decision, 48 VA. L. REV. 398, 403–04 (1962) ("in view of the limited resources of the Commission, the unfortunate existence of more positive and

SEC, not a judicial opinion. It involved a regulated industry closely supervised by the SEC. Neither the text of the statute nor its legislative history mandated a broad insider trading prohibition.[4]

In *SEC v. Texas Gulf Sulphur Co.*,[5] however, the Second Circuit set a major precedent accepting the SEC's argument that insider trading violated Rule 10b–5. In March 1959, agents of Texas Gulf Sulphur Co. (Texas Gulf Sulphur)—a mining corporation—began aerial surveys of an area near Timmins, Ontario. Evidence of an ore deposit was found. In October 1963, Texas Gulf Sulphur began ground surveys of the area. In early November, a drilling rig took core samples from depths of several hundred feet. Visual examination of the samples suggested commercially significant deposits of copper and zinc. Texas Gulf Sulphur's president ordered the exploration group to maintain strict confidentiality, even to the point of withholding the news from other Texas Gulf Sulphur directors and employees. In early December, a chemical assay confirmed the presence of copper, zinc, and silver. At the subsequent trial, several expert witnesses testified that they had never heard of any other initial exploratory drill hole showing comparable results. Over the next several months, Texas Gulf Sulphur acquired the rights to the land under which this remarkable ore deposit lay. In March and early April 1964, further drilling confirmed that Texas Gulf Sulphur had made a significant ore discovery. After denying several rumors about the find, Texas Gulf Sulphur finally announced its discovery in a press conference on April 16, 1964.

Throughout the fall of 1963 and spring of 1964, a number of Texas Gulf Sulphur insiders bought stock and/or options on company stock. Others tipped off outsiders. Still others accepted stock options from the company's board of directors without informing the directors of the discovery. Between November 1963 and March 1964, the insiders were able to buy at prices that were slowly rising, albeit with fluctuations, from just under $18 per share to $25 per share. As rumors began circulating in late March and early April, the price jumped to about $30 per share. On April 16th, the stock opened at $31, but quickly jumped to $37 per share. By May 15, 1964, Texas Gulf Sulphur's stock was trading at over $58 per share—a 222% rise over the previous November's price. Any joy the insiders may have taken from their profits was short-lived, however, as the SEC sued them for violating Rule 10b–5.

In *Texas Gulf Sulphur*, the Second Circuit held that when an insider has material nonpublic information, Rule 10b–5 requires that the insider must either disclose such information before trading or abstain from trading until the information has been disclosed. Thus was born what is now known as the "disclose or abstain" rule: an insider in possession of

reprehensible forms of fraud, and the inherent problems concerning proof and evidence adhering to any controversy involving a breach of duty of disclosure, there is little prospect of excessive litigation evolving pursuant to [*Cady, Roberts*]'').

4. *See* Stephen M. Bainbridge, *Incorporating State Law Fiduciary Duties into the Federal Insider Trading Prohibition*, 52 WASH. & LEE L. REV. 1189, 1228–34 (1995).

5. 401 F.2d 833 (2d Cir.), *cert. denied*, 394 U.S. 976 (1968).

material nonpublic information must disclose such information before trading or, if disclosure is impossible or improper, abstain from trading.

The policy foundation on which the Second Circuit erected the disclose or abstain rule was equality of access to information. The federal insider trading prohibition purportedly was necessary to ensure that "all investors trading on impersonal exchanges have relatively equal access to material information."[6] Put another way, Congress purportedly intended "that all members of the investing public should be subject to identical market risks."[7]

To consider the potentially expansive scope of the equality of access principle, suppose a Texas Gulf Sulphur representative had approached a landowner in the Timmins area to negotiate purchasing mineral rights to the land. Texas Gulf Sulphur's agent does not disclose the ore strike, but the landowner knows Texas Gulf Sulphur has been drilling in the area and has heard rumors that it has been buying up a lot of mineral rights. She puts two and two together, reaches the obvious conclusion, and buys some Texas Gulf Sulphur stock. Under a literal reading of *Texas Gulf Sulphur*, is our landowner liable for illegal insider trading?

Probably. The *Texas Gulf Sulphur* court stated that the insider trading prohibition applies to "anyone in possession of material inside information," because § 10(b) was intended to assure that "all investors trading on impersonal exchanges have relatively equal access to material information."[8] The court further stated that the prohibition applies to anyone who has "access, directly or *indirectly*," to confidential information if she knows that the information is unavailable to the investing public.[9] The only issue thus perhaps would be a factual one turning on the landowner's state of mind: did she know she was dealing with confidential information. If so, the equal access policy would seem to justify imposing a duty on her.

B. THE SUPREME COURT SETS LIMITS

In *Chiarella v. United States*,[10] the Supreme Court concluded that the equal access test went too far. Vincent Chiarella was an employee of Pandick Press, a financial printer. In preparing tender offer disclosure materials, Pandick used codes to conceal the names of the companies involved, but Chiarella broke the codes. He purchased target company shares before the bid was announced, then sold the shares for considerable profits after announcement of the bid.

Chiarella was caught and convicted of violating Rule 10b–5 by trading on the basis of material nonpublic information. The Second Circuit affirmed his conviction, applying the *Texas Gulf Sulphur* equality of access to information-based disclose or abstain rule. Under that

---

6. *Id.* at 847.

7. *Id.* at 852.

8. *Id.* at 847.

9. *Id.*

10. 445 U.S. 222 (1980).

standard, applied by the Court of Appeals, Chiarella lost because he had superior access to information than those with whom he traded.

The Supreme Court reversed. In doing so, the court rejected the notion that § 10(b) was intended to assure all investors equal access to information. The court could not affirm Chiarella's conviction without recognizing a general duty between all participants in market transactions to forego trades based on material, nonpublic information, which it declined to do.[11]

Chiarella thus made clear that the disclose or abstain rule is not triggered merely because the trader possesses material nonpublic information. When a 10b–5 action is based upon nondisclosure, there can be no fraud absent a duty to speak, and no such duty arises from the mere possession of nonpublic information.[12] Instead, the disclose or abstain theory of liability for insider trading was now premised on the inside trader being subject to a duty to disclose to the party on the other side of the transaction that arose from a relationship of trust and confidence between the parties thereto.[13] Chiarella was neither an employee, officer, nor director of any of the companies in whose stock he traded. He worked for Pandick Press, which itself was not an agent of any of those companies. Pandick worked for acquiring companies, not the takeover targets in whose stock Chiarella traded. He therefore had no duty to disclose to those with whom he traded.[14]

Three years later, in *Dirks v. SEC*,[15] the Supreme Court reaffirmed and refined *Chiarella*'s sharp limitation of the insider trading prohibition. Raymond Dirks, who was a securities analyst, began investigating Equity Funding of America after receiving a tip that it was engaged in widespread fraudulent corporate practices from Ronald Secrist, a former officer of Equity Funding. Dirks passed the results of his investigation to the SEC and the Wall Street Journal, but also discussed his findings with his clients. A number of those clients sold their holdings of Equity Funding securities before any public disclosure of the fraud, thereby avoiding substantial losses. After the fraud became public and Equity Funding went into receivership, the SEC charged that Dirks had violated the federal insider trading prohibition by repeating the allegations of fraud to his clients.

Under the old *Texas Gulf Sulphur* equal access to information standard, tipping of the sort at issue in *Dirks* would present no conceptual problems. The tippee had access to information unavailable to those with whom he traded and, as such, was liable. After *Chiarella*, however, the tipping problem was more complex. Neither Dirks nor his customers were agents, officers, or directors of Equity Funding. Nor did they have any other form of special relationship of trust and confidence with those with whom they traded. They were pure strangers.

11. *Id.* at 233.

12. *Id.* at 235.

13. *Id.* at 230.

14. *Id.* at 232–33.

15. 463 U.S. 646 (1983).

In reversing Dirk's SEC-imposed censure, the Supreme Court reaffirmed its rejection of the equal access standard:

> We were explicit in *Chiarella* in saying that there can be no duty to disclose where the person who has traded on inside information "was not [the corporation's] agent, . . . was not a fiduciary, [or] was not a person in whom the sellers [of the securities] had placed their trust and confidence." Not to require such a fiduciary relationship, we recognized, would "depar[t] radically from the established doctrine that duty arises from a specific relationship between two parties" and would amount to "recognizing a general duty between all participants in market transactions to forgo actions based on material, nonpublic information."[16]

Recognizing that the *Chiarella* formulation posed problems for tipping cases, the court held that tipping could violate the insider trading prohibition, but further held that a tippee's liability is derivative of the tipper's, "arising from his role as a participant after the fact in the insider's breach of a fiduciary duty."[17] A tippee therefore can be held liable only when the tipper breached a fiduciary duty by disclosing information to the tippee, and the tippee knows or has reason to know of the breach of duty.[18] On the *Dirks* facts, this formulation precluded imposition of liability. To be sure, Secrist was an officer and, hence, a fiduciary of Equity Funding. But the mere fact that an insider tips nonpublic information is not enough to impose liability under *Dirks*. What *Dirks* proscribes is not merely a breach of confidentiality by the insider, but rather a breach of the duty of loyalty imposed on all fiduciaries to avoid personally profiting from information entrusted to them.[19] Looking at objective criteria, courts must determine whether the insider personally benefited, directly or indirectly, from his disclosure.[20] Secrist tipped off Dirks in order to bring Equity Funding's misconduct to light, not for any personal gain. Absent the requisite personal benefit, liability could not be imposed.[21]

Just as there had been nothing historically or doctrinally inevitable about *Texas Gulf Sulphur*'s imposition of the equal access standard, there also was nothing inevitable about the Supreme Court's rejection of that standard. The equal access standard was consistent with a trend towards affirmative disclosure obligations and away from *caveat emptor* (buyer beware) that was sweeping across a broad swath of the common law. In rejecting this trend, Justice Powell arguably shifted the focus of insider trading liability from deceit to agency, a point that becomes especially significant later in our analysis.[22] Nothing in the text of the statute or the rule explicitly mandated that shift.

---

16. *Id.* at 654–55.
17. *Id.* at 659.
18. *Id.* at 660.
19. *Id.* at 662.
20. *Id.*

21. *Id.* at 666–67.

22. A. C. Pritchard, *United States v. O'Hagan: Agency Law And Justice Powell's Legacy For The Law Of Insider Trading,*78 Bos. Univ. L. Rev. 13 (1998).

C. THE MISAPPROPRIATION THEORY EMERGES

After *Chiarella* and *Dirks*, the SEC began advocating a new theory of insider trading liability that came to be called "misappropriation." Its origins are commonly (but incorrectly) traced to Chief Justice Burger's *Chiarella* dissent. Burger contended that the way in which the inside trader acquires the nonpublic information on which he trades could itself be a material circumstance that must be disclosed to the market before trading. Accordingly, he argued, "a person who has misappropriated nonpublic information has an absolute duty [to the persons with whom he trades] to disclose that information or to refrain from trading."[23] The majority declined to address Burger's argument, because it had not been presented to the jury and thus could not sustain a criminal conviction.[24]

The way was thus left open for the SEC to urge the lower courts to adopt the misappropriation theory as an alternative basis of insider trading liability. In *United States v. Newman,*[25] employees of an investment bank misappropriated confidential information concerning proposed mergers involving clients of the firm. As had been true of Vincent Chiarella, the Newman defendants' employer worked for prospective acquiring companies, while the trading took place in target company securities. As such, the Newman defendants owed no fiduciary duties to the investors with whom they traded. In this instance, moreover, neither the investment bank nor its clients traded in the target companies' shares contemporaneously with the defendants.

Unlike Chief Justice Burger's *Chiarella* dissent, the Second Circuit did not assert that the Newman defendants owed any duty of disclosure to the investors with whom they traded. Moreover, the Second Circuit did not assert that the Newman defendants had defrauded the investors. Instead, the court held that by misappropriating confidential information for personal gain, the defendants had defrauded their employer and its clients and that that fraud sufficed to impose insider trading liability on the defendants with whom they traded.[26]

Like the traditional disclose or abstain rule, the misappropriation theory thus required a breach of fiduciary duty before trading on inside information became unlawful.[27] Under the misappropriation theory, however, the defendant need not owe a duty either to the investor with whom he traded or to the issuer of the traded securities. Instead, the misappropriation theory applied when the inside trader violated a fiduciary duty owed to the source of the information.[28] If the misappropriation theory had been available against Chiarella, for example, his convic-

---

23. Chiarella v. United States, 445 U.S. 222, 240 (1980) (Burger, C.J., dissenting).

24. *Id.* at 236.

25. 664 F.2d 12 (2d Cir. 1981), *cert. denied*, 464 U.S. 863 (1983).

26. *Id.* at 17.

27. *See* SEC v. Switzer, 590 F. Supp. 756, 766 (W.D. Okla. 1984) (not unlawful to trade on the basis of inadvertently overheard information).

28. *E.g.*, United States v. Carpenter, 791 F.2d 1024, 1028–29 (2d Cir. 1986), *aff'd on other grounds*, 484 U.S. 19 (1987).

tion could have been upheld based on the breach of the duty he owed Pandick Press.

1. Why the SEC Pushed the Misappropriation Theory

The misappropriation theory thus became the vehicle by which the SEC sought to recapture as much as possible of the ground it had lost in *Chiarella* and *Dirks*. A former SEC Commissioner admitted as much, acknowledging that the misappropriation theory was "merely a pretext for enforcing equal opportunity in information."[29]

The SEC's support for the misappropriation theory likely was not accidental.[30] During the 1980s, the Commission embarked upon a limited program of deregulating the securities markets. Among other things, it adopted a safe harbor for projections and other soft data, adopted the shelf registration rule, adopted the integrated disclosure system, and expanded the exemptions from registration under the Securities Act. The deregulatory trend motivated one long-time critic of the SEC to compliment the Commission for being "well on the road toward a sensible disclosure system with much of the dead wood, idiosyncrasies, overregulation, and overdrafting eliminated."[31] At about the same time, however, the SEC adopted a vigorous enforcement campaign against insider trading. Not only did the number of cases increase substantially, but also the Commission adopted a "big bang" approach under which it focused on high visibility cases that would produce substantial publicity. In part, this may have been due to an increase in the frequency of insider trading, but one suspects the Commission's renewed interest in insider trading was motivated in large measure by a desire to preserve its budget during an era of deregulation and spending restraint. By virtue of the misappropriation theory, the Commission restored much of the prohibition's pre-*Chiarella* breadth and thereby ensured that its budget-justifying enforcement program would continue unimpeded.

By this point, moreover, the insider trading prohibition had come to benefit important interest groups. The post-*Chiarella* insider trading rules have been supported and driven in large part by market professionals, a cohesive and politically powerful interest group, which is effectively insulated from insider trading liability in the post-*Chiarella* regime. Only insiders and quasi-insiders such as lawyers and investment bankers have a greater degree of access to nonpublic information that might affect a firm's stock price than do market professionals. By basing insider trading liability on breach of fiduciary duty, and positing that the requisite fiduciary duty exists with respect to insiders and quasi-insiders but not with respect to market professionals, the prohibition protects the latter's ability to profit from new information about a firm.

29. Charles C. Cox & Kevin S. Fogarty, *Bases of Insider Trading Law*, 49 OHIO ST. L.J. 353, 366 (1988).

30. *See* Bainbridge, *supra* note 4, at 1246–51; see also MICHAEL P. DOOLEY, FUNDAMENTALS OF CORPORATE LAW 816–857 (1995);

JONATHAN R. MACEY, INSIDER TRADING: ECONOMICS, POLITICS, AND POLICY (1991).

31. Homer Kripke, *Has the SEC Taken All the Dead Wood Out of Its Disclosure System?*, 38 BUS. LAW. 833 (1983).

2. The Poor Fit Between Insider Trading and Securities Fraud

The emergence of the misappropriation theory highlighted the increasingly anomalous nature of the insider trading prohibition in the overall scheme of securities regulation. Both Securities Exchange Act § 10(b) and Rule 10b–5 thereunder sweep broadly, capturing "any" fraudulent or manipulative conduct "in connection with" the purchase or sale of "any" security. Nonetheless, the Supreme Court has warned against expanding the concept of securities fraud beyond that which the words of the statute will reasonably bear.[32] Once courts began accepting the misappropriation theory, that warning took on special significance. From a strict textualist perspective, the validity of the misappropriation theory appeared to depend upon whether (1) the deceit, if any, worked by the misappropriator on the source of the information constitutes deception as the term is used in § 10(b) and Rule 10b–5 and (2) any such deceit is deemed to have occurred "in connection with" the purchase or sale of a security.

In *United States v. Bryan*, the Fourth Circuit defined fraud—as the term is used in § 10(b) and Rule 10b–5—"as the making of a material misrepresentation or the nondisclosure of material information in violation of a duty to disclose."[33] So defined, fraud is present in a misappropriation case only in a technical and highly formalistic sense. Although a misappropriator arguably deceives the source of the information, any such deception is really quite inconsequential. The source of the information presumably is injured, if at all, not by the deception, but by the conversion of the information by the misappropriator for his own profit. Hence, it is the breach of fiduciary duty, if any, by the misappropriator that is truly objectionable, while any deception is purely incidental. So understood, the misappropriation theory appears to run afoul of the Supreme Court's holding in *Santa Fe* that a mere breach of duty cannot give rise to Rule 10b–5 liability.[34]

In *Santa Fe*, the court held that Rule 10b–5 did not reach claims "in which the essence of the complaint is that shareholders were treated unfairly by a fiduciary."[35] But this is the very essence of the complaint made in insider trading cases. The court also held that extension of Rule 10b–5 to breaches of fiduciary duty was unjustified in light of the state law remedies available to plaintiffs.[36] Insider trading plaintiffs likewise have state law remedies available to them.[37] Granted, those remedies vary from state to state and are likely to prove unavailing in many cases,

---

32. United States v. Bryan, 58 F.3d 933, 945 (4th Cir. 1995) (citing Central Bank of Denver, N.A. v. First Interstate Bank of Denver, N.A., 511 U.S. 164 (1994)).

33. *Id.* at 946.

34. Santa Fe Industries v. Green, 430 U.S. 462 (1977). The federalism implications of insider trading regulation are discussed in Bainbridge, *supra* note 4, at 1258–61; Richard W. Painter et al., *Don't Ask, Just Tell: Insider Trading after United States v. O'Hagan*, 84 Va. L. Rev. 153, 174–86 (1998).

35. *Santa Fe*, 430 U.S. at 477.

36. *Id.* at 478.

37. Bainbridge, *supra* note 4, at 1218–27.

but the same was true of the state law remedy at issue in *Santa Fe*.[38] Finally, the court expressed reluctance "to federalize the substantial portion of the law of corporations that deals with transactions in securities, particularly where established state policies of corporate regulation would be overridden."[39] But this is precisely what the federal insider trading prohibition did. *Santa Fe* thus is a serious doctrinal problem for proponents of an insider trading prohibition grounded in securities fraud.[40]

Santa Fe was not the only doctrinal challenge to the misappropriation theory. In *Central Bank of Denver v. First Interstate Bank*,[41] the Supreme Court held that there was no implied private right of action against those who aid and abet violations of Rule 10b–5. *Central Bank* thus substantially limited the scope of secondary liability under the rule, at least insofar as private party causes of action are concerned. For our purposes, however, the case is more significant for its methodology than its holding. The court held that the scope of conduct prohibited by § 10(b) (and thus Rule 10b–5) is controlled by the text of the statute. Where the plain text does not resolve some aspect of the Rule 10b–5 cause of action, courts must "infer 'how the 1934 Congress would have addressed the issue had the 10b–5 action been included as an express provision of the 1934 Act.' "[42]

Applying the *Central Bank* standard, the Eighth Circuit, in *United States v. O'Hagan*, interpreted the statutory prohibition of fraud created by a § 10(b) narrowly to exclude conduct constituting a "mere breach of a fiduciary duty," instead capturing only conduct constituting a material misrepresentation or the nondisclosure of material information in violation of a duty to disclose.[43] Because the Eighth Circuit believed the misappropriation theory permits the imposition of § 10(b) liability based upon a breach of fiduciary duty without any such deception, it held that the theory was inconsistent with the plain statutory text of § 10(b) and, accordingly, invalid as per *Central Bank*.[44]

The Eighth Circuit further invoked *Central Bank* to strictly construe the statutory limitation that the requisite deception be committed "in connection with" a securities transaction,[45] which requirement the court contended the misappropriation theory rendered "nugatory."[46] Specifically, the court held that § 10(b) reaches "only a breach of a duty to parties to the securities transaction or, at the most, to other market

---

38. *Id.* at 1259.

39. *Santa Fe*, 430 U.S. at 479.

40. *See Bryan*, 58 F.3d at 946, 949.

41. 511 U.S. 164 (1994).

42. *Id.* at 178 (quoting Musick, Peeler & Garrett v. Employers Ins., 508 U.S. 286, 294 (1993)). The court admits this is an "awkward task." Lampf, Pleva, Lipkind, Prupis & Petigrow v. Gilbertson, 501 U.S. 350, 357 (1991). Justice Scalia put it more colorfully: "We are imagining here." *Id.* at 360. Central Bank constrained this imagi-

native process by requiring courts to "use the express causes of action in the securities acts as the primary model for the § 10(b) action." *Central Bank*, 511 U.S. at 178.

43. U.S. v. O'Hagan, 92 F.3d 612, 617–18 (8th Cir. 1996), *rev'd*, 521 U.S. 642 (1997).

44. *Id.*

45. *Id.* at 618.

46. *Id.* at 617.

participants such as investors."[47] Absent such a limitation, the court opined, § 10(b) would be transformed "into an expansive 'general fraud-on-the-source theory' which seemingly would apply infinite number of trust relationships."[48] Such an expansive theory of liability, the court further opined, could not be justified by the text of statute.[49] In the typical misappropriation case, of course, the source of the information is not the affected purchaser or seller. Often the source is not even a contemporaneous purchaser or seller and frequently has no state in any affected securities transaction. Even assuming the misappropriator has deceived the source of the information, one thus must stretch the phrase "in connection with" pretty far in order to bring that fraud within the statute's ambit. As the Fourth Circuit put it in *Bryan*: "The misappropriation of information from an individual who is in no way connected to, or even interested in, securities is simply not the kind of conduct with which the securities laws, as presently written, are concerned."[50]

The Eighth and Fourth Circuits' interpretation of § 10(b) had much to commend it. The courts carefully considered the Supreme Court's relevant precedents, especially *Santa Fe* and *Central Bank*. At least insofar as the misappropriation theory imposes liability solely on the basis of a breach of fiduciary duty to the source of the information, without any requirement that the alleged perpetrator have deceived the persons with whom he traded or other market participants, the theory ran afoul of those precedents.

Yet, these cases potentially challenged not just the misappropriation theory but the entirety of the insider trading prohibition. Although the Fourth Circuit was careful to opine that *Bryan* left intact both the disclose or abstain theory of liability and tipping liability thereunder, arguably this was not the case. The duty at issue in tipping cases is not a duty to disclose, but rather, a duty to refrain from self-dealing in confidential information owed by the tipper to the source of the information. As such, tipping is subject to the same line of attack as the *Bryan* court invoked against the misappropriation theory. Even the basic disclose or abstain theory of liability was called into question by *Bryan*. Granted, insider trading in violation of the disclose or abstain rule involves an element of deception. By definition, the defendant has failed to disclose nonpublic information before trading. The nondisclosure argument is not a very powerful explanation for insider trading liability, however. Persons subject to the disclose or abstain theory often are also subject to a duty of confidentiality, which precludes them from disclosing the information. As we have seen, the insider trading prohibition thus becomes a rule to abstain from trading, rather than a rule requiring disclosure or abstention. In other words, given that the defendant had no

---

47. *Id.* In *Bryan*, the Fourth Circuit similarly opined § 10(b) is primarily concerned with deception of purchasers and sellers of securities, and at most extends to fraud committed against other persons closely linked to, and with a stake in, a securities transaction. 58 F.3d at 946.

48. *O'Hagan*, 92 F.3d at 619 (quoting *Bryan*, 58 F.3d at 950).

49. *Id.*

50. 58 F.3d at 950.

right to disclose, it is the failure to abstain from trading, rather than the nondisclosure, which is the basis for imposing liability. The inexorable logic of both *Bryan* and the Eighth Circuit's *O'Hagan* opinion thus called into question not just the misappropriation theory, but the entire federal insider trading prohibition.[51]

D. THE POLICY BASIS FOR REGULATING INSIDER TRADING

Just as the development of the misappropriation theory exposed the doctrinal anomalies inherent in the insider trading prohibition, it also exposed the lack of a coherent policy justification for the prohibition. Securities fraud is concerned with protection of investors and preservation of investor confidence in the integrity of the securities markets.[52] Yet, as the Fourth and Eighth Circuit's analyses implied, the insider trading prohibition had come to be more about theft of information than investor protection.[53]

Under the post-*Chiarella* framework, investors' rights varied widely depending on the identity of the trader, the nature of the inside information, and the source of that information. Consider *United States v. Carpenter.*[54] R. Foster Winans wrote the Wall Street Journal's "Heard on the Street" column, a daily report on various stocks that was said to affect the price of the stocks discussed. Journal policy expressly treated the column's contents prior to publication as confidential information belonging to the newspaper. Despite that rule, Winans agreed to provide several co-conspirators with prepublication information as to the timing and contents of future columns. His fellow conspirators then traded in those stocks based on the expected impact of the column on the stocks' prices, sharing the profits.

Any duties Winans owed in this situation ran to an entity that had neither issued the securities in question nor even participated in stock market transactions. What Winans' breach of his duties to the Wall Street Journal has to do with the federal securities laws is not immedi-

---

51. Put another way, the nondisclosure argument is circular. As *Chiarella* made clear, and *Dirks* affirmed, not all failures to disclose are fraudulent. Rather, a nondisclosure is actionable only if the trader is subject to a duty to disclose. In turn, a duty to disclose exists only where the trader is subject to a fiduciary duty to refrain from self-dealing in confidential information. Absent such a fiduciary duty, insider trading simply is not fraudulent. Once again, this leaves the disclose or abstain rule subject to the same line of attack as was adopted by the Fourth and Eighth Circuits.

52. *See, e.g.,* Central Bank of Denver, N.A. v. First Interstate Bank of Denver, N.A., 511 U.S. 164, 173 (1994) ("the broad congressional purposes behind the [securities laws are] to protect investors from false

and misleading practices that might injure them").

53. In a telling passage of his partial dissent to a leading Second Circuit opinion endorsing and fleshing out the misappropriation theory, Judge Winter had acknowledged that the misappropriation theory lacked "any obvious relationship" to the statutory text of § 10(b) because "theft rather than fraud or deceit" had become "the gravamen of the prohibition." United States v. Chestman, 947 F.2d 551, 578 (2d Cir. 1991) (Winter, J., concurring in part and dissenting in part), *cert. denied*, 503 U.S. 1004 (1992).

54. 791 F.2d 1024 (2d Cir. 1986), aff'd, 484 U.S. 19 (1987).

ately apparent. The incongruity of the misappropriation theory becomes even more apparent when one considers that its logic suggests that the Wall Street Journal could lawfully trade on the same information used by Winans. If we are really concerned with protecting investors and maintaining their confidence in the market's integrity, the inside trader's identity ought to be irrelevant. As *Texas Gulf Sulphur* recognized, from the investors' point of view, insider trading is a matter of concern because they have traded with someone with superior access to information. From the investor's perspective, it does not matter whether it is Winans or the Journal on the opposite side of the transaction. Both have greater access to the relevant information than do investors.

The logic of the misappropriation theory also suggests that Winans would not have been liable if the Wall Street Journal had authorized his trades. In that instance, his trades would not have constituted an improper conversion of nonpublic information and the essential breach of fiduciary duty would not be present. Again, however, from an investor's perspective, it would not seem to matter whether Winans' trades were authorized or not.

In sum, if investor protection or confidence in the market were the real issues, one would be hard-pressed to defend the pre-*O'Hagan* state of the law. An expansive version of the old equal access test seems far better-suited to advancing those values, but it (supposedly) expired in *Chiarella*. Something else had to be going on.

Pre-*O'Hagan*, there was a growing consensus that the federal insider trading prohibition was more easily justified as a means of protecting property rights in information than as a way of protecting investors.[55] Consider the prototypical insider trading transaction, in which an insider trades in her employer's stock on the basis of information learned solely because of her position with the firm. There is no avoiding the necessity of assigning the property right to either the corporation or the inside trader. A rule allowing insider trading assigns the property right to the insider, while a rule prohibiting insider trading assigns it to the corporation.

The rationale for assigning the property right to the firm is precisely the same as the rationale for prohibiting patent infringement or theft of trade secrets: protecting the economic incentive to produce socially valuable information. As the theory goes, the readily appropriable nature of information makes it difficult for the developer of a new idea to recoup the sunk costs incurred in developing it.[56] If an inventor develops a better mousetrap, for example, he cannot profit on that invention

---

55. *See* Bainbridge, *supra* note 4, at 1252, and authorities cited in *id*. at 1252 n.266. The question for most scholars no longer was whether some form of insider trading regulation is necessary and appropriate to protect property rights in nonpublic information, but whether we should make a federal case of it. *See* Larry E. Ribstein, *Federalism and Insider Trading*, 6 SUP. CT. ECON. REV. 123, 171 (1998) ("Misappropriation of information is wrong, but we should not make a federal case out of it.").

56. ROBERT COOTER & THOMAS ULEN, LAW AND ECONOMICS 119–28 (2d ed. 1997).

without selling mousetraps and thereby making the new design available to potential competitors. Assuming both the inventor and his competitors incur roughly equivalent marginal costs to produce and market the trap, the competitors will be able to set a market price at which the inventor likely will be unable to earn a return on his sunk costs. *Ex post*, the rational inventor should ignore his sunk costs and go on producing the improved mousetrap. *Ex ante*, however, the inventor will anticipate that he will be unable to generate positive returns on his up-front costs and therefore will be deterred from developing socially valuable information. As Judge Ralph Winter explained in his separate opinion in *United States v. Chestman*:

> Information is ... expensive to produce, and, because it involves facts and ideas that can be easily photocopied or carried in one's head, there is a ubiquitous risk that those who pay to produce information will see others reap the profit from it. Where the profit from an activity is likely to be diverted, investment in that activity will decline. If the law fails to protect property rights in commercial information, therefore, less will be invested in generating such information.[57]

Accordingly, society provides incentives for inventive activity by using the patent system to give inventors a property right in new ideas. By preventing competitors from appropriating the idea, the patent allows the inventor to charge monopolistic prices for the improved mousetrap, thereby recouping his sunk costs. Trademark, copy-right, and trade secret law all are justified on similar grounds.

Granted, this argument may not provide quite as compelling a justification for the insider trading prohibition as it does for the patent system. Legalizing insider trading likely would have a much smaller impact on the corporation's incentive to develop new information than would, say, legalizing patent infringement. It seems plausible, however, that insider trading will have at least some impact on the incentive to produce new information. Again, Judge Winter explains:

> [I]nsider trading creates a risk that information will be prematurely disclosed by such trading, and the corporation will lose part or all of its property in that information. Although trades by an insider may rarely affect market price, others who know of the insider's trading may notice that a trader is unusually successful, or simply perceive unusual activity in a stock and guess the information and/or make piggyback trades. A broker who executes a trade for an [insider] may well draw relevant conclusions. Or, as in the instant matter, the trader ... may tell his or her broker about the inside information, who may then trade on his or her account, on clients' accounts, or may tell friends and relatives. One inside trader has publicly attributed his exposure in part to the fact that the bank through which he

57.　947 F.2d 551, 576–77 (2d Cir. 1991)　503 U.S. 1004 (1992).
(Winter, J., dissenting in part), *cert. denied,*

made trades piggybacked on the trades, as did the broker who made the trades for the bank. Once activity in a stock reaches an unusual stage, others may guess the reason for the trading—the corporate secret. Insider trading thus increases the risk that confidential information acquired at a cost may be disclosed. If so, the owner of the information may lose its investment.[58]

Even if one is skeptical that insider trading poses the sort of threats Winter identifies, the affirmative case for assigning the property right to the corporation is demonstrably stronger than the one for assigning it to the insider, as has been explained earlier.[59] The law therefore should assume (although the assumption sometimes may be wrong) that assigning the property right to the firm maximizes the social incentives for the production of valuable new information.

There are essentially two ways of assigning a property right to information: allowing the owner to enter into transactions without disclosing the information, or prohibiting others from using the information. In effect, the federal insider trading prohibition vests a property right of the latter type in the owner of nonpublic information. To be sure, enforcement of the insider trading prohibition differs rather dramatically from enforcement of, say, trespassing laws. In context, however, the prohibition's enforcement mechanisms are not inconsistent with a property rights analysis. Where public policy argues for giving someone a property right, but the costs of enforcing such a right would be excessive, the state often uses its regulatory powers as a substitute for granting a property right. Insider trading poses just such a situation. Private enforcement of the insider trading laws is rare and usually parasitic on public enforcement proceedings.[60] Indeed, the very nature of insider trading makes public regulation essential precisely because private enforcement is almost impossible. The insider trading prohibition's regulatory nature thus need not preclude a property-rights-based analysis.

In fact, there were striking doctrinal parallels between insider trading law pre-*O'Hagan* and other forms of property rights in information. Using another's trade secret is actionable only if taking the trade secret involved a breach of fiduciary duty, misrepresentation, or theft, for example, which was "an equally apt summary of the law of insider trading after *Chiarella* and *Dirks*."[61] In light of such parallels, Winter speculated that the property rights rationale explained both the Supreme Court's decisions in *Chiarella* and *Dirks* and the Second Circuit's adoption of the misappropriation theory.[62]

---

58. *Id.* at 577 (footnote and citations omitted).

59. Bainbridge, *supra* note 4, at 1255–56.

60. Michael P. Dooley, *Enforcement of Insider Trading Restrictions*, 66 VA. L. REV. 1, 15–17 (1980).

61. DOOLEY, *supra* note 30, at 776.

62. United States v. Chestman, 947 F.2d 551, 578 (2d Cir. 1991) (Winter, J., dissenting in part), *cert. denied*, 503 U.S. 1004 (1992).

Perhaps, it is thus not surprising that many aspects of the pre-*O'Hagan* prohibition were more consistent with the property rights justification for the prohibition than they were with a securities fraud-based justification. The basic function of a securities fraud regime is to ensure timely disclosure of accurate information to investors. Yet, the insider trading prohibition did not lead to increased disclosure. Consider the classic disclose or abstain rule as the Second Circuit pronounced it in *Texas Gulf Sulphur*: The rule's name was something of a misnomer, of course. The Second Circuit presumably phrased the rule in terms of disclosure because a key element of an omission case under Rule 10b–5 is that the defendant owed a duty of disclosure to the investor on the other side of the transaction. As a practical matter, however, disclosure was rarely an option. In *Texas Gulf Sulphur*, for example, the company had no affirmative duty to disclose the ore strike. As the Second Circuit correctly noted, the timing of disclosure was a matter for the business judgment of corporate managers, subject to any affirmative disclosure requirements imposed by the stock exchanges or the SEC.[63] In this case, moreover, a valuable corporate purpose was served by delaying disclosure: confidentiality prevented competitors from buying up the mineral rights and kept down the price landowners would charge for them. The company therefore had no duty to disclose the discovery, at least up until the time that the land acquisition program was completed. Given that the corporation had no duty to disclose, and had decided not to disclose the information, the insiders' fiduciary duties to the corporation precluded them from disclosing it for personal gain.

Disclosure by an insider who wishes to trade thus was only feasible if there was no legitimate corporate purpose for maintaining secrecy. These situations, however, presumably are relatively rare—it is hard to imagine many business developments that can be disclosed immediately without working some harm to the corporation. In most cases, the disclose or abstain rule really does not provide the insider with a disclosure option. Instead, the rule collapses into a rule of abstention. Accordingly, as a former SEC Commissioner admitted, "the insider trading rules probably do not result in more information coming into the market: The 'abstain or disclose' rule for those entrusted with confidential information usually is observed by abstention."[64]

It is also telling that many of the prohibition's doctrinal oddities make sense if protection of property rights is the true policy goal.[65]

---

63. SEC v. Texas Gulf Sulphur Co., 401 F.2d 833, 850 n.12 (2d Cir.), *cert. denied*, 394 U.S. 976 (1968).

64. Cox & Fogarty, *supra* note 29, at 353.

65. To be sure, not all aspects of the federal prohibition can be so explained. For example, because property rights generally include some element of transferability, it may seem curious that federal law at least in some circumstances does not allow the owner of nonpublic information to authorize others to use it for their own personal gain. *See, e.g.,* 17 C.F.R. § 240.14e–3(d) (tender offeror may not divulge its takeover plans to anyone likely to trade in target stock). This does not undermine the general validity of the property rights justification. Rather, if protection of property rights is taken as a valid public-regarding policy basis for the prohibition, it gives us a basis for criticizing departures from that norm.

Consider, for example, the apparent incongruity that in Carpenter, Winans could be held liable for trading on information about the Wall Street Journal's "Heard on the Street," but the Journal could have lawfully traded on the same information. As we saw above, this result makes no sense from a traditional securities law perspective. From a property rights perspective, however, the result in *Carpenter* makes perfect sense; because the information belonged to the Journal, it should be free to use the information as it saw fit, while Winans' use of the same information amounted to a theft of property owned by the Journal.

A property rights-based approach also helps make sense of a couple of aspects of *Dirks* that are quite puzzling when approached from a securities fraud-based perspective. One is the court's solicitude for market professionals. After *Dirks*, market analysts were essentially exempt from insider trading liability with respect to nonpublic information they develop because they usually owe no fiduciary duty to the firms they research. *Dirks* thus essentially assigned the property right to such information to the market analyst rather than to the affected corporation. From a disclosure-oriented perspective, this is puzzling—the analyst and/or his clients will trade on the basis of information other investors lack. From a property perspective, however, the rule is justifiable because it encourages market analysts to expend resources to develop socially valuable information about firms and thereby promote market efficiency.[66]

An even more significant puzzle, which also becomes more easily explicable from a property rights perspective, was the Supreme Court's failure in *Chiarella* and *Dirks* to precisely define the basis upon which liability was to be imposed. Did it suffice to show that a fiduciary relationship existed between the inside trader and those with whom she traded (or the source of the information in the case of the misappropriation theory)? Or was it necessary to show that the trade breached a specific fiduciary duty arising out of such a relationship? If the latter, what duty was the relevant one? The court was never very clear on this issue, but a number of passages in *Dirks* implied that it was a breach of the fiduciary duty against self-dealing—not merely the existence of a fiduciary relationship or a breach of a duty of confidentiality—that was at issue. The court, for example, described the elements of an insider trading violation as: "(i) the existence of a relationship affording access to inside information intended to be available only for a corporate purpose, and (ii) the unfairness of allowing a corporate insider to take advantage of that information by trading without disclosure."[67] Another passage likewise describes insider trading liability as arising from "the 'inherent unfairness involved where one takes advantage' of 'information intended to be available only for a corporate purpose and not for the personal benefit of anyone.'"[68] Yet, another noted that insiders are

66. *See* MACEY, *supra* note 30, at 36.

67. Dirks v. SEC, 463 U.S. 646, 653 (1983) (quoting Chiarella v. United States, 445 U.S. 222, 227 (1980)).

68. *Id.* at 654 (quoting In re Merrill Lynch, Pierce, Fenner & Smith, Inc., 43 S.E.C. 933, 936 (1968)).

"forbidden by their fiduciary relationship from using undisclosed corporate information for their personal gain."[69] The focus in each instance is on the duty to refrain from self-dealing. From a disclosure-oriented approach, in which maximizing disclosure is the principal policy goal, such a focus makes no sense, because requiring such a breach limits the class of cases in which disclosure is made. In contrast, from a property rights perspective, these passages make perfect sense, because they focus attention on the basic issue of whether the insider had converted information belonging to the corporation.

E. *O'HAGAN*

In *United States v. O'Hagan*,[70] the Supreme Court revisited the post-*Chiarella* insider trading prohibition in order to determine the validity of the misappropriation theory. James O'Hagan was a partner in the Minneapolis law firm of Dorsey & Whitney. In July 1988, Grand Metropolitan PLC (Grand Met) retained Dorsey & Whitney in connection with its planned takeover of Pillsbury Company. Although O'Hagan was not one of the lawyers on the Grand Met project, he learned of their intentions and began buying Pillsbury stock and call options on Pillsbury stock. When Grand Met announced its tender offer in October, the price of Pillsbury stock rose to nearly $60 per share. O'Hagan then sold his Pillsbury call options and common stock, making a profit of more than $4.3 million. O'Hagan subsequently was indicted and convicted on various charges, the most pertinent of which for our purposes was that he violated § 10(b) and Rule 10b–5 by trading on misappropriated nonpublic information.[71] On appeal, the Eighth Circuit reversed O'Hagan's conviction, becoming the second court of appeals (joining the Fourth Circuit) to reject the misappropriation theory. The Supreme Court granted *cert* to resolve the resulting circuit split.

The court now had an opportunity to rethink the entire problem. How did the federalism principles of *Santa Fe* apply to insider trading? What about the statutory interpretation methodology of *Central Bank*? Unfortunately, the court's answers to these questions managed to (1) create new and potentially challenging doctrinal problems; (2) exacerbate the doctrinal tensions between the prohibition on the one hand and both *Central Bank* and *Santa Fe* on the other, and (3) weaken the protections

---

69. *Id.* at 659.

70. 521 U.S. 642 (1997), *rev'g*, 92 F.3d 612 (8th Cir. 1995).

71. O'Hagan was also indicted for violations of Rule 14e–3, which proscribes insider trading in connection with tender offers, and the federal mail fraud and money laundering statutes. The Eighth Circuit overturned O'Hagan's convictions under those provisions. As to Rule 14e–3, the court held that the SEC lacked authority to adopt a prohibition of insider trading that does not require a breach of fiduciary duty. *O'Hagan*, 92 F.3d at 622–27. As to O'Hagan's

mail fraud and money laundering convictions, the Eighth Circuit also reversed them on grounds that the indictment was structured so as to premise the charges under those provisions on the primary securities fraud violations. *Id.* at 627–28. Accordingly, in view of the court's reversal of the securities fraud convictions, the latter counts could not stand either. The Supreme Court reversed on all points, reinstating O'Hagan's convictions under all of the statutory violations charged in the indictment. United States v. O'Hagan, 521 U.S. 642 (1997).

the prohibition provides owners of nonpublic information. In most respects, the court left Rule 10b–5 in a worse state than it found it.

1. The Holding

The Supreme Court reversed the Eighth Circuit, thereby confirming that the misappropriation theory is a valid basis on which to impose insider trading liability. The majority (per Justice Ginsburg) acknowledged that misappropriators such as O'Hagan have no disclosure obligation running to the persons with whom they trade. Instead, it grounded liability under the misappropriation theory on deception of the source of the information. A fiduciary's undisclosed use of information belonging to his principal, without disclosure of such use to the principal, for personal gain constitutes fraud in connection with the purchase or sale of a security and thus violates Rule 10b–5.

Although the court thus rejected the Fourth and Eighth Circuits' position, the version of the misappropriation theory it endorsed differed from that which had been crafted by the lower courts. The majority explained that its version of the misappropriation theory addressed the use of "confidential information for securities trading purposes, in breach of a duty owed to the source of the information."[72] Accordingly, "a fiduciary's undisclosed, self-serving use of a principal's information to purchase or sell securities, in breach of a duty of loyalty and confidentiality, defrauds the principal of the exclusive use of that information."[73] Someone thus can be held liable under this version of the misappropriation theory only where they have deceived the source of the information by failing to disclose their intent to trade on the basis of the information disclosed by the source. This requirement follows, the majority opined, from the statutory requirement that there be a "deceptive device or contrivance" used "in connection with" a securities transaction.[74] The Supreme Court thus rejected Chief Justice Burger's argument in *Chiarella* that the misappropriation theory created disclosure obligation running to those with whom the misappropriator trades.[75] Instead, it is the failure to disclose one's intentions to the source of the information that constitutes the requisite disclosure violation under the *O'Hagan* version of the misappropriation theory.

O'Hagan posed at least as many new questions as it answered old ones. Among these were:

Liability for brazen misappropriators? The *O'Hagan* majority made clear that disclosure to the source of the information is all that is required under Rule 10b–5. If a brazen misappropriator discloses his trading plans to the source, and then trades on that information, Rule 10b–5 is not violated.[76] As we shall see, this is an odd result that jibes

---

72. *Id.* at 652.

73. *Id.*

74. *Id.* at 653.

75. *Id.* at 654 n.6.

76. *Id.* at 655 ("full disclosure forecloses liability under the misappropriation theory .... If the fiduciary discloses to the source that he plans to trade on nonpublic infor-

with neither the property rights nor the securities fraud rationale for regulating insider trading.

Liability for authorized trading? Suppose, for example, a takeover bidder authorized an arbitrageur to trade in a target company's stock on the basis of material nonpublic information about the perspective bidder's intentions. Warehousing of this sort is proscribed by Rule 14e–3, but only insofar as the information relates to a perspective tender offer. Whether such trading in a non-tender offer context violated Rule 10b–5 was unclear. The *O'Hagan* majority at least implicitly validated authorized trading of this sort. It approvingly quoted, for example, counsel for the United States' comment that "to satisfy the common law rule the trustee may not use the property that [has] been entrusted [to] him, there would have to be consent."[77]

The fiduciary relationship requirement: Does a duty to disclose to the source of the information arise before trading in all fiduciary relationships? Consider ABA Model Rule of Professional Conduct 1.8(b), which states: "A lawyer shall not use information relating to representation of a client to the disadvantage of the client unless the client consents after consultation. . . ." Does a lawyer's use of confidential client information for insider trading purposes always operate to the client's disadvantage? If not, O'Hagan did not violate § 10(b). The *O'Hagan* majority simply ignored this problem.

Criminal or civil?: In rejecting the Eighth Circuit's argument that Rule 10b–5 is primarily concerned with deception of market participants, the majority noted that the discussion in *Central Bank* upon which the Eighth Circuit relied dealt only with private civil litigation under § 10(b). The court then went on to discuss its holding in *Blue Chip Stamps* that only actual purchasers or sellers of securities have standing to bring private causes of action under Rule 10b–5.[78] The court concluded: "Criminal prosecutions do not present the dangers the court addressed in *Blue Chip Stamps*, so that decision is 'inapplicable' to indictments for violations of § 10(b) and Rule 10b–5."[79] This passage opens the door for misappropriators to argue that *O'Hagan* should be limited to criminal prosecutions, because the majority acknowledged the limitations imposed by *Central Bank* and *Blue Chip Stamps* on private party litigation.

2. Status of Central Bank and Santa Fe

The *O'Hagan* majority essentially orphaned *Central Bank*. Justice Ginsburg largely ignored the statutory text, except for rather glib assertions with respect to the meaning of the phrases "deception" and

---

mation, there is no 'deceptive device' and thus no § 10(b) violation").

77. *Id.* at 654. Footnote 7 to the majority opinion, however, suggests that on these facts O'Hagan would need approval from both Dorsey & Whitney and Grand Met. *Id.* at 655 n.7.

78. *Id.* at 664 (discussing Blue Chip Stamps v. Manor Drug Stores, 421 U.S. 723 (1975)).

79. *Id.* (citations omitted).

"in connection with." She likewise ignored the cogent arguments advanced by both the Eighth and Fourth Circuits with respect to the implications of *Central Bank* for the misappropriation theory.[80] Most importantly, she ignored the interpretive methodology expounded in *Central Bank*.[81] One is therefore left to wonder whether the strict textualist approach taken by *Central Bank* was an aberrational departure from the more policy-sensitive approach that exemplified Supreme Court securities law decisions prior to *Central Bank*.[82]

With regard to *Santa Fe*, Justice Ginsburg correctly described that case as "underscoring that § 10(b) is not an all-purpose breach of fiduciary duty ban; rather it trains on conduct involving manipulation or deception."[83] Instead of acknowledging that insider trading is mainly a fiduciary duty issue, however, she treated it as solely a disclosure issue. It is thus the failure to disclose that one is about to inside trade that is the problem, not the trade itself: "A fiduciary who '[pretends] loyalty to the principal while secretly converting the principal's information for personal gain' ... 'dupes' or defrauds the principal."[84] As Justice Ginsburg acknowledged, this approach means that full disclosure must preclude liability.

Granted, insider trading involves deception in the sense that the defendant by definition failed to disclose nonpublic information before trading. As we have seen, however, persons subject to the disclose or abstain theory often are also subject to a state law-based fiduciary duty of confidentiality, which precludes them from disclosing the information. As to them, the insider trading prohibition thus becomes a rule to abstain from trading, rather than a rule requiring disclosure or abstention. Even if such a duty did not exist, moreover, identifying the parties to whom the requisite disclosure must be made presents an insurmountable obstacle in cases involving trading on an impersonal stock exchange. As such, *O'Hagan* collapses the prohibition into a rule that all fiduciaries must abstain from trading on material nonpublic information. In other words, it really is the failure to abstain from trading, rather than the nondisclosure, which is the basis for imposing liability. The nondisclosure thus remains wholly incidental to the violation, which remains a

---

80. To the extent the majority discussed Central Bank's implications for the problem at hand, it focused on dismissing the Eighth Circuit's argument that Central Bank limited Rule 10b–5's regulatory purview to purchasers and sellers. *Id.*

81. Strikingly, *Central Bank*'s author (Justice Scalia) dissented from the majority's Rule 10b–5 holding, relying on the "unelaborated statutory language." *Id.* at 679.

82. The majority's interpretation of the phrase "in connection with," as used in § 10(b), is especially troubling. Fraudulent conduct having only a slight connection with a securities transaction thus is now within the scope of Rule 10b–5. There has long been a risk that Rule 10b–5 will become a universal solvent, encompassing not only virtually the entire universe of securities fraud, but also much of state corporate law. The minimal contacts O'Hagan requires between the fraudulent act and a securities transaction substantially exacerbate that risk. The uncertainty thus created as to Rule 10b–5's parameters fairly raises vagueness and related due process issues.

83. *O'Hagan*, 521 U.S. at 655.

84. *Id.* at 653–64.

breach of fiduciary duty. *Santa Fe* thus remains a serious obstacle for the misappropriation theory.

Justice Ginsburg may or may not have recognized this problem. In either case, her opinion provides a solution, but only at the expense of gutting *Santa Fe* of its principal meaning. Her majority opinion dismissed *Santa Fe* as a mere disclosure case: "in *Santa Fe Industries*, all pertinent facts were disclosed by the persons charged with violating § 10(b) and Rule 10b–5; therefore, there was no deception through nondisclosure to which liability under those provisions could attach."[85] In effect, by ignoring them, Justice Ginsberg has relegated to the sideline the serious federalism concerns that drove *Santa Fe.*

The conceptual conflict between the Supreme Court's insider trading jurisprudence and its more general Rule 10b–5 precedents thus remained unresolved post-*O'Hagan*. Unfortunately, in the subsequent 10–plus years, the Supreme Court has not returned to the basic problem of defining insider trading. Those tensions thus remain very much alive today.

3. *O'Hagan* and the Property Rights Rationale

In this essay, I have not tried to hide the ball—it should be clear by now that I believe the Supreme Court should have used Judge Winter's opinion in *Chestman* as a model for deciding *O'Hagan*. As we have seen, Judge Winter acknowledged that the misappropriation theory lacked any real connection to, or justification under, traditional securities fraud concepts. Instead, as he also recognized, protection of the source of the information's property rights therein is the strongest justification for a continued prohibition of insider trading. Using language that smacked of path dependence, Judge Winter opined that the technical doctrinal problems posed by the misappropriation theory should be overlooked so as to preserve the policy benefits the theory provided.

The Supreme Court thus should have treated the prohibition's location in the federal securities laws as a historical accident, which has some continuing justification in the SEC's comparative advantage in detecting and prosecuting insider trading on stock markets.[86] The court then should have focused on the problem as one implicating fiduciary duties with respect to property rights in information, rather than deceit or manipulation. The court should have forthrightly acknowledged that this interpretation of the federal insider trading prohibition ran afoul of *Central Bank* and *Santa Fe*. Unfortunately, as the Eighth and Fourth Circuit opinions persuasively demonstrated, there does not appear to be any way of preserving the misappropriation theory—and perhaps the prohibition itself—without running afoul of those precedents.

---

85. *Id.* at 655 (citations omitted).

86. *See* Bainbridge, *supra* note 4, at 1262–66 (arguing that the SEC has a substantial comparative advantage in detecting and prosecuting insider trading, which makes insider trading a unique form of fiduciary duty violation).

The court could have justified setting aside those precedents in this context by accepting the full implications of Chief Justice Rehnquist's observation that Rule 10b–5 is "a judicial oak which has grown from little more than a legislative acorn."[87] In other words, the court could have treated the insider trading prohibition as a special case of judge-made federal common law, whose continued existence is justified by prudential considerations rather than either the precise statutory language of § 10(b) or doctrinaire federalism.

The majority chose not to do so. Instead, as we have seen, it voluntarily strapped itself into the securities fraud straightjacket. In doing so, its contribution to resolving the doctrinal tension between the insider trading prohibition and its *Central Bank* and *Santa Fe* precedents consisted solely of providing ammunition for those who wish to gut those opinions.

The only remaining question is whether the majority did as much damage to the policy basis of the prohibition as it did to the doctrine. As it turns out, the majority opinion is something of a mixed bag. Both proponents and opponents of the property rights rationale will be able to quote passages indicating support for their position, but neither should take much comfort from *O'Hagan*. The basic problem is that the majority appears to have no clearer understanding of the policy issues at stake than it did of the doctrinal ones.

The majority opinion began promisingly enough, with an acknowledgement that confidential information belonging to corporations "qualifies as property."[88] The court's authorized trading dictum also is consistent with the property rights rationale, while being demonstrably inconsistent with traditional securities law-based policy justifications for the insider trading prohibition.[89] There is a general presumption that property rights ought to be alienable. If we are concerned with protecting the source of the information's property rights therein, accordingly, we generally ought to permit the source to authorize others to trade on that information.[90] In contrast, legalizing authorized trading makes little sense if the policy goal is the traditional securities fraud concern of protecting investors and maintaining their confidence in the integrity of the markets. Would an investor who traded with O'Hagan

87. Blue Chip Stamps v. Manor Drug Stores, 421 U.S. 723, 737 (1975).

88. *O'Hagan*, 521 U.S. at 654.

89. Indeed, one might almost argue that the majority gave too much protection to property rights in information. The logic of the *O'Hagan* majority suggests that any undisclosed use of a principal's property by an agent constitutes the requisite deception. Suppose, for example, O'Hagan had ordered the shares in question by a long distance telephone call to his broker and billed the call to the firm without its knowl-edge or consent. (The example is taken from Painter et al., *supra* note 34, at 178.) In such a case, there has been a deception that was consummated when the thief bought the securities. As such, the thief—by Justice Ginsburg's logic—has used a deceptive device in connection with the purchase of a security and has violated Rule 10b–5, which seems patently absurd.

90. *See* Stephen M. Bainbridge, *Insider Trading under the Restatement of the Law Governing Lawyers*, 19 J. Corp. L. 1, 37–39 (1993) (noting that mandatory rules may be appropriate in some cases).

feel any better about doing so if she knew that Dorsey and Whitney had authorized O'Hagan's trades?

The authorized trading dictum has significant, but as yet little-noticed implications. Query, for example, whether it applies to all insider trading cases or just to misappropriation cases. Suppose that in a classic disclose or abstain case, such as *Texas Gulf Sulphur*, the issuer's board of directors adopted a policy of allowing insider trading by managers. If they did so, the corporation has consented to any such inside trading, which under Justice Ginsburg's analysis appears to vitiate any deception. The corporate policy itself presumably would have to be disclosed, just as broad disclosure respecting executive compensation is already required,[91] but the implication is that authorized trading should not result in 10b–5 liability under either theory.

The authorized trading dictum might have even broader implications if its logic is extended to Rule 10b–5 generally. Consider, for example, the dictum's implications for a case like *Jordan v. Duff and Phelps, Inc.*,[92] which involved a non-insider trading Rule 10b–5 claim arising out of a merger involving a close corporation. Jordan was a securities analyst who worked for Duff & Phelps, a credit and securities rating firm. Jordan purchased shares in Duff & Phelps pursuant to a shareholders agreement that included, *inter alia*, a mandatory buy back provision triggered by termination of employment, under which a terminated employee would receive book value for his shares. Unbeknownst to Jordan, Duff & Phelps was negotiating a merger with Security Pacific. If affected, shareholders would receive a price considerably in excess of book value. Jordan quit, tendered his stock to the company, received the book value thereof, and later learned that Duff & Phelps was going to be acquired in a leveraged buy-out. Jordan sued under Rule 10b–5, alleging that the failure to disclose the merger negotiations was an omission of a material fact that the company had a duty to disclose. The most interesting aspect, for our purposes, of the resulting opinion is the claim made by Judge Posner's dissent that: "The terms of the stockholder agreement show that there was no duty of disclosure, and since there was no duty there was no violation of Rule 10b–5."[93] In effect, Judge Posner is asserting that the scope of the duty to disclose may be defined by contract. Because the shareholder agreement did not require disclosure, there was no duty to disclose.[94] It is but a short step from that holding to the converse proposition that a party to whom a duty of disclosure is owed may contractually waive that entitlement. The majority (per Judge Easterbrook) agreed with the principle, but thought it inapplicable on the facts:

---

91. Notice that in authorized trading cases that would fall within the misappropriation theory rather than the disclose or abstain rule (i.e., an authorization by the source of market information), neither the source of the information nor the inside trader would have any obligation to disclose to the market or to those with whom the trader transacts. This observation further illustrates the rather tenuous connection between inside trading and securities fraud.

92. 815 F.2d 429 (7th Cir. 1987), *cert. dismissed*, 484 U.S. 901 (1988).

93. *Id.* at 444 (Posner, J., dissenting).

94. *Id.* at 446–47.

It is a violation of duty to steal from the corporate treasury; it is not a violation to write oneself a check that the board has approved as a bonus. We may assume that duties concerning the timing of disclosure by an otherwise-silent firm also may be the subject of contract. Section 29(a) of the Securities Exchange Act of 1934 forbids waivers of the provisions of the Act, and here the critical provision is § 10(b) and the SEC's Rule 10b–5. But a provision must be applicable to be "waived," and the existence of a requirement to speak is a condition of the application of § 10(b) to a person's silence during a securities trade. The obligation to break silence is itself based on state law, and so may be redefined to the extent state law permits. But we need not decide how far contracts can redefine obligations to disclose. Jordan was an employee at will; he signed no contract.[95]

Jordan stands in sharp contrast with the widely-shared assumption that the federal securities laws are mandatory, rather than enabling, and thus not subject to contractual opting out. The authorized trading dictum in *O'Hagan*, however, supports the Easterbrook/Posner position. If mere disclosure of trading intentions suffices to foreclose Rule 10b–5 liability, as Ginsburg stated, then consent to trading must likewise foreclose such liability. If consent to trading on a case-by-case basis forecloses liability, blanket (albeit informed) *ex ante* consent should do likewise. In neither case has the source of the information been deceived. If *ex ante* consent would foreclose insider trading liability, the logical implication is that a consensual waiver of a disclosure obligation should also foreclose Rule 10b–5 liability.

I do not propose here to delve more deeply into the thorny doctrinal and policy issues raised by this reading of *O'Hagan*. Instead, it suffices to predict that this reading of the majority opinion will not command widespread acceptance. The misappropriation theory announced in *O'Hagan* is premised on fraud on the source of the information. In *Carpenter*, for example, liability would be premised on the fraud perpetrated on the Wall Street Journal. Acting through appropriate decision making processes, the Journal could authorize inside trading by its agents. By contrast, however, *Chiarella* focused the classic disclose or abstain rule on fraud perpetrated on the specific investors with whom the insiders trade.[96] Authorization of inside trading by the issuer's board of directors, or even a majority of the shareholders, does not constitute consent by the specific investors with whom the insider trades. Nothing in *O'Hagan* explicitly suggests an intent to undermine the *Chiarella* interpretation of the traditional disclose or abstain rule. To the contrary, Justice Ginsburg expressly stated that the two theories are "complementary."[97] Because the disclose or abstain rule thus remains conceptually distinct from the misappropriation theory, the authorized trading dictum can be plausibly limited to the latter context.

95. *Id.* at 436 (Easterbrook, J.) (citations omitted).

96. Chiarella v. United States, 445 U.S. 222, 232 (1980).

97. *O'Hagan*, 521 U.S. at 652.

Irrespective of whether the foregoing prediction is ratified, the mere fact that the issue arose in the first instance is instructive. Did Justice Ginsburg intend to validate the property rights approach to insider trading? Did she intend to validate contractual waivers of Rule 10b–5 duties? I doubt it. She probably did not even realize that her dictum had implications going beyond the misappropriation context.[98]

Declining to ascribe intentionality to the portions of the majority opinion pointing towards a property rights basis for the prohibition is further justified by the fact that the opinion quickly shifted gears towards treating the problem as one sounding in traditional securities fraud: "Deception through nondisclosure is central to the theory of liability for which the government seeks recognition," and which the majority accepted.[99] Indeed, the incoherence of the majority opinion on policy issues is well-illustrated by its arguable revival of the long-discredited equal access theory of liability. In justifying her claim that the misappropriation theory was consistent with § 10(b), for example, Justice Ginsburg opined that the theory advances "an animating purpose of the Exchange Act: to insure [sic] honest securities markets and thereby promote investor confidence."[100] She went on to claim that "investors likely would hesitate to venture their capital in a market where trading based on misappropriated nonpublic information is unchecked by law,"[101] because those who trade with misappropriators suffer from an informational disadvantage "that cannot be overcome with research or skill."[102] The parallels to *Texas Gulf Sulphur* are obvious. If we want to protect investors from informational disadvantages that cannot be overcome by research or skill, moreover, the equal access test is far better suited to doing so than the *Chiarella/Dirks* framework.

Yet, predictably, the majority showed no greater fidelity to equality of access to information than it did to protection of property rights. Pre-*O'Hagan* it was widely assumed that the misappropriation theory would impose liability on those who steal nonpublic information (such as the sort of industrial espionage Charlie Sheen's character perpetrated in Oliver Stone's movie Wall Street). In *O'Hagan*, however, the majority made clear that disclosure to the source of the information is all that is required under Rule 10b–5. If a misappropriator brazenly discloses his trading plans to the source, and then trades (either with the source's approval or over its objection), Rule 10b–5 is not violated.

The brazen misappropriator dictum is inconsistent with both an investor protection rationale for the prohibition and the property rights justification. As to the former, investors who trade with a brazen misappropriator presumably will not feel any greater confidence in the

---

98. For an argument that bounded rationality and institutional incentives leave the Supreme Court almost incapable of dealing with securities fraud cases, see Stephen M. Bainbridge & G. Mitu Gulati, *How Do Judges Maximize? (The Same Way Everybody Else Does—Boundedly): Rules of Thumb in Securities Fraud Opinions*, 51 Emory L.J. 83 (2002).

99. *O'Hagan*, 521 U.S. at 654.

100. *Id.* at 658.

101. *Id.*

102. *Id.* at 658–59.

integrity of the securities market if they later find out that the misappropriator had disclosed his intentions to the source of the information. As to the latter, requiring the prospective misappropriator to disclose his intentions before trading provides only weak protection of the source of the information's property rights therein. To be sure, in cases in which the disclosure obligation is satisfied, the difficult task of detecting improper trading is eliminated. As the majority pointed out, moreover, the source may have state law claims against the misappropriator. In some jurisdictions, however, it is far from clear whether inside trading by a fiduciary violates state law.[103] Even where state law proscribes such trading, moreover, the Supreme Court's approach means that in brazen misappropriator cases we lose the comparative advantage the SEC has in litigating insider trading cases and the benefit of the well-developed and relatively liberal remedy under Rule 10b–5.

In sum, the internal inconsistencies that plague the majority opinion preclude any reading of *O'Hagan* that ascribes rational intentionality thereto. The opinion fails to cohere as to either policy or doctrine. It forecloses neither the equal access nor the property rights policy rationale for the rule, while also failing to privilege either rationale. Just as a child might break his toy by attempting to force a square peg into a round hole, the Supreme Court made a hash of insider trading law (and Rule 10b–5 generally) by attempting to force insider trading into a paradigm—securities fraud—that does not fit.

103. *See* Bainbridge, *supra* note 4, at 1216–27 (discussing state law on insider trading by corporate counsel, officers, and directors).

Chapter 9

SHAREHOLDER LITIGATION: THE ACCIDENTAL ELEGANCE OF *ARONSON v. LEWIS*

By
David A. Skeel, Jr.

A. INTRODUCTION

"You don't know us," confided the narrator in a long-running television commercial. "We don't make a lot of the products you buy. We make a lot of the products you buy better." The ad's sponsor was a company no ordinary consumer would have ever heard of, but it was (according to the ad) a key component in cassette tapes, Sony electronics equipment and other well-known products. The company was not the household name, but it made the household name products better.

The Delaware Supreme Court decision in *Aronson v. Lewis* occupies a similar status in American corporate law.[1] Unlike many key corporate law decisions, *Aronson*'s issuance in 1984 was not heralded by stories in the *Wall Street Journal* and *New York Times,* nor in any other newspaper of note. Even now, few people other than corporate law experts are likely to recognize the name. Yet *Aronson* plays a pivotal role in many corporate law decisions that get a lot more attention. When shareholders sued Disney's board of directors, alleging that the directors had breached their fiduciary duties by approving an extravagant severance package for one-time Hollywood wunderkind Michael Ovitz, *Aronson* provided the framework for both trial court and Supreme Court rulings that were featured prominently in the press.[2] More recently, allegations that many

* S. Samuel Arsht Professor of Corporate Law, University of Pennsylvania. Thanks to Larry Hamermesh, Larry Mitchell, Leo Strine, the reviewer, and participants at the Murphy Conference on Corporate Law at Fordham University School of Law for comments and discussion on earlier drafts; to Bill Draper for library help; and to the University of Pennsylvania Law School for generous summer funding.

1. 473 A.2d 805 (Del. 1984).

2. *See, e.g.,* In re The Walt Disney Company Derivative Litigation, 825 A.2d 275 (Del. Ch. 2003). The subsequent trial in the Delaware Chancery Court even inspired a Woody Allen spoof in the *New Yorker*.

companies backdated the stock options they awarded to their executives prompted both federal and state court litigation against the companies. As with *Disney*, a Delaware trial court decision was covered in both the general press and the business media;[3] as with *Disney*, *Aronson* lay at the heart of the extensively publicized case. Indeed, *Aronson* may well be the single most frequently cited corporate law case of the past three decades.

Aronson established the parameters for filing derivative litigation against the directors of a corporation (or a third party, but derivative suits against third parties are now rare). A shareholder who sues derivatively alleges that the directors have breached a duty to the corporation, and seeks to pursue the litigation on the corporation's behalf. In effect, the shareholder argues that the corporation should have brought the suit itself, but because it failed to do so, the shareholder would like to step into the company's shoes. The shareholder's right to sue is based on, or "derivative", of the corporation's right—hence, the name.

The derivative mechanism would be unnecessary if companies could be expected to enforce directors' fiduciary duties themselves. But because the corporation's directors are the ones who decide whether the corporation should sue, and because most people do not make a practice of suing themselves, the cases would not be brought unless courts permitted shareholders to bypass the corporation and its board of directors. On the other hand, if courts let shareholders file derivative suits whenever they wished, corporate directors might spend their entire lives defending themselves in litigation. The first great dilemma in derivative litigation is trying to construct a framework that lets potentially meritorious suits go forward, but discourages nuisance or strike suits which are filed simply in an effort to extract a settlement from the company.

The second dilemma arises in derivative litigation against publicly held companies. If the shareholders of these companies have relatively small stakes, they may be unwilling to pursue even meritorious litigation if they must finance it themselves. To counteract this problem, American courts have long permitted plaintiff's attorneys to take their fees from the proceeds of any recovery in the litigation. In effect, this assures that every shareholder contributes to litigation (since the recovery is reduced by the cost of the attorneys' fees), rather than just the shareholders who brought the suit. While this solved one problem, it created another. Plaintiff's attorneys became the real parties in interest in many derivative cases, since they were the biggest beneficiaries if the case succeeded, and they often seemed to focus more on garnering the biggest possible fees for themselves than on the interests of the shareholders they ostensibly represented. Moreover, control of the litigation by plaintiff's attorneys increased the risk of strike suits because the attorneys, unlike

Woody Allen, *Surprise Rocks Disney Trial*,   **3.** Desimone v. Barrows, 924 A.2d 908
New Yorker, Dec. 13, 2004.   (Del.Ch.2007).

a shareholder, would not be hurt if they brought litigation that harmed the company.

Aronson v. Lewis is nested deep within the longstanding effort to devise a framework that sensibly mediates between the competing concerns of encouraging meritorious litigation and screening out strike suits. To provide context, this chapter will briefly survey the history of the derivative litigation, a history that shows US and UK courts adopting very different stances toward derivative litigation and the policing of corporate directors. In the UK, the principal remedy for directorial misbehavior is private action by large shareholders or intervention by regulators, and courts have repeatedly stymied shareholder litigation. US courts, by contrast, helped to facilitate shareholder litigation. After pausing to consider the rise of federal securities litigation (which is "direct" rather than derivative in nature but poses many of the same problems as derivative litigation), we will turn to a controversial Delaware Supreme Court case that set the stage for *Aronson*. In one of the more intriguing quirks of recent corporate law history, the very same justice who had written the first decision two years earlier was also the winning lawyer in *Aronson*, arguing for a position that sharply limited the applicability of his earlier ruling.

B. THE EARLY HISTORY OF THE DERIVATIVE SUIT

An 1843 English case, *Foss v. Harbottle*, looms large in the history of Anglo–American derivative litigation.[4] To be sure, derivative litigation does not really begin with *Foss*. Depending on the flexibility of one's definition, these lawsuits can be traced back an additional century or two, or perhaps even to Rome or the Babylonians. Even in the U.S., most notably but not exclusively in New York, courts had blessed lawsuits that we would now call derivative before 1843. But for two reasons, *Foss* is a convenient starting point. First, courts on both sides of the Atlantic treated the case as a watershed throughout the nineteenth century. Second, the divergent paths of doctrinal development after *Foss* in the U.S. and U.K. provide a revealing perspective on alternative strategies for policing corporate managers.

In *Foss*, a group of shareholders of a nonprofit corporation sought to sue its managers, alleging that the managers had misused their power. Although the court recognized the right of shareholders to sue under some circumstances, it concluded that these particular shareholders were not entitled to proceed because their allegations related to concerns that affected all of the company's shareholders, and the shareholders as a group had not taken formal action. A shareholder plaintiff, the court held, can only sue if the action in question could not have been approved

---

4. 2 Hare 461, 67 Eng. Rep. 189 (Ch. 1843). The best article on the early history of American derivative litigation is a short article published fifty years ago. Bert S. Prunty, *The Shareholders' Derivative Suit:* *Notes on Its Derivation*, 32 N.Y.U. L. Rev. 980 (1957). The details of the next several paragraphs are drawn in large part from this work.

by the shareholders as a group, or if the managers had engaged in fraudulent misrepresentation. (As an alert reader will have noticed, *Foss*'s reputation as the wellspring of derivative litigation is mildly ironic, given that the case says more about the restrictions on derivative litigation than about the legitimacy of this device.)

In England, subsequent nineteenth century cases very clearly bore the imprint of *Foss*, hewing closely to both its letter and its spirit. An 1867 case construed *Foss*'s reference to managerial fraud to authorize minority shareholders to sue a majority block that had defrauded them.[5] In a case decided eight years later, the court treated majority/minority fraud and the fraud exception as one and the same. Under *Foss*, the court said, shareholders can only sue if: 1) the actions in question are ultra vires; or 2) the wrong has been committed by a majority group against the minority.[6] English courts have continued to limit shareholders' right to sue in this fashion ever since. Although several legislative adjustments have been made in recent years in an effort to widen the scope of derivative legislation, they have had very little impact on the frequency of derivative litigation. Derivative litigation has always been extremely uncommon in England, and it remains so today.[7]

Although American derivative litigation seems to have developed from the same roots, a very different tree, with vastly more foliage, emerged in this country in the course of the nineteenth century. Unlike their English brethren, American courts never limited shareholder litigation to cases involving ultra vires acts or fraud by a controlling majority. Several of the early cases were not even aimed at managerial misbehavior; shareholders' real target was a third party. In the best known of the suits, *Dodge v. Woolsey*,[8] a shareholder sought to challenge a state statute that imposed an income tax on the corporation. Because the company's directors were unwilling to pursue the litigation, the Supreme Court agreed that the shareholder could take up the cudgel himself.

While US courts were far more permissive than their British counterparts, shareholders' right to sue derivatively was never absolute. The courts recognized that simply letting any shareholder sue whenever the directors were not willing to do their bidding would wreck havoc on corporate governance. Early on, they began to impose procedural restrictions. Most importantly, shareholders were required to make demand on the directors before suing—that is, a shareholder could not head to the courthouse until she had first asked directors to take action themselves. "I think it is necessary to show, in order to warrant the interference of individual stockholders," a New York judge said in an early case, "that the constituted representatives of the company, whose especial duty it is to vindicate its rights, have been requested to institute proceedings for

---

5. Atwool v. Merryweather, L.R. 5 Eq. 464 (1867).

6. 616 Russell v. Wakefield Waterworks Co., L.R. 20 Eq. 479 (1875).

7. These recent developments and the paucity of UK derivative litigation are

chronicled in John Armour, *Enforcement Strategies in UK Company Law: A Roadmap and Empirical Assessment* (unpublished manuscript, 2007).

8. 59 U.S. (How.) 331 (1856).

that purpose, and have refused to do so."[9] Even with these restrictions, however, shareholders had far more ability to bring a derivative action in the United States than did their counterparts in England.

Not only did US courts define derivative standing quite broadly, but they subsequently encouraged derivative litigation in another way: by giving attorneys an incentive to participate. In ordinary American litigation, each party bears the costs of its own attorneys. While this rule works tolerably well under most circumstances, it discourages the shareholders of widely held corporations from pursuing derivative litigation, even if the managers of their company have acted very badly. If a shareholder holds only a few shares, the costs of pursuing the litigation will almost always dwarf her pro rata share of the expected recovery from the lawsuit. And even if she has a large enough stake to justify taking the laboring oar, she may hesitate to do so, in the hope that someone else will, and will bear the costs, instead. American courts vitiated this problem by applying the "common fund" exception to the usual rule that the plaintiff who brings a suit is saddled with its costs. Under the common fund doctrine, the proceeds of a recovery with numerous beneficiaries is first used to pay attorneys' fees and other costs, before anyone else gets a recovery. In effect, paying the lawyers first forces all of the shareholders to bear the cost, since they (or the corporation) recover only after-attorney dollars.

English judges never went for any of this. Just as they held the line on derivative standing, they never fudged the rules on attorneys' fees to make it easier for shareholders to bring derivative litigation. In England, the ordinary rule for attorneys' fees is that the loser in a lawsuit pays the lawyers for both sides. England's "loser pays" rule is a particularly unattractive prospect for derivative suit plaintiffs. If the suit fails, as many lawsuits do, the shareholder plaintiff is responsible for not just one, but two sets of attorneys' fees. Even shareholders who are not afraid of risk will think twice about making such a wager.

Why were US courts so much more accommodating to the derivative mechanism than their British counterparts? The contrast can perhaps be traced, in part, to differences in corporate evolution in the two countries. As first documented in a famous study by Adolph Berle and Gardiner Means,[10] the shareholdings of many of America's large corporations were widely dispersed by the beginning of the twentieth century. Shareholders' small stakes and distance from the daily operations of the company made it difficult for them to monitor the company's managers. The

9. House v. Cooper, 30 Barb. 157, 158 (N.Y. 1858). U.S. Supreme Court recognition of the demand requirement is often traced to *Hawes v. City of Oakland*, 104 U.S. 450, 460–61 (1881). Some states also required that demand be made on the other shareholders, and precluded suit unless a majority of the shareholders approved. The shareholder demand lost much of its bite over time, however, because courts carved out numerous exceptions. Shareholder demand is generally waived, for instance, if the corporation has numerous shareholders and making demand would therefore be costly or inconvenient.

10. Adolph Berle & Gardiner Means, The Modern Corporation and Private Property (1932).

expansion of derivative litigation, together with the payment of attorneys' fees if the litigation was successful, gave shareholders a tool for policing their managers. "Equity came to the relief of the shareholder," as the Supreme Court put it in 1949, and "allowed him to step into the corporation's shoes and to seek in its right the restitution [against managers who profit personally at the expense of their trust] he could not demand in his own."[11]

In contrast to the US, family control was the norm even with the largest UK corporations until much later.[12] Because shareholders were more actively involved in the company's affairs and could use ordinary internal governance mechanisms such as corporate voting to police its managers, they had less need for a robust external enforcement mechanism like derivative litigation. UK shareholdings did eventually disperse after World War II, but they were still more concentrated than in the US, due in part to tax and dividend policies that encouraged institutions rather than individuals to hold stock.[13]

Differences in corporate ownership do not seem to entirely explain the divergence between the US and UK, however, because the expansion of derivative standing in the US began well before widely scattered shareholdings became a characteristic feature of large US corporations in the early twentieth century. An additional factor may have been the dilemma that gave rise to *Dodge v. Woolsey* and other derivative suits against third parties. The directors' failure to sue in *Dodge* does not seem to have reflected disagreement about the validity of the state income tax in question. The directors worried (one suspects), instead, that it would be a fool's errand for the corporation itself to seek relief in the courts of the state that had imposed the tax. But if the suit were brought by shareholders who lived in another state, the calculus immediately changed, for one simple reason: unlike the corporation itself, out-of-state shareholders could invoke diversity jurisdiction and challenge the statute in federal court. From this perspective, a generous interpretation of derivative standing facilitated challenges to potentially unconstitutional legislation that might not have been possible otherwise. No doubt other factors came into play as well. In short, the divergent evolution of the derivative mechanism in the US and UK seems to have reflected the response of common law courts to the peculiar dynamics of the corporate landscape in each country.

By the 1940s, American derivative litigation had acquired the unsavory reputation that has dogged it ever since. Business leaders harnessed this dissatisfaction by commissioning a study of derivative litigation in New York. Overseen by Franklin Wood for the Chamber of Commerce of the State of New York, the study became known, appropriately enough,

11. Cohen v. Beneficial Industrial Loan Corp., 337 U.S. 541, 548 (1949).

12. *See, e.g.,* Brian R. Cheffins, *History and the Global Corporate Governance Revolution: The UK Perspective*, 43 Bus. Hist.

103 (2001)(UK ownership did not become diffuse until after World War II).

13. This view and its implications for shareholder litigation are outlined in Armour, *supra* note 7.

as the Wood Report. "Although derivative actions have been hailed in some quarters as a wholesome corrective," Wood wrote, "their increase has been accompanied by a considerable body of literature commending improvements and substitutes for such actions, which suggests that . . . the remedy has become maladjusted to the disease. It is hardly possible, certainly, to attribute the increase of such litigation to a decline in business morals since the days of [notorious robber barons] Jim Fisk and Jay Gould."[14]

Wood and his peers examined 1,266 lawsuits brought by shareholders in two New York counties and the U.S. District Court for the Southern District of New York over the ten year period from 1932 to 1942. More than half of the cases (693) involved closely held corporations, but Wood directed most of his attention to the 573 publicly held company cases. The pecuniary recoveries in these cases amounted to only 5% of the amounts alleged in the 2% of cases that were successfully tried, and another 3% in the 6% of cases that produced court approved settlements. The paucity of recoveries, Wood concluded, with the sarcastic tone that makes his report entertaining reading more than sixty years later, "is a record of sorts."[15] The report criticizes the frequency with which the suits were brought by shareholders with little stake in the company, complaining that "the smallest of small investors have suddenly become masters of the most intricate details of corporate finance, and the most alert of sentinels to employ attorneys and attack corporate management on the slightest suspicion of a big lawsuit."[16] The potential benefits to the plaintiffs of success in a recent case, he noted, were $3.57, $.41, $2.51, $.17 and $.65.[17] In reality, Wood concluded, the plaintiffs had very little to do with the litigation at all. They were essentially a front for the plaintiff's attorneys, who were the real beneficiaries of the derivative suits because their fees were paid in full if the litigation provided a benefit to the company. The attorneys' "shoddy burlesque of a professional relationship to the clients," as Wood put it, "makes the ambulance-chaser by comparison a paragon of propriety. He at least represents a real client, with usually real injuries, and a legitimate interest in 50% of the recovery."[18] The attorneys' fees were "among the largest possible for practitioners in any field of law,"[19] and the corporation usually indemnified the directors' fees as well, which meant it essentially bore the costs of both sides.

14. Chamber of Commerce of New York State, Survey and Report Regarding Stockholders' Derivative Suits 96 (1944)(cited hereafter as WOOD REPORT).

15. *Id.* at 7. Wood did acknowledge that private settlements in other cases undoubtedly increased the overall shareholder recoveries.

16. "Women," he notes, "are prominent among these one-suit students of law and finance." *Id.* at 46. Although women are the only group Wood explicitly singles out for disapprobation, Larry Mitchell detects a persistent undercurrent of anti-Semitism

against the largely Jewish plaintiffs' bar throughout the report. Lawrence E. Mitchell, *Gentleman's Agreement: The Anti–Semitic Origins of Restrictions on Stockholder Litigation*, at 10 (unpublished manuscript, 2007)(finding that "21 of the plaintiffs in the 32 listed actions have traditionally Jewish surnames, with an additional seven . . . having arguably Jewish surnames).

17. *Id.* at 49.

18. *Id.* at 47.

19. *Id.* at 11.

It should be noted that Wood had no quarrel with derivative litigation in the close corporation context, as this litigation was usually brought by minority shareholders with a significant stake who alleged misbehavior by the majority. For publicly held firms, on the other hand, derivative litigation needed radical surgery. Indeed, Wood's report was in the nature of a brief (a brief commissioned by the Chamber of Commerce, a leading business group). The solution, he concluded, was to limit standing to shareholders who owned stock at the time of the alleged wrongdoing, and to require the shareholder plaintiff to post security for costs in the event the litigation were found to have been without merit.

With an alacrity that reflected the influence of business, the seriousness of the flaws in the derivative mechanism, the persuasiveness of Wood's handiwork, or some combination of the three, the New York legislature enacted the nation's first security for expenses statute the same month the report was issued. Under the New York provision, a plaintiff was required to post "security for reasonable expenses, including attorneys' fees," unless the plaintiff owned at least "5% or $50,000 worth of the company's stock."[20] For those who viewed derivative litigation as an essential tool for monitoring the managers of large corporations, the new provision was a worrisome development. In an article published within months of the Wood Report, a leading scholar of shareholder litigation lambasted the Wood report and predicted that the reforms it inspired meant "the death knell of stockholders' derivative suits in New York."[21] Few shareholders held 5% of the stock of the nation's largest corporations, the article pointed out, and only the wealthy ("who presumably can be persuaded not 'to upset the apple cart' "[22]) could hold $50,000 worth of stock. The article concluded that, given the cost of posting bond, and the inevitable riskiness of these suits, few shareholders will be willing to sue. "Since all means of control other than the stockholder's suit are expressly rejected by the Report . . ., the practical abolition of stockholders' suits constitutes an invitation to corporate management to repeat the scandalous behavior exposed during the past ten years on governmental investigations and in 46 successful civil suits in the three courts studied"[23] by the Wood report.

Although derivative litigation may indeed have been chilled for a time, the prophesies of its demise were greatly exaggerated. Twenty years later another commentator reported, based on anecdotal evidence and a quick survey of the West's *Decennial Digest*, that the number of derivative suits had grown dramatically from 1956–1966, as compared to the previous decade.[24] Courts and legislatures had lowered the barriers to

---

20. Ch. 668, sec. 61–b [1944] N.Y. Laws 1455 (later amended by NY Bus. Corp. Law sec. 67).

21. George D. Hornstein, *The Death Knell of Stockholders' Derivative Suits in New York*, 32 Calif. L. Rev. 123 (1944). *See also* Sergei S. Zlinkoff, *The American Investor and the Constitutionality of Section 61–B of the New York General Corporate Law*,

54 Yale L.J. 352 (1945)(criticizing the legislation).

22. Hornstein, infra note 21, at 143.

23. Hornstein, infra note 21, at 144.

24. Daniel J. Dykstra, *The Revival of the Derivative Suit*, 116 U. Pa. L. Rev. 75 (1967).

derivative litigation in a variety of ways. To ease the bite of the security for expenses statutes, for instance, they let shareholders band together to clear the $50,000 threshold. Courts also held that these state procedural strictures did not apply to litigation brought under the federal securities acts. The freedom from state procedural impediments enjoyed by litigation based on the securities acts was one of several developments that would make securities litigation especially attractive for aggrieved investors, as we shall see in a moment. For now, the principal point is simply that by the mid 1960s, derivative litigation was once again alive and well.

C. SECURITIES CLASS ACTIONS AND THE EXPANDING SCOPE OF SECURITIES LAW

Derivative litigation has never been the only option for suing corporate directors who have allegedly violated their fiduciary duties. If a shareholder has been personally harmed by the directors' misbehavior, she can sue directly rather than bringing a derivative action on behalf of the firm. By suing directly, a plaintiff (and her attorney, of course) sidesteps all of the nettlesome prerequisites that complicate derivative litigation: no need to worry about demand on the directors, security for expenses, or any of the other special obstacles to derivative litigation. If the plaintiff wins, moreover, any recovery comes straight to her rather than going first (and sometimes only) to the corporation.

From the plaintiff's perspective, suing directly thus is a dream by comparison to the derivative mechanism. But it has two obvious limitations. The first is that the plaintiff must persuade the court that the injury is indeed direct. The line between direct and derivative in caselaw is fuzzy, to put it charitably, but courts tend to treat allegations of general mismanagement as derivative (the initial victim of the harm is the company itself; shareholders are harmed only indirectly, since the deterioration in the value of the company lowers the value of their shares), while interference with the incidents of a share of stock, such as its voting rights, is characterized as a direct harm. Second, the small stakes of most shareholders in a large corporation make solo litigation unattractive both for them and for an attorney.

The advent of large scale securities litigation in the 1960s addressed both of these concerns, dramatically reshaping the landscape of shareholder litigation. The Securities Acts of 1933 and 1934 had introduced a handful of causes of action for investors who are harmed in connection with the purchase, sale, or voting of securities.[25] These causes of action are direct, but the provisions that explicitly invited investors to sue were confined to relatively limited events such as the purchase of stock in connection with an initial public offering. They were also subject to

---

25. These provisions, which include sections 11, 12, 13 and 15 of the 1933 Act and sections 9, 16, 18 and 20 of the 1934 Act, are listed and described in David S. Ruder, *Civil Liability Under Rule 10b–5: Judicial Revision of Legislative Intent?*, 57 Nw. U.L. Rev. 627, 648–49 (1963).

restrictions quite similar to the derivative suit prerequisites, such as a security for expenses provision (as well as a short statute of limitations).

The dramatic expansion of federal securities litigation would come not from any of these provisions, however, but from two broad antifraud provisions in the 1934 Act, section 10(b) and section 14(a), neither of which explicitly authorized private shareholder litigation. Shareholder plaintiffs and their lawyers argued that they had an implied right to sue under these two antifraud provisions. "[I]t is likely that the Congressmen involved [in the enactment of the securities acts] would ... have been amazed if told that the acts which they were passing would have the effect of granting an implied private right of action," the leading academic critic of these suits groused.[26] But courts increasingly allowed the suits to go forward, and the Supreme Court gave its imprimatur in 1964.[27] To make matters better, at least from the defendants' perspective, courts held that these suits were not subject either to the procedural restrictions that applied to the other, explicitly authorized causes of action, or, as we have seen, to the state law restrictions imposed on derivative litigation.[28]

The SEC fueled the growth of federal securities litigation by steadily expanding the scope of the 1934 Act in general, and Rules 14 and 10b–5 in particular. Although the proxy rules apply only to publicly held companies, the SEC defined publicly held to include not only companies listed on the national exchanges, but any company with at least $1 million in assets and 500 shareholders.[29] Of even greater moment, the Commission, under its activist Chairman William Cary, interpreted Rule 10b–5 to prohibit inside trading both by insiders and wide range of other actors, and it used the rule to police any misdisclosure made by the company. In one of its most important rulings, the SEC marveled at its own handiwork, praising the "wholly new and far-reaching body of federal corporation law," and quoted from a recent case that had described Rule 10b–5 as "a potent weapon for enforcement of many fiduciary duties."[30]

The last piece in the puzzle was the class action device. If the litigation was framed as a class action representing many or all of a company's shareholders as opposed to solo litigation, it would be worthwhile for attorneys to pursue even if any given shareholder's stake was small. In the 1960s, the usefulness of the class action strategy was

26. *Id.* at 654.

27. J.I. Case Co. v. Borak, 377 U.S. 426 (1964).

28. Here, too, David Ruder sounded a dissenting note. It is "not unreasonable to suggest," he wrote, "that Congress might be interested in providing limitations on liability similar to those contained in the 1933 and 1934 acts." David S. Ruder, *Pitfalls in the Development of a Federal Law of Corporations by Implication Through Rule 10b–5*, 59 Nw. U.L. Rev. 185, 207 (1964).

29. 15 U.S.C. sec. 77l(g)(added by 1964 amendments to the 1934 act). The dollar amount has been adjusted in recent years to account for inflation, and is currently $10 million. 17 C.F.R. sec. 240.12g–1.

30. In the Matter of Cady, Roberts & Co., CCH FED. SEC. L. REP. Para 76803, at 81016 (1961)(quoting McClure v. Borne Chemical Co., Inc., 292 F.2d 824, 834 (3d Cir. 1961)).

greatly enhanced by the redrafting of Federal Rule of Civil Procedure 23.2.[31] Although originally intended to strengthen enforcement of the civil rights laws, the new Rule 23 quickly became an important feature of securities litigation, as well as direct shareholder litigation under state law.[32] Securities class actions had all of the benefits of a derivative suit, but none of the pesky limitations. They quickly became the avenue of choice for many lawsuits that might previously have been brought as state law derivative suits.

In the 1970s, the pendulum shifted back, as the Supreme Court began to narrow the scope of securities litigation. Of particular importance for our purposes, the Court held that Rule 10b–5 could not be used to police violations by directors or officers of their fiduciary duties.[33] Fiduciary duty was the province of state corporate law, according to the Court, and Congress did not intend to subsume it into the antifraud provisions of the securities laws. In other cases, the Court limited relief to investors who had actually bought or sold securities (denying relief to those who claimed they were tricked into holding their stock rather than selling by the defendants' misstatements) and held that Rule 10b–5 required a showing of scienter—it was not enough to show that the defendant had acted negligently.[34]

Both federal securities class actions and state law derivative suits have continued to be controversial. In the decades after the Wood Report, researchers conducted several subsequent studies of shareholder litigation. In the best known and most influential of these studies, Roberta Romano studied every shareholder suit brought against a publicly held firm from the late 1960s through 1987, and compared them to a random sample of publicly held companies.[35] Based on her findings that large majorities of the cases settle and that the per share recoveries in the settlements are generally small, Romano states that the "data support the conclusion that shareholder litigation is a weak, if not ineffective, instrument of corporate governance."[36] Defenders of shareholder litigation argue, among other things, that many of the settlements in the cases actually are quite large in absolute terms; and that

---

31. These changes also added Federal Rule 23.1, which requires the plaintiff in a derivative suit to describe "efforts, if any, made by the plaintiff to obtain the action the plaintiffs desires from the directors . . . and the reasons for the plaintiff's failure to obtain the action or for not making the effort." The rule thus incorporates the demand requirement for derivative cases brought in federal court, while leaving the content of the requirement to state law.

32. The most prominent source of state law corporate class actions is litigation over an acquisition or sale. These suits are direct because the price obtained for shareholders is not a corporate cause of action. A recent study of litigation in Delaware found that nearly 79% of the fiduciary duty actions filed in Delaware were class actions, and nearly all of these arise in the acquisition context. Robert B. Thompson & Randall S. Thomas, *The Public and Private Faces of Derivative Lawsuits*, 57 VAND. L. REV. 1747, 1762 & Tbl 2 (2004).

33. Santa Fe Industries, Inc. v. Green, 430 U.S. 462 (1977).

34. Blue Chip Stamps v. Manor Drug Stores, 421 U.S. 723 (1975)(purchase-sale requirement); Ernst & Ernst v. Hochfelder, 425 U.S. 185 (1976)(scienter).

35. Roberta Romano, *The Shareholder Suit: Litigation without Foundation?*, 7 J.L. ECON. & ORG. 55 (1991).

36. *Id.* at 84.

the threat of suit may deter managerial misbehavior even if the litigation does not produce substantial benefits for the particular corporation involved. For present purposes, we should note (while sidestepping the debate over efficacy) that Romano's study, like much discussion of shareholder litigation, lumps federal securities class actions and state derivative suits together. While I too have emphasized some of the commonalities, there may be good reasons for viewing them differently in the end, as we shall see.

D. *ZAPATA v. MALDONADO*

If the general background to Delaware's decision in *Aronson v. Lewis* was the never ending debate about whether shareholder litigation is a valuable tool for policing managers or simply a get rich quick scheme for plaintiffs' attorneys, the immediate background was a case called *Zapata Corp. v. Maldonado.*[37] *Zapata* was the Delaware Supreme Court's much-awaited response to a clever new strategy by corporate directors to take control of (and thus to kill) derivative litigation that previously would have proceeded without interference.

Zapata nicely illustrates the strategy. *Zapata* arose after the directors of Zapata Corporation moved back the exercise date of their stock option plan, so that they could exercise the options before they announced the company's intention to make a tender offer for its own shares at a hefty premium over the current price. If they bought the stock while the stock price was still low, the directors would have a much lower tax bill on their gains (the difference between the lower stock price, rather than the higher one, and their exercise price). Unfortunately, the same maneuver also would reduce the size of the company's tax deduction for the cost of compensation (which was a deductible business expense), since the deduction was based on the same calculation as the directors' personal tax bill. Pushing back the exercise date personally benefited the directors, in other words, but hurt the company to precisely the same extent. Shareholders brought a derivative suit against the Zapata directors alleging that the options sleight-of-hand violated their duty of loyalty.

In the past, directors who had been caught with their hands in the cookie jar like this had no avenue to slow or stymie the litigation's onward march. They had all participated in the decision to move back the exercise date, so demand would clearly be excused. But Zapata's directors had one last trick up their sleeves. Four years after the litigation was initially filed, the directors appointed two new directors to vacancies created by the resignations of several of their peers. The board then created an "Independent Investigation Committee" consisting solely of the two new directors. This committee would determine whether the litigation should continue.

37. 430 A.2d 779 (Del. 1981).

In a much discussed New York decision, the court had given considerable deference to a similarly constituted special litigation committee.[38] Under the New York approach, the court would assess the independence of the directors on the committee and the thoroughness of their investigation. But the committee's substantive decision on the litigation would enjoy the same business judgment rule deference as other directorial decisions.

The New York approach spurred cries of alarm from advocates of derivative litigation. The "independent" committees set up by directors who had been sued invariably concluded that the litigation would simply be too costly, or the prospects of recovery too slim, to justify continuation. Some observers attributed the defendant-colored glasses with which the committees seemed to view litigation to a "structural bias" in board decision making: many board members were beholden to or had long-standing relationships with the company's chief executive and board members tended to come from the same professional and social circles. Given this bias, observers argued, courts should give little deference to the committee's conclusions. "[T]o follow ... the path suggested by the cases to date," one commentator warned, "will certainly mean the virtual death of the derivative suit."[39] If the litigation implicates a majority of the directors, he concluded, the board should never be permitted to dismiss it.[40]

In *Zapata*, Justice William Quillen announced that Delaware would neither defer to the decisions of special committees nor ignore their recommendation. "If, on the one hand, corporations can consistently wrest bona fide derivative actions away from well-meaning derivative plaintiffs through the use of the committee mechanism," he wrote, "the derivative suit will lose much, if not all, of its generally recognized effectiveness as an intra-corporate means of policing corporate directors. If, on the other hand, corporations are unable to rid themselves of meritless or harmful litigation and strike suits, the derivative action, created to benefit the corporation, will produce the opposite, unintended result."[41]

To strike this balance, *Zapata* established a two part test for reviewing a committee recommendation to terminate the litigation. The court should first assess the independence, good faith, and reasonable investigation of the committee, as under the New York approach. But

38. Auerbach v. Bennett, 393 N.E.2d 994 (N.Y. 1979).

39. George W. Dent, Jr., *The Power of Directors to Terminate Shareholder Litigation: The Death of the Derivative Suit?*, 75 Nw. U.L. Rev. 96, 146 (1980).

40. *Id.* at 122, 141–42. In an initial draft of its Principles of Corporate Governance, the American Law Institute's reporters adopted a similar position, holding that a special litigation committee could only be appointed by disinterested directors, and at

least one court followed their lead. *See* Miller v. Register & Tribune Syndicate, Inc., 336 N.W.2d 709 (Iowa 1983). The reporters later eliminated the blanket prohibition. These developments are discussed in Dennis J. Block & H. Adam Prussin, *Termination of Derivative Suits Against Directors on Business Judgment Grounds: From Zapata to Aronson*, 39 Bus. L. 1503, 1518–21 (1984).

41. Zapata Corp. v. Maldonado, 430 A.2d 779 (Del. 1981)(citations omitted).

this would not end the inquiry due, at least in part, to the concerns about psychological bias. Because the "question naturally arises whether a 'there but for the grace of God go I' empathy might play a role" when "directors are passing judgment on fellow directors in the same corporation," Quillen wrote, the analysis should proceed to a second step: "The Court should determine, applying its own independent business judgment, whether the motion should be granted."[42]

This is a radically different standard than the New York approach. The second step speaks in terms of business judgment, but it is the court's own business judgment, not the judgment of corporate businessmen or businesswomen, that determines the litigation's fate. In effect, *Zapata* ripped the decision out of the committee's hands. It also had put the chancery court in the position of deciding whether a corporation should pursue derivative litigation. But it only had these effects in cases where demand would otherwise have been excused. Although *Zapata* itself had nothing to say about the demand futility requirement, this was understandable enough given the circumstances of the case. If ever there were a case where demand would be excused, *Zapata* was it. But the line between demand excused and demand required cases was quite murky in Delaware law, as elsewhere. In Delaware, this distinction had suddenly become extraordinarily important, thanks to the second step of the *Zapata* test.

It was into this breach that *Aronson* sailed.

E. THE CHANCERY COURT DECISION

The complaint in *Aronson* tells a simple tale of behavior that could be viewed as either blandly unobjectionable or patently nefarious, depending on one's point of view and the facts lying behind the plaintiff's five page opening salvo. The plaintiff was a shareholder of Meyers Parking System, Inc., a nationwide network of parking lot facilities that had been spun off from Prudential Building Maintenance Corporation in 1979. Leo Fink, who owned 47% of Meyers' stock and had retired from Prudential in April, 1980, had contracts with both corporations. He had signed a consulting contract with Prudential, 25% of which would be billed to Meyers, and an employment contract with Meyers. The Meyers contract entitled Fink to $150,000 per year, plus a bonus of 5% of every dollar of Meyers's pretax profits over $2,400,000. If either side terminated the agreement, Fink would be employed as a consultant at $150,000 per year for the first three years, $125,000 for the next three, and $100,000 thereafter, whether or not Fink (who was 75 when the agreement began on January 1, 1981) was able to perform any services. He also had received $225,000 in interest free loans. These arrangements, according to the complaint, "were improper, unnecessary, a waste of corporate assets and made for no valid business purpose."[43]

---

42. *Id.* at 787.

43. Complaint, p.3.

The plaintiff sued without first asking the Meyers directors to take action themselves—that is, without making demand. This was not an oversight, of course. The plaintiff insisted that demand should be excused in this case. His explanation, as set forth in paragraph 13 of the complaint, was as follows:

Demand has not been made upon the directors of Meyers to bring this action because such attempt would be futile for the following reasons:

(a) All of the directors in office are named as defendants herein and they have participated in, expressly approved and/or acquiesced in, and are personally liable for, the wrongs complained of herein.

(b) Defendant Fink, having selected each director, controls and dominates every member of the Board and every officer of Meyers.

(c) Institution of this action by present directors would require the defendant directors to sue themselves, thereby placing the conduct of this action in hostile hands and preventing its effective prosecution.[44]

In response, the defendants asked the Chancery Court to dismiss the complaint for failure to make demand. In their briefing in the Chancery Court, the defendants repeatedly emphasized two points: first, the allegations really implicated Fink, not the board as a whole; and second, the attempt to implicate the rest of the board "has relied on conclusory and self-manufactured claims of 'futility' in an effort to avoid the salutory requirements of Rule 23.1," which requires that a derivative suit plaintiff either make demand or state with particularity the reasons for not making demand.[45] "[T]he only fact alleged in support of the allegation of control and domination of Meyers' Board by Mr. Fink," the defendants argued, was "the selection of each member by Mr. Fink."[46]

In his reply memo, the plaintiff reiterated the strong circumstantial links between Fink and the other nine members of Meyers' board. "Fink, through his 47% ownership of Meyers' outstanding stock," plaintiff argued, "dominates and controls each director and officer of Meyers, having selected each such officer and director."[47] Not only is 47% of the stock enough to give effective control of a publicly held company, but Fink, together with the four other directors who also were directors of Meyers, owned 57.5% of the outstanding stock. Plaintiff's response also raised further questions about the legitimacy of Fink's contract with Meyers, stating that "Fink performs little or no services for Meyers and because of his advanced age, cannot be expected to perform any services."[48]

44. Complaint, Para. 13, p.4.

45. Defendants' Memorandum of Law in Support of Their Motion to Dismiss Plaintiff's Complaint, p.9 (Oct. 7, 1982).

46. *Id.* at page 12.

47. Plaintiff's Answering Brief in Opposition to Defendants' Motion to Dismiss the Complaint, p.2 (Oct. 26, 1981).

48. *Id.* at page 4.

By the end of the briefing and oral argument, the key issue seemed clear: what kind of allegations suffice to show that a board of directors is too tainted to make an objective decision whether to pursue a cause of action, so that demand on the board is excused? As with the parties' briefs, it was this issue that occupied much of Vice Chancellor Hartnett's opinion. The Vice Chancellor rejected the links the plaintiff had sought to establish between Fink and the board as a whole. Fink's 47% stock ownership was not by itself sufficient to call into question the impartiality of the board of directors, and plaintiff's allegation that he dominated and controlled the other directors was "merely conclusory and [did] not allege control with particularity" because it was not supported by any "cogent facts."[49] The allegation that Fink was in league with the other officer directors was similarly unavailing because there were "no allegations in the complaint which show that these four directors [were] aligned with Fink."[50]

At this point, the opinion took a surprising turn. After concluding that the plaintiff did not adequately allege that the board itself was tainted, the Vice Chancellor said that a court "often must look for evidence of why approval would have been wrongful," and conducted his own inquiry into the underlying contract.[51] In his view, the provision in Fink's compensation agreement which guaranteed payment even if Fink was unable to perform any services "may have constituted the approval of a transaction wasteful on its face."[52] Because this provision may have been "one which no reasonable man could have approved in the belief that the corporation was getting a *quid pro quo*," the court concluded, demand was excused and the defendants' motion to dismiss must be denied.

In a short addendum attached to the opinion after the defendants asked for the reargument, the Vice Chancellor suggested that his decision to take his own look at the underlying transaction, rather than just the plaintiff's allegations about the directors' complicity, was inspired at least in part by *Zapata*. In order to properly balance shareholders' interest in bringing corporate causes of action with the directors' right to " 'rid [the corporation] of detrimental litigation,' " as *Zapata* instructs, "[e]ach case in which there has been no demand must ... be carefully scrutinized and analyzed according to its own unique set of facts, taking into account the totality of the circumstances and the competing interests."[53]

Before we follow the parties to the Delaware Supreme Court, it is worth mentioning that the *Aronson* case itself seems to have exhibited only one of the qualities that make shareholder litigation controversial. Harry Lewis, the plaintiff, whose only evident involvement in the litiga-

---

49. Lewis v. Aronson, 466 A.2d 375, 382 (Del. Ch.1983).

50. *Id.*

51. *Id.* at 383.

52. *Id.* at 384.

53. *Id.* at 385 (quoting another case that he had recently decided, *Bergstein v. Texas Intern. Co.*, 453 A.2d 467 (Del Ch. 1982), which in turn quotes and discusses *Zapata*).

tion was his serving as the named plaintiff, cropped up in so many cases in the 1970s and early 1980s that he was rumored to be simply a "street name" used by plaintiffs' lawyers. He did exist, however, and by one count his name appeared in 81 judicial opinions in securities cases and derivative litigation.[54]

F. DEFINING DEMAND FUTILITY: THE SUPREME COURT DECISION

The argument in the Delaware Supreme Court was curious in one respect, and as we shall see later, dramatic in another. It was curious in that the unusual trajectory of the Chancery Court opinion put the parties in an odd posture before the Delaware Supreme Court. "The defendants say that they agree with much of the opinion below," as the plaintiff (and appellee in the Delaware Supreme Court) put it, "but disagree with the result ... For his part, the plaintiff finds himself in disagreement with much of the opinion below, but, at the same time, agrees with the result."[55] The defendants praised the Vice Chancellor's conclusion that Fink's 47% stock ownership did not constitute a factual basis for suggesting that he dominated and controlled the board of directors. Even if Fink had owned an absolute majority and could single-handedly select the directors, they argued, this would not show that the directors failed to exercise independent judgment. There was simply no adequate factual allegation that the directors could not be trusted to make an appropriate decision whether to pursue the litigation. They also agreed that acquiescence in or approval by the directors of the challenged transactions is not a basis for excusing demand. It was only in the opinion's final twist, with the court's conclusion that it could infer the possibility of waste from a provision in the contract, the defendants argued, that the lower court lost its way.

The plaintiff, despite having won below, spent much of his brief insisting, contrary to the Vice Chancellor's conclusion, that Fink's 47% stock ownership clearly enabled him to dominate and control the rest of the board. Having shown that the defendant had a controlling block of stock, the plaintiff argued, he should not be required to show actual domination—that is, that the directors selected by the defendant failed to exercise independent judgment—until after he had an opportunity for full discovery. "To force the plaintiff to plead more facts" at the outset of the case, before having the opportunity for discovery, he complained, "which is the inevitable consequence of the Vice Chancellor's ruling on the control issue, represents judicial insistence on the necessity to plead

54. Deborah DeMott, Shareholder Derivative Actions: Law and Practice, para. 1:5 n.1 (2003)(describing the mystery surrounding Harry Lewis). Allegations that leading shareholder litigation firm Milberg Weiss paid "professional plaintiffs" to serve as the nominal plaintiffs in its suits led to indictments in 2006 and contributed to the loss by the firm of its once dominant role in federal securities litigation. *See, e.g.,* Nathan Koppel, *Milberg's Case for Kickbacks,* WALL ST. J., Aug. 4–5, 2007, at A3 (discussing debate whether such fees are problematic).

55. Plaintiff Below–Appellee's Answering Brief, Aronson v. Lewis, No. 203, 473 A.2d 805 (Del. S.Ct. Oct. 5, 1983), at 9 (cited hereafter as Plaintiff Below's Brief).

voluminous evidence contrary to the letter and spirit of the Rules of the Court of Chancery."[56]

Both concluded with dire predictions of the effect on future derivative litigation if their view was rejected. "Contrary to *Zapata*," the defendants warned, "the decision below minimizes a board's ability to manage by redefining self-interest in such an expansive manner that demand on the board will almost always be excused."[57] Under the Vice Chancellor's conclusion that a board's independence could be called into question if a transaction appears to have been wasteful, the defendants warned ("and here," they emphasized, "the possible inference of wastefulness was based on an allegation concerning a single provision in an employment contract"), "demand will never be required, and a derivative suit will always go forward with the board being unable to exercise judgment to refuse to bring it or to terminate it, no matter what the real interests of the corporation may be."[58]

The plaintiff feared precisely the opposite. If alleging that Fink held 47% of Meyer's stock and personally selected all of the directors was not adequate to excuse demand, demand would rarely, if ever, be excused. This view, according to the plaintiff, "mocks *Zapata*," since under such an onerous demand requirement, "the two-step procedure established by *Zapata*, confined as it is to demand futile cases, would rarely be invoked."[59] The Delaware Supreme Court "must insure," the plaintiff concluded, "that the demand on directors issue will not 'make the derivative suit an endangered species of legal action.' "[60]

In addition to insisting that catastrophic consequences would attend the rejection of their view, each side also sought (as the quotes in the previous two paragraphs suggest) to wrap itself in the mantle of *Zapata*. This was to be expected, of course. The key question left open in *Zapata* was when is and is not demand excused, and it was evident to everyone that *Aronson* was the case that would answer this question. The outcome in this case, moreover, would significantly influence *Zapata*'s relevance in the future. If *Aronson* defined demand futility narrowly (the defendant's plea), demand would rarely be excused and *Zapata* would wither on the vine. A broad exception to demand, by contrast, would heighten the importance of *Zapata*.

This is where the drama came in. In the two years since *Zapata* was decided, the opinion's author, Justice Quillen, had retired from the Delaware Supreme Court and returned to private practice. Justice Quillen was now a partner at Potter Anderson, the firm handling the Meyers directors' defense. Quillen had not yet made his transition when the defendants first moved to dismiss the plaintiff's complaint and did not appear in the chancery court proceedings. But his was the lead name on the defendants' Delaware Supreme Court brief, and Quillen himself

---

56. *Id.* at 16.

57. Appellants' Opening Brief, at 33, Aronson v. Lewis, 473 A.2d 805 (Del. S.Ct. 1984).

58. *Id.*

59. Plaintiff Below's Brief, p.19.

60. *Id.* at 47.

presented the oral argument. Much of his argument focused on *Zapata*. One can only imagine what the justices were thinking when Justice Quillen said, with understandable self confidence, "Both sides in the briefing have emphasized the *Zapata* case," and proceeded to opine on the true significance of the case. Contrary to the chancery court opinion, he argued, "*Zapata* Policy Point 1" was that a derivative plaintiff does not have "an unfettered right to bring a derivative suit" even if demand is excused. *Zapata* Policy Points 2 and 3 were that "disinterested directors should have the opportunity to receive a demand and exercise their business judgment with regard to derivative litigation;" and that "disinterestedness should be defined to implement and not eradicate the managerial policy of the statute."[61] Not only had Quillen, unlike the three justices before whom he now appeared, written the *Zapata* opinion, but he was the only person present who had participated in the deliberations. Remarkably, neither of other two justices who decided *Zapata* was on the panel that would decide *Aronson*.

In the two years since it was decided, *Zapata* had proven quite unpopular ("a spectacular failure," in the words of one subsequent commentator).[62] There was general agreement with the court's skepticism of special litigation committees, but the conclusion that the chancery court should exercise its own business judgment seemed to fly in the face of generations of teaching about the respective roles of courts and corporate boards: that directors, not courts, were the ones who made business decisions.

Justice Quillen certainly did not echo these complaints in his argument. Nor did he suggest for a moment that the Delaware Supreme Court should revisit *Zapata*. But his argument for a narrow exception to the demand requirement would, if the Delaware Supreme Court agreed, significantly reduce the future relevance of *Zapata*. He was asking the Court to sharply limit the reach of the case that he himself had decided.

After the author of *Zapata* sat down, plaintiff's attorney Joseph Rosenthal was immediately pressed to defend the Chancery Court's conclusion that demand was excused because waste could be inferred from the contract. What factual basis, Justice Moore asked, did he have for the claim that Fink was incapable of working for Meyers and thus that the contract intended to pay him for doing nothing? Fink was already 75 years old, Rosenthal said (an argument that Quillen had already parried by pointing out that many people continue to work long after they turn 70, including Delaware's governor and a majority of the U.S. Supreme Court), and that Fink also worked for Prudential. Justice Moore also worried that under the broader exception to demand advocated by the plaintiff, demand would be excused any time a derivative action was brought against a company that had a controlling shareholder.

---

61. Aronson v. Lewis, Supreme Court Transcript, at 9, 11 (Nov. 14, 1983).

62. Edward B. Rock, *The Logic and (Uncertain) Significance of Institutional* *Shareholder Activism,* 79 Geo. L.J. 445, 503 (1991).

When it issued its opinion several months later, the Delaware Supreme Court returned a decisive victory for the defendants and for a sharply constrained demand futility exception. After noting that this case addressed the "crucial issue [left] unanswered" by *Zapata,* the court flatly rejected the Chancery Court's conclusion that the court should excuse demand if it could reasonably infer from the underlying transaction that the directors had permitted a waste of the corporation's assets.[63] "In our view," Justice Moore wrote, "demand can only be excused where facts are alleged with particularity which create a reasonable doubt that the directors' action was entitled to the protections of the business judgment rule."[64] As it often does with its judicial formulas, the Court distilled the issue of business judgment to a two-part test: "[I]n determining demand futility the Court of Chancery ... must decide whether, under the particularized facts alleged, a reasonable doubt is created that: (1) the directors are disinterested and independent and (2) the challenged transaction was otherwise the product of a value business judgment. Hence, the Court of Chancery must make two inquiries, one into the independence and disinterestedness of the directors and the other into the substantive nature of the challenged transaction and the board's approval thereof."[65] Only if the plaintiff alleges particularized facts suggesting either that a majority of the board was tainted or that the transaction could not satisfy the business judgment rule will demand be excused.

There is no "there but for the grace of God" language in the Delaware Supreme Court's *Aronson* opinion. To the contrary, Justice Moore went out of his way to reject arguments that structural bias invariably taints the decision-making even of ostensibly independent boards. "Critics will charge that we are ignoring the structural bias common to corporate boards throughout America," he wrote, "as well as the other unseen socialization processes cutting against independent discussion and decisionmaking in the boardroom. The difficulty with structural bias in a demand futile case is simply one of establishing it in the complaint for purposes of Rule 23.1. We are satisfied that discretionary review by the Court of Chancery of complaints alleging specific facts pointing to bias on a particular board will be sufficient for determining demand futility."[66] If Justice Moore's opinion makes any assumption about the psychology of a corporate board, the assumption seems to be this: if a majority of the directors are independent, they are likely to constitute a critical mass that is capable (unless shown otherwise) to resist even a controlling shareholder or a powerful chief executive.[67]

Here, the plaintiff failed to allege sufficiently particularized facts to satisfy either prong. Because the facts in this case—most prominently, Fink's inability to perform the contract and Fink's domination of the

----

63. Aronson, 473 A.2d at 807.

64. *Id.* at 808.

65. *Id.* at 814.

66. *Id.* at 815 n.8.

67. *See* Leo E. Strine, Jr., *The Inescapably Empirical Foundation of the Common Law of Corporations,* 27 DEL. J. CORP. L. 499, 506 (2002)(drawing this conclusion).

board—were simply conclusory allegations, demand was required and the plaintiff's suit should have been dismissed for failure to make demand.

G. DO DERIVATIVE SUITS STILL MATTER?

With *Aronson*, Delaware's framework for determining when shareholders can pursue derivative litigation was complete. The framework and its legacy will be considered in more detail below. But we first take up a more basic issue: do derivative suits still matter?

It is not that shareholder litigation is on its death bed, as commentators repeatedly warned throughout the twentieth century. The question, instead, is why anyone would file derivatively given the other litigation options that are now available. Since the 1960s, as the securities class action has blossomed, it has increasingly been used to police misbehavior that traditionally might have given rise to derivative litigation. Although the Supreme Court explicitly held in the 1970s that Rule 10b–5 could not be used to police fiduciary duty violations, securities litigation has achieved the same effect indirectly. The ever increasing list of items that must be disclosed, ranging from financial conditions and optional business projections under Regulation S–K, to executive compensation, requires a steady stream of information about the company's decision making. A plaintiff's attorney who believes that managers have mismanaged a company or made a questionable business decision can often frame her complaint in disclosure terms, pointing to misstatements in or omissions from the company's securities filings. Given that securities class actions avoid nearly all of the procedural obstacles that complicate a derivative suit, it is no wonder the attorneys so often invoke the securities law. "[T]he federal securities law and enforcement via securities fraud class actions today," in the words of an important recent article, "have become the most visible means of regulating corporate governance."[68]

So why would anyone file derivatively? One reason, not surprisingly, is that some cases cannot easily be framed either as a securities class action or as a direct action under state law. The most obvious example is alleged misbehavior by a closely held corporation. Because these corporations are not subject to the securities law disclosure requirements, disgruntled shareholders cannot frame their complaints as securities violations. Second, derivative litigation and securities class actions are often brought simultaneously, based on the same behavior, as the parties try to secure a favored venue, for instance, or simply because different lawyers are involved. Finally, in some cases, the misbehavior may be so egregious that the procedural requirements for filing derivatively do not pose a serious barrier.

In practice, derivative litigation is most prominent in cases involving close corporations, and with duty of loyalty allegations. A recent study of

---

68. Robert B. Thompson & Hillary A. Sale, *Securities Fraud as Corporate Gover-* *nance: Reflections upon Federalism,* 56 VAND. L. REV. 859, 860 (2003).

shareholder litigation in Delaware found, for instance, that roughly thirty percent of the derivative suits filed in 1999–2000 involved close corporations, nearly all alleging duty of loyalty violations, and that roughly half of the public corporation cases also raised duty of loyalty issues.[69] Many of the most prominent recent derivative cases have, as with *Aronson* itself, involved compensation issues.

Notice the irony here: the derivative mechanism evolved at least in part in the U.S. to address the collective action problems endemic to publicly held corporations in the late nineteenth and early twentieth centuries. Yet it now is often used to address the problems of close corporations—and in particular the kinds of majority oppression concerns that were the focus of the earliest derivative cases.[70]

H.   THE LEGACY OF *ARONSON*

The cliché that no case is decided in isolation has rarely been more true than with the Delaware Supreme Court's decision in *Aronson*. We have already seen how an earlier case, *Zapata*, made *Aronson* necessary and no doubt influenced the stance in *Aronson*. A second, equally striking influence on *Aronson* seems to have an emerging perception on the Court that all of Delaware fiduciary duty law could be organized around a single principle, the business judgment rule. In *Aronson*, and in several of the Court's most important takeover cases starting the following year, the Court sought to define its doctrinal advances in terms of the business judgment rule.[71] "In our view," the Court wrote in *Aronson*, "the whole question of demand futility is inextricably bound to issues of business judgment and the standards of that doctrine's applicability."[72] In *Unocal*, the Court prefaced its analysis of duties of the directors of a takeover target with the statement that "the business judgment rule . . . is applicable in the context of a takeover" and concluded that "the board acted in the exercise of sound business judgment."[73] In *Moran*, which legitimized the poison pill, the "primary issue," in the Court's view, was "the applicability of the business judgment rule;"[74] and the Court said in

---

69. Robert B. Thompson & Randall S. Thomas, *The Public and Private Faces of Derivative Lawsuits*, 57 VAND. L. REV. 1747 (2004). *Id.* at 1762 tbl 3 (table showing that 25/83 lead cases were nonpublic); 1766 tbl 5 (84% of close corporation cases allege self dealing); 1772 tbl 11 (49% of derivative suits against public companies allege self dealing).

70. A major difficulty with derivative litigation in disputes by a minority shareholder against the majority shareholders of a closely held corporation is that derivative recoveries go to the corporation rather than the complaining shareholders, which gives the majority block control of any recovery. While some states have responded to this problem by permitting the minority shareholders of a closely held corporation to sue directly, even if the cause of action is deriv-

ative, Delaware does not recognize the exception. *See, e.g.* Abelow v. Symonds, 156 A.2d 416 (Del. Ch. 1959).

71. Indeed, *Aronson* is most widely cited for its articulation of the business judgment rule, which it defines as "a presumption that in making a business decision the directors of a corporation acted on an informed basis, in good faith and in the honest belief that the action taken was in the best interests of the company." 473 A.2d at 812.

72. *Id.*

73. Unocal Corp. v. Mesa Petroleum Co., 493 A.2d 946 (Del. 1985). The quotes appear at p.954 and p.949.

74. Moran v. Household International, Inc., 500 A.2d 1346, 1350 (Del. 1985).

Revlon that "the business judgment rule may be applicable to the actions of corporate directors responding to takeover threats [if] the principles upon which it is founded—care, loyalty and independence . . . [are] first . . . satisfied."[75]

The overall project had mixed success. Perhaps the entire corpus of fiduciary duty regulation can be routed through the business judgment rule, but it is not always clear that the game is worth the candle. The business judgment rule is incidental to the real analysis in the takeover cases, which turns on the reasonableness of the target directors' response to an unwanted takeover. In *Aronson*, however, framing the demand inquiry in terms of the business judgment rule has proven to be a brilliant stroke. Unlike with the takeover cases, the question whether the directors would be entitled to the benefits of the business judgment rule is essential to determining whether their decision (in this case, the refusal to sue) should be respected. Viewing the demand futility through the lens of the business judgment rule thus makes perfect sense. In retrospect, the *Aronson* demand futility standard can be seen as a side effect—a remarkably happy one, I will argue—of the Court's larger quest for a unified field theory of directors' fiduciary duties in corporate law.[76]

The first prong is where much of the action is. The classic case for excusing demand is a challenge to a transaction in which the directors each have a financial interest, as in *Zapata*. If all of the directors truly are implicated, nearly everyone agrees that demand should be excused. The more difficult case comes when a key manager is implicated but many of the other directors are not. Some observers believe that, because of the structural bias on boards, demand should ordinarily be excused in this case. *Aronson* refused to presume structural bias, as we have seen. Only if a majority of the board is either interested or can be shown to be controlled by the interested director is demand excused under *Aronson*'s first prong.

It is worth noting that the standard for directorial disinterest in Delaware is broader and more flexible than the strict formula for disinterestedness mandated by the stock exchanges after the corporate scandals.[77] A so-called "gray" director—one who has ties to the company,

75. Revlon, Inc. v. MacAndrews & Forbes Holdings, Inc., 506 A.2d 173, 180 (Del. 1985).

76. In characterizing *Aronson* as accidental, I do not mean to suggest that the Delaware Supreme Court was unaware of the importance of its analysis in the case. By 1984, the great takeover battles of the 1980s were on the horizon, and the court may well have recognized that a broad ("pro-shareholder") demand futility exception would have been difficult to reconcile with rulings that gave the directors of a target discretion to defend against an unwanted takeover bid. My point is simply that the Court's doctrinal strategy—at tempting to ground each of the cases in the business judgment rule—was notably unsuccessful elsewhere, but produced luminous results in *Aronson*.

77. Under the New York Stock Exchange standard, a director is not independent if she has any "material relationship" with the company, or if she, among other things, receives more than $100,000 per year in direct compensation from the company, is employed by a firm that is an auditor of the company, or is employed by a company that receives $1 million or more from the company. N.Y. Stock Exchange Listed Company Manual, sec. 303A.02.

such as working for a law firm that represents it, but is not an insider—may qualify as disinterested under Delaware's standards but will not meet the stricter stock exchange standard. A director that satisfies the stock exchange standards, on the other hand, will invariably meet the more flexible Delaware standard. Because the stock exchanges now require that a majority of the directors on every board meet their strict new standards, the first prong of *Aronson* is likely to recede somewhat in importance. Except with transactions that implicate all of the directors, plaintiffs will rarely be able to show that a majority of the board is interested. In these cases, demand will only be excused if they can show that a majority of the board is not independent—that is, they are controlled by the alleged wrongdoer. This showing will be much easier in cases involving closely held companies, since the shareholders of these companies generally have a close familiarity with the business and the relationships among its directors.

The second prong, which asks whether "the challenged transaction was otherwise the product of a valid exercise of business judgment," functions as a catch-all or escape valve. Even if the plaintiff cannot cast a reasonable doubt on the disinterest or independence of a majority of the directors, demand may be excused if the decision making process or the decision itself is, in a sense, inexcusable. The most prominent recent example of such a case was a derivative suit alleging that the directors of Disney violated their fiduciary duties in approving an enormous severance payment to Michael Ovitz, who had been lured to Disney by CEO Michael Eisner two years earlier. Although there was no serious question about the directors' disinterest and the plaintiff could not demonstrate their lack of independence, the decision making process was so flawed that the Delaware Supreme Court concluded that demand should be excused.

Notice the relationship between *Aronson*'s second prong and structural bias on the board of directors. What *Aronson*'s first prong taketh away—refusing to assume that boards are controlled by their key managers—the second prong giveth back. If board decision making is distorted by structural bias, demand will sometimes be excused, as in *Disney*, even if the plaintiff can not point to particularized facts demonstrating that the outside directors lack independence.

Other than complaints by plaintiff's lawyers that the demand futility exception is now far too narrow, the principal objection to *Aronson*'s demand standard is that it, together with *Zapata*, discourages plaintiff's attorneys from ever making demand on the directors. If the plaintiff makes demand and the directors conclude that the suit should be dismissed, as they always do, their decision will stand unless it is wrongful. Under an alternative favored by some commentators and adopted by the ALI, demand would be required in every case but would not give the directors any greater ability to terminate the litigation.[78]

---

78. American Law Institute, Principles of Corporate Governance, sec. 7.03 (requir-ing demand except in limited circum-stances). *See also* Cuker v. Mikalauskas,

While universal demand would give repentant directors an opportunity to make changes and perhaps obviate the need for litigation in some cases, it seems unlikely that this would often be the effect. More often it would simply delay litigation.

I. THE PLAINTIFF'S ATTORNEY AUCTION

Even if we conclude that *Aronson* is a masterful solution to the problem of determining which derivative suits should go forward, it is important to keep in mind that reducing the likelihood of strike suits is only one of two longstanding concerns about derivative litigation: the other is the conflict of interest between plaintiff's attorneys and their ostensible clients, the company's shareholders. Is there a way to solve this problem as well?

Over the past seventy years, commentators have floated a variety of proposals that would either displace plaintiff's attorneys or provide more oversight over their decision to sue, their handling of the case, or both. In the 1930s, several commentators proposed that the government itself should get in the shareholder litigation business, either by creating an agency to police directorial misbehavior or by authorizing government officials such as the attorney general to sue on shareholders' behalf.[79] More recent years have seen proposals to create a committee of shareholders or independent experts to pass judgment on the litigation.[80] (The presumption in federal securities class actions that the largest shareholder will serve as the lead plaintiff is in a similar spirit.) The Achilles heel of the proposals is a suspicion that they would be cumbersome to put in place and might not improve shareholder litigation all that much.

The proposal that has gained the most traction takes precisely the opposite tack. Rather trying to create a more traditional attorney-client relationship, with the client monitoring the attorneys actions, this approach advocates that the role of plaintiff's attorney be auctioned to the law firm that offers the highest price.[81] After the winning bid is distributed to shareholders or the company, the client would essentially disappear. The attorneys themselves would pursue the litigation, and would keep any recovery. Because the attorneys would be litigating on their own behalf once they paid the shareholders, their conflict of interest would disappear. They would focus on obtaining the best possible result in the case. Although no court has conducted this kind of auction to

---

692 A.2d 1042 (Pa. 1997)(adopting the ALI approach for derivative suits involving Pennsylvania corporations).

79. Harris Berlack, *Stockholders' Suits: A Possible Substitute*, 35 Mich. L. Rev. 597, 609, 610 (1937). *See also* Roscoe Pound, *Visitatorial Jurisdiction Over Corporations in Equity*, 49 Harv. L. Rev. 369, 393 (1936)(arguing that the Attorney General has visitatorial jurisdiction over corporations and could intervene when "mismanagement seriously affects the economic or-

der and threatens loss to the investing public").

80. *See, e.g.,* Rock, *supra* note 55, at 490–504 (discussing pros and cons of shareholder committees).

81. The leading analysis and defense of this approach is Jonathan R. Macey & Geoffrey P. Miller, *The Plaintiff's Attorney's Role in Class Action and Derivative Litigation: Ecomonic Analysis and Recommendations for Reform*, 58 U. Chi. L. Rev. 1 (1991).

determine the lead counsel in a shareholders' suit (and practical obstacles such as prohibitions on buying stakes in litigation would interfere), courts in several securities fraud cases have asked law firms to submit applications disclosing the percentage of any recovery they expected to receive, and courts have selected lawyers based on these applications.[82]

While the lowest fee approach is a more realistic alternative to traditional approaches to selecting lead counsel than is a true auction, it also has more limitations. It does not fully eliminate the plaintiff's attorney's conflict of interest, for instance, since the attorney still will have an interest in maximizing her own fees rather than the overall recovery. The auction also could leave shareholders with incompetent counsel if poor lawyers underbid their competitors and the court did not assess the quality of the firm. If courts did take a closer look at the law firm quality, on the other hand, low bid auctions perhaps could help to moderate fees. Although the strategy has been used only in federal class actions to date, in principle it could be used in a derivative case as well.

J.　*ARONSON* AND THE FEDERAL SECURITIES LAW REFORMS

In the twenty-five years since *Aronson*, the framework for handling derivative litigation has remained relatively constant, while Congress has twice intervened to reshape the basic parameters of securities class action litigation. In 1995, Congress enacted the Private Securities Litigation Reform Act, which establishes a rebuttable presumption that the investor who has the largest stake in a securities class action will be named as the lead plaintiff in the action. The 1995 Act also requires that securities plaintiffs "state with particularity facts giving rise to a strong inference that the defendant acted with the requisite state of mind"— that is, that the defendant knowingly or recklessly violated the securities laws.[83] Both of these provisions are designed to stymie strike suits, the first by increasing the likelihood that the plaintiff will exercise meaningful oversight over the class attorneys, and the second by making it easier to kick out suits that are sloppy or obviously non-meritorious. In 1998, Congress again intervened, forcing most plaintiffs' to bring their federal securities class action cases in federal courts after numerous plaintiffs had circumvented the strictures of the 1995 act by filing in state court.

Whether the reforms have increased the proportion of meritorious suits is still a matter of debate. The existing empirical studies are somewhat mixed, with some evidence that the reforms are achieving their intended effect and some that there has been little measurable change.[84] Studies focusing on particular provisions, rather than the

---

82. The best known example is In re Oracle Securities Litigation, 131 F.R.D. 688 (N.D. Cal. 1990).

83. Private Securities Litigation Reform Act of 1995 (PSLRA), Pub. L. No. 104–67, 109 Stat. 737 (1995), sec. 101(a) &

(b)(amending 1934 act sections 27(a) and 27D(a)).

84. The studies to date are surveyed in Stephen Choi, *Do the Merits Matter Less After the Private Securities Litigation Reform Act*, J.L. Econ. & Org. (forthcoming

reforms as a whole, also do not find dramatic effects. A recent study of the lead plaintiff provision suggests that the presence of an institutional lead plaintiff slightly increases the expected settlement amount in the case, but that overall settlement amounts have not increased since the 1995 reform and the ratio of the settlement to the estimated magnitude of the company's provable losses from alleged misbehavior has actually decreased.[85]

Superficially, the securities class action reforms have magnified the differences between federal securities cases and state law derivative actions, since none of the new bells and whistles apply to old fashioned derivative cases. In reality, the federal changes can be seen as evidence that the two forms of shareholder litigation are evolving in the same direction. This parallel evolution is most evident with the new pleading standard, which serves, in a sense, as a substitute for *Aronson*'s demand requirement. Like *Aronson*, it imposes a heightened pleading standard that is designed to discourage sloppy pleading and to ensure that only serious allegations survive. In each context, moreover, the determination whether litigation should go forward is made primarily by a court, in response to a motion to dismiss in the early stages of the case.

The real differences in securities class actions and derivative suits are found less in procedural niceties than elsewhere. As we have seen, the continuing expansion of the securities laws has created liability for behavior that would not be actionable under state law. This suggests an obvious but rarely noted conclusion about contemporary shareholder litigation. To the extent one worries about contemporary shareholder litigation, the place to look for answers is in the substantive provisions of the securities acts. Reversing the trend toward ever more expansive disclosure requirements would do far more to rein in shareholder litigation than any of the procedural changes that garner most of the attention.[86]

K. CONCLUSION

Shareholder litigation is probably the least loved form of litigation. In the popular perception, plaintiff's attorneys sue at the drop of a hat—or more precisely, the drop of a stock price—and they pocket huge fees in cases that provide only a token recovery for shareholders. Shareholder litigation is not the only way to police corporate directors, but it is deeply

---

2007). Choi presents evidence that the act may have discouraged some non-nuisance claims that lacked "hard evidence" of fraud.

85. James D. Cox & Randall S. Thomas (with Dana Kiku), *Does the Plaintiff Matter? An Empirical Analysis of Lead Plaintiffs in Securities Class Actions*, 106 COLUM. L. REV. 1587 (2006).

86. Alternatively, one could disimply investors' private right of action, as Joe Grundfest suggested some years ago. *See, e.g.,* Joseph A. Grundfest, *Disimplying Pri-*

vate Rights of Action Under the Federal Securities Laws: The Commission's Authority, 107 HARV. L. REV. 963 (1994)(suggesting the SEC has the power to disimply). Reversing the private right of action would leave the SEC as the principal enforcer of the provisions (like sections 10 and 14) that do not explicitly provide for a private cause of action. As difficult as this is to imagine, it may well be what the drafters of the securities acts contemplated, and it is essentially the approach one sees in the U.K.

entrenched in this country. It is hard to imagine shifting to an alternative strategy, such as the use of governmental regulators one finds in the U.K.

Against this unpromising backdrop, *Aronson v. Lewis* has been a rather remarkable success. Its two prong test works effectively both for the close corporations that supply half of all derivative disputes, and for the high profile cases that get all of the attention. Nearly twenty-five years after *Aronson*, it seems fair to say that lumping derivative suits with federal securities class actions together gives derivative litigation a bad rap. All in all, at least in Delaware, the derivative mechanism works better than ever before.

Chapter 10

THE GROWTH OF THE FIDUCIARY DUTY CLASS ACTIONS FOR FREEZE OUT MERGERS: *WEINBERGER v. UOP, INC.*

By

*Vikramaditya Khanna**

The *Weinberger* v. *UOP, Inc.*[1] decision occurred at a critical juncture in the Delaware jurisprudence on freeze out mergers. Its status as an iconic case is fortified by its role as being the harbinger of an era of increased judicial scrutiny of freeze out mergers.[2] This chapter examines and analyzes the impact of *Weinberger* and its progeny on the judicial analysis of freeze out mergers. Section A begins by briefly describing what a freeze out merger is and how it was regulated before *Weinberger*. Section B details the primary facts and holdings from *Weinberger*. Section C analyzes the impact of this decision on freeze out mergers and how one might assess whether this impact is desirable or not. Section D examines the development of freeze out merger jurisprudence following *Weinberger* and inquires into the issues that are being raised by the on-

* Professor of Law, University of Michigan Law School. S.J.D. Harvard Law School, 1997. Email: vskhanna@umich.edu or vskhanna2007@yahoo.com. My thanks to Jon Macey for very helpful comments and suggestions.

1. 457 A. 2d 701 (Del. 1983).

2. Freeze out mergers have generated a tremendous amount of academic commentary. *See* Lucian Arye Bebchuk & Marcel Kahan, *Adverse Selection and Gains to Controllers in Corporate Freezeouts, in* CONCENTRATED CORPORATE OWNERSHIP (R. MORCK, ED.) 247–259 (2000); John C. Coates IV, *"Fair Value" as an Avoidable Rule of Corporate Law: Minority Discounts in Conflict Trans-* actions, 147 U. PA. L. REV. 1251 (1999); Ronald J. Gilson & Jeffrey N. Gordon, *Controlling Controlling Shareholders*, 152 U. PA. L. REV. 785 (2003); Adam C. Pritchard, *Tender Offers by Controlling Shareholders: The Specter of Coercion and Fair Price*, 1 BERKELEY BUS. L.J. 83 (2004); Faith Stevelman, *Going Private at the Intersection of the Market and the Law*, 62 BUS. LAW. 775 (2007); Guhan Subramanian, *Fixing Freezeouts*, 115 YALE L. J. 2 (2005)[hereinafter *Fixing Freezeouts*]; Guhan Subramanian, *Post-Siliconix Freeze-outs: Theory & Evidence*, 35 J. LEG. STUD. 1 (2007)[hereinafter *Post-Siliconix*].

going developments in this arena. Section E concludes with some thoughts about the future regulation of freeze out mergers.

A.   FREEZE OUT MERGERS

The term "freeze out" merger refers to a merger where the acquiring party is the controlling shareholder of the target (or "to be acquired") party.[3] For example, if the target firm is ABC Ltd. and it has a 55% controlling shareholder (123 Ltd.) and that controlling shareholder decides to merge with ABC Ltd. then that merger would be called a freeze out merger. The result of this merger is usually that the non–123 shareholders of ABC (i.e., the minority) are given cash for their 45% of ABC shares.[4] Freeze out mergers have many synonyms in the literature including "cash out" merger, "squeeze out" merger, controlled merger and "going private" transactions.[5] The last synonym indicates what happens to a firm when all the minority shareholders have been cashed out—that firm has one shareholder and does not publicly trade (i.e., the firm has "gone private").

Such transactions present a potential problem for corporate law because the acquiring party (i.e., 123 Ltd.) can determine when the transaction will occur, can determine the price to be paid for the target's shares, and can force through the merger even against the wishes of the minority.[6] This is because approving a merger generally only requires a favorable vote from the *majority* of the outstanding shareholders.[7] A controlling shareholder can usually manage this (in our example 123 Ltd. has 55% of the shares).

In light of this, the ability to use a merger to rid a company of its minority shareholders can be used in an exploitative manner. For example, the controlling shareholder could propose a relatively low price for the merger or pick a time for the merger when the target's market price is very low (e.g., right after a stock market decline). Indeed, some suggest that the "going private" wave in the early to mid 1970s is an example of this.[8] In addition, a controller may time a freeze out just before some rather profitable opportunities arise for the firm—this would deny minority shareholders the gains of these opportunities.[9] Further, the controller could engage in value reducing corporate deci-

---

3. *See* William T. Allen, Reinier Kraakman & Guhan Subramanian, Commentaries and Cases on the Law of Business Organization 496–97 (2d ed., 2007).

4. Other kinds of consideration may be given too, but quite often the consideration is cash.

5. *See* Allen, Kraakman & Subramanian, *supra* note 3.

6. *See id.*; Bebchuk & Kahan, *supra* note 2; Coates, *supra* note 2, at 1274; Subramanian, *Fixing Freezeouts, supra* note 2, 30–48.

7. For a discussion of the historical background on freeze out mergers see Allen, Kraakman & Subramanian, *supra* note 3, at 497–98; Subramanian, *Fixing Freezeouts, supra* note 2, at 8–10.

8. *See* A.A. Sommer, Jr., Law Advisory Council Lecture, Notre Dame Law School (Nov. 1974) in [1974–75 Transfer Binder] Fed. Sec. L. Rep. (CCH) 80,010 at 84,695 (Nov. 20, 1974).

9. *See* Allen, Kraakman & Subramanian, *supra* note 3, at 71–73 (discussing *Page* v. *Page* which presents a similar example of opportunistic behavior).

sions, which have the effect of depressing the target's market price before a freeze out.[10] With a lower market price the controller would offer less to the minority.

Absent some restraint on these kinds of behavior, one might expect that people would be reluctant to become shareholders in a firm with a controlling shareholder, they may demand additional protections before becoming shareholders, or they may pay a very low price for the shares to reflect the future possibility of being frozen out.[11] This may make raising capital more difficult especially when one is trying to raise capital from a disaggregated group of potential minority investors who are most likely going to be passive.[12] The effects of such mergers are discussed later but for now it is sufficient to note that a freeze out merger may be used to expropriate minority shareholders.

The natural follow-on question is then, why not prohibit freeze out mergers altogether? If they do not have redeeming qualities, a simple response would be to ban them. It turns out, however, that freeze out mergers may have beneficial effects and hence regulation of them would need to be somewhat nuanced.

One of the potential benefits is that engaging in a freeze out merger/going private transaction may shed some regulatory burdens that a firm is currently bearing. For example, a publicly traded firm is subject to the rules of Sarbanes–Oxley (SOX). If the firm thinks that these rules are imposing too great a cost on it then it may benefit the firm to no longer be publicly traded.[13] This would require the firm to engage in a going private transaction. Moreover, it is not per se unfair if a firm chooses this route to avoid SOX as SOX envisions that it should not apply to non-publicly traded firms. There are other kinds of regulations that may have similar concerns.

Yet another benefit might be that a controller may only engage in some beneficial changes to the firm if she does not need to share the gains with minority shareholders.[14] For example, imagine a corporate decision that would benefit the firm by $50 million, but would cost the firm $36 million and cost the controller additionally another $10 million in her time and effort. This change is worth doing (the net benefit is $4

10. *See* Coates, *supra* note 2, at 1316; Subramanian, *Fixing Freezeouts, supra* note 2, at 33–34.

11. *See* Pritchard, *supra* note 2, at 84–85.

12. *See* Bebchuk & Kahan, *supra* note 2, at 247–251. The connection between investor protection and stock market development has generated much interest. For brevity I refer only to the articles often credited with bringing the issue to greater attention. *See* Rafael La Porta, Florencio Lopez-de-Silanes, Andrei Shleifer & Robert Vishny, *Legal Determinants of External Finance*, 52 J. Fin., 1131–50 (1997); Rafael La Porta, Florencio Lopez-de-Silanes, Andrei Shleifer & Robert Vishny, *Law and Finance*, 106 J. Pol. Econ., 1113–55 (1998).

13. For some discussion of the costs of SOX to the US equity markets see The Competitive Position of the US Public Equity Markets, Report of the Committee on Capital Markets Regulation, available at http://www.capmktsreg.org/research.html.

14. *See* Frank H. Easterbrook & Daniel R. Fischel, *Corporate Control Transactions*, 91 Yale L.J. 698, 700 (1982); Benjamin Hermalin & Alan Schwartz, Buyouts in Large Companies, 25 J. Legal Stud. 351, 358 (1996).

million), but a controlling shareholder who holds 51% of the stock would be unwilling to do it. The controller would receive roughly $25 million (51% of the $50 million gain) and spend roughly $28 million ($10 million of her own and $18 million due to being a 51% shareholder of the firm). If, however, the controller wanted to take the firm private then she *would* make the change. Of course, the firm may be able to work out a way to pay the controller the $10 million (although this may not be as easy as it sounds), but absent that, going private may be preferable.

One can imagine other scenarios where a freeze out could be beneficial, but the important point is that sometimes these transactions may be desirable and thus we would not want to prohibit them, but rather regulate them in a manner that reduces the instances of undesirable freeze outs while still keeping most of the desirable ones. This leads to the question of whether the regulation that existed before *Weinberger* achieved this and whether *Weinberger* improved upon the pre-existing state of affairs.

Prior to *Weinberger* the primary method of protecting minority shareholders, besides contractual protections they might negotiate, was appraisal rights. Appraisal rights are available for dissenting shareholders in corporate mergers in the Delaware General Corporation Law and in all other states' Corporate Law statutes.[15] Briefly, these statutes usually provide the minority shareholder with an opportunity to have the court determine the fair value of the shares and have the court order the controlling shareholder to pay that fair value to the minority. If the process works well, one of the primary fears behind a freeze out (low price to the minority) can be assuaged by the fair value the court orders to be given to the minority. The problems, however, arise in how appraisal works.[16]

First, appraisal rights could be avoided by a controlling shareholder by structuring the transaction in particular ways. For example, if the acquisition was structured as a sale of assets, no appraisal action would be required by statute in Delaware.[17] Another example is that in Delaware, appraisal actions can be avoided if the controlling shareholder offers the minority stock in another publicly traded corporation.[18] Thus, by structuring the acquisition as a sale of assets or by offering stock as consideration, the controlling shareholder could largely avoid appraisal actions.

Second, even if appraisal actions were available, they were cumbersome and expensive for a shareholder to initiate. The shareholder must

15. *See* ALLEN, KRAAKMAN & SUBRAMANIAN, *supra* note 3, at 485.

16. *See* Coates, *supra* note 2, *passim* (discussing concerns with the calculation of fair value and minority discounts and putting forward proposals for reform); Lawrence A. Hamermesh & Michael L. Wachter, *The Fair Value of Cornfields in*

Delaware Appraisal Law, 31 J. CORP. L. 119 (2005).

17. *See* DELAWARE GENERAL CORPORATION LAW (DGCL) § 262 (c). Delaware case law does not require it either—see *Hariton v. ARCO Electronics, Inc.* 182 A. 2d 22 (*Del. Ch.* 1962).

18. *See* DGCL § 262(b)(2).

first dissent from the merger and then file their appraisal action.[19] This action had to be brought individually as there was no method of aggregating the appraisal actions of all shareholders.[20] This meant that for many small shareholders it was not economical to bring an appraisal action. The costs of hiring an attorney and pursuing the case would likely exceed the increase in value the shareholder might expect to receive. Thus, a person owning 20 shares in a firm who was cashed out for $20 a share would not be willing to hire an attorney for $100 per hour for 20 hours to generate a fair value of $40 per share. This would mean spending $2000 on attorney's fees to generate an additional $800 in value. In light of this, many minority shareholders would not avail the appraisal remedy.

Third, even if a minority shareholder could bring an action and found it economical to do so (perhaps they owned enough shares to make the legal costs worth it), they still had to contend with a rather awkward valuation process. There were concerns both in determining what shareholders had a right to claim and how that claim would be valued. First, shareholders by statute were entitled only to the fair value of the shares at the time of the merger but independent of any gains from the merger.[21] However, some of the gains arising after a merger may be because of some business plans put in place before the merger. Accounting for this and the gains arising from certain synergies (e.g., asset synergies) presented courts with areas where determining how much of the gain should "fairly" belong to minority shareholders would be difficult. In *Glassman* v. *Unocal Exploration Corporation*,[22] the Delaware Supreme Court held that minority shareholders are entitled to all non-speculative elements of the future value that were existing at the time of the merger.[23] Although this still leaves much open for debate (what is "non-speculative"), Delaware seems to have settled on this general formulation.

However, once we know what elements of value count in appraisal the next question is how to value these elements. One possible approach would be to simply approximate fair value by reference to the market price of the shares on the date of the merger. However, the courts were not willing to rely on market price as a measure of fair value.[24] Given that controlling shareholders could chose to do a freeze out when stock prices are depressed, reliance on market price may not be the best talisman for fair value. If courts are not willing to rely on market price then they need to find an alternative. Initially the Delaware courts relied on the Delaware Block Method[24.5] which tried to avoid reliance on future

---

19. *See* DGCL § 262(d); ALLEN, KRAAKMAN & SUBRAMANIAN, *supra* note 3, at 487.

20. *See id.*

21. *See* DGCL § 262(h); ALLEN, KRAAKMAN & SUBRAMANIAN, *supra* note 3, at 488–92.

22. 777 A. 2d 242 (Del. 2001).

23. *See id.,* at 248.

24. For concerns with market price as a measure of firm value in freeze out mergers see Bebchuk & Kahan, *supra* note 2; Coates, *supra* note 2.

24.5 Under the Delaware Block Method approach, three elements of value were examined: market value, asset value, and earnings value. These values were then av-

cash flows (the things investors presumably care most about) and relied on more historical measures of value (earnings, asset values, and so forth).[25] It appeared that Delaware courts may have thought that relying on future cash flows was too speculative.

In light of the foregoing, it appears that the appraisal remedy was not a very strong protection for minority shareholders—its coverage was spotty, it was expensive and cumbersome to use and its valuation methods were somewhat awkward. However, minority shareholders might, in some instances, be able to rely on another method of protecting their interests.

If the freeze out merger was accompanied by fraud or over-reaching, there was some precedent for the Delaware courts to allow a fiduciary duty class action against the controlling shareholder.[26] At first cut, this seems strange because appraisal appeared to be the exclusive remedy under the Delaware statute. Moreover, the point of appraisal was to obtain fair value for the minority (the primary concern associated with freeze out mergers) so it was not immediately obvious why a fiduciary action was necessary. If the concern was that appraisal did not function well, it seems the more natural way of addressing the problem would be to reform the appraisal process rather than to allow a parallel cause of action. However, Delaware courts seemed to permit both actions, perhaps on the notion that the presence of fraud or over-reaching merited additional punishment for the controlling shareholder over and above any remedies provided in the appraisal proceedings.[27] Moreover, historically, fiduciary duty actions generally predate the appraisal process so one might not assume that the appraisal process replaced all of fiduciary duty in this arena.

If fraud or over-reaching was present, the fiduciary duty class action would exist and normally the controlling shareholder would have to show that there was a valid business purpose for the merger to have a chance of surviving the fiduciary duty action.[28] The test for determining whether the controlling shareholder had breached a fiduciary duty was whether the transaction was entirely fair (i.e., fair process and fair price).[29] If the controlling shareholder could not show this, the plaintiff would be entitled to judgment for breach of fiduciary duty.

The fiduciary class action presented some advantages over the appraisal remedy. Fiduciary class actions are class actions and hence permit aggregation of minority shareholder claims making it more economical for shareholders to be part of a suit.[30] Moreover, these suits

eraged in order to determine the fair value of the equity of the company.

25. *See* ALLEN, KRAAKMAN & SUBRAMANIAN, *supra* note 3, at 488–89; 507–08.

26. *See Singer* v. *Magnavox Co.,* 380 A.2d 969 (Del. 1977); *Tanzer* v. *International General Industries, Inc.* 379 A.2d 1121 (1977).

27. *Cf.* ALLEN, KRAAKMAN & SUBRAMANIAN, *supra* note 3, at 486–87.

28. *See Singer, supra* note 26; *Tanzer, supra* note 26.

29. *See Weinberger, supra* note 1, at 711.

30. *See* ALLEN, KRAAKMAN & SUBRAMANIAN, *supra* note 3, at 487.

could not be avoided by simply offering stock as consideration or structuring the transaction as a sale of assets. Further, the remedy was more flexible than appraisal and could be crafted by the court to suit the situation. Although these are strengths relative to the appraisal process, the requirement that there be fraud or over-reaching may have served to limit the scope of the fiduciary duty class action for freeze out mergers.

Thus, prior to *Weinberger,* a controlling shareholder might be able to engage in a freeze out merger and face limited risk of a fiduciary duty class action and only have to contend with the appraisal process. In the 1970s, increasing stress was placed on this method of policing freeze outs because the stock market declined and a surge in going private/freeze out mergers followed. This led to increased attention and scrutiny on these kinds of transactions. In this context the *Weinberger* line of cases arose.

B.   ENTER *WEINBERGER v. UOP, INC.*

Weinberger brought about a number of important changes in the regulation of freeze out mergers. The critical facts were that Signal owned 50.5% of UOP and it wanted to merge with UOP to obtain 100% of its shares. Signal's management began exploring the potentiality of a merger and gathered information on whether, and at what price, an acquisition of UOP's remaining stock would be desirable for Signal. This was accomplished through a "feasibility study" conducted by two of Signal's officers and directors—Mr. Arledge and Mr. Chitiea—who were also directors on UOP's board. The feasibility study relied on information that Mr. Arledge and Mr. Chitiea obtained in their positions as UOP directors. Moreover, the study was to be used for the exclusive benefit of Signal and indeed the results were not shared with UOP. Based on this, Signal offered $21 per share which was the same price it had paid for obtaining 50.5% of UOP (the study noted that any price up to $24 per share was a good deal). Following this, Signal moved for reasonably quick responses from UOP's board and a shareholder vote. The vote was in favor of the Signal merger with a little over the majority of the minority shareholders voting to approve the merger. Although in the end, only 2.2% of UOP's shareholders opposed the merger, the plaintiff brought suit seeking a remedy for breach of fiduciary duty by Signal in the pursuit of this freeze out merger.

The Delaware Supreme Court took the opportunity presented in this case to change the law relating to freeze out mergers in significant ways. In particular, the court held that:

1. Normally appraisal proceedings would be the monetary remedy for minority shareholders.

2. However, the fiduciary duty class action would still be available to the minority shareholders in some instances including when there is evidence of fraud, over-reaching, self-dealing, misrepresentation or similar kind of behavior.

3. When appraisal is sought the court shall award the minority their proportionate interest in the going concern value of the

firm. This requires the court to take into account a multitude of factors including those which at the time of the merger are susceptible to proof, not "speculative" and could shed light on the fair value of the firm.

4. When appraisal is sought the court shall not be limited to the Delaware Block Method of assessing value. Indeed, the court may chose to rely on the Discounted Cash Flow[30.5] approach or any generally accepted financial technique.

5. In a fiduciary duty class action the critical issue is the entire fairness of the transaction. That includes fair dealing and fair price.

6. Fair dealing includes disclosure, providing adequate time for consideration of the offer, and not using confidential information from the target. Signal's feasibility study based on information obtained from UOP (by Mr. Arledge and Mr. Chitiea) that is used exclusively for Signal's benefit smacks of unfair dealing. Moreover, there were some time constraints on UOP. Both of these together suggest that Signal breached its fiduciary duty to UOP.

7. If a breach of fiduciary duty is found the remedy will be "in conformity" with the factors relevant to appraisal and may even include recissory damage elements.

8. Having a valid business purpose for a freeze out is not necessary to avoid a breach of fiduciary duty.

This is quite a number of holdings for a single decision. The overall tenor of the decision is to equate the remedies, to the extent possible, between appraisal and fiduciary duty class actions. Although the procedural differences remain (e.g., class actions versus individualized claims), the remedies are more similar. This arguably furthers the protection of minority shareholders by providing them with equivalent remedies whichever cause of action is chosen. Also, the decision liberalizes how fair value is assessed thereby reducing some of the clumsiness of the prior methods of valuing shares. The decision also lays out in greater detail the fiduciary duties of controlling shareholders and removes some undergrowth (e.g., the "proper business purpose" element). Moreover, the decision provides examples of what might amount to a violation of fair dealing. All aspects of *Weinberger* cannot be covered in this chapter; as such, focus will be on the effects it had on fiduciary duty class actions, freeze out mergers, and the progression of case law thereafter.

C. ARE THE CHANGES WROUGHT BY *WEIN-BERGER* DESIRABLE?

To examine the desirability of *Weinberger* one needs a sense of the problems and promises of freeze out mergers and their regulation. There

---

30.5 The Discounted Cash Flow approach is a method of valuation that takes the net present value of the free cash flow of a company.

are a number of potential concerns associated with freeze outs and going private transactions. First, minority shareholders may be cashed out of the firm at a low price or at an inopportune time.[31] If this behavior is not regulated, one might expect minority shareholders to contract for some protection against this behavior when they join the firm (e.g., contract for a veto over going private decisions) or to pay less for the firm's shares.[32] The discount on share prices may not perfectly match the expropriation risk, but one would still expect some degree of discounting to occur.[33] This makes raising capital more costly for the firm and forces greater dilution on the firm's current shareholders for raising a certain amount of money. This, by itself, may not raise much societal concern as the minority is paying less, in effect, for the risk of being expropriated.[34]

However, there are other concerns associated with freeze outs that may impose inefficiencies that are of concern to society. For example, if the controller makes business decisions with a view to reduce the firm's value so that the minority can be frozen out at a lower price, the social loss associated with the poor business decision is a cause of societal concern.[35] Indeed, absent some protections there may be too many freeze outs from society's perspective.[36]

If society regulates these transactions (as in *Weinberger*), minority shareholders have greater legal protection from expropriation via a freeze out merger.[37] The effect of this is that minority shareholders would presumably need to seek less protection via contract and would pay more for the shares (i.e., the discount on share prices would be less relative to no regulation). The cost of capital would then be somewhat less and the social losses from wasteful business decisions would decline.

Of course, increasing protection for minority shareholders is not without cost. There is the cost of adjudicating fiduciary claims and concerns that the fiduciary duty class action may be used to bring frivolous or extortionary suits.[38] One can imagine an attorney who initiates a class action to extract a settlement from the controlling shareholder following a freeze out merger. The cost of litigation and the adverse publicity may be sufficient to induce a controlling shareholder to settle a claim even if it is lacking in merit. For example, if the legal cost of defending against a frivolous fiduciary class action is $3 million and

---

31. *See* Robert Charles Clark, Corporate Law, § 12.2, 507–08 (1986).

32. *See* Frank H. Easterbrook & Daniel R. Fischel, The Economic Structure of Corporate Law 146 (1991); Pritchard, *supra* note 2, at 84–85.

33. *See* Coates, *supra* note 2, at 1307; Subramanian, *Fixing Freeze-outs, supra* note 2, at 24–29.

34. *See* Pritchard, *supra* note 2, at 84–85.

35. *See* Coates, *supra* note 2, at 1316.

36. *See* Subramanian, *Fixing Freeze-outs, supra* note 2, at 32–38.

37. Note that the remedy from *Weinberger* may make it more difficult for a controlling shareholder to know how much cashing out the minority may cost when they make their freeze out offer.

38. *See* Pritchard, *supra* note 2, at 83–84, 87; Elliott J. Weiss & Lawrence J. White, *File Early, Then Free Ride: How Delaware Law (Mis)Shapes Shareholder Class Actions*, 57 Vand. L. Rev. 1797, *passim* (2004). *But see* Subramanian, *Fixing Freeze-outs, supra* note 2, at 45–46 (noting that litigation costs (excluding the costs of executive distraction from the suit) do not appear large relative to other costs).

the costs of bearing adverse publicity and distraction to executives is $5 million, then settling a frivolous suit for something less than $8 million would be worth it.

In addition, the protections given to minorities under *Weinberger*, which provides them with the power to deter or disrupt a freeze out (i.e., "hold up" power), can have efficiency consequences. For example, minority hold up and the threat of litigation may deter (or disrupt) some controllers from engaging in a freeze out when it would be socially efficient to do so.[39] These are losses from regulation that merit societal concern.

In essence, the methods for preventing exploitation of minorities may reduce certain costs (e.g., cost of capital and efficiency losses from poor business decisions), but increase other costs (e.g., litigation costs and deterring or disrupting desirable freeze outs). The socially desirable level of regulation would reflect an optimal balance between these concerns. Thus, the choice between *Weinberger* style protection and lighter legal protection is largely a choice between bearing higher hold up and frivolous litigation costs under *Weinberger* for a potentially lower cost of capital and less wasteful business decisions.

Of course, from a policy perspective we need not limit ourselves to only the *Weinberger* level of protection and light protection—we might chose intermediate points along the continuum of little protection to very strong levels of protection. For example, one might view appraisal rights as being an intermediate point between *Weinberger* and little protection. Because appraisal does not permit shareholders to aggregate claims it may present lower costs from frivolous claims. The absence of aggregation presents the plaintiff with a smaller "club" to use against the controlling shareholder and should result in fewer frivolous claims. Further, the fact that shareholders seek appraisal individually suggests that only minority shareholders with larger claims will bring suit which may operate in an analogous manner to the lead plaintiff provisions in securities class actions.[40] Moreover, because appraisal rights cannot block a merger, they pose a lesser cost to controlling shareholders in terms of disrupting or deterring freeze outs. Thus, we expect a lesser hold up risk. However, minority shareholders receive somewhat less protection than under a fiduciary duty class action so minority shareholders may discount the shares they purchase compared to *Weinberger* style protection and there may be some value reducing decisions, but not as much as when there is little protection.

The continuum of policy choices leads us to at least two important points. First, favoring *Weinberger* style protection implies that we value reducing the cost of capital and wasteful business decisions more than

39. *See* Subramanian, *Fixing Freezeouts, supra* note 2, at 42–48.

40. For greater discussion of the lead plaintiff provision see Stephen J. Choi, Jill E. Fisch & Adam C. Pritchard, *Do Institutions Matter? The Impact of the Lead Plaintiff Provision of the Private Securities Litigation Reform Act,* available at http:// papers.ssrn.com/sol3/papers.cfm?abstract_id=706901.

the increase in frivolous litigation costs and desirable freeze outs deterred or disrupted. Second, this balance might change over time and with the background institutional structure. If there are other rules (besides rules on freeze out mergers, such as disclosure rules)[41] that work to limit the expropriation of minority shareholders then *Weinberger* style protection may have few additional benefits, but large additional costs. However, when there is a background of minimal protection of minority shareholders against expropriation, the *Weinberger* style protections may generate substantial gains relative to their costs.

Delaware's preference for *Weinberger* style protection may indicate that *at that point in time* the value of reducing expropriation risks of minority shareholders via freeze out mergers (and the cost of capital and wasteful business decisions) may well have justified the potential increase in the costs of hold up and frivolous suits. Viewing the *Weinberger* case in this manner, we can then examine how future cases refined the analysis and whether the balance of costs may have changed over time.

D. CASES FOLLOWING *WEINBERGER* AND RECENT CONTROVERSIES

Following *Weinberger* there have been a number of cases that extended the availability of fiduciary duty class actions to cases beyond fraud or over-reaching. Indeed, it seems safe to say that now the fiduciary duty class action is largely available in most cases where a controlling shareholder engages in a freeze out. The case of *Kahn* v. *Lynch*[42] is an example of this; this case also includes pronouncements on how controlling shareholders may be able to somewhat insulate themselves from fiduciary duty class actions.

In *Lynch*, Alcatel was Lynch's controlling shareholder with 43% of Lynch's stock. Alcatel had an effective veto over Lynch's ability to engage in a merger because Lynch's charter required 60% shareholder approval before a merger could be consummated.

Alcatel, however, was interested in merging Lynch with one of its wholly owned subsidiaries. Alcatel proposed such a merger and Lynch created an independent committee to advise it (and negotiate with Alcatel) over the proposed merger. The independent committee hired its own advisors to help in making their recommendations. Although Alcatel began by making a stock for stock offer, that was soon changed to a cash offer of $14 per share to Lynch's remaining shareholders. Lynch's independent committee met with its advisors and concluded that this price was too low. The committee presented Alcatel with a counter offer of $17 per share to which Alcatel countered with $15 per share. Through a few more rounds of this kind of negotiation Alcatel raised its offer to $15.50 per share.

---

41. *See e.g.,* SEC Rule 13e–3, 17 C.F.R. § 240.13e–3 (2005) (requiring substantial disclosures to the minority in the context of a freeze out).

42. 669 A.2d 979 (Del. 1995).

Although the committee still wanted a higher price, it appears Alcatel made it clear that if the committee did not recommend this price to the Board, Alcatel would proceed with an unfriendly tender offer at a lower price. The committee consulted its advisors and decided that it was best to take the $15.50 per share offer. After all, the threat that the lower priced tender offer might succeed may have been credible. This is because Lynch's shareholders might realize that Alcatel could veto merger proposals from other parties and hence Alcatel was the only real option on the table. It was better to accept Alcatel's offer, the committee decided, as no one else could likely make a successful offer at that stage.[43]

Following the committee's recommendation to the Board, suit was initiated by minority shareholders claiming breach of fiduciary duty by Alcatel. The court began by noting that the standard of review in a freeze out merger is entire fairness and that the defendant (the controlling shareholder) bears the burden of proving that the transaction is entirely fair (both fair dealing and fair price). However, as suggested in *Weinberger* (and affirmed in *Lynch*), if the controlling shareholder creates an independent committee to negotiate with it on behalf of the target firm on an arm's length basis, then that would provide evidence that the transaction was indeed fair. If such a committee existed (or there was approval by the majority of the minority shareholders), the burden of proving entire fairness would shift from the controlling shareholder to the plaintiffs.[44]

The next issue for the court was whether the independent committee on the facts was sufficient to shift the burden to the plaintiff. The court held that it was not, stating that for an independent committee to be able to shift the burden, the controlling shareholder must not be able to dictate the terms of the merger and the committee must have real bargaining power reflecting an arm's length bargain. The facts indicated that the committee did not have such power because Alcatel obtained the committee's favorable recommendation only after threatening a lower priced tender offer. In light of this, the burden of proving entire fairness continued to reside with the controlling shareholder.

Lynch has a number of important points for understanding the regulation of freeze out mergers. First, no longer is it necessary for the plaintiff to show fraud or over-reaching to be able to access the fiduciary duty class action.[45] Second, even if an independent committee has real bargaining power, that will not grant the controlling shareholder the

---

43. This argument assumes that Alcatel would veto a merger proposal that was even higher than its offer because it wanted to obtain Lynch. Presumably, it is possible that a third party could have made a proposal that would induce Alcatel to accede to the merger—the price offered would simply have to be fairly high. One might view the committee's acceptance of Alcatel's proposal as the committee's opinion that a much higher proposal was not likely.

44. For the treatment of majority of minority ratification see *Rosenblatt v. Getty Oil Co.*, 493 A.2d 929 (Del. 1985).

45. *See Rabkin v. Olin Corp.*, C.A. No. 7547, 1990 WL 47648, at *12 (Del. Ch. Apr. 17, 1990).

business judgment rule, but rather only shift the burden of entire fairness to the plaintiff.

One of the reasons for this approach is a notion that *Lynch* elaborates: inherent coercion. The idea is that even if the controlling shareholder does not engage in any over-reaching, the minority might still feel compelled to agree to the transaction because the minority knows that if they refuse the controller's offer, the controlling shareholder has other ways in which to punish and expropriate the minority (e.g., taking a higher salary for himself). In light of that, freeze out mergers cannot really receive the business judgment rule because inherent coercion will always make the transaction appear somewhat less than at arm's length.

Second, the court's pronouncements on what real bargaining power consists of are instructive for future cases. The independent committee cannot be forced into a decision by the controlling shareholder and the committee must have the funds needed to obtain advice from outside experts on relevant topics.

The *Lynch* case is the high point for the protection of minority shareholders in freeze out mergers. In this respect *Lynch* represents an extreme point on the continuum of policy choices one might utilize—it is even more protective and expansive than *Weinberger*. However, the trend toward increasing minority protection was about to change, albeit slowly.

In the late 1990s, controlling shareholders began trying to complete a freeze out in two steps rather than one.[46] First, the controlling shareholder would conduct a tender offer to obtain a total of 90% of the shares of the target firm (e.g., if the controller had 55% of the target's stock then the controller would make a tender offer for an additional 35% of target stock). Second, once 90% of the stock was obtained, the controlling shareholder would conduct a short form merger under § 253 of the Delaware General Corporation Law. In theory this might evade the application of a fiduciary duty class action because a tender offer does not require the use of corporate machinery (as a merger does) and hence may not involve the kind of coercion one envisages with a merger where, if a majority of the shareholders vote in favor of a merger, it will occur even against the will of the minority.[47]

Indeed, the early cases examining these tender offer freeze outs (TOFOs) seemed to hold that the Delaware courts would grant TOFOs the deferential business judgment review standard because tender offers are already regulated by parts of the Federal Securities Laws and do not involve the kind of coercion envisaged by the *Weinberger* line of cases.[48] Over time it appears that some practitioner's thought that the TOFO

46. *See* Gilson & Gordon, *supra* note 2, at 817–828; Pritchard, *supra* note 2, at 83; Subramanian, *Fixing Freeze-outs, supra* note 2, at 17–22.

47. *See* ALLEN, KRAAKMAN & SUBRAMANIAN, *supra* note 3, at 517–523; Pritchard, *supra* note 2, at 101.

48. *See Solomon v. Pathe Communications Corp.*, 672 A.2d 35 (Del. 1996); *Glassman, supra* note 22; *In re* Siliconix Inc. S'holders Litig.*, No. Civ. A. 18700, 2001 WL 716787, at *6 (Del.Ch. June 19, 2001).

route was the best route for a controlling shareholder to take a company private quickly and without too much attendant litigation.[49] Indeed, recent empirical evidence shows that TOFO mergers occurred at a lower price compared to classical freeze out mergers.[50] Thus, by the mid 1990s, there were two methods of obtaining a freeze out: the classical method (a freeze out merger) and the TOFO method.

The *Pure Resources*[51] case crystallized this bifurcated approach. In *Pure*, Unocal was the controlling shareholder of Pure Resources and owned about 65% of the stock. Unocal then made a tender offer to obtain at least 90% of the stock to be followed by a short form merger—the TOFO method. The critical issue was whether the TOFO method should continue to be governed by the relatively deferential business judgment standard or whether it should be governed by the *Weinberger/Lynch* entire fairness approach.

Vice Chancellor Strine's opinion raised a number of important issues in the process of adjudicating this case. In particular, Vice Chancellor Strine did not find the policy arguments for treating freeze out mergers and TOFOs differently to be convincing. He argued that there is inherent coercion in the TOFO merger as well. After all, if the minority shareholders reject the controlling shareholder's tender offer, the controller could exact revenge on them (e.g., giving himself a higher salary, engaging in less visible extractionary measures) just as in the case of a rejected freeze out merger offer. In light of this implicit threat, the kinds of concerns present in *Lynch* (e.g., inherent coercion), would also be present in a TOFO merger.

In spite of this, Vice Chancellor Strine chose to continue to apply the deferential approach to TOFO transactions if a number of conditions were met. First, the controlling shareholder would need to condition the merger on obtaining a non-waivable majority of the minority approval of the merger. Second, the controlling shareholder would need to promise to consummate a § 253 short form merger quickly and at the same price as the tender offer. Third, the controller must not make any threats or engage in any retributive behavior.

Although the decision continues the current two track approach to freeze outs, a few comments are important. First, the difference now between the approach to TOFOs and the classical freeze out merger is not so much in the conditions to obtain favorable review (both are required to have approvals from disinterested parties and not have threats accompanying them), but rather in the effect of meeting these conditions. For the TOFO, it means essentially no judicial review under the business judgment standard, but for the classical freeze out it means the plaintiff must prove the transaction was not entirely fair. Second, Vice Chancellor Strine's opinion largely set the groundwork for trying to unify the standards applied to TOFOs and classical freeze outs. However,

49. *See* Pritchard, *supra* note 2, at 101–103; Subramanian, *Fixing Freeze-outs, supra* note 2, at 24–25.

50. *See* Subramanian, *Post*-Siliconix, *supra* note 2.

51. 808 A.2d 421 (2002).

Vice Chancellor Strine appeared to suggest that if unification of standards was to occur he might prefer that it be towards the deferential business judgment standard for both TOFOs and classical freeze outs rather than toward entire fairness for both.

Vice Chancellor Strine's reasons for this appear more clearly if we look at recent decisions that evince greater concern and skepticism about the suits brought by minority shareholders.[52] The increasing concern is that these suits are often lacking in merit and simply increase the costs of the system. After all, if a controlling shareholder meets the conditions set out in *Pure*, is there much left to be determined at a trial about entire fairness? Indeed, in the recent *Cox* decision, the court opined that if an independent committee and the majority of the minority shareholders had approved a freeze out merger (TOFO or classical), there is little need for further judicial scrutiny.[53]

These recent cases indicate a change in direction away from granting strong protection to minority shareholders back towards the business judgment standard. If the *Cox* suggestions become accepted law, freeze out mergers would be much like any other conflicted transaction when the conflicted party is a director—if appropriate approvals have been obtained, the transaction gets the business judgment rule.[54] This would make freeze out mergers one area where the standard of review for transactions involving controlling shareholders is the same as that for reviewing transactions involving directors. In most other areas, when a conflicted transaction involves a controlling shareholder the best approvals will only shift the burden of proving entire fairness to the plaintiff.

These developments can be analyzed in a number of different ways. For example, one might praise these developments as engineering a more appropriate balance between hold up costs and expropriation costs in the context of freeze out mergers regardless of transactional form. Alternatively, one might critique these developments as unjustifiably creating one standard of review for the freeze out method of expropriating minority shareholders (business judgment with appropriate approvals) and another standard for other methods of expropriating minority shareholders (entire fairness even with appropriate approvals).

In the space of this chapter, one cannot adequately address all of these points; however, one point about the developing trend in freeze out mergers must be addressed. Perhaps the moves toward the business judgment rule simply reflect Delaware's increased experience with freeze outs and greater protections for minority shareholders arising from other areas of law (e.g., enhanced disclosure obligations).[55] One might

---

52. *See In re Cysive, Inc. Shareholders Litigation*, 836 A. 2d 531 (Del. Ch. 2003); *In re Cox Communications, Inc. Shareholders Litigation*, 879 A. 2d 604 (Del. Ch. 2005).

53. *See Cox, supra* note 52, at 644–47. This approach shares a middle ground approach that is similar to Gilson & Gordon,

supra note 2 and Subramanian, *Fixing Freeze-outs, supra* note 2.

54. *See* ALLEN, KRAAKMAN & SUBRAMANIAN, *supra* note 3, at 324–27.

55. *See e.g.*, SEC Rule 13e–3, 17 C.F.R. § 240.13e–3 (2005). Enhanced disclosure may make pricing expropriation risk easier

consider Delaware jurisprudence as a system that generally prefers the business judgment rule except when new and important transactions come about (e.g., takeover defenses, freeze out mergers).[56] When these new transactions arise, Delaware has little experience with them and hence reviews them with enhanced scrutiny. However, once sufficient experience has been obtained, Delaware may revert back to something akin to the business judgment rule. Whether this learning curve theory, combined with enhanced disclosure to minorities, explains the developments in freeze out jurisprudence may become more clear only in the future.

E. CONCLUDING THOUGHTS

The *Weinberger* case represents a number of changes in the way in which freeze out mergers are regulated. It made changes to both the appraisal remedy as well as fiduciary duty class actions and spurred the development of a detailed and thoughtful line of Delaware cases on freeze out mergers. Indeed, the number of changes wrought by *Weinberger* is quite remarkable. It thus earns its status as an iconic case the hard way—by making numerous and substantial changes to the law. However, since *Weinberger*, a number of other cases have expanded its holdings and more recently narrowed them to where we may be on the brink of regulating freeze out mergers through standards akin to the business judgment rule. Although this may be but the natural progression of case law back to a familiar standard, it underscores a change in how courts view freeze out mergers and the kinds of protection they merit.

---

as well as deter some opportunistic behavior by the controller.

56. *Cf.* Edward B. Rock, *Saints and Sinners: How Does Delaware Corporate Law Work?*, 44 UCLA L. Rev. 1009 (1997).

Chapter 11

OUT WITH THE BATHWATER: EROSION OF SHAREHOLDERS' TAKEOVER POWER

By
Logan Beirne*
Jonathan Macey**

Distinct from the rest of the world, United States public corporations possess a separation between managerial control and share ownership. In the American corporation, those who own it do not control it and those who govern it do not own it.[1] That is, while one set of people provide most of the risk capital to finance the corporation's asset purchases and enable all of the company's activities, another group of non-owner directors and managers typically control these assets and undertake the strategies to utilize this investment to earn returns.[2] In nations such as France, Germany, Italy, and Japan, large company ownership is dominated by large banks, powerful families, cross-holding corporate collectives, and governments. Distinct from such characteristic ownership in Europe and Asia, U.S. companies' ability to raise large sums of capital from widely disparate investors permits the democratization of capital, as large companies control resources raised from middle class investors, whose contributions to insurance premiums, pension funds, and mutual funds pay for the stock that capitalizes corporate America.[3]

The United States' unique "shareholder culture" theoretically places the shareholders at the epicenter of the corporate governance model. Unlike those views held in other nations, the United States

* Yale Law School 2008.

** Sam Harris Professor of Corporate Law, Securities Law and Corporate Finance, Deputy Dean, Yale Law School.

1. Adolf A. Berle & Gardiner C. Means, The Modern Corporation and Private Property 112–16 (Transaction Publishers 1991) (1932).

2. Jonathan Macey, Corporate Governance: Promises Kept, Promises Broken (forthcoming, Princeton University Press).

3. *Id.*

maintains a broad—albeit not universal—consensus that the public corporation should be governed for the benefit of shareholders.[4] This view is illustrated in various surveys, including one in which 76 percent of U.S. senior managers answered "the shareholders" when asked the question "who owns the large public corporation?"[4.5] As a means of comparison, 97.1 percent of corporate managers in Japan, 78 percent of French managers, and 82 percent of German managers answered "all of the stakeholders" to the same question, thereby elevating workers, customers, suppliers, local communities, and other non investors to the level of importance reserved for shareholders in the United States.[5]

Surprisingly, this venerated shareholder power has come under attack in the United States from both Congress and the judiciary. Due to the agency relationship created between the American separation of owner and management, there is inevitably conflict between shareholders and the agents who run their corporations. The shareholders have historically possessed a range of measures for recourse when their agents (management) are failing to act in their best interests. However, with Congress's passage of the Williams Act[6] in 1968 and the Delaware Supreme Court's line of cases known as the "takeover trilogy" (discussed in Section D, infra) in the mid–1980s, shareholder power has been curtailed. Both Congress and the Delaware Supreme Court, which is the most authoritative court in the U.S. in the area of corporate governance, effectively hindered shareholders' ability to maximize the value of their shares. Specifically, investors now possess diminished ability to utilize a powerful mechanism for increasing shareholder value: the hostile takeover.

This chapter commences by analyzing the functioning of the market for corporate control. It then delves into the emergence and impacts of the tender offer, corporate America's response to the tender offer and the impact of the Williams Act. The chapter then traces the subsequent emergence of the leveraged buyout (LBO) and the modern hostile takeover. It details corporate America's response to this new threat and then analyzes the Delaware Supreme Court's response in the "takeover trilogy." The chapter concludes by comparing this U.S. takeover juris-

---

4. "[S]ubject only to the legal and contractual responsibilities of the company to third parties."

4.5 Macey, Corporate Governance: Promises Kept, Promises Broken (2008), *supra* note 2.

5. *Id.*("Likewise, survey data about managers' views of the importance of dividends and the importance of job security for workers confirms the distinction noted here about America's exceptional approach to the governance of the corporate enterprise. In France, Germany and Japan most managers think that their primary obligation is to provide job security for workers, while in the U.S. managers are much more focused on the shareholders' interests in general and on paying dividends in par-

ticular. For example, in the U.S. 89 percent of corporate senior managers said that providing dividends for shareholders was more important than providing job security for workers. In Japan only three percent of senior managers thought that dividends were more important than job security. Similarly, a survey of 1000 companies in the U.S. by Japan's Economic Planning Agency reported that U.S. firms view their stock price as far more important than market share, while Japanese companies view market share as more important than share price.")

6. Williams Act of 1968, Pub. L. No. 90–439, § 3, 82 Stat. 454, 456 (1968).

prudence with that of Germany and Japan as a means of elucidating the distinctiveness of the American system.

A. THE MARKET FOR CORPORATE CONTROL

The market for corporate control is a pure market process that tends to function well without government intervention. Rather, regulatory intervention, when it occurs, tends to reflect the efforts of special groups such as managers and labor unions to impede the markets in order to protect incumbent management at firms that are either actual or potential targets. The market for corporate control is simply risk arbitrage on a very grand scale. Risk arbitrage involves the time-honored process of "buying low and selling high." Unfortunately, the response by corporate managers to efforts by entrepreneurs to enter this market has been to "buy *law*" in order to prevent take-over professionals from buying low.

In efficient capital markets, poor performance is hard to hide. When firms fare poorly, such poor performance is reflected in the firm's share prices and in a host of other indicators, including accounting data—particularly reported earnings—and sales performance in comparison to rival companies. All of these indicators are highly accessible and visible to a host of sophisticated outsiders watching the company. These outsiders include analysts, arbitrageurs, and venture capitalists. When these indicators lag relative to industry and sector competitors, potential acquirers have a strong incentive to act; by acquiring the shares of a poorly managed firm at a depressed price that reflects the firm's poor performance, the acquirer can institute the changes necessary to restore top corporate performance. Generally, these changes require that the top management of the target company be replaced by a new management team.

Thus, a properly functioning market for corporate control clearly provides benefits for the shareholders of companies whose shares are purchased by the outside bidder. Such shareholders receive a substantial premium, generally around fifty percent of the price at which the target firm's shares had been trading before the bid.[7] Moreover, even non-selling shareholders benefit when there is a hostile acquisition of a public company in which they own shares. Such non-selling shareholders benefit when the new management team takes over and reorganizes the target company. In doing so, successful bidders will provide better discipline for management, seek strategic synergies with other companies, and sell assets, subsidiaries, divisions, and other components of the target that are not adding value to shareholders. In efficient capital markets, share prices for non-selling shareholders go up when these strategic changes are announced by competent bidders.

7. Theodor Baums & Kenneth E. Scott, *Taking Shareholder Protection Seriously? Corporate Governance in the U.S. and Germany*, 17 J. APPLIED/CORP. FIN. 44, 59 n.55 (2005); Gregg A. Jarrell et al., *The Market for Corporate Control: The Empirical Evidence Since 1980*, 2 J. ECON. PERSP. 49, 52 (1988).

Takeovers benefit shareholders whether they end up selling their shares to an acquirer or not. When a company is open to the threat of a takeover, management and directors' best defense against losing their positions due to a hostile takeover is to keep share prices high, thereby making the company more expensive for the acquirer. As the cost of acquisition increases, the acquirer finds the acquisition less profitable. (When the shares are undervalued relative to their potential, the profit potential is greater.) In this way, managers have great incentive to make sure that shareholders' shares recognize their maximum value; otherwise, an acquirer may recognize the arbitrage opportunity and acquire the company, likely causing management to lose their jobs. In this way, an efficient market for corporate control that relies on stock price to determine control of corporate American rather than being impeded by artificial barriers to takeovers, allows shareholders to keep their agents in check. Absent artificial barriers, discussed in Section D, *infra*, directors and management have the incentive to abide by their fiduciary duties to shareholders by maximizing shareholder value. Otherwise, an efficient market for corporate control will help ensure their ouster. Despite these benefits, the power of this takeover mechanism has been continuously eroded since the tender offer was invented in the 1960s.

B.   THE EMERGENCE OF THE TENDER OFFER

Prior to the introduction of the tender offer, launching a proxy fight for the election of directors was the only way that a challenger could hope to oust an underperforming incumbent management team.[8] As a corporate governance device, proxy fights suffer from two distinct disadvantages relative to takeovers. First, incumbent management enjoys a number of structural advantages over outsiders in proxy contests. Incumbent management controls the timing of the contest, and can charge election expenses to the company. The incumbents also have better information about who the company's shareholders are and what issues are likely to appeal to particular groups of shareholders. Moreover, when a company is involved in a proxy fight, shareholders are required to choose between the incumbent management team, which is a known entity, and a group of unknown outside raiders.[9]

But the more profound deficiency in proxy contests as a corporate governance device is that those launching proxy contests lack credibility relative to those launching takeover contests in the form of tender offers. Potential acquirers making tender offers for a controlling block of a company's shares have enormous credibility because they are risking their own capital to acquire the controlling block. Having gained control of the company, tender offerors stand to benefit by managing the business in such a way as to increase the value of their shares, and the shares of their fellow shareholders.

8. Baums & Scott, *supra* note 7, at 58–
49.   **9.** *Id.*

By contrast, an entrepreneur who launches a proxy contest need not, in theory, own any shares in the target company whose board she seeks to displace. Rather, the outside "raider" asks that shareholders take it on faith that a successful proxy battle will lead to improvements in corporate governance. Thus, proxy contests are rarely successful unless organized and conducted by raiders who have significant investments in the shares of the target firms. Only those raiders can make a credible commitment to the target firm shareholders that their goal is to maximize the value of the entire firm, rather than to obtain the private benefits of control simply to loot the firm.

Thus, the emergence of the hostile tender offer in the 1960s should be viewed as a major innovation in the history of corporate governance. It provided the first large-scale, self-effectuating corporate control device. The hostile tender offer is large-scale because it affects all shareholders and because it involves the deployment of massive resources by outside bidders. These resources are required to monitor potential target companies, to evaluate which incumbent management teams are operating so inefficiently that they warrant being displaced in a hostile bid, to effectuate the hostile acquisition, and to implement the strategic plan to redeploy the target company's assets to higher value uses.

The market for corporate control is self-effectuating because it emerges spontaneously from market forces without the need for any action taken or resources deployed on the part of the subject company. An efficient market for corporate control is such an effective corporate governance device that it facilitates the separation of equity ownership and managerial responsibility in unique ways not replicable by other corporate governance devices. In particular, the tender offer, which is the pivotal device in the market for corporate control, obviates the need for target company shareholders to make comparisons of the relative merits of competing management teams before deciding whether to approve a proposed change-in-control transaction. Rather, as Baums and Scott have observed, "[w]ith the development of the tender offer in the 1960s, [shareholders] didn't have to make a comparison between alternative management teams but merely a comparison between the price being offered by the acquirer and the market price under current management."[10]

Under this system, acquirers seeking control of target companies began to fare much better than they had when the principal strategy available to them was the proxy contest. These advances, of course, were made at the expense of the target management. As the market for corporate control became more effective as a governing device, life became less comfortable for incumbent management, who felt increasing pressure to maintain high share prices in order to reduce the probability that they would face a hostile tender offer for control.

10. *Id.*

C. MANAGEMENT STRIKES BACK: THE WILLIAMS ACT AND BEYOND

In 1968, "[m]anagement struck back" against the unfettered operation of the market for corporate control by supporting the passage of the Williams Act, which deterred corporate takeovers by dramatically increasing both the out-of-pocket costs and the legal risks that bidders face when launching a tender offer.[11] Specifically, the Williams Act appropriates valuable property rights in information belonging to bidders by requiring such bidders to disclose such information to the financial markets. Among other things, the Williams Act requires that individuals, groups, and firms making tender offers supply the markets with their identities, their plans for the target firm, and their sources of financing. The requirements of the Williams Act made it easier for target firm management to entrench themselves by giving them "earlier warning" about an outside bid, and more time to resist.[12]

As a consequence of the Williams Act and other anti-takeover efforts, hostile takeovers began a steady decline from 14% to 4% of all mergers and acquisition activity.[13] In addition to their legislative efforts, managers championed a number of changes to their charters and bylaws designed to impede the market for corporate control. As Baums and Scott have observed, managers and their attorneys implemented staggered boards of directors; abolished the right of shareholders to remove directors without cause, to hold special meetings, or to act by written consent without meeting; and employed supermajority shareholder vote requirements to approve clean-up mergers which members of the prior board had not approved.[14]

Two factors prevented managers from being able to fully accomplish their goal of retarding the market for corporate control. First, fundamental changes to a company's corporate governance structure require that a company change its articles of incorporation, which, in turn, requires shareholder approval. Rational shareholders would not approve proposed changes to the governance structure of a company that would make them worse off by impeding the operation of the market for corporate control. Second, there were important innovations in the market for corporate control—particularly the emergence of the leveraged buy-out and junk bond financing—which facilitated the takeover market and tended to counteract the pernicious effects of managerial entrenchment efforts. However, corporations responded to these new threats and, with the help of the Delaware Supreme Court, have been able to curtail investors' ability to utilize the hostile takeover.

---

11. *Id.* at 58.

12. Baums & Scott, supra note 7, at 58.

13. Henry G. Mann, *Bring Back the Hostile Takeover*, WALL ST. J., June 26, 2002, at A18.

14. Baums & Scott, supra note 7, at 58–59.

D. EMERGENCE OF THE MODERN TAKEOVER: THE JUDICIARY IS NEXT TO TAKE AIM

In a series of landmark cases from 1985–1986, known as the "takeover trilogy," the Delaware Supreme Court revolutionized the law governing changes in corporate control. With its decisions in Unocal Corp. v. Mesa Petroleum Co.,[15] Moran v. Household International, Inc.,[16] and Revlon, Inc. v. MacAndrews & Forbes Holdings, Inc.,[17] the court held that corporate boards of directors are bound by fundamental duties of loyalty and care to their corporation and its shareholders. In doing so, the court failed to detail any specific blueprint with which to evaluate a board's adherence to these duties, articulating only a general rule that directors should be judged based upon the circumstances relating their obligation of acting with due diligence and good faith.[18] Such hazy rulings left it up to the courts to police the directors' implementation of anti-takeover tactics on a case by case basis without setting clear guidelines for protecting shareholders. This regime, in which it is left to individual courts to determine whether a decision is consistent with the directors' fiduciary responsibilities, has "turned out to be of little substance."[19]

In the end, the Delaware Supreme Court abdicated its duty to protect shareholders from directors' takeover tactics detrimental to these investors' interests. In the "takeover trilogy", the court upheld directors' methods of thwarting coercive bids. These rulings, moreover opened the door for the court to uphold such methods against bids that were non-coercive and quite beneficial to shareholders. The court also enabled directors to make more costly and difficult those acquisitions that would benefit shareholders, thereby ignoring the chilling effects that such defensive measures have on the market for corporate control.[20] In this way, via judicial fiat, the Delaware courts, opened the door for those who run corporations to negate the owners of the corporations' "most powerful corporate governance device in the shareholders' corporate governance arsenal."[21] "Delaware jurisprudence seems to be willing, in substance . . . to give management something approaching an absolute veto over hostile tender offers despite overwhelming evidence that they confer large benefits on target shareholders."[22]

The following section explores the historical context of the "takeover trilogy" by delving into the hostile takeovers of the 1980's. It then explores the defensive response of corporate managers and directors. Finally, it examines the specific cases of the trilogy.

15. Del.Supr., 493 A.2d 946 (1985).

16. Del.Supr., 500 A.2d 1346 (1985).

17. Del.Supr., 506 A.2d 173 (1985).

18. Barkan v. Amsted Industries, Inc. 567 A.2d 1279.

19. Theodor Baums & Kenneth E. Scott, *Taking Shareholder Protection Seriously? Corporate Governance in the U.S.* *and Germany*, 17 J. APPLIED CORP. FIN. 44, 59 (2005).

20. Jonathan R. Macey, The Politicization of American Corporate Governance, 1 Vir. Law & Bus. Rev. 10, 35 (2006).

21. *Id.* at 36.

22. Baums & Scott, supra note 5, at 59.

1. Historical Context: The Barbarians Cometh

In 1985, the year of the events surrounding *Unocal* and *Moran*, the level of merger and acquisition activity in the United States set a record high—as of that point in time—with a staggering 3,397 transactions valued at a combined $144 billion.[23] This record was to be short-lived, as it was eclipsed in 1986, the year of the events surrounding *Revlon*. In 1986, 4,024 transactions with a combined value of $190 billion were completed.[24] What further distinguished these record levels of M & A activity during the time of the "takeover trilogy", was the significant increase in the use of leverage. This buyout boom was marked by the emergence of the leveraged buyout (LBO), which made up 13.5% of the successful takeovers in 1985 and more than 20% in 1986.[25] While private equity investment is not a recent financial tool, this was the period in which Kohlberg Kravis and Roberts (KKR) invented the modern private equity buy-out industry.[26] During this era, KKR and other "barbarian investors" sought out companies not being managed to their full monetary potential and borrowed billions to acquire these undervalued firms. They then used their control to sell off pieces of each company, slash the workforce, and use other means to bring a greater return to the shareholders in order to recoup their investment. These investors were driven by the following common inefficiencies in corporate America: management had sought to (a) reduce their risk at the expense of potentially increasing returns to investors by not fully leveraging the company, (b) increase their own power and resources by conglomerating beyond optimal size, and (c) have their pay set with little regard to company performance. While passive and disseminated shareholders allowed such inefficiencies to persist, the aggressive shareholder sought to make the companies more responsive to (their) shareholder interests and, of course, to capitalize on the resulting boost in their shares' valuation.

How were investors such as KKR able to effectuate such change? By buying up majority or at least significant minority positions, institutional investors like KKR had the ability to help shape the board of directors, a powerful and direct tool in shaping subsequent governance practices. "The problem of managerial slack inheres in two features of the public corporation structure—strong centralized management and the absence of effective devices for ensuring that managers are accountable to owners in exercising their powers."[27] Institutional investors of the day sought to eliminate such a situation and to reduce the resultant agency costs by controlling management's oversight. "Often board members are explicitly selected by the [investor] for their industry or functional expertise, and they bring considerable hands-on experience and know-

---

23. 1986 Profiles, Mergers & Acquisitions 57 (May/June 1987). These statistics include only transactions valued at $1 million so the United Staes M & A activity was actually higher.

24. *Id.*

25. *Id.*

26. See George Anders, Merchants of Debt: KKR and the Mortgaging of American Business.

27. 81 Notre Game L. Rev. 1431, 1476.

how. This means that they aren't as likely to be captive to management's agenda as those chosen by the CEO."[28] Through this influence over the board of directors, the investors imposed their disclosure and accountability agendas. Often backed by the contracts stipulating the companies' responsibilities in return for capital, the investors required the dissemination of company information and required managers to disclose any possible conflicts of interest or other issues. In addition, used their board presence to establish performance-based best practices for management and shape the board's formal proceedings.[29]

What made these aggressive shareholders particularly effective in both monitoring and threatening management was that often, they did not merely interfere at a high level during quarterly board meetings. Rather, in their bid to boost their returns, these investors often became extensively involved in the tactical day-to-day functioning of the company. "In monitoring investments, private equity investors work with CEOs, effectively serving various capacities that range from executive coach to consultant to investment banker, providing ongoing advice [and] analysis."[30] The relationship extended beyond intermittent discussion to also encompass ad hoc strategy consultations and leveraging the investors' network to build managerial capital.[31] Whether considering an acquisition or merely deciding what to name a new product, the relationship facilitated the injection of shareholder input into company decisions (often to their mutual benefit).

Aggressive shareholders also impacted companies more indirectly via alteration of their financial structures. Agency theory is concerned with the conflicts between shareholders and their agents; managers. Distributing money to shareholders is at a cost to managers' power, as it reduces the amount of capital under their control and leads to increased monitoring when management must obtain new outside capital. Managers have an incentive to expand the business—even when a smaller size may be of more benefit to shareholders—because it both increases the resources under their control and, since compensation is typically correlated with sales growth, is likely to line their own pockets.[32] Furthermore, a larger business increases the costs of a takeover, thereby better protecting the managers' jobs. Aggressive shareholders' active participation, however, can negate much of this. With the "carrot" approach, investors can structure ownership to reduce such agency costs: aligning management's interests with those of shareholders via compensation. In order to create a stronger connection between company performance and managerial pay, aggressive shareholders can "force managers to put significant skin in the game—and then reward them handsomely when they succeed."[33] In fact, a Boston Consulting Group study found that managers at private equity portfolio companies have an average of one to

---

28. BCG, 5.
29. Moon, 80.
30. *Id.*
31. *Id.*

32. Michael C. Jensen, *Agency Costs of Free Cash Flow, Corporate Finances, and Takeovers*, 76 AM. ECON. REV. 323.
33. BCG, 9.

two years of salary invested in their company while "the relationship between pay and performance at most public companies remains weak."[34] This aligns management's pecuniary interests with those of the shareholders, thereby helping to "unleash the . . . energies of their senior executives and allow managers to participate in the upside of the business."[35] While this compensation may be championed by an engaged private equity investor with even just a minority position, it often occurs as a result of LBOs. "With LBOs, the buyout firms typically owned 80–90% of the target, and operating management owned about 10%."[36] The resultant company was one in which management's ownership increased, thereby resulting in an "ownership structure that was clearly aligned with the interests of the management and owners."[37]

This "carrot" enticement may be accompanied by the "stick's" threats. Another mechanism by which takeover investors tame management involves higher debt levels. The typical LBO targets are "firms or divisions . . . that have stable business histories and substantial free cash flow—situations where agency costs of free cash flow are likely to be high."[38] As discussed, managers in such firms have an incentive to spend free cash flow on value-dissipating investments. However, the high debt service requirements induce managerial discipline as management must instead use the cash flows as the shareholders want them to—to service the debt that they had used as leverage.

Via these numerous mechanisms, aggressive institutional investors were able to significantly impact the corporate governance of their portfolio companies in order to elevate the company's share price. They used their influence prior to investment and their shareholder power after investment to affect the board and management. These investors' unique relationship with their investment led them to actively engage the company to alter corporate governance according to their pecuniary interests. Management began to work with their boards of directors, who are supposed to represent the will of the shareholders, to find a means of resisting such shareholder control.

2. The Target Companies' Response: The Poison Pill Mechanism

The uniquely American "democratization of capital" nevertheless requires a "republicanization of representation" in the sense that the investors are typically so disparate that they elect representatives to represent their interests in the board of directors because it is impractical and infeasible to self represent such typically small minority stakes. Under U.S. law, corporations are not managed by the shareholders, but rather by the direction of boards of directors, who are literally the governors of the corporation. The board has the authority to manage the business of the corporation and can initiate strategic plans and cause the

34. *Id.*
35. *Id.*
36. *Id.* at 324.

37. *Id.*
38. *Id.*

corporation to pursue, or to change, its business plans. The board has plenary authority to act for the corporation in all matters not requiring shareholder approval. In fact, in the U.S., directors' power to manage the business and affairs of the corporation is virtually absolute.

The problem with boards is their unique susceptibility to capture by the managers they are supposed to monitor. The problem of capture is so pervasive and acute that no board, not even those that appear highly qualified, independent and professional, should be relied upon entirely. Because proximate monitors, which directors are, participate in corporate decision-making, they take ownership of the strategies and plans that the corporation pursues. In doing so, these proximate monitors are rendered incapable of objectively evaluating their own strategies and plans. In particular, boards of directors have long been responsible for selecting and evaluating the performance of top management. After top managers have been selected, retained and promoted, boards become committed to and responsible for these managers. For this reason, as board tenure lengthens, it becomes increasingly less likely that boards will remain independent of the managers they are charged with monitoring. Couple this with the high probability of a loss of a member's board seat in the takeover, and it is easy to see why board members actively work with management to implement defensive measures against takeovers. Amidst the rising tide of LBOs, in the early 1980's, management across America quickly worked with their semi-captured boards to thwart takeovers via a powerful mechanism that came to be called the poison pill.

Technically called a shareholder rights plan, the term "poison pill" is the nickname for a particular device utilized by public companies to avoid a hostile takeover by making themselves unattractive to the investor who wants to make the hostile acquisition. Poison pills prevent hostile takeovers by increasing the costs of acquiring a large block of shares in a target company. A poison pill involves the issuance by a company of a new class of stock—usually preferred shares—that provide holders with the rights to purchase additional shares, either in the target company—so-called "flip-in" pills—or in the acquirer—so-called "flip-over" pills—whenever certain triggering events occur. The most common triggering event is the acquisition of a certain threshold percentage (usually twenty or thirty percent) of target firm shares by any acquirer that the target company board finds unacceptable. Should an outside bidder make acquisitions that exceed the designated threshold without the permission of the target firm's board of directors, the target firm's shareholders are able to purchase additional shares at hugely discounted prices. The device is called a poison pill because these discount purchases have the intended effect of diluting the ownership interests of the outside bidder, who is specifically precluded from participating in the discount purchases permitted to the other investors.

Because poison pills have been technically evaluated as representing merely the issuance of a new class of shares, which most companies can do without shareholder approval, poison pills may be implemented by corporate boards without any shareholder action. When adopted, the rights initially attach to the corporation's outstanding common stock, cannot be traded separately from the common stock, and are priced so that exercise of the option would be economically irrational. As mentioned above, the pill or shareholder rights become exercisable and can trade separately from the common stock only when a triggering event occurs.

A pill's flip-over feature typically is triggered when the target is merged into the acquirer or one of its affiliates after the acquirer obtains the specified percentage of the target's common stock. When this triggering event occurs, the target firm's shareholders become entitled to purchase common stock of the acquiring company, typically at a deeply discounted price. These purchases have the effect of impairing the acquirer's capital structure and drastically diluting the interest of the acquirer's previous stockholders. In other words, the pre-existing shareholders in the acquiring firm are harmed by flip-over poison pills because triggering the flip-over pill gives target shareholders the option to purchase shares of the acquiring company at deeply discounted prices, which dilutes the interests of the pre-existing shareholders of the acquirer. Whereas flip-over pills are triggered by the merger of the acquirer and the target, flip-in pills are triggered merely by the acquisition of a specified percentage of the issuer's common stock. When a flip-in pill is triggered, all target firm shareholders except the acquirer are permitted to buy shares in the target at a deeply discounted price.

Poison pills impede the market for corporate control by eliminating the possibility of hostile takeovers in firms with poison pills in place. Significantly, the shareholder rights distributed by companies as poison pills can be redeemed by the target at little or no cost to the issuing company. Redeeming the rights eliminates the poison pill, and permits an acquisition to proceed. In other words, the consequence of the poison pill is to require acquirers to obtain the approval of target company boards of directors before proceeding. The harm to acquiring firm shareholders from the triggering of a poison pill is so severe that the poison pill has never been intentionally triggered.[39]

Thus, the poison pill has effectively destroyed the hostile takeover. Those companies with the most venal management teams are immune from ouster in a hostile takeover. Only companies with benign, other-regarding boards of directors will redeem their poison pill rights plans and permit outside acquirers to effectuate a change in control.

3. The Trilogy Begins: *Unocal*

On April 8, 1985, Mesa Petroleum Company, which owned thirteen percent of Unocal, made an offer to acquire Unocal Corporation. Mesa stated in a proxy statement to Unocal's shareholders that it would—in typical LBO fashion—borrow heavily based upon Unocal's assets, thereby increasing the company's debt levels in order to help pay for the

---

39. Baums & Scott, supra note 5, at 59.

acquisition. Mesa structured the deal as a "front loaded" cash tender offer for thirty-seven percent of Unocal's stock at $54 per share.[40] The "back end" of the offer would then "eliminate the remaining publicly held shares by an exchange of securities purportedly worth $54 per share."[41] However, these securities, referred to by Unocal as "junk bonds," were highly subordinated, thereby making them more risky and potentially less valuable. This two-part offer would likely have the coercive effect of "stampeding shareholders into tendering at the first [cash] tier, even if the price is inadequate, out of fear of what they will receive at the back end of the transaction."[42] As the following subsection demonstrates, the beauty of the two-step takeover (in the eyes of the bidder) is that it places the shareholders of the target firm in a prisoner's dilemma that leads them to tender their shares.

a. *Unocal* and the Prisoner's dilemma

As Unocal feared, an offer such as this creates the situation in which Mesa, as the initial bidder, has an advantage because the best strategy for each target shareholder is to choose to tender even though a better solution would be for them to all reject the offer. Game theorists use the term 'prisoner's dilemma' to describe such a situation where the inability of individuals to coordinate their decisions leads to a suboptimal result from the perspective of the decision-makers.[43] To illustrate with a simplified—yet parallel—version of Mesa's offer, suppose that the current price of a firm's stock is $30 per share. The firm has 101 shares outstanding and "M" has acquired as a 'toe hold' one of these shares in an open-market transaction. She purchased the stock after investing $40 in research indicating that under her ownership/management the value of the firm would increase to $37 per share. The remaining 100 shares are divided evenly between two people, A and B, neither of whom is able to contact the other one without incurring prohibitive costs.[44]

In this situation M could make, as Mesa did, a two-tier offer for all of the remaining shares. M would promise to pay a premium for the first

---

40. Unocal Corp. v. Mesa Petroleum Co., 493 A.2d 949 (Del. 1985).

41. *Id.*

42. *Id.* at 956.

43. Brudney and Chirelstein were the first to describe the situation facing target shareholders as a prisoner's dilemma. See Brudney & Chirelstein, Fair Shares in Corporate Mergers and Takeovers, supra note 27, at 337 (describing "whipsaw effect" of two-tier bid on shareholders). For a description of the prisoner's dilemma game, see P. SAMUELSON, ECONOMICS 482–83 (8th ed. 1970); P. ARANSON, AMERICAN GOVERNMENT: STRATEGY AND CHOICE 54 (1981).

44. In the context of actual tender offer situations in publicly held firms, the prisoner's dilemma results from the high costs to diverse shareholders of communicating among themselves. The prisoner's dilemma is exacerbated in the publicity held firm because individual shareholders who expend resources to communicate information to fellow shareholders bear all the costs of such communication, but share the benefits collectively with all other shareholders. The efficiency of capital markets makes the dilemma even more acute. Investors who expend resources to uncover information and then attempt to capture the value of their investment by purchasing shares signal the nature of their discovery to other investors; this prevents the initial investor from capturing the full value of her informational investment. *See* Scholes, *The Market for Securities: Substitution versus Price Pressure and the Effects of Information on Share Prices*, 45 J. BUS. 179 (1972).

fifty shares, but she would also announce that she would follow with a take-out merger for the remaining fifty shares at the pre-tender offer price of $30. Suppose that the bid is to purchase the first fifty shares for $40 each and the remaining 50 for $30 per share, acquiring all shares at an average price of $35.[45] When (and if) the acquisition is completed, the price will climb to $37 under M's management, giving M a gross return of $207 ($200 on the 100 shares purchased from A and B, plus $7 on the initial share), and profits of $167 once her research costs are subtracted.

The threatened bid, however, provides useful information to others that the firm may be undervalued.[46] The news causes other parties to look at the firm, and A and B may be convinced that at least one of the third parties, T, would place a higher value on the firm than does M and would be willing eventually to make a better offer, say an average of $39 per share instead of M's $35 per share.[47]

M often has the advantage of having developed her information first and so will be able to offer and complete acquisition of control before T can make his own bid. If A doesn't tender to M and B does, B receives $40 for his shares and A receives only $30. On the other hand, if A and B both tender, B still receives an average of $35 for his shares. Under these circumstances, B is better off tendering his shares, regardless of whether A tenders or not. By tendering, B earns at least $5 and perhaps $10 over the current market price for the shares; by not tendering he loses any premium. A, of course, is in exactly the same position and will act in the same way. The result is that both will tender. Under current law, the offeror, M, will be required to purchase the shares pro-rata. A and B will each receive $40 for 25 of the shares they own and $30 for the remaining 25 shares. If the two could communicate, they would both agree not to tender any of their shares and hold out for the later, higher offer of $39 per share from T. The inability of A and B to coordinate their activities, however, results in a total loss to them of $400. This simplified example explains Unocal's concern over Mesa's two-tiered offering. Mesa's offer encouraged everyone to jump at the cash front end offer due to their fear of being left with the less desirable junk bonds given at the back end offer. Not surprisingly, Unocal acted swiftly to counter this threat.

45. The question of how an initial bidder chooses the blended price in two-tier bid is of considerable interest in itself, but is not addressed here. At a minimum, to create a prisoner's dilemma, the first-tier bid must be higher than the blended bid expected from a third party. The minority shareholders' "appraisal rights" also set a lower limit for the second-tier bid. *See* W. CARY & W. EISENBERG, CASES AND MATERIALS ON CORPORATIONS 1452–62 (5th ed. 1980) (discussing appraisal rights); *see also* Manning, *The Shareholder's Appraisal Remedy: An Essay For Frank Coker*, 72 YALE L. J. 223, 229 (1962) (consequence of appraisal remedy was to "consolidate and liberate" management); Eisen-berg, *The Legal Roles of Shareholders and Management in Modern Corporate Decision-making*, 57 CALIF. L. REV. 1, 85 (1969) (appraisal called "remedy of desperation").

46. "The bid itself . . . may reveal much of what the offeror has learned. . . . Indeed, the existence of an offer by itself tells other prospective bidders where to look, even if it conveys no other information." *Management Role, supra* note 14, at 1178 & n.45; *see also* Bradley, *Interfirm Tender Offers and the Market for Corporate Control*, 53 J. BUS. 345, 347 (1980); Scholes, *supra* note.

47. T's willingness to pay $39 per share of course implies that the firm is worth more than $39 to T.

b. The Battle for *Unocal*

Five days after Mesa's original offer, Unocal's board of directors met to discuss the proposed merger. The board received detailed presentation from legal counsel on their obligations under both Delaware law and federal securities laws. They next heard presentations from the company's investment bankers, who outlined valuation techniques and explained their finding that Unocal was worth $60 per share in cash. Based upon their bankers' recommendation, Unocal rejected Mesa's offer and instead passed a resolution that if Mesa acquired 64 million shares through its offer, Unocal would implement a self-tender offer for the remaining 49% of its own stock for $72 per share. This was $18 higher than Mesa's offer and at a $12 premium to the banker's valuation of the company. It would also cause the company to incur over $6 billion in additional debt, which would make the company even less attractive for an LBO since the acquirer would be able to borrow less off of Unocal's assets to pay for an acquisition. It would also hurt the company's longer term prospects by reducing exploratory drilling. Unocal excluded Mesa from the $72 per share offer for a "valid business purpose" since its stated objective was to compensate shareholders at the "back end" of Mesa's offer. "[U]nder the proration aspect of the exchange offer (49%) every Mesa share accepted by Unocal would displace one held by another stockholder. Further, if Mesa were permitted to tender to Unocal, the latter would in effect be financing Mesa's own inadequate proposal."[48]

Mesa filed suit to challenge this exchange offer as well as their exclusion. The issue was whether Unocal's directors had breached their fiduciary duties with their actions. Holding for Unocal, the Supreme Court of Delaware articulated the basic rule that in the event of a takeover attempt, as long as the directors reasonably believe that there is a danger to the corporation's effectiveness, they may take any defensive measure, such as the poison pill, that is reasonable in relation to the hostile takeover threat.[49]

Specifically, the court held,

> When a board addresses a pending takeover bid it has an obligation to determine whether the offer is in the best interests of the corporation and its shareholders. In that respect a board's duty is no different from any other responsibility it [sic] shoulders, and its decisions should be no less entitled to the respect they otherwise would be accorded in the realm of business judgment. There are, however, certain caveats to a proper exercise of this function. Because of the omnipresent specter that a board may be acting primarily in its own interests, rather than those of the corporation and its shareholders, there is an enhanced duty which calls for judicial examination at the threshold before the protections of the business judgment rule may be conferred.

48. *Id.* at 951.

49. Arthur M. Borden, Going Private 4–68.

This Court has long recognized that: 'We must bear in mind the inherent danger in the purchase of shares with corporate funds to remove a threat to corporate policy when a threat to control is involved. The directors are of necessity confronted with a conflict of interest, and an objective decision is difficult.' In the face of this inherent conflict directors must show that they had reasonable grounds for believing that a danger to corporate policy and effectiveness existed because of another person's stock ownership. However, they satisfy that burden 'by showing good faith and reasonable investigation. . . .' Furthermore, such proof is materially enhanced, as here, by the approval of a board comprised of a majority of outside independent directors who have acted in accordance with the foregoing standards.[50]

The court recognized a need to find a way to give deference to the board's business judgment while ensuring that the board acted reasonably in relation to the corporation's stakeholders (not only shareholders but also employees, customers, creditors, etc.).[51] In this case, Unocal was indeed facing a coercive bid that could potentially damage the shareholders' interests and the court found that the board had acted properly to protect the corporation's interests. In effect, this decision opened the door for corporations to take anti-takeover measures and left it up to the courts to decide whether the boards were acting in shareholders' best interests. If *Unocal* opened the door for the poison pill, however, the *Moran* decision can be credited with blasting the door off its hinges.

4. The Attack on the Poison Pill Widens: *Moran*[52]

In August of 1984, the board of directors of Household International, Inc. adopted a complicated "Rights Plan"—effectively, a poison pill—aimed at thwarting any takeover attempts.[53] Without a shareholder vote on the matter, the board created a complicated mechanism by which they would flood the market with newly issued Household shares if any shareholder started buying large blocks (20% or 30%) of its stock, thus diluting the bidder's existing holdings and making the acquisition prohibitively expensive.[54] This plan was not created amidst a battle with a corporate raider that potentially posed a threat to the company, as was the case in *Unocal*, but was merely a preventive measure to guard the company from a theoretical foe.[55] As previously discussed, the mere threat of a takeover drives management to maximize shareholder value. The Household Board's move, however, would remove such incentive along with shareholders' ability to benefit from a bidder willing to purchase their company at a price above its trading value. Additionally, the measure would block an all cash bid that would have yielded shareholders a premium. Accordingly, shareholder and board member

---

50. *Id*. at 955–956.

51. *Id*. at 956.

52. Moran v. Household International, Inc., 500 A.2d 1346 (Del. 1985).

53. *Moran*, at 1348.

54. *Id*. at 1349.

55. *Id*.

John Moran filed suit to invalidate the poison pill, which he argued would stifle bids that might maximize shareholder value.[56]

Explaining that directors were protected by the business judgment rule,[56.5] the Delaware Supreme Court upheld Household's poison pill. The court held that despite the lack of any existing threat, the board of directors "adopted the Plan in the good faith belief that it was necessary to protect Household from coercive acquisition [and] the Plan is reasonable in relation to the threat posed."[57] Despite the long-held notion that the shareholders were the rightful owners of the company, and the directors' goal was to maximize shareholder value, the court deferred to Household's directors' decision to chill even friendly buyouts that would net those shareholders a premium.

The court observed that permitting companies to implement poison pill rights plans without shareholder votes would not have deleterious corporate governance effects because such plans would be subject to intense scrutiny by the courts. In particular, with respect to the poison pill rights plan adopted by Household International, the Court asserted that:

> [T]he Rights Plan is not absolute. When the Household Board of Directors is faced with a tender offer and a request to redeem the Rights, they will not be able to arbitrarily reject the offer. They will be held to the same fiduciary standards any other board of directors would be held to in deciding to adopt a defensive mechanism, the same standard as they were held to in originally approving the Rights Plan.[58]

But who will decide whether the board is upholding these duties? Certainly not the shareholders, who did not even have a chance to vote on the Rights Plan. Instead, with regard to poison pills at least, the Delaware Supreme Court replaced the shareholders as epicenter of the corporate governance model. The court stripped shareholders of their power to protect their own interests and placed them at the mercy of the courts to police the market for corporate control. These sweeping powers inherent in the broadest implications of *Moran* were pruned back to a degree in *Revlon, Inc. v. MacAndrews & Forbes Holdings, Inc.*[59]

5. The Trilogy Capstone: *Revlon* Duties

Revlon v. MacAndrews could serve as a bedtime story to remind directors of their duties to the shareholders they represent. The cast of characters would include Revlon as the damsel in distress facing "the

---

56. *Id.*

56.5 The business judgment rule is a legal principle under which a court will refuse to review the actions of a corporation's board of directors in managing the corporation unless there is some allegation that the directors acted in bad faith and/or violated their duty of care. See Aronson v. Lewis, 473 A.2d 805, 812 (Del.1984) (defining the business judgment rule as "a pre-

sumption that in making a business decision the directors of a corporation acted on an informed basis, in good faith and in the honest belief that the action taken was in the best interest of the company").

57. *Id.*

58. *Id.* at 1354.

59. 506 A.2d 173 (Del. 1985).

impending threat"[60] from a barbarian (Pantry Pride) who is looking to carve her up, and a "white knight" (Forstmann)[61] who attempts to save her. In June of 1985, Pantry Pride made a friendly offer to purchase Revlon. The CEO of Revlon dismissed the $40–50 per share offer as below the company's intrinsic value and developed a strong personal dislike for Pantry Pride's CEO. Pantry Pride's board then authorized a hostile bid for Revlon. In reaction, Revlon's board met and was advised by their investment banker that Pantry Pride's offer was "a grossly inadequate price for the company."[62] The banker explained that Pantry Pride would likely use junk bond financing, as in *Unocal*, to purchase Revlon, which it would then break up and obtain a premium by selling the company in pieces. In response to this perceived threat, the Revlon board, which was dominated by "insider" directors who held management positions within the company or significant business relationships with it, adopted a poison pill.

The company repurchased 5 million of the 35 million outstanding shares and adopted a "Note Purchase Rights Plan" by which each shareholder—except the acquirer—would receive a note entitling them to $65 per share effective when anyone "acquired beneficial ownership of 20% or more of Revlon's shares, unless the purchaser acquired all the company's stock for cash at $65 or more per share."[63] Thus, if Pantry Pride attempted to purchase Revlon, this Plan would saddle them with these payments unless it paid $65 per share in cash, thereby making the purchase cost ineffective. Pantry Pride made a hostile offer, which the shareholders rejected under the director's advisement. Revlon then issued Notes that placed restrictions ("covenants") on how much more debt the company could incur. This had the effect of making an LBO less attractive since Pantry Pride would be able to borrow less based on Revlon's assets in order to purchase the company.[64]

Meanwhile, Revlon began friendly negotiations with Forstmann and the Revlon directors agreed to be acquired by $56 per share. They provided Forstmann with detailed financials to which Pantry Pride had no access and agreed to effectively remove the Notes Purchase Plan and to waive the Notes debt covenants, thereby paving the way for Forstmann's takeover. In the end, Revlon would be broken up anyway and Revlon's management would receive "golden parachutes," which were described as "agreements providing substantial bonuses and other benefits for managers and certain directors upon a change in control of a company."[65] On this news, the value of the Notes dropped over 23% and the Wall Street Journal reported threats of litigation from creditors. Pantry Pride responded by raising its bid to 56.25 per share, and Forstmann responded by raising its bid to $57.25. Revlon made an

60. *Revlon* at 175.

61. *Id*. at 182.

62. *Id*. at 175.

63. *Id*. at 177.

64. *Id*. at 180–81 ("Pantry Pride was a small, highly leveraged company bent on a 'bust up' takeover by using 'junk bond' financing to buy Revlon cheaply, sell the acquired assets to pay the debts incurred, and retain the profit for itself.")

65. *Id*. at 178 n.5.

agreement for Forstmann to support the price of the faltering Notes and provided Forstmann with a "lock-up" agreement that would end the bidding war by making it extremely difficult for anyone else to purchase Revlon's assets. Pantry Pride filed suit, challenging Revlon's use of the lock-up agreement as well as the Rights and Notes covenants.[66] While also seeking a restraining order to prevent Revlon from being sold to Forstmann, Pantry placed a conditional bid of $58 per share.

Surprisingly in light of the momentum from Unocal and Moran, the Delaware Supreme Court found for Pantry Pride. First, it found the Note Purchase Rights Plan issue was moot since Revlon had eventually agreed to redeem them if the bids exceeded $57, and all bids did surpass that amount. Second, the court found that Revlon's offer of Notes with restrictive debt covenants was originally protected by "the directors' general broad powers to manage the business and affairs of the corporation."[67] While it was forestalling a hostile takeover, Revlon's board was acting within its Unocal duties that "require the directors to determine the best interest of the corporation and its stockholders."[68] However, this duty was transformed once Revlon began negotiating with Fortsmann and it became clear that the company was going to be broken up regardless. "It no longer faced threats to corporate policy and effectiveness, or to the stockholders' interests, from a grossly inadequate bid. The whole question of defensive measure became moot. The directors' role changed from defenders of the corporate bastion to auctioneers charged with getting the best price for the stockholders...."[69] For this reason, the court enjoined the lockup agreement since it would have "ended the auction for Revlon ... to the ultimate detriment of its shareholders."[70]

Pruning back the broadest implications of Unocal, the court denied Revlon's argument that it acted in good faith by using the Notes agreement to benefit *note*holders "because *Unocal* permits consideration of other corporate constituencies [besides stockholders]."[71] Taking a step back towards the historically American shareholder-centric view, the court held that "[a] board may have regard for various constituencies in discharging its responsibilities, provided there are rationally related benefits accruing to the stockholders."[72] The court concluded that:

> [T]he Revlon board was confronted with a situation not uncommon in the current wave of corporate takeovers. A hostile and determined bidder sought the company at a price the board was convinced was inadequate. The initial defensive tactics worked to the benefit of the shareholders, and thus the board was able to sustain its *Unocal* burdens in justifying those measures. However, in granting [a] lock-up to Forstmann, we must conclude that under all the circumstances the directors allowed considerations other than the

66. *Id.* at 178. Pantry Pride also challenged Revlon's cancellation fee.

67. *Id.* at 181.

68. *Id.*

69. *Id.*

70. *Id.* at 185.

71. *Id.* at 182.

72. *Id.*

maximization of shareholder profit to affect their judgment, and followed a course that ended the auction for Revlon, absent court intervention, to the ultimate detriment of its shareholders. No such defensive measure can be sustained when it represents a breach of the directors' fundamental duty of care.[73]

With *Revlon*, the Delaware Supreme Court moved slightly back towards the more shareholder-centric American model of corporate governance. However, it still did not clarify directors' specific duties to shareholders, again leaving it up to the courts to decide this question on a case-by-case basis. *Revlon* forced only those that had agreed to sell the company to work to maximize shareholder value. Only after the board and management decided to sell were they required to act as auctioneers with a duty to maximize share price. Indeed, *Revlon* does not affect those boards and managers who refuse to sell the company. Companies that refuse to be acquired may utilize poison pills that chill even takeover bids that would have netted shareholders a premium if unimpeded by this artificial mechanism. In fact, *Revlon* reaffirmed those powers defined in *Unocal* and *Moran* for directors and management to defend against all sales via poison pills. This effectively frees companies from the threat of takeover so they no longer have the incentive to maximize share prices as a means of protecting their jobs. Rather than allowing an open market for corporate control to help ensure directors and managers are fulfilling their fiduciary duties to shareholders, in its "takeover trilogy" holdings, the Delaware Supreme Court allowed shareholders' agents to provide themselves with artificial protection and left it up to courts to determine if any violations of fiduciary duties to shareholders arise.

E. CONCLUSION

Takeovers provide benefits for target firm shareholders, whether they sell their shares or not. Absent regulatory distortions, the best strategy for target management to use to avoid being ousted in a hostile takeover is to keep share prices high. Higher share prices deter hostile bids by making such bids more costly, thereby destroying the arbitrage potential that exists when shares are undervalued relative to their true potential.[74]

The market for corporate control as a corporate governance device only improves the quality of corporate performance at those publicly held firms that are *not* guarded by the takeover-chilling effects of the Williams Act and/or a poison pill. Because share prices represent the best

---

73. *Id.* at 185.

74. *See,* Frank H. Eastbrook & Daniel R. Fischel, *The Proper Role of a Target's Management in Responding to a Tender Offer,* 94 HARV. L. REV. 1161, 1169 (1981). ("Managers will attempt to reduce agency costs in order to reduce the chance of takeover, and the process of reducing agency costs leads to higher prices for shares.") *See* *also* Daniel R. Fischel, The Corporate Governance Movement, 35 VAND. L. REV. 1259, 1264 (1982) (arguing that the market for corporate control "simultaneously gives managers of all firms who wish to avoid a takeover an incentive to operate efficiently and to keep share prices high").

available—and indeed the only—real time, unbiased assessment of a company's performance and future prospects, by providing strong incentives for target managers to keep such share prices high, the market for corporate control is an elemental component of any corporate governance system in which the owners of residual claims in the company are not in positions of management. Improved corporate governance is a byproduct of an efficient market for corporate control. Such improved governance, however, is not limited to those firms that actually receive premium bids from outside acquirers. Rather, the genius of the market for corporate control as a corporate governance device is that it improves the quality of corporate performance at all publicly held firms whose shares are "contestable."[75]

The reason that the benefits of the monitoring provided by potential bidders is not limited to the shareholders in firms fortunate enough to receive a bid from a hostile bidder is because managers who want to avoid being displaced in a hostile takeover must keep the prices of their firms' shares high in order to avoid being ousted in a tender offer. Because managers and boards know that they will be ousted following a successful hostile acquisition, they will work harder to maximize shareholder value in order to avoid that possibility. Thus, a takeover threat will not only discipline management, it will also discipline the non-monitoring board.[76] This mechanism has been hindered to a degree by Congressional and Judicial intervention.

75. In this context, the term "contestable" means susceptible to the market for corporate control. A firm's shares are contestable in the market for corporate control if a majority of the shares are in the hands of independent (nonmanagement-affiliated) value-maximizing shareholders. Where, for example, a majority of the voting shares of a company are in the hands of small-stake shareholders or institutional investors focused on share price performance, the company's shares are contestable. By contrast, the company's shares are not contestable where shares are parked with friendly institutional investors or where incumbent management and their allies have shares with supermajority voting rights that prevent an outside acquirer from obtaining a majority of the voting shares.

76. As important as the market for corporate control clearly is, it nonetheless is possible to overstate the role played by this particular market in corporate governance. In particular, the market for corporate control was not capable of dealing with the recent corporate governance problems at firms like Enron and WorldCom, which involved artificially inflated earnings, profits, and other measures of corporate performance. See E.S. Browning, *Abreast of the Market: Investor Confidence Remains Fickle*, WALL ST. J., Sept. 9, 2002, at C1 ("Scandals at Enron, WorldCom, Global Crossing, Tyco International, Adelphia Communications, ImClone Systems and a host of other companies have raised questions about whether corporate earnings reports and corporate executives can be trusted."). The market for corporate control exerts powerful disciplinary pressure on under-performing management by providing arbitrage possibilities where share price lags because companies have slothful or corrupt management. The depressed share prices in such companies present attractive investment opportunities for entrepreneurial corporate raiders, who profit by purchasing a controlling interest in under-performing companies and installing more competent and motivated management. See Andrei Shleifer & Robert W. Vishny, *A Survey of Corporate Governance*, 52 FIN. 737, 756 (1997) (noting that the raider benefits when the share prices of the target firm rise to reflect the improved earnings generated by the new management team). However, the market for corporate control only disciplines bad management when the target firm's share prices are depressed. Because accounting fraud causes share prices to be artificially inflated rather than depressed, the takeover entrepreneurs who drive the market for corporate control have no incentive to launch the hostile takeovers that discipline managers employing questionable accounting practices to over-inflate their companies' share prices. *Id.*

Chapter 12

THE "TRANS UNION" CASE:
SMITH v. VAN GORKOM

By

Fred S. McChesney*

While you see a chance, take it . . .
Because it's all on you.**

Few, if any, cases have shocked the corporate world as much as *Smith v. Van Gorkom.*[1] The 1985 decision by the Delaware Supreme Court was greeted with disbelief and disdain by corporate practitioners and academics alike. Daniel Fischel, for example, called the decision "one of the worst decisions in the history of corporate law."[2] Jonathan Macey and Geoffrey Miller wrote, "The outcome of the case was exactly the opposite to what virtually every observer of Delaware law would have predicted."[3] Its repercussions continue to reverberate, some twenty years later.

This chapter explores two aspects of *Smith v. Van Gorkom.* First is a discussion of the reasons the decision was so wrong-headed, and the impact its errors had. Second, the chapter notes the ways that the law reacted to, and to a considerable extent ultimately corrected, the mischief created by *Trans Union.*

A. LEVERAGED BUYOUTS

Trans Union (TU) is a diversified Fortune 500 company headquartered in Chicago. Originally, it was especially prominent in the railway car leasing business (the firm's initial name was the Union Tank Car Company), but over time it became one of the most important firms

---

* Northwestern University: Class of 1967 James B. Haddad Professor, Law School; Professor, Kellogg School of Management.

** Winwood & Jennings, *While You See a Chance* (F.S. Music Ltd.). Steve Winwood popularized the song in February 1982, when it reached #7 on the Billboard chart.

1. 488 A.2d 858 (Del. 1985). The case is often referred to as the *Trans Union* decision, the name of the firm involved in the events described here.

2. Fischel, 40 Bus. Law. 1437 (1985).

3. Macey & Miller, Trans Union Reconsidered, 98 Yale L.J. 127 (1988).

gathering and reporting personal credit information. In that new line, it was generally very profitable.

The relevant points concerned in *Smith v. Van Gorkom* revolve around a "leveraged buyout" (LBO) of Trans Union. To understand what *Smith v. Van Gorkom* involved, therefore, it is useful to start with the mechanics of an LBO in general.

The term "leveraged buyout" includes any acquisition of a company (often called the "target company"), via purchases of stock from current shareholders, in which a large portion of the purchase is financed by debt ("leverage") obtained by the acquiring firm from outsider lenders (e.g., a bank). LBOs are considered by management, boards of directors, and controlling shareholders in virtually every instance in which a large, publicly-held company changes control.[4] There is nothing generically different about an LBO as compared to any other transaction financed with a large percentage of outside-borrowed funds. For example, LBOs are not unlike buying a home through the use of a mortgage. With the mortgage, the house purchase is a leveraged transaction using money borrowed from a bank and secured by the value of the purchased home. Similarly, a substantial portion of the debt used for an LBO is secured by the assets of the target company, which will generate cash flows that are used to service the debt.

As the post-acquisition cash flow of the purchased business pays down the debt, the value of the equity position can often rise considerably. Once the acquisition debt is reduced to a more manageable level, the company can be taken public, sold, or re-leveraged to provide for further expansion.[5]

There are at least three prevailing motivations for using an LBO to conduct an acquisition. First, a firm may be more valuable under new ownership and management, generating additional funds or higher asset prices to repay the debt. Second, an LBO provides investors the opportunity to reap larger rewards by chipping in a small amount of their own capital, which is "leveraged" ten, twenty, or perhaps fifty times with debt obtained from outsiders. In effect, leverage allows acquiring investors to profit by putting relatively little of their own funds into the acquisition transaction, with the rest financed with outside lenders' money. Finally, LBOs can result in substantial tax advantages, such as the deduction of interest on the acquisition indebtedness.[6]

B. THE MECHANICS OF A LEVERAGED BUYOUT

In LBO cases, the initial impetus for the acquisition can come either from management of the target company (in effect purchasing the shares of its own shareholders) or from outside acquirers. Assuming that at some price over current market value shareholders of the target firm

---

4. See generally R. Kuhn, *Mergers, Acquisitions, and Leveraged Buyouts* (1990).

5. Kuhn, supra.

6. Scharf, C.A., Shea, E.E. and Beck, G.C., 1991, *Acquisitions, Mergers, Sales, Buyouts, and Takeovers: A Handbook with Forms*. Englewood Cliffs: Prentice Hall.

would be willing to sell their shares, such that there is interest in a transaction among both potential acquirers and potential sellers, a series of steps will ensue. But first, two questions present themselves: can the acquiring firm borrow enough money to offer target company shareholders a premium over their current share prices, and will that premium be high enough that target-firm shareholders will sell their shares in sufficient numbers to give acquirers the control they seek in the target firm?

To understand how these questions are sorted out, Figure 1 may be useful. Essentially, an LBO entails three separate groups involved in acquiring a controlling bloc of a target firm (call it ABC Corporation), and three different groups involved in having the firm acquired. On the acquiring side, there are the acquirers themselves, lenders to finance the acquisition, and a holding company (whose purpose will be explained below.) These three groups are shown in Figure 1. On the selling side, there is, of course, the target firm itself, plus the target firm's management, which acquirers hope will recommend to ABC's shareholders that they sell their shares. And finally, of course, there are the shareholders themselves.

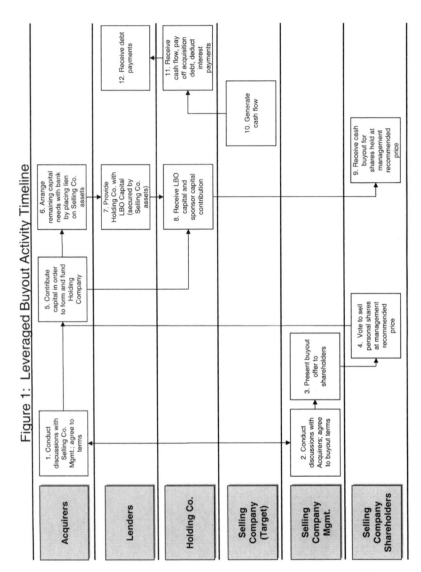

Figure 1: Leveraged Buyout Activity Timeline

On the acquirer side, the process of a leveraged buyout typically starts with an individual or group interested in becoming the owners of target Firm ABC.[7] Let Firm ABC be a large, publicly-held firm with thousands of shareholders. To raise the loan funds necessary to finance the acquisition of so many shares, the acquirers and target-firm management will contact a lender (call it Lender) to see how much money Lender would provide to finance the acquisition. That amount will then determine how much the acquirers can offer the shareholders of the target firm (ABC Corporation) for their shares.

But how is that amount determined? In that respect, one must understand the further mechanics of an LBO. The acquiring company

---

7. The grouping to acquire Firm A might be A's current management (di-rectors and officers). If so, the transaction is referred to as a "management LBO".

will form a holding company as the acquisition vehicle (call it "Vehicle") for obtaining control of ABC. The acquisition vehicle company will be established to hold the proceeds of the loan; initially, those loan proceeds will be its only or its principal assets. With those assets pledged by the lender, Vehicle will suggest to the board of directors of ABC a price at which Vehicle would be willing to purchase ABC shares. If management of target firm ABC (essentially, ABC's board of directors) finds that the price offered to purchase the ABC shareholders' shares represents an attractive price to shareholders, it will recommend that shareholders accept the acquiring company's tender offer for the ABC shares.[8] Ordinarily, shareholders of a target company will agree with its board of directors when the board recommends sale of the shares, and will indicate its willingness to sell at the price offered by Vehicle. Vehicle will then tender for the ABC shares at the given price and complete its acquisition of ABC shares.

A key point, then, is that following its loan, Vehicle now controls the assets of ABC Corporation–indeed it may merge the two firms. But the assets of ABC are now available to satisfy the obligations of Vehicle, principally the loan from Lender. Indeed, it is the very security provided by those assets that gives Lender the incentive to lend to Vehicle, which when founded usually has few or no assets of its own.

C. THE TRANS UNION LEVERAGED BUYOUT

The general schema in Figure 1 describing leveraged buyouts can be adapted as in Figure 2 to explain the LBO in *Smith v. Van Gorkom*.[9]

8. This process describes a "friendly takeover," one in which target-firm management is working with the acquiring group to effectuate a sale of the target-firms shares by recommending the sale of the shares to the acquirers. This is not the only way a takeover can occur. If target-firm's management resists the sale by refusing to ratify and recommend it to its shareholders, outside acquirers can go around target-firm management and bid directly to shareholders for their shares, i.e., organize a "hostile takeover."

9. The facts reported here are those in the Delaware Supreme Court's opinion. It is assumed here that the Delaware Supreme Court's rendition of the facts accurately captures the essentials of the decision facing the Trans Union board. The unpublished opinion of the Delaware trial court (the Chancery Court) opinion was apparently very brief and virtually devoid of factual background, even though, said the Supreme Court, "[t]he nature of this case requires a detailed factual statement." 488 A.2d at 864.

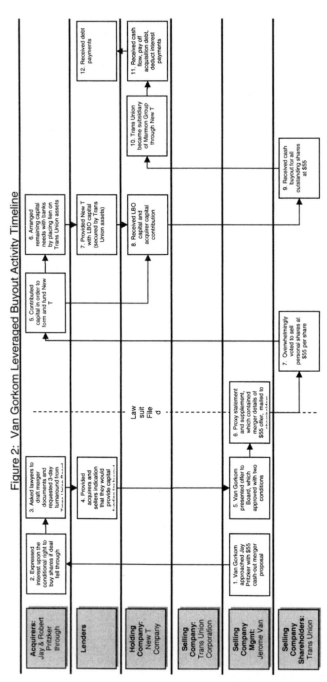

Figure 2: Van Gorkom Leveraged Buyout Activity Timeline

Trans Union (TU) and in particular its board chairman and chief executive offer, Jerome Van Gorkom, had an asset of potential value to Trans Union shareholders, a complicated tax-code provision known as investment tax credits (ITCs). Van Gorkom had spent years trying to find ways to unlock the value contained in Trans Union accumulated ITC's, but doing so required a firm to have sufficient offsetting revenues.

Absent changes in tax law (for which Van Gorkom had lobbied publicly), Trans Union could not realize the value of its ITCs, given the firm's future expected revenue flows and the tax-based accelerated depreciation schedules being applied to firm assets. Critically, also, the ITCs were non-transferable—they could not be sold separately to another firm.

Because its ITCs were non-transferable, Trans Union ultimately required some sort of acquisition or merger with another firm to maximize their value.[10] After consideration of various possibilities, Van Gorkom outlined to the Trans Union board the possible desirability of selling Trans Union to a company with a large amount of taxable income against which the ITC's could profitability be applied. The attractiveness of such a sale might be even greater if the acquisition could be financed using other people's money, i.e., via a highly leveraged buy-out of Trans Union shareholders.

In September 1980, Van Gorkom proposed such a deal to Jay Pritzker, whom he knew socially, and more importantly, who was known as one looking for undervalued companies regardless of the industry. One of the world's richest men, Pritzker had (following service as a naval aviator in World War II) started acquiring small companies such as timber mills. Soon, Jay Pritzer, with his brother Robert, established Marmon Corporation, holding interests in businesses as diverse as Hyatt Hotels, Braniff Airlines, Levitz Furniture, Ticketmaster and various casinos in Las Vegas and Atlantic City. Moving into a Fortune 500 company specializing in consumer credit would add another piece to the very diversified Marmon portfolio.

But could the acquisition of Trans Union be done with most of the financing coming from outside investors? Could such financing rise to a sufficient level that current Trans Union shareholders would be willing to sell their shares? If so, the funds would be received by a subsidiary vehicle ("New T Company") formed by the Pritzker parent firm, the Marmon Group. Discussions with lenders revealed that outside financing would be available, which would enable Pritzker to offer a price over then-current market prices for Trans Union shares. Pritzker would tender $55 per share, a sizeable premium over market—some $21 over the mid-range of Trans Union share prices for 1980 and almost $18 more than its closing price on the last trading day before the Pritzker offer was announced.[11] Thereafter, New T could be merged with TU, or New T could hold the TU shares as a wholly-owned subsidiary.[12] Covering the

10. Trans Union's difficulties with accelerated tax credits as well as accelerated depreciation "are indispensible to understanding the condition of Trans Union, and the [directors'] motivations underlying the sale of the company." Hamermesh, Why I Do Not Teach Van Gorkom, 34 GA.L.REV. 477 (2000). Yet, while briefly mentioned early in the Delaware court opinion, Trans Union's problems in these respects never resurface once the court's discusses why directors were at fault.

11. "[Trans Union's] high and low range for 1980 through September 19 (the last trading day before announcement of the merger) was $38 ¼–$29 ½." 488 A.2d at 866 n.5. The price at the September 19 close was 37 ¼. 488 A.2d at 867.

12. Ultimately, in 2005, Marmon "spun off" the shares of Trans Union, its wholly-owned subsidiary, to Marmon shareholders.

loan proceeds from the lender to New T would now be the considerable value of the Trans Union assets under its new Pritzker ownership.

However, Pritzker demanded that the Trans Union board move swiftly in considering his offer. He was concerned that his bid would put Trans Union in play, ultimately to be acquired by another bidder, and he did not want to be a "stalking horse" in that way. Van Gorkom, on the other hand, was concerned about any deal that would not leave the Trans Union board free to accept another offer higher than Pritzker's $55 per share proposal, should one in fact emerge.[13] After negotiating over this point with Van Gorkom, Pritzker agreed that Van Gorkom would present the Pritzker offer to the TU board for accelerated action, but at the same time the board would for 90 days be free to accept (but not solicit) competing bids for ninety days.

On September 20, 1980, the TU board met in a special session called for by Van Gorkom. The board was to consider Pritzker's proposed merger offer, although Van Gorkom did not announce in advance the purpose of the meeting. After two hours, during which they were advised by their attorney Brennan "that they might be sued [by Trans Union shareholders] if they failed to accept the offer," the board approved the Pritzker proposal.[14] Van Gorkom executed the agreement that evening, only one week after Pritzker was first approached.

On October 10, the offer was amended to allow Trans Union to nullify the deal with Pritzker if a more favorable offer was made and reduced to a definite agreement before the shareholders met in February. No such offer emerged, although Salomon Brothers was engaged to search for possible suitors. Two groups did express interest in acquiring Trans Union's shares. The would-be acquirers both expressed contingent interest in ultimately offering $60 for the shares. One investment group, including Kohlberg, Kravis Roberts & Company plus some Trans Union senior management, proposed an offer contingent on obtaining outside financing, an offer withdrawn soon thereafter when one of the Trans Union managers pulled out of the investment group. Some weeks later, GE Credit Corporation said that although it thought it might be prepared to offer $60 per share, it needed an extension of time beyond the shareholder meeting to formalize its offer, an extension Pritzker naturally refused to grant. GE then terminated negotiations, saying it would not continue "in the absence of the willingness [of the Pritzker interests] to terminate the proposed $55 cash merger."[15] At a shareholder meeting held on February 10, 1981, shareholders voted to approve the Pritzker merger proposal, with some 90 percent of the shares voted in favor.

---

13. It is important to recall that the Trans Union events occurred at the dawn of the modern corporate takeover era. Courts had yet to propound the set of rules now taught routinely in corporations classes concerning directors' duty of care in takeover situations. E.g., Revlon, Inc. v. MacAndrews & Forbes Holdings, Inc., 506 A.2d 173 (Del. 1985). Van Gorkom's sensitivity to directors' need to maximize shareholder welfare, five years before the Delaware court enunciated specific rules, is noteworthy.

14. 488 A.2d at 868.

15. 488 A.2d at 885.

(Trans Union had over 13 million shares outstanding, but not all shareholders voted.)

A few Trans Union shareholders believed, however, that the board had not acted properly in organizing and approving the arrangement with Pritzker, which the board then submitted to shareholders. When those Trans Union shareholders brought suit to challenge the board's action in approving the Pritzker proposal, the Delaware Court of Chancery dismissed the suit.[16] On appeal, however, the Delaware Supreme Court held that in making their decision on September 20, the directors "were grossly negligent in approving the 'sale' of the Company upon two hours' consideration, without prior notice, and without the exigency of a crisis or emergency."[17]

D. THE APPLICABLE STANDARD OF "GROSS NEGLIGENCE"

There was much at stake for the TU directors (Van Gorkom et al.) in the case before the Delaware Supreme Court, in which the court would decide whether the directors had violated their duty of care to shareholders. First the directors' *personal* liability was at stake. Were the shareholders to succeed in their claims that the directors had erred, it was the directors themselves who would have to pay those millions of dollars at stake.[18]

To prevail in a case like *Trans Union,* plaintiff-shareholders must show that directors violated their "duty of care." To find for plaintiffs, however, would require the court to find that the directors were grossly negligent. As directors, Van Gorkom and company were agents of Trans Union (and so, indirectly, they were agents of its shareholders). As agents, they were required to apply their skills to advance the interests of the firm. Under typical principles of corporate law, this would mean that, in making decisions, they acted reasonably. Any mistake they may have made was not automatically actionable. Perfection is not the standard; even reasonable people make mistakes. Consequently, directors ordinarily will argue successfully that they have fulfilled their duty of care, as long as their decision was not motivated by any personal gain rather than gain to shareholders.[19]

16. Plaintiff Smith had in December 1980 unsuccessfully sought to enjoin the Pritzker deal, because of the cash acquisition's tax consequences to shareholders as compared to a stock-for-stock acquisition. W. Owen, Autopsy of a Merger—Trans Union: The Deal That Rocked the Corporate World 161–64.

17. 488 A.2d at 874.

18. Many firms, including Trans Union in this case, carry insurance covering their directors and officers in the event of personal liability. But, as was also true of Trans Union here, that insurance may not be sufficient to cover the full extent of damages in the event of liability, leaving the remainder as the personal liability of the directors and officers.

19. This is the well-established rule of director liability based on claims of director error, in the absence of plausible claims that directors were motivated by personal gain. There was no issue of personal gain in the case of *Smith v. Van Gorkom*.

It bears emphasis, too, that the relevant state law (Delaware), requires not just negligence by a director but *gross* negligence. This is a higher hurdle that plaintiffs must clear than a standard of mere negligence, the standard found in many other states. For a Delaware firm like Trans Union, the actions complained of must not only fall short of what a reasonable person would do in a similar situation, but fall *grossly* short of what a reasonable person (here, a director) would have done in such a situation.

Further, any gross negligence must have damaged the plaintiffs. Plaintiffs, that is, must show not only that defendants have acted with gross negligence under Delaware law, they must also show that their gross negligence has damaged plaintiffs. In other words, there will be no liability if defendant shareholders have not been damaged. "No harm, no foul" is the rule in corporate law when defendants have allegedly violated their duty of care, and plaintiffs must show the amount of the harm.

Finally, it is the plaintiffs' (here, Trans Union shareholders') burden to prove all of the above. Plaintiffs must show that their version of the facts is "more likely than not." If the details of a particular case show it was only "as probable as not" that directors were grossly negligent, or only "as probable as not" that there was any harm to plaintiffs, then plaintiffs have not satisfied their burden of proof and judgment should be awarded to defendants.

Given all these requirements, it is hardly surprising that shareholder-plaintiff suits against their corporate directors almost never succeed. *Trans Union*, therefore, was a rare exception to the rule.

E. WHERE TRANS UNION DIRECTORS ALLEGEDLY WENT WRONG

What made *Trans Union* one of those rare exceptions? The Delaware court stressed a series of procedural difficulties that, in the court's mind, made the directors' decision deficient.[20] The Delaware court focused on several issues, all pertaining to what had happened at the directors meeting on September 20, 1980 when the Pritzker offer was approved.

The court pointed out that the meeting was called quickly, that its purpose was not well explained in advance, and that the directors were largely dependent on Van Gorkom's explanation as to why the arrangement with Pritzker was good for Trans Union and its shareholders. The court also stressed that the directors lacked, and did not ask for, various sorts of documentation, such as a fairness opinion and a valuation report from outside experts. Both could have been provided, although that would have meant Pritzker's timetable could not have been met and his offer would be withdrawn. Neither the lack of subsequent competing

---

20. These are summarized in 488 A.2d 873 *et seq.*

bids nor the shareholder vote in favor of the Pritzker proposal excused the directors' dereliction of their duty on September 20.

The Delaware Supreme Court summarized:

"[W]e must conclude that the Board of Directors did not reach an informed business judgment on September 20, 1980 in voting to 'sell' the Company for $55 per share pursuant to the Pritzker cash-out merger proposal. Our reasons, in summary, are as follows: The directors (1) did not adequately inform themselves as to Van Gorkom's role in forcing the 'sale' of the Company and in establishing the per share purchase price; (2) were uninformed as to the intrinsic value of the Company; and (3) given these circumstances, at a minimum, were grossly negligent in approving the 'sale' of the Company upon two hours' consideration, without prior notice, and without the exigency of a crisis or emergency."

488 A.2d at 874.

Concerning damages, the Delaware Supreme Court remanded the case to the Chancery Court for "an evidentiary hearing to determine the fair value of the shares represented by the plaintiffs' class, based on the intrinsic value of Trans Union on September 20, 1980... [D]amages may be entered "to the extent that the fair value of Trans Union exceeds $55 per share" as of that date.[21] Ultimately, the Chancery Court approved a settlement of $23.5 million as "fair, reasonable and in the best interest" of the shareholders.[22]

F. PROCEDURAL VERSUS LEGAL STANDARDS GOVERNING THE TRANS UNION BOARD

As noted above, corporate lawyers reacted to *Van Gorkom* with disbelief and vehement disagreement.[23] The decision was criticized generally as indecipherable.[24] The remedy ordered (and the justification for

21. 488 A.2d at 893.

22. 11 Del. J. Corp. L. 1000 (1986).

23. E.g., "The Delaware Supreme Court's decision in *Trans Union* was met by astonishment in the corporate bar." R. Gilson & B. Black, The Law and Finance of Corporate Acquisitions 1054 (2d ed. 1995); "The response of the corporate bar to *Van Gorkom* was one of shocked incredulity. 'The Delaware Supreme Court ... exploded a bomb.'" Robert W. Hamilton, Cases and Materials on Corporations 698 (6th ed. 1998), quoting an unpublished newsletter of Bayless Manning to clients. For one of any number of similar reactions, see Fischel, supra note 2; Herzel & Katz, Smith v. Van Gorkom: The Business of Judging Business Judgment, 41 Bus. Law 1187, 1188 (1986) ("To most [including the authors] the court's decision seems misguided"); W. Carney, Mergers and Acquisitions 156 (2000)

("The Trans Union decision was widely criticized").

24. E.g., Gilson & Black, supra note 23, at 1056 ("*Trans Union* is difficult to interpret"); Macey and Miller, supra note 3, at 127 ("one of the most important—and mystifying—corporate law cases of the decade"). The uncertainty about what the case means extends to whether *Van Gorkom* should even be read as a duty-of-care case in the first place. Kirk, The *Trans Union* Case: Is It Business Judgment Rule as Usual? 24 Am. Bus. L.J. 467 (1986). See also Gilson & Black, supra note 23, at 1054–55: ("Although the court does not say so explicitly, the clear implication of the opinion is that Van Gorkom was looking out for his own interests rather than those of Trans Union. As in most cases finding a violation of the business judgment rule, there are strong hints of breach of the duty of loyalty.... That Van Gorkom may have put his

doing so) seemed confused.[25] But in particular, the facts recited by the court did not indicate that the prevailing Delaware standard in duty-of-care cases had been breached. As two leading commentators summarize in a frequently cited article,

> While the majority opinion claimed to have articulated a "gross negligence" standard as governing the case, the facts did not support a finding of negligence, much less gross negligence. There was no suggestion that the board of five inside and five outside directors acted out of any improper motive. Their credentials and business experience were superb. The merger had been negotiated by Van Gorkom, the Trans Union chairman, an attorney and certified public accountant who had many years of experience with the corporation and owned a substantial block of stock.

> Most important, the economic rationale for the merger was obvious: Trans Union possessed valuable tax credits that it could not use but that could be sold to the bidder through a merger. The board acted quickly, not because it failed to understand the gravity of its decision, but because the bidder had insisted that it respond to the proposal within three days. The board had been warned by counsel that failure to approve the merger might result in personal liability. The purchase price of $55 a share, representing a fifty percent premium over market, hardly seemed inadequate, particularly since the firm's shares were publicly traded, and had never traded at a price higher than $39½. After the board originally approved the merger, it met again to reconsider the matter. Shareholders overwhelmingly approved the merger.

> In short, the facts, the ostensible legal standard and the holding are contradictory.[26]

That is, the duties that directors owe their corporation could hardly have been breached by Trans Union's directors bringing to bear such a wealth of knowledge and experience, in the face of Pritzker's demand for speed and the premium he was offering.

---

own interests above those of the shareholders (although the record apparently would not support that conclusion) would explain his liability.") But, as Gilson and Black note, breach of loyalty cannot explain the liability of the other directors, particularly the outside directors.

25. With its remand to the Chancery Court for a determination of Trans Union's "intrinsic value," that determination to be made "in accordance with *Weinberger v. UOP*,"(488 A.2d at 893), the Delaware Supreme Court has been criticized for both its economics and its law. Economically, there is no such thing as "intrinsic value." The value of anything, including a firm's shares, is what somebody will pay for it. "If any of this were true—if there were a single 'intrinsic value' that could be summed or otherwise derived from a column of figures and entered as the bottom line on a 'valuation study'—then the directors' reliance on market premia would, of course, be subject to severe criticism... In fact, however, the court's understanding of the underlying economics is so muddled that its line of reasoning runs off track." M. Dooley, Fundamentals of Corporation Law, 247 (1995). Legally, *Weinberger* was a duty of loyalty case, not a duty of care case, as was *Van Gorkom*.

26. Macey and Miller, supra note 3, at 129–30.

As correct as such criticisms of the Delaware Supreme Court's decision are, they omit consideration of an issue that the Delaware court also ignored. Even had the Delaware court believed (despite the evidence in the case) that directors had breached their duty of care toward Trans Union and thus its shareholders, breach of duty is only a necessary condition for liability, not a sufficient condition.[27] To violate the duty of care because of supposed gross negligence, any breach must also have caused some damage to the firm and its shareholders.[28] The court did not address that issue in its opinion, basing its conclusion on the factors noted above, such as the board's speed in concluding that the Pritzker offer was a good one for shareholders as well as the board's failure to consider various other possible sources of information before deciding to recommend the Pritzker offer to shareholders.[29] But whether shareholders were harmed or not was a point never addressed in the case.

In other words, the court ignored what, both to shareholders at the time and to analysts afterwards, would seem the essential point: what difference did the factors on which the court rested liability make?[30] Undertaking all the procedural steps that the court said the board should have undertaken would have taken more time than Pritzker's offer allowed. The board therefore would have been forced to reject Pritzker's time-constrained offer at its September 20 meeting.[31] The question shareholders would have asked of their directors on September 20 was: what would be gained by following all of the procedural steps recited by the Delaware court? If the answer to that question would be nothing, then the board fulfilled its duty to shareholders, assuming it did

---

27. "So far, we have discussed what it takes to show that directors or officers breached their duty of care. Liability, however, does not result simply from such a breach.... [S]uch a breach must be the cause of damages in order for there to be liability." F. Gevurtz, Corporation Law 301 (2000).

28. E.g., Barnes v. Andrews, 298 F. 614 (S.D.N.Y. 1924) (director's "neglect" not shown to have caused any loss to the firm); Francis v. United Jersey Bank, Francis v. United Jersey Bank, 432 A.2d 814 (N.J. 1981) (director's negligence a proximate cause of firm's losses).

29. "This lack of a need for causal proof is not a matter that should go unexplored, yet nothing in *Van Gorkom* itself addresses the question...." Hamermesh, supra note 10, at 487. The *Van Gorkom* focus on informational inputs rather than shareholder-benefit outputs contained the seeds of future legal mischief. "[I]t may be that the court's lack of focus on the causation issue laid the groundwork for its subsequent and widely criticized determination in *Cede & Co. v. Technicolor* that a plaintiff in a duty-of-care case need not establish a causal relation between the failure to exercise care

and the injury." Id., 488, citing Cede & Co. v. Technicolor, Inc., 634 A.2d 345, 371 (Del. 1993). "The *Cede* court's rejection of tort law causation principles ... seems bizarre." Gevurtz, supra note 27, at 302.

30. In asking what difference it would make had the directors behaved as the Delaware Supreme Court said they should have, one can assume *arguendo* that the directors truly did breach their duty. Although the ensuing discussion treats the consequences of the assumed breach in terms of proximate cause (see note 29 *supra* and accompanying text), the analysis could just as easily have been phrased in terms of damages, which, it is argued here, were zero. In that case, there would be no breach of the duty of care, any more than there would be if breach was not the cause of any damage. Focus on causation as opposed to damages, that is, leads to the same conclusion that the Trans Union directors should not have been held liable.

31. "Thirty-six hours on a late summer weekend. That was all the time the board of directors of Trans Union had to decide, for if they didn't, the offer that had been tendered by the Pritzkers would vanish from the table...." Owen, supra note 16.

all it could do to maximize the value of the firm to them, in light of what the directors already knew or reasonably could have learned at the time.

The premium that Pritzker put on the table was a handsome one and the size of the premium in *Van Gorkom* is often treated as tantamount to proof that the board had fulfilled its duty by recommending acceptance.[32] But the question—both economically and legally—is not whether the offer was a good one, but rather whether, taking reasonable steps to meet its duty of care, the board could have gotten a better offer. What a reasonable board would have done naturally depends on the consequences of accepting Pritzker's offer when compared to the effects of rejecting it.[33] The remand instruction from the Delaware Supreme Court referred to what was "fair, reasonable and in the best interests of shareholders," indicating that the court believed the standard was the price that could have been obtained, had the board performed in the way it (the Delaware Supreme Court) said it should have. "[T]he 'intrinsic value' of Trans Union can be reduced to the difference between its current market value and how much more another firm would have been willing to pay because of that firms' special use of Trans Union's assets—in this case the investment tax credits."[34]

G. EXPECTED EFFECTS OF REJECTING THE PRITZKER OFFER: A SIMPLE MODEL

Because the possibility of a higher offer was just that—only a possibility—it is useful to think of the Trans Union board's decision in terms of the probability of different outcomes. The board had before it two possible decisions: accept the Pritzker offer or reject it. For shareholders, there were three possible implications. Shareholders could (1) gain nothing, if the Pritzker offer were rejected; (2) reap the $18 premium that Pritzker's offer would afford; or (3) hold out for an even greater premium from some other bidder. As with any decision whose consequences will only be known subsequently, the TU board's decision to accept or reject Pritzker's offer and recommend it to shareholders at the time could be based only on educated estimates of the decision's future impact. A board decision to accept Pritzker's offer would lead to various potential consequences, while a board decision to reject the offer would lead to various alternative potential consequences. Those consequences are summarized in Table 1.

The decision to accept is shown as Decision 1, while the decision to reject is shown as Decision II.

---

32. "Indeed, given that the deal appeared to be so favorable, the board surely was entitled to some leeway in the formality of the procedures which it used to evaluate the matter." Macey and Miller, supra note 3, at 131.

33. Hamermesh, supra note 10, at 483–84, 488–90.

34. Dooley, supra note 25, at 246–4.

TABLE 1:

Consequences of Decision Facing Trans Union Board

(Accept [I] or Reject [II] Pritzker Offer)

		[Decision I]	[Decision II]
BOARD DECISION:		Accept Pritzker Offer	Reject Pritzker Offer
FINANCIAL CONSEQUENCES:			
[A]	Shareholder Gain = $0	Impossible— Shareholder gain certain	Possible—Pritzker walks, no other bidder appears.
[B]	Shareholder Gain = $18	Probable—Pritzker offer accepted	Possible—Pritzker remains, or he walks and another bidder makes similar offer.
[C]	Shareholder Gain > $18	Possible—another bidder appears and outbids Pritzker	Possible—Pritzker or another bidder makes higher offer.

Each decision entailed possible consequences, depending on what happened next. If the board accepted Pritzker's offer, TU shareholders could not lose (outcome [IA]). The sole question was the amount of the gain. If the Pritzker offer was accepted, a gain of at $18 was guaranteed (outcome [IB]).[35]

Pritzker's offer did allow the board to entertain higher offers subsequently, but the probability of such offers emerging would have seemed relatively small to the TU directors, for several reasons. First, the offer's premium over market was almost 50 percent. This was not only a healthy gain to shareholders; it was a gain very much on the high side of takeover premia generally during this period.[36] Second, Pritzker had insisted on Trans Union not seeking higher offers, although it could accept an alternative offer, should one materialize. Third, the possible gain available from acquiring Trans Union and its accumulating ITCs was information that had been in the market for a long time without exciting any bidder interest. Indeed, for years Trans Union had publicized the additional value available to any firm that could use its excess ITCs.

It was therefore unlikely that a better offer than Pritzker's $18 premium would emerge after September 20. Upon remand, the Chancery

---

35. It is assumed that shareholders would overwhelmingly approve the Pritzker offer, as in fact they did.

36. A comprehensive study of successful takeover premia found that "from 1980 to 1985 the average premium was 30 percent." Jarrell, Brickley & Netter, The Market for Corporate Control: The Empirical Evidence Since 1980, 2 J. Econ. Perspectives 49, 51 (1988). See also Jensen & Ruback, The Market for Corporate Control: The Scientific Evidence, 11 J. Fin. Econ. 5 (1983). "Many published studies have documented the effects of tender offers and mergers on stock prices. The consensus is that these transactions confer large stock-price gains on target shareholders, averaging about 30 to 50 percent over pre-offer prices during the eighties." Jarrell, Takeovers and Leveraged Buyouts, in D. Henderson, ed., The Fortune Encyclopedia of Economics 607–08 (1993). For one such study, see Jarrell & Poulsen, The Returns to Acquiring Firms in Tender Offers: Evidence from Three Decades, 18 *Fin. Mgmt.* 12 (1989) (hereinafter Returns to Tender Offers).

Court stated that, but for the class action, "it is reasonable to assume that the class of former Trans Union stockholders would have received nothing beyond the merger consideration of $55 per share."[37] Still one cannot rule out the possibility of a higher offer (outcome [IC]).

What if the board had rejected Pritzker's offer (decision column [II] in Table 1)? Perhaps most importantly, rejection of Pritzker's offer entailed the possibility that a beneficial takeover would not take place at all. Compared to accepting the Pritzker deal, "all other alternatives involved substantially more risk."[38] And as compared to accepting the Pritzker bid, where any risk was on the upside in that a better offer might emerge, rejecting the Pritzker bid entailed a substantial downside risk. Shareholders could lose the $18 offered by Pritzker, if no other offer materialized for Trans Union (outcome [IIA] in Table 1).

Following a board rejection of the Pritzker offer, however, two other outcomes were possible. The $18 gain might still have been realized (outcome [IIB]), in either of two ways. Pritzker could renew his offer for ultimate acceptance by the TU board, perhaps following the lengthier sort of board deliberation and information-gathering process that the Delaware court said should have been undertaken. Or, even if Pritzker declined to make a second offer at $55, another bidder might emerge and make a similar offer entailing a gain of $18 per share.[39]

Alternatively, a shareholder gain of even more than $18 might have been realized following the board's rejection of Pritzker's $55 offer (outcome [IIC] in Table 1). This could happen if either Pritzker or another bidder countered the board's rejection by making a higher offer. One must assume that the probability of that result (outcome [IIC]) is higher than the likelihood of getting a higher offer after accepting Pritzker's offer (outcome [IC]).[40] After rejecting Pritzker's offer, the board would be free to actively seek higher offers, which acceptance of Pritzker's offer forbade.

These, then, were the considerations that would have faced the Trans Union directors on September 20, 1980. Satisfying its legal obligation, a board of directors would have accepted the Pritzker offer if the expected value of doing so exceeded the expected value of rejecting the offer.[41] Those expected values in turn depended on the probabilities

37. 11. Del. J. Corp. L. 1000, 1003.

38. Gilson & Black, supra note 23, at 1055. General Electric, in insisting that the Pritzker offer be rebuffed as a condition of GE's making it own bid, essentially was asking shareholders to run this risk.

39. Pritzker or another bidder might also have launched a hostile offer for Trans Union, at a price containing less than an $18 premium over market. That possibility is not included here. Van Gorkom and the Trans Union board were clearly interested in a friendly takeover, making a hostile bid unnecessary.

40. More technically, the probability distributions of potential subsequent offers are different, depending whether the TU board has accepted or rejected the Pritzker offer. This point is explored further in note 42, *infra.*

41. "The argument is not that the Pritzkers' offer represented the best possible price that Trans Union could have received. It is entirely possible that some other buyer would have been willing to pay more.... And it is equally possible that other buyers would have placed a lower value on Trans Union. The decision faced

associated with each of the outcomes of accepting (Decision I in Table 1) or rejecting (Decision II in Table 1) the offer. The value-maximizing decision rule is shown in Table 2, which reflects the ordinary method of computing expected values as applied to the decision facing the Trans Union Board.[42]

Table 2:

Optimal Decision Rule for Trans Union Board

(Accept [I] or Reject [II] Pritzker Offer)

DECISION: Accept Pritzker Offer If
            Expected Value (Acceptance) > Expected Value (Rejection),
               i.e., if $Pr^*(IA) + Pr^*(IB) + Pr^*(IC) > Pr^*(IIA) + Pr^*(IIB) + Pr^*(IIC)^{\#}$

IA and IIA, = $0, IIA and IIB = $18, **X** is unknown.

EXAMPLE: Accept Pritzker Offer If
            $0^*(0) + .9^*(\$18) + .1^*(\$X) > .33^*(\$0) + .33^*(\$18) + .34^*(\$X)$ **X** > **\$42.75**$^{\#\#}$
            Therefore, accept Pritzker offer unless an alternative offer of some **$80 (greater than a $42.75 premium over market price of $37.25)** is likely.

$^{\#}$ *Pr* refers to the probability of a particular outcome; outcomes as indicated in parentheses (e.g., IA) are those summarized in Table 1.

$^{\#\#}$ Solving for **X**,
   $0 + .9^*\$18 + .1^*\mathbf{X} > 0 + .33^*\$18 + .34^*\mathbf{X}$
   $\$16.2 + .1^*\mathbf{X} > \$5.94 + .34^*\mathbf{X}$
   $(\$16.2 - \$5.94) > .24^*\mathbf{X}$
   $\$10.26/.24 > \mathbf{X}$
   $\$42.75 > \mathbf{X}$

by the board was not different from the decision faced by homeowners who receive a firm offer for their house. While it is conceivable that someone else will ... offer a higher price, it's also conceivable that no such buyer will be found within a reasonable period of time or ever. In the meantime, the homeowners, like the directors, risk losing an opportunity to sell now on favorable terms." Dooley, supra note 25, at 247.

42. "Expected value is simply the weighted average of the best guesses about future payments to be received...." Carney, supra note 23, at 25. Expected values are calculated by multiplying (weighting) the value of each possible outcome by its respective probability of occurring. The method is found in any text on finance, including legal texts. E.g., Carney, id., W. Brudney & W. Bratton, Corporate Finance 51–57 (4th ed. 1993). Perhaps more importantly, it is a method familiar to Delaware courts, as it utilizes the same methodology as the Delaware block method traditionally (but no longer exclusively) employed in appraisal proceedings for valuing firms under alternative assumptions. E.g., Francis I. duPont & Co. v. Universal City Studios, Inc. 312 A.2d 344 (Del. Ch. 1973).

As Table 2 illustrates, a value-maximizing board deciding what was good for Trans Union shareholders on September 20 would have to resolve two sorts of issues.[43] First, what were the probabilities attached to the different possible outcomes? Second, what were the shareholder gains associated with the different outcomes? Making different assumptions about these two sets of parameters is revealing. Four different hypothetical possibilities are discussed here.

Suppose, first, the example shown in Table 2. Assume that if the TU board had voted in favor of recommending the Pritzker offer, there was a 90 percent chance the bidder would succeed in completing the takeover at a share price of $55, an $18 premium over market as of September 19. Therefore, there was a 10 percent chance a higher offer might be made. Alternatively, if the TU board rejected the Pritzker offer, assume that the three possible outcomes had essentially equal probabilities. It was just as likely that (a) no other offer would emerge (so shareholders would gain nothing); (b) a takeover would eventually be completed by some other bidder at the same $18 premium; or (c) that a higher offer would emerge.

The equal-probability alternative for Decision II is not chosen idly here. If the TU board was truly under-informed on September 20, it would by definition not have optimal information as to the respective likelihoods of the three possible outcomes.[44] There would be no reason to assume that any of the three outcomes was more likely than another.[45] The assumption of equal probabilities also satisfies a necessary condition of the model, that the probability of getting a better offer than Pritzker's would be higher without Pritzker's condition prohibiting Trans Union from searching for a better offer.[46]

43. If the board had perfect (or even reasonably good) information about all possible outcomes and their associated probabilities, value maximization would entail comparison of the values of two different probability distributions, that associated with Decision I and that associated with Decision II. But almost certainly the Trans Union board could not have known (and could not have found out, regardless of Pritzker's time constraints) what the entire probability distributions associated with the two decisions were. This was a case of decision under uncertainty, not risk. See generally F. Knight, Risk and Uncertainty (1921).

44. The board would of course have known of the three outcomes. Attorney Brennan told them that there was a good chance they would be sued if they rejected the offer and no other offer materialized (outcome [IIA]). The $18 premium was on the table (outcome [IIB]), and the possibility of higher offers (outcome [IIC]) was clear from Pritzker's concession to Van Gorkom's condition that the board be free to accept a higher offer within ninety days.

45. The available evidence suggests that in deciding among a set of new or unfamiliar outcomes, people tend to underestimate the relevant probabilities. Tvesky & Fox, Weighing Risk and Uncertainty, 102 *Psych. Rev.* 269 (1995). However, decision-makers also have a tendency to attach probabilities to the various outcomes that are more equal than the true distribution of underlying probabilities. Thus, overly large probabilities are ascribed to relatively low and relatively high payoff events, while unduly low probabilities are attributed to the more likely outcomes between the low and high extremes. Tversky & Kahneman, Advances in Prospect Theory: Cumulative Representation of Uncertainty, *5 J. Risk & Uncertainty* 297 (1992).

46. The probabilities of .1 and .34 assumed for outcomes [IC] and [IIC] respectively mean that an active campaign to market Trans Union would at least triple the likelihood of an offer higher than Pritzker's $55.

Under these probability assumptions, should the board have accepted or rejected the Pritzker offer? As Table 2 indicates, the question boils down to the price at which any higher offer might be made. Pritzker's offer represented a *guaranteed* minimum gain to shareholders of $18. They might gain more, either by accepting the Pritzker offer and then standing ready to consider higher competing offers (outcome [IC] in Table 1), or by rejecting the Pritzker offer and then more actively marketing Trans Union as a takeover candidate (outcome [IIC]).

As the example in Table 2 shows, with the assumed probabilities for the various outcomes, the board should have accepted the Pritzker offer unless it felt that a higher offer would be more than $80 per share (more than a $42.75 premium over the closing price for Trans Union shares on September 20).[47] A premium of that magnitude—over 100 percent above Trans Union's going share price—would have been utterly remarkable.

To be more precise, one can compare the Trans Union premium over its takeover premium relative to market value for acquired firms generally during this early period of corporate takeovers. In one study using a sample of 526 successful tender offers from 1963 to 1986, shareholders of the acquired firms enjoyed a mean abnormal return (i.e., return earned with market fluctuations held constant) of 29 percent, with a standard deviation of .95 percent.[48] Assuming normality in the distribution of outcomes, only .5 percent of all firms enjoyed a premium (abnormal return) greater than 32 percent in 1963–1986. Applying this data to Trans Union in particular, the probability of an abnormal return of over 100 percent is extraordinarily small.[49]

One can alter the assumed probabilities to see what a value-maximizing board would have done under alternative assumptions, including rather extreme ones. To take a second example, suppose that the chance of a higher premium, even if Pritzker's offer was accepted (outcome [IC] in Table 1), was 20 percent—double that shown in Table II's example. Suppose, likewise, that the chances of getting a higher offer if Pritzker's offer was rejected (outcome [IIC] in Table 1) was a very high 80 percent (with equal 10–percent probabilities for the other two outcomes if the Pritzker offer was rejected). Under those assumptions, a board should

47. Expected value of Decision I = .9($18) + .1($42.75) = $20.48.

Expected value of Decision II = .33($0) + .33($18) + .34($42.75) = $20.54.

48. Returns in Tender Offers, supra note 36, at 16 (Exhibit 2).

49. The comparison between the Trans Union premium and takeover premia generally during this time is in some respects crude; some qualifications are in order. As noted in the text, studies of abnormal returns use regression analysis to control for market fluctuations. Abnormal returns also are calculated over a period surrounding the actual announcement date of the take-

over, to capture the fact that the full premium over market typically registers over time, not on a single day. (In the study cited, Returns to Tender Offers, *supra* note 36, that period runs from twenty days before the announcement to ten days after the announcement.) These and other refinements in takeover event studies (themselves based on the capital asset pricing model) are not captured in the discussion here concerning the one-day, 100 percent ($18) premium represented by Pritzker's offer for Trans Union. Indeed, the capital asset pricing model was only coming to be understood and used outside academia at the time of Trans Union events.

reject Pritzker's offer only if a premium of over $21 (that is, a bid over $58) were deemed prospectively available.[50]

The simple model is useful in answering the critical question in the *Trans Union* case: what alternative bid should be assumed in analyzing the TU board's decision? That question must be answered to assess what damage, if any, shareholders suffered from the board's decision. The best available evidence indicates that the most likely bid greater than the $55 Pritzker offer was $60 (a premium of $23), the figure proposed both by the Kohlberg, Kravis Roberts investment group and by GE Credit. It was possible on September 20 that a $60 offer would be available if the Pritzker offer were refused, but those higher offers were merely possibilities. And in fact, neither of the $60 offers was actually made.

As a third hypothetical situation, then, assume again that the Trans Union board deemed a $60 bid 10 percent likely in the event that the Pritzker offer were accepted (outcome [I]C in Table 1), but five times (50 percent) more likely in the event the Pritzker offer were refused (outcome [II]C). The expected value of the premium from accepting the Pritzker offer would be $18.50, while the expected value of refusing it (using the same assumptions as applied previously) would be only $17.00.[51] So, it certainly would have been value-reducing to shareholders for the board to reject Pritzker's offer with an even-money expectation (a 50–50 chance) of getting a bid of $60. In fact, unless there were a two-out-of-three likelihood of getting $60 if Pritzker's offer were rejected, a rational board would still not turn down Pritzker's offer.[52] (Recall the advice of Trans Union's lawyer that the board would be sued if they did *not* recommend the Pritzker offer to shareholders.)

At what prospective higher price should the board have rejected Pritzker's offer of $55? To answer this question, it is essential to consider that the Delaware Chancery Court eventually approved a settlement of $23.5 million from the defendants in the case, finding that the sum was "fair, reasonable and in the best interests of the class."[53] Given the number of shares represented by the plaintiff class, 12,734,404, the court in effect held that an additional $1.85 over Pritzker's $55 offer (a total premium of $19.85 rather than Pritzker's $18) could have been had, but for defendants' alleged gross negligence.

But how likely would that higher premium have to be for its expected value to exceed a certain $18 premium? In a fourth and final hypothetical exercise, assume that a $19.85 premium, as opposed to Pritzker's $18, were available. If an additional $1.85 struck the court as fair and reasonable, and was a sum acceptable to plaintiff shareholders

---

50. Expected value of Decision I = .8($18) + .2($21) = $18.60.

Expected value of Decision II = .10($0) + .10($18) + .8($21) = $18.60.

51. Expected value of Decision I = .9($18) + .1($23) = $18.50.

Expected value of Decision II = .25($0) + .25($18) + .5($23) = $17.00.

52. Expected value of Decision I = .9($18) + .1($23) = $18.50.

Expected value of Decision II = .16($0) + .16($18) + .68($23) = $18.52.

53. See text accompanying note 22, *supra*.

themselves, one wonders how likely an offer of $56.85 rather than Pritzker's $55 would have to be before a board would rationally reject the Pritzker offer. Employing the same methodology as above, one finds that the TU board would have had to assume an 85 percent probability that the better offer was available.[54]

In effect, the Delaware Supreme Court held it was gross negligence for the TU board to reject a certain offer of $55, because there must have been an 85 percent chance that a higher bid of $56.85 could have been obtained. To say that there was a 85 percent chance of a higher bid "out there" is to say that there was virtually no chance that Trans Union shareholders would come up empty, with Pritzker withdrawing his offer and no other bid materializing. That is, the board was grossly negligent for concluding that Pritzker's offer was the best possible one, after trying unsuccessfully both before and after the Pritzker deal to interest *any* investor in bidding for Trans Union at *any* price above market, and treating as negligible any risk that shareholders might wind up with no gain at all.

More to the legal point, even if the court believed that the TU board was wrong, that did not make its determination grossly negligent. Again, perfection is not the legal standard by which directors' duty of care is measured. One might assume *arguendo* that reasonable people could differ on whether a minimally higher bid was available with a relatively high probability, such that Pritzker's bid did not offer the greatest expected value to shareholders. But that is legally irrelevant. The issue is whether a director in a like position on the TU board would have been grossly derelict in his duty to take the bird in the hand rather than hold out for a higher offer in the bush. Given the numbers (both on higher bids and relevant probabilities) presented here, it is difficult to agree that any gross neglect of duty occurred.

The foregoing criticisms have principally to do with the substance of the decision made by the TU directors. But the Delaware Supreme Court's principal objections to the TU board's September 20 decision concern process, not substance, in particular how much information the TU board had before it before voting, how much of that information it absorbed before the vote, how long it took in its deliberations, and so forth.[55] Monitoring of inputs is an inferior system of principals' surveillance of their agents, compared to direct measurement of the output for which principals contract.[56] Particularly in a takeover situation, shareholders do not care about informational inputs used by directors; they care only about maximizing the value they will receive for their shares.

---

54. Expected value of Decision I = $.9(\$18) + .1(\$19.85) = \$18.19$.

Expected value of Decision II = $.075(\$0) + .075(\$18) + .85(\$19.85) = \$18.22$.

55. "[T]he focus of the court's finding of 'gross negligence' is the directors' failure to become sufficiently informed, rather than any failure in examining the informa-

tion gathered.... There is no analysis in *Van Gorkom* to give the 'gross negligence concept any precise content.'" Hamermesh, supra note 10, at 486 (footnote omitted).

56. E.g., Alchian & Demsetz, Production, Information Costs and Economic Organization, 62 Am. Econ. Rev. 777 (1972).

This obvious point is black-letter law in Delaware: when a sale of control impends, directors must "seek the transaction offering the best value reasonably available to the stockholders."[57] Had the *Van Gorkom* court focused on the real substance of the board's decision—what Pritzker's premium represented for Trans Union shareholders—the hypothetical (but realistic) numbers presented here make it highly unlikely that the outcome of the decision could be viewed as grossly negligent.[58] The furor over *Van Gorkom*, therefore, usefully recalls that shareholders care about results, not about how they were reached.[59]

H. *VAN GORKOM* AND THE CONTRACTUAL THEORY OF THE FIRM

The *Van Gorkom* opinion is usefully revisited for a second reason, one harking back to a debate predating that decision but continuing well beyond it. Corporations, with their limited liability for shareholders, were initially possible in Anglo–American law only by grant from the crown (in England) or legislature (later in England and in America).[60] Thus, many regard the corporation as a "creature of the state,"[61] the state's principal responsibility therefore being parental—regulatory—supervision of its offspring.[62]

57. Paramount Communications, Inc. v. QVC Network, Inc. 637 A.2d 34, 43 (Del. 1993).

58. The numbers are more than realistic; they are conservative. The set of alternatives offered if Pritzker's proposal was refused entailed more risk. A higher offer might later be made, but then again no offer might materialize. If Trans Union's shareholders, like investors generally, were risk-averse, the values shown in the four examples above for Decision II should be reduced appropriately for the risk they entailed. In addition, the hypothetical examples above do not adjust for the time value of money, i.e., for the fact that any better bid would be made and acted on sometime later than Pritzker's offer, and so would be of less value to shareholders, *ceteris paribus*. The latter point is all the more important, given the rising level of interest rates during the early 1980s. "[T]he prime rate had increased about 72% from September 20, 1980, the date of the Pritzker proposal, to December 19, 1980–from 12–1/2% to 21–1/2%—and was averaging 20.16% in January." Owen, supra note 16, at 180. Not only would higher interest rates lower the value of subsequent offers to shareholders, but they reduced the likelihood that highly-leveraged offers would be available in the first place.

59. "But as most commentators would agree, these procedures have led not to more effective management oversight and

better business decisions, but, instead, to a classic triumph of form over function...." Elson, Courts and Boards: The Top 10 Cases, 22 *Directors and Boards* 1, 27 (1997).

60. Adam Smith noted that "this prerogative of the crown seems to have been reserved... for extorting money from the subject." A. Smith, The Wealth of Nations 123–24 (Cannan ed. 1937).

61. "[T]here are some commentators who assert that the freedom to engage in a joint business venture in corporate form is a 'privilege' bestowed by the state. From this vacuous concept, they purport to derive the conclusion that the state has a right, even a duty, to control corporations. That line of reasoning is metaphysical jibberish." W. Klein, Business Organization and Finance: Legal and Economic Principles 108 (1980).

62. "Twenty years ago, legal scholars were herdlike in regarding corporate law as a species of consumer protection in which the law's role was to protect helpless investors by hogtying a predatory corporate management.... This view was echoed in article after article by professors from leading law schools calling for stringent federal laws regulating the conduct of corporate management." Winter, Foreward, in R. Romano, The Genius of American Corporate Law ix (1993). For more recent discussions of the role of mandatory government rules in corporate law, see, e.g., the articles ex-

Others see corporations as a nexus of contracts among private parties (shareholders, directors, officers).[63] In this contractarian view of the firm, the role of government, beyond enforcement of contracts' explicit terms, is to provide statutory default provisions defining or interpreting corporate rights and obligations that were not specified by contract among the participants in the firm.[64] A key part of the contractarian model of corporate law is competition among the states to attract corporations, which Roberta Romano calls "the genius of American corporate law."[65]

The debate over the state's role vis-à-vis the corporation has sometimes been more incendiary than illuminating, in part because the debaters often argue at different levels. Distinctions between normative and positive analysis are sometimes blurred, for example.[66] The normative side of the debate has proven less useful, partly because there are no rules that determine who wins the debate.[67]

The positive side of the debate between regulators and contractarians is more interesting. The criterion by which positive models are evaluated is predictive ability.[68] Thus, conclusions about which model is more correct are possible by assessing their predictions against observed events. Which theory best describes what it is that government actually does concerning corporations, when its legislature passes laws and its courts enforce them? Is the state behaving as a public regulator, or as a facilitator of private contract?

cerpted and cited in R. Romano, ed. Foundations of Corporate Law 101–121 (1993).

63. E.g.,Butler, The Contractual Theory of the Corporation, 11 Geo. Mason L. Rev. 99 (1989); F. Easterbrook & D. Fischel, The Economic Structure of Corporate Law (1991). That a firm (such as a corporation) can be thought of as a "nexus of contracts" has become something of a cliché in the university, but for good reason: it captures much of the basic logic at stake. Ramseyer, Corporate Law, in The New Palgrave Dictionary of Economics and the Law, vol. I 504 (1998) (citations omitted).

64. For a good summary, see Ramseyer, supra note 63, and the bibliography he provides. Modern arguments in favor of the contractarian view of the firm now include recommendations that corporate charters be permitted to include pre-emptive "freeze provisions," safeguarding the corporation and its shareholders against unwanted non-mandatory legislative changes in state corporation laws. Kades, Freezing the Company Charter, 79 N.C. L. Rev. 111 (2000).

65. R. Romano, The Genius of American Corporate Law (1993); see also Romano, Competition for State Corporate Law, The New Palgrave Dictionary of Economics and the Law, vol. I (1998).

66. Compare, e.g., Eisenberg, The Structure of Corporation Law, 89 Colum. L. Rev. 1461 with McChesney, Economics, Law, and Science in the Corporate Field: A Critique of Eisenberg, 89 Colum. L. Rev. 1530 (1989).

67. This point is discussed further in McChesney, Positive Economics and All That, 61 Geo. Wash. L. Rev. 272 (1992). Those that see the corporation primarily in contractual terms, and thus the role of the state as enforcing contracts and providing missing terms, may claim victory on the basis that such a regime maximizes the wealth of the participating parties (shareholders, etc.). But no force in life demands that maximizing wealth be the sole—or even principal—value to be sought. Regulators who oppose contractarians on the ground that wealth maximization is not the relevant value to be advanced by the state vis-à-vis corporations essentially advance an unassailable argument, as long as the costs of their pursuing non-maximizing behavior are outside the realm of discussion.

68. The classic citation is Friedman, The Methodology of Positive Economics, in Essays in Positive Economics (1953). For further discussion, see McChesney, supra note 67, at 275–81.

There has been relatively little systematic positive work addressing these issues.[69] In that respect, the legal process touched off by *Van Gorkom* makes the case particularly interesting. The Delaware holding is essentially regulatory, imposing on corporate boards various procedures that must be followed if the duty of care is to be fulfilled.[70] After *Van Gorkom,* "general counsels made recommendations to boards of directors that they hire expensive financial advisers, commission extensive studies, and otherwise improve the paper record of their decisional process in order to reduce the risk of liability in situations similar to *Van Gorkom.* It was a widely held belief that the cost of this exercise exceeded the benefits to the decisional process."[71]

If the Delaware decision were the last word, the regulatory model of the government vis-à-vis corporations would seem validated. But the *Van Gorkom* decision was not the last word. The holding sparked repercussions along other margins consistent with the governmental role predicted by the contractarian model. Given the dominance of Delaware in corporate law and the radical swerve from accepted duty-of-care principles in the *Van Gorkom* opinion, the Delaware opinion not surprisingly spurred immediate reactions. Obtaining directors' and officers' (D & O) insurance became very difficult.[72] Partly as a reflection of the upheavals in the insurance market, it also became more difficult for corporations to attract directors to their boards, and existing directors resigned from boards.[73]

69. For a notable exception, see Baysinger & Butler, The Role of Corporate Law in the Theory of the Firm, 28 J. L. & Econ. 179 (1985). The Baysinger–Butler article is discussed in Romano, Competition for State Corporate Law, The New Palgrave Dictionary of Economics and the Law, vol. I 366 (1998).

70. "*Trans Union* is not, at bottom, a business judgment case.... Its function is to regulate a target's response to certain types of takeover bids, namely 'rush' offers with short time fuses." Macey & Miller, *Trans Union* Reconsidered, 98 Yale L.J. 127 (1988). "*Trans Union* may be the Delaware Supreme Court's first attempt at counseling directors about the right way to sell the corporation." Gilson & Black, supra note 23, at 1055 (footnote omitted).

71. Hamilton, Reliance and Liability Standards, supra note 23, at 29. Accord, Herzel & Katz, supra note 23, at 1191: "Such formalism has a lot of costs. Most obviously, it will mean more reliance on and more fees for lawyers, investment bankers, accountants, management consultants, and economists, and who knows, maybe sociologists, statisticians, psychologists, demographers and population geneticists. In short, experts of every stripe, whose advice might shed some light on some aspect of the board's decision." For a similar evaluation, see Macey and Miller, supra note 3, at 135.

72. The risk of liability for corporate directors was reflected in a more than ten-fold increase in D & O insurance premiums from 1984 to 1986. Bradley & Schipani, The Relevance of the Duty of Care Standard in Corporate Governance, 75 Iowa L. Rev. 1 (1989). In addition to the risks *Van Gorkom* created, the decision caused such uncertainty about its ultimate impact that many insurance firms suspended the writing of D & O insurance. (At the time of *Van Gorkom*, the author was in the midst of incorporating a non-profit association, a process delayed because practically no insurance firms were writing new D & O insurance policies covering the particular organization seeking incorporation.) Unavailability of D & O insurance was a problem into 1987, according to some sources. E.g., Glaberson, "Liability Rates Flattening Out as Crisis Eases," *N.Y. Times*, Feb. 9, 1987, p. A1, col. 5 (companies that could not find insurance "at any price" beginning to find it). The fact that insurance was often unavailable, rather than just more expensive to reflect increased but measurable risk, attests to the great uncertainty about future liabilities in the wake of *Van Gorkom.*

73. E.g., Hamilton, Reliance and Liability Standards for Outside Directors, 24 Wake Forest L. Rev. 5, 28 (1989). Baum & Byrne, "The Job Nobody Wants", *Bus. Wk.*, Sept. 8, 1986, p. 56.

Needless to say, judicial imposition of costs exceeding benefits is hardly what shareholders themselves would want for their firms. The obligations imposed in shareholders' names were not duties that shareholders had contracted for, nor were they ones that corporate law had previously provided as a default option governing board behavior in the case of a takeover. Nothing in Trans Union's charter prescribed particular duties for disinterested directors in the event of a takeover. Hence, the law's default rule—gross negligence in Delaware—defined management's obligations to its shareholders. In holding for shareholders against management, the *Van Gorkom* court effectively tore up contracts existing between shareholders and directors of other Delaware corporations relying on the gross negligence default provisions established by state law.

Under the contractarian model of the firm, two things predictably would follow. First, the Delaware court's attempt generally to abrogate existing contractual rights and obligations between management and shareholders predictably would fail. Only Trans Union shareholders would benefit *ex post* from the Delaware court's ruling. Shareholders in other firms, now faced with the *Van Gorkom* opinion, would realize that mandatorily they now had more protection from directors' decisions than shareholders were willing to pay for. In a contractual setting, management in subsequent contracts would demand more in compensation for the new legal risks than shareholders would be willing to pay.[74]

As shareholders confronted the implications of *Van Gorkom,* a second development was predictable. In the contractarian model, faced with a decision that swept away existing contracts between shareholders and their management, competing state legislatures would seek to restore the value-maximizing *status quo ante.* Delaware's imposition of an inefficient law (one whose costs exceeded its benefits) created a profit opportunity for politicians in other states to install rules guaranteeing that *Van Gorkom* could not happen in their jurisdictions. That competition would force Delaware to mitigate the effects of the inefficient rule it created.

And so it all happened. The year after *Van Gorkom* was decided, Indiana became the first state to confer additional protections on directors in duty-of-care cases; Delaware followed two months later.[75] Eventually, almost all states did likewise.[76] Delaware's "charter option" statute, allowing shareholders (in the firm's certificate of incorporation)

---

74. The point is simply an application of the more general point that the law (legislative or judicial) cannot redistribute income generally by abrogating contractual terms in a particular case. E.g., M. Polinsky, An Introduction to Law and Economics 122–23 (2d. ed. 1989) ("[I]t is frequently difficult, if not impossible, to use legal rules to redistribute income in contractual disputes.... [T]he parties will take any distributional effects of breach of contract remedies into account when they negotiate the contract price....")

75. For further discussion of this important point, see Butler, *Smith v. Van Gorkom, Jurisdictional Competition, and the Role of Random Mutations in the Role of Corporate Law,* 45 Wash. L.J. 267 (2006).

76. Hamermesh, supra note 10, at 490.

to limit or eliminate personal liability of corporate directors in duty-of-care situations,[77] was the model adopted most often.[78]

In short, *Van Gorkom* may have ordained additional shareholder protections against management breach of the duty of care. But even if it did, the costs of those protections exceeded their benefits. Delaware created a profit opportunity for other jurisdictions by mandating inefficient shareholder protection. The predictable state competition subsequently undid the inefficiency, forcing Delaware to restore the superior product it had been providing.[79] Thus was demonstrated again the genius of American corporate law.

I. CONCLUSION

States' and shareholders' reactions to the harm done by the *Van Gorkom* decision bear out what the probability-weighted hypotheticals proposed in this chapter attempted to illustrate. The decision imposed a costly set of procedures on firms in takeover situations, procedures that for Trans Union shareholders themselves had no net benefits. Rather than replicate a series of subsequent *Van Gorkom* cases—or perhaps worse decisions relying on the Delaware result—states (notably, but not initially, Delaware) competed to make available to shareholders a set of judge-proof, statutorily safeguarded protections for directors exercising their judgment under their duty of care. Shareholders have responded to the opportunity overwhelmingly by making the charter amendments permitted by statute. So has been restored the situation prevailing in corporate law before the *Trans Union* case: virtually zero-chance of liability for directors in duty-of care cases.

As the years pass, then, the importance of *Smith v. Van Gorkom* itself may seem to dim.[80] But its lessons endure—or ought to, in any event.

---

77. Del. Code Ann. tit. 8 § 102(b)(7).

78. Hanks, Evaluating Recent State Legislation on Director and Officer Liability Limitation and Indemnification, 43 Bus. Law. 1207, 219–20 (1988).

79. This is not to say, of course, that because all ended well, no harm was done.

Persons hurt in automobile accidents may ultimately recover completely and their cars be can repaired or replaced, but the process of personal and vehicular restoration is naturally costly.

80. E.g., Hamermesh, supra note 10, at 495–96.

Chapter 13

INVESTOR PROTECTION AND THE PERILS OF CORPORATE PUBLICITY: *BASIC INC. v. LEVINSON*

By

*Donald C. Langevoort**

The Supreme Court's 1988 decision in *Basic Inc. v. Levinson*[1] is a fixture in federal securities law casebooks, addressing the liability that follows under Rule 10b–5 when a company falsely denies that it is engaged in merger negotiations. Two important issues were presented to the Court—first, whether and when preliminary merger negotiations and similar kinds of speculative information will be considered material so as to give rise to antifraud liability when they are misrepresented; second, whether courts should apply a presumption of reliance on the misrepresentation by investors so as to make "fraud on the market" class actions readily certifiable. Teaching materials often separate the two portions of the Court's opinion, which means that subtle and perhaps troubling connections between the two issues are often not noticed. This essay looks at each separately, and then together, starting with materiality.

A. MATERIALITY

1. The Litigation

A common assumption among teachers and scholars is that *Basic* involved a deliberate lie by Basic's management to protect the confidentiality of negotiations that were ongoing with Combustion Engineering, which came to fruition in late December 1978 and gave Basic shareholders a large premium over the prevailing market price. Actually, Basic's

* Thomas Aquinas Reynolds Professor of Law, Georgetown University Law Center. Thanks to Seung–Hyun Ryu for excellent research assistance.

1. 485 U.S. 224 (1988).

defense throughout the lawsuit was that it simply had told the truth—that there were no negotiations going on with Combustion when, months earlier, it denied them, nor anything else happening that it thought constituted a pending corporate development that might explain why the company's stock price was temporarily spiking.

To understand this issue as it eventually came to the Supreme Court, it is important to consider the procedural posture as the case moved forward in the courts below. Prior to the adoption of the Private Securities Litigation Reform Act in 1995, at least, defendants faced with large fraud on the market damage claims had very limited procedural options in trying to get a case dismissed before trial. One option was to say that the class should not be certified because there was insufficient commonality or typicality among plaintiffs claims, which raises the second issue in *Basic*. Another option was a Rule 12(b)(6) motion to dismiss, but that was hugely tilted to plaintiffs' favor by requiring the judge to assume the truth of the facts plaintiffs allege. The only other tactic, really, was a motion for summary judgment. But that, too, favors plaintiffs in that it requires no material factual dispute on the record, and plaintiffs' lawyers are usually very good at making damning factual allegations. Thus summary judgment was nearly impossible prior to extensive discovery, and hard enough even after discovery. A judge inclined to dismiss plaintiffs' case would often have to push hard against the law of civil procedure in order to find grounds for doing so, either by declaring plaintiffs' factual claims unsubstantiated in the post-discovery record or by calling the disputed issues matters of law rather than fact. The trial judge in *Basic* was very much so inclined, and the materiality portion of the case is about how he sought to justify summary judgment.[2]

Most of the facts were not disputed, though the inferences to be drawn from them were. Combustion Engineering had long had an interest in buying Basic—first approaching Basic in the mid–1960s—but antitrust obstacles stood in the way. In 1976, the FTC signaled a change in its policy regarding relevant product markets in the chemical industry, leading Combustion to renew its interest. Apparently, Combustion was by this time not the only one interested in Basic: one way or another, a number of other foreign and domestic companies made contacts as well. Basic apparently began to fear a hostile tender offer.

During late 1976 and early 1977, Basic and Combustion officials had a handful of informal contacts at which Combustion's vice-president, Kelly, raised the possibility of an acquisition. Basic at one point gave to Kelley some proprietary information, showing an interest in continuing the discussions, but these initial overtures were never embraced by Basic's managers, whose position was that Basic wanted to remain independent. A few weeks after the last of these early contacts, in October 1977, rumors surfaced on Wall Street that *another* large chemical company, Flintkote, was interested in acquiring Basic, which apparently caused a brief run-up in Basic's stock price. This led Basic to make

---

2. *Levinson v. Basic Inc.*, FED. SEC. L. REP. (CCH) par. 91801 (N.D. Ohio 1984).

the first of the three denials at issue in the case, saying to a Cleveland newspaper that the company "knew no reasons for the stock's activity and that no negotiations were underway with any company for a merger" and that Flintkote had formally denied that it would be making a bid for Basic. There were no more contacts with Combustion for the remainder of that year.

Early in 1978, Combustion considered making another approach to Basic, but an internal Combustion document showed that senior management withheld approval of this as a high priority initiative, saying that "because of Basic management's attitude," the possibility of an acquisition "does not appear to be an active area at present." Soon afterwards, there were some contacts at which Basic raised the possibility of acquiring some of Combustion's refractory facilities, using its stock to pay for them. These discussions continued for a few months, with Combustion listening to Basic's proposal but eventually rejecting Basic's informal bid as too low. In the course of these discussions, Combustion reminded Basic's management that it was still interested in acquiring Basic, and in June, Kelly suggested a price of $28 per share. Basic officials said that this was far too low to merit consideration. In the course of these discussions during the spring of 1978, Basic again conveyed information about its internal financial situation to Combustion, though it later argued that this was to pursue its own acquisition plans and not with a view toward the possibility of a merger, which it was not seriously considering.

Combustion was persistent, and internal documents later revealed in the litigation—but not shared with Basic at the time—showed that acquiring Basic was gradually becoming an important corporate objective. In July 1978, Kelly initiated telephone conversations with Basic executives to talk further and indicated that Combustion was moving toward making a serious offer on a friendly basis. Basic again gave Kelly some internal information about future earnings and revenues, later saying that if an offer was to be forthcoming, they wanted it to reflect Basic's real value and not be a low-ball bid. But the last contact between Combustion and Basic came that month with Combustion making no offer. No more discussions were scheduled.[3]

Two months later, in late September, there was another run-up in Basic's stock price, leading the New York Stock Exchange to inquire as to whether the company had any explanation. Max Muller, who had been involved in the conversations with Combustion during the summer, responded that he knew of no "present or pending corporate developments" that would explain it, and this statement was made public in a press release at the Exchange's request. This was the second denial at

---

3. This is when another denial occurred, though not one that was considered by the Supreme Court. On July 14, the price of Basic stock again spiked, and Basic's Theodore Thomas responded to a New York Stock Exchange inquiry that he knew of no pending corporate developments that would explain the spike. According to the district court, Thomas had not been advised of the conversations that were ongoing with Combustion when he said what he did, so that he genuinely had no such knowledge.

issue in the litigation. The third and last denial came in a report to shareholders in early November, which simply repeated what had been said in the September press release: that Basic management knew of no developments that would account for the occasional heavy trading volume and stock price movements.

By the time of this third denial, there had been no contacts between Combustion and Basic to discuss a merger for more than three months. Nothing at Basic indicated that any thought was still being given to the proposal Combustion had made during the summer. But in late November, Combustion came back yet again and put an informal offer on the table that Basic's management considered high enough to warrant attention (at around $35 per share), which a few weeks later led to the commencement of serious negotiations. Upon receiving this November offer, Basic contacted its investment banker, Kidder Peabody and for the first time told them about Combustion's interest in pursuing a merger. By mid-December, negotiations were in earnest with board approval from both companies for their bankers to haggle over price, and on December 18, Basic formally accepted Combustion's proposal for a friendly tender offer at $46 per share.

From this, you can see why Basic argued that it never lied or intentionally misled. Its account was that it was listening to Combustion's sporadic expressions of interest, but that until late November 1978 nothing Combustion was saying was anywhere near attractive enough for the discussions to turn serious. Late November, then, is when negotiations began, not before. So when the "no negotiations" or "no pending corporate developments" statements were made prior to that point, it was the truth. Basic emphasized two facts with respect to the good faith of the two fall 1978 denials: first, that it hadn't heard from Combustion since July about any interest in an acquisition when it made those statements and was not aware of any renewed interest; second, that it had not even told its own investment bankers, Kidder Peabody, about Combustion's interest in a merger until late November. That, it argued, is hard to explain if Basic had actually thought itself seriously engaged in merger negotiations with Combustion for months (or years) before.

Of course plaintiffs told a different story in their lawsuit, saying that the word negotiation has a more expansive meaning and that investors had been misled by being deprived of information about what they characterized as serious and frequent meetings by the two companies looking at the possibility of a merger. To defendants' frustration, plaintiffs' factual allegations in the lawsuit largely ignored that there had been separate negotiations over the possibility of Basic buying some of Combustion's refractories, instead painting these contacts as key meetings progressing toward the merger. Plaintiffs also pointed to the sharing of proprietary information in both 1977 and 1978 as demonstrating Basic's commitment to serious deal-making. Their best piece of evidence was a cryptic note written by Combustion's Kelly to the his own CEO in July 1978, around the time of the last contact, suggesting that Basic had acquiesced in a "go slow" approach to a merger possibility in order to give Basic's stock price a chance to go back down after recent surges and noting that Basic's position on public disclosure would continue to be that Basic knew nothing that could be causing these run-ups.

After discovery, Basic moved for summary judgment on its "no lie" claim. As noted earlier, this was hardly a favorable procedural posture, requiring that there be no material factual dispute in the record, and plaintiffs were insistent on their right to tell their story to a jury. But in a lengthy, if disjointed, opinion, the district judge agreed entirely with Basic's account and dismissed the case. He looked closely at the voluminous record and determined that at no time prior to December 1978 were there ongoing merger negotiations with Combustion as that term is commonly understood, so that what Basic said was literally true. He rejected plaintiff's inferences that Basic had shown a commitment to finding a deal with Combustion as strained and unreasonable, examining each assertion against the documentary evidence and deposition testimony.

Rule 10b–5, however, bars not only literal lies but also half-truths: omissions of facts necessary to make statements made not misleading.[4] So plaintiffs argued that investors were misled by the omission of the substantive discussions whether or not, technically, they were negotiations. They reminded the court that Basic had said "no corporate developments," not just "no negotiations." This, finally, is where the district court brought materiality into the analysis. It noted that *even if* these contacts between Basic and Combustion somehow fell into the category of preliminary merger negotiations—which it doubted—the Third Circuit had recently held that preliminary merger negotiations (i.e., those where there was not yet an agreement in principle on price and structure) were immaterial as a matter of law.[5] Relying on this precedent, the court said that the half-truth argument was unavailing because whatever was going on between Basic and Combustion would not be a material fact.

The notion of something being immaterial as a matter of law is worth pondering. Materiality is about what is important to reasonable investors,[6] and hence seems very much a fact question—there indeed was much dicta to that effect in the case law at the time. That would make it out-of-bounds for summary judgment so long as there was an omission that plaintiffs allege was misleading. But even back then (and certainly in years following) there was a surprisingly large incidence of courts granting dismissals on materiality as a matter of law. This was a tool district judges could use to get rid of cases they thought lacking in merit without the time and expense of a trial. The district judge was happy to

---

4. See Donald Langevoort, *Half-Truths: Protecting Mistaken Inferences by Investors and Others*, 52 STAN. L. REV. 87 (1999).

5. *Greenfield v. Heublein, Inc.*, 742 F.2d 751 (3d Cir. 1984); *Staffin v. Greenberg*, 672 F.2d 1196 (3d Cir. 1982).

6. The standard definition of materiality is taken from *TSC Industries, Inc. v. Northway, Inc.*, 426 U.S. 438, 449 (1976): "An omitted fact is material if there is a substantial likelihood that a reasonable investor would consider it important ..."

have the precedent to invoke to eliminate this alternative argument against dismissal.

The district court separately granted summary judgment to Basic based on lack of scienter. Rule 10b–5 cases require plaintiffs to show that a misrepresentation or omission was either intentional or reckless. Hinting that he saw the question as one of the motivation of Basic's managers in issuing their denials, the judge said he found no evidence in the record that they were saying anything but what they thought was true—they consulted with counsel, thought of the words "negotiations" and "developments" in their literal sense, and honestly never considered the on-and-off (and theretofore unpromising) discussions with Combustion as anything more than preliminary expressions of interest, not a necessary qualifier to their denials. Here, again, the court emphasized that with respect to the fall 1978 denials there had been no word for months from Combustion, after Basic management had firmly dismissed any thought of a merger at a price in the mid-twenties. The court also stressed that each time a denial was issued it was in response to market fluctuations apparently caused by rumors of *other* companies' possible interests in Basic. There was never any evidence that analysts or anyone else in the market ever had any idea of Combustion's interest.

The appeal to the Sixth Circuit was painful for Basic and its lawyers.[7] The court of appeals' opinion begins with a recitation of facts largely lifted from plaintiffs' brief, stating without qualification that Basic and Combustion had had numerous serious contacts and discussions throughout the class period, all looking toward a merger between the two companies. The Sixth Circuit made no reference to the district judge's detailed examination of the record and summarily concluded that Basic's denials *were* false and misleading.[8] Thus, the only important issue to the appellate court was whether the misrepresentations were material. Here, the court suggested that the mere fact that Basic thought it important to address the issue established materiality.[9] It then parted company with the Third Circuit on materiality as a matter of law, emphasizing that it did not want to countenance an ability to lie about something that so easily can become important to investors. So, it concluded, the district court had erred in granting summary judgment on materiality. The same with scienter, because the Sixth Circuit read the district court's ruling as derivative of its materiality holding, thus requiring reversal on both. In fact, the scienter ruling was mostly on the grounds that even assuming a material omission there was insufficient evidence in the record of any desire to deceive investors or conscious awareness that investors would be misled by what was said. At this point, the interesting scienter question essentially drops out of the case.

7. *Levinson v. Basic Inc.*, 786 F.2d 741 (6th Cir. 1986).

8. *Id.* at 747.

9. *Id.* at 748 ("When a company whose stock is publicly traded makes a statement, as Basic did, that 'no negotiations' are underway [etc.] . . . information concerning ongoing acquisition discussions becomes material *by virtue of the statement denying their existence*").

The Supreme Court granted certiorari on materiality to resolve what was now a split between the circuits. In their briefs and oral argument, Basic's lawyers pointed out the liberties plaintiffs (and the Sixth Circuit) had taken with the facts in contrast to the district court's careful review of the record. But most of the argument was devoted to the proper standard for materiality, which because of the split in the circuits is what had justified Supreme Court review. By this time, there was a second court of appeals holding that preliminary merger negotiations were immaterial as a matter of law, *Flamm v. Eberstadt*,[10] written by the recently-appointed Judge Frank Easterbrook for the Seventh Circuit. Whereas the Third Circuit's decisions on this issue had been a bit confusing, Easterbrook offered a clearly articulated law and economics lesson on why preliminary merger negotiations are best left in the dark. Basic's lawyers embraced all this authority and pushed the Court to follow the teachings.

The Supreme Court did not follow the teachings, however, and unanimously affirmed the Sixth Circuit.[11] Its essential point was that materiality is about what is important to investors, nothing more and nothing less. Accepting without question the Sixth Circuit's recitation of the facts—i.e., that there were real and serious on-going discussions between Basic and Combustion that had been concealed from investors—the only question was whether these *could* rise to the level of importance at which reasonable investors would be interested. The Court first rejected the "agreement in principle" test as based on policies having nothing to do with materiality properly understood.[11.5] One policy argument was that investors are too easily misled by speculative considerations of mergers that might or might not come about. This, the Court said, is too paternalistic, assuming that investors are little more than nitwits. A more serious policy—the one that Easterbrook had emphasized—was the need to preserve some zone of secrecy for merger negotiations that generally work to benefit investors. But the Court asked what this had to do with materiality. Materiality is not supposed to carry the baggage of policy design but simply ask about the significance of what is misrepresented or concealed. Finally, the Court rejected the justification based on predictability, saying that although clarity is desirable, accuracy is more important and on questions of significance, only a close look at facts and circumstances will do.

As to the proper test for materiality, the Court did not like the Sixth Circuit's *ipso facto* locution, and instead—following the urging of the SEC in the government's amicus brief—invoked a standard that the

---

10. 814 F.2d 1169 (7th Cir. 1987). Judge Easterbrook said that the issues in *Flamm* and *Basic* were different: *Flamm* involved concealment while *Basic* involved a lie. He declined to reach the question of whether a lie is permissible. In fact, the cases are closer factually than Easterbrook suggests.

11. As discussed in the next section, only six Justices of the Court heard the

Basic case. However, in contrast to the decision on reliance, the materiality holding was unanimous.

11.5 The agreement in principle is one of the stages of private negotiations. It spells out the terms and conditions of the sale.

Second Circuit had devised in the seminal *Texas Gulf Sulphur* case, when it analyzed the materiality of core drilling sample results that seemed preliminarily (but not conclusively) to point to a rich mineral ore discovery.[12] The materiality of any speculative information, the Court said, requires balancing probability and magnitude—that is, an assessment of the likelihood at the time that the event will come to pass and the impact on the company and its shareholders if it does. On probability in the context of merger negotiations, the Court said that fact-finders might look at evidence such as "board resolutions, instructions to investment bankers, and actual negotiations between principals or their intermediaries . . . "[13] With respect to magnitude, the size of the companies and potential premiums would be probative. But the Court said little more than this. Because the probability-magnitude test is one that neither court below had employed, it remanded for further consideration of whether summary judgment had properly been granted.

Before doing so, however, the Court dropped a footnote that has had a good deal of influence ever since. Footnote 17 makes clear that a finding of materiality does not by itself give rise to a duty to disclose, so that companies are free to remain silent about pending merger negotiations. They just can't lie about them. The Court recognized that this puts a company in a bind if, as in this case, stock exchange officials or journalists insist that the company respond to rumors or stock price movements. "No comment" would be truthful but may not work to conceal what the company might want to conceal. But the Court responded simply that "creating an exception to a regulatory scheme founded on a pro-disclosure regulatory philosophy, because complying with the regulation is 'bad for business,' is a role for Congress, not this Court."[14]

2. Some Questions

The materiality portion of *Basic* is persuasive enough if one believes, as the Court did, that materiality is just about what is important to investors. If one asks an investor whether he or she would find significant discussions a company is having that might lead to a big merger, the answer almost surely would be yes. More concretely, insider trading profits surely can be (and often are) made from trading on the basis of information about negotiations that have not yet reached the stage of agreement on price and essential terms.

In turn, the probability-magnitude test also seems intuitively right as an approach to importance. Note that the Court said that probability and magnitude must be "balanced". What does that mean? A little thought makes clear that this should be a simple expected value calculation: the fact-finder should determine probability and magnitude and then multiply. A 50% chance of a $1 billion premium for shareholders should be thought through by asking whether .5 times $1 billion—$500

12. *SEC v. Texas Gulf Sulphur Co.*, 401 F.2d 833 (2d Cir. 1968) (en banc).

13. 485 U.S. at 239.

14. *Id.* at 239 n.17.

million, in other words—is material. The answer would be yes for most companies.

But famously, the probability portion of the probability-magnitude test is miserably difficult to apply. Take *Basic*. When in September 1978 the company issued its second denial that there were any pending or present corporate developments, it hadn't heard anything or had any contacts with Combustion for three months. Its last meeting had involved mention of a price that was far short of what Basic's management thought of as acceptable, and Basic had indicated that it wanted to remain independent. Yet Combustion had a palpable continuing interest, reason to expect that Basic would continue to listen, and thus might well be back. So with those facts (and any others from the earlier recitation) what probability should one assign to the likelihood of that merger actually taking place? One could do nothing but take a rough guess, which is not particularly comfortable when hundreds of millions of dollars of potential liability could rest on being right. It might get easier once the two parties actually sit down to negotiate price and structure, but until they come to agreement, it's still guesswork.

That brings us to another often-made point. Any judicial fact-finder will be making the materiality determination in hindsight, after the event that once was speculative has come to pass with certainty. Psychologists teach that human beings have a difficult time ignoring their subsequent knowledge, and will likely overestimate the probability that the event would happen once they know that it actually did. This is called the hindsight bias.[15] A lawyer making a real-time materiality determination had better factor in the hindsight bias risk, at which point educated guesswork simply gives way to an abundance of caution.

Now consider the rule rejected by the Court, the agreement-in-principle test. There were a number of concerns raised about the approach besides the purists' point that it goes to something other than what is important. For instance, if preliminary merger negotiations are immaterial as a matter of law, could insiders freely trade on the information? The district court in *Basic* took pains to distinguish corporate disclosure from insider-trading cases, suggesting that there should be a dual standard of materiality based on whether the defendant is trading or not.[16] But that certainly threatens the coherence of materiality as a concept—a point the SEC hammered home in its amicus brief.

The bigger issue was the one the Court touched on in footnote 17. What the agreement in principle test says is that companies are free to misrepresent the status of a possible deal to investors up until a fairly late point in the negotiations. One justification for this is because, on average, maintaining secrecy makes a positive outcome, a merger agree-

15. See G. Mitu Gulati et al., *Fraud by Hindsight*, 98 Nw. U. L. Rev. 773 (2004).

16. For a thoughtful essay on *Basic* that follows up on the possibility that materiality should vary depending on context, including whether the person making the misrepresentation stands to benefit, see Victor Brudney, *A Note on Materiality and Soft Information Under the Federal Securities Laws*, 75 Va. L. Rev. 723 (1989).

ment, more likely than if the negotiations are publicly exposed, and that increased likelihood benefits investors as a class. That was the "good for business" policy reasoning that the Court said should be left for Congress, but isn't it right? Actually, it's a bit more complicated. When a company wants to maximize value via a sale of control, a public auction-type process is often the better route, suggesting a benefit to openness rather than secrecy. But potential acquirors may well be reluctant to engage in the process if they worry that they will be out-bid by someone else, and thus demand secrecy or other kinds of deal protections. As the endless academic and policy debates over lock-ups in corporate control transactions have shown, the answer to what is best policy is quite ambiguous.

Those debates have also pointed out that sometimes secrecy raises an agency cost problem: executives of the target company may well prefer privacy for selfish reasons, because they can use the exclusivity to assure that their preferred acquiror (the one willing to keep them on or make large severance payments) has a leg up. Indeed, the best argument in *Basic* that the discussions were in fact more serious than the district court found in its review of the evidence—and that Basic management did deliberately conceal the discussions—would be that management had come to fear a hostile takeover and saw Combustion as a potential "white knight" that would not bust up the company or fire existing management were it to make the acquisition. Their first choice was to remain independent, but if there was to be a sale of control, they wanted it to be to Combustion and no one else. That might explain why Basic management was coy enough to let Combustion think it was worth coming back and why they failed to make public any hint about Combustion's interest.[17] While a plausible reading of the facts, this would probably not be an example of preserving secrecy for *shareholders'* benefit.

That said, there are no doubt instances where concealment of the truth is good for the company's current shareholders. *Basic* was criticized in a lively scholarly debate after the case came down for failing to take this seriously or realize that that the truth is proprietary information over which company management ought be able to assert control when it really is in shareholders' best interests.[18] After all, if—as the Court acknowledged—there is normally no duty to disclose information

---

17. An intriguing piece of evidence is that although Basic had not told Kidder Peabody about Combustion's acquisition interest during the summer, it did refer to Combustion in discussions with Kidder about possible takeover defenses as a potential white knight. Moreover, the reason given for not letting Kidder know of the interest was confidentiality—presumably Basic did not want even its own bankers to think that it was receptive to offers lest it be seen as in play and invite hostile interest. Obviously, then, Basic did not completely trust Kidder to be a loyal adviser. Perhaps they were wise: Basic's main banker at Kidder apparently was Martin Siegel, who years later would go to jail in the massive insider trading scandals of the 1980s.

18. *See* Jonathan Macey & Geoffrey Miller, *Good Finance, Bad Economics: An Analysis of the Fraud-on-the-Market Theory*, 42 STAN. L. REV. 1059 (1990); Ian Ayres, *Back to Basics: Regulating How Corporations Speak to the Market*, 77 VA. L. REV. 945 (1991).

regardless of its materiality (i.e., the information can be thought of as privileged) why not enhance that privilege by allowing the company to conceal it effectively by dissembling? There are many possible answers, some practical, some moral. My sense is that the issue comes up much more frequently that we commonly think,[19] even in notorious post-Basic "scandals" like Enron and Worldcom or the more recent options backdating situations. Although it is commonplace to ascribe managerial selfishness and greed as the motivation in these scandals, it is not hard to notice shareholder-regarding reasons as well: keeping the company on a rapid growth trajectory, attracting the best employees, avoiding credit downgrades, etc. But the closer we look, the more ambiguity we see. Is management just rationalizing that the truth has to be hidden for the good of the shareholders, when in fact they mainly fear the risk to their careers should the truth be known? In the end, how should a court decide whose interest the concealment really was in? Much more could be (and has been) said on this question, which was truncated because *Basic* decided it was an issue for Congress to consider, not the courts.

It is unhelpful to wander too much further in this direction because this doesn't seem to be what was happening in the dealings between Combustion and Basic. Again, the only impartial observer to take a close look at the record developed during discovery, the trial judge, was convinced that Basic was telling what it honestly thought was the truth in denying negotiations or other pending corporate developments because the natural and normal meaning of those words implies a mutual commitment to an active effort to arrive at a bargain, and as of the three points in time at which the denials were made, there was neither commitment nor significant activity. Just as important, Basic had little reason to think that whatever conversations they had had with Kelly months before would be the reasons for the occasional stock price runups that the company was being asked to explain.

Because the case was remanded on the issue of materiality, of course, Basic could still pursue this point, showing that the "probability" prong was sufficiently—low when each of the denials occurred so that the test produces a no materiality outcome. But the Sixth Circuit wanted no part of this argument, and held on remand that the fraud and materiality issues would have to go to trial.[20] Given the liability exposure created by the fraud-on-the-market theory—the other issue in *Basic*—and fear of the hindsight bias, this was too much risk, and Basic settled with the plaintiffs shortly thereafter for between $2 and $4.5 million, depending on the number of claims eventually submitted.[21]

19. *See* Donald C. Langevoort, *Resetting the Corporate Thermostat: Lessons from the Recent Financial Scandals About Self–Deception, Deceiving Others and the Design of Internal Controls*, 93 Geo. L.J. 285, 295–97 (2004).

20. *Levinson v. Basic Inc.*, 871 F.2d 562 (6th Cir. 1989).

21. *See* Notice of Settlement Approval and Proof of Claim Requirement, Wall St. J., April 3, 1990, at B15. Of this amount, between $1.4 and $1.9 million was set aside for plaintiffs' attorneys fees.

In this sense, *Basic* is a good illustration of a familiar problem with private securities class actions, the misfit between the standard tools of civil procedure (notice pleading, limitations on motions to dismiss and summary judgment) and the desire to have prompt, accurate resolution of highly factual questions before tens of millions of dollars of the corporation's (and therefore shareholders') money are spent on discovery and trial. No one has yet come up with the ideal solution. In 1995, Congress did raise the pleading standards for these kinds of cases in order to give trial judges more control over what cases go on to discovery and trial—requiring that plaintiffs put forward sufficient facts in their complaints to give rise to a strong inference of scienter, and staying discovery while defendant's motion on the pleadings is considered.[21.5] That might have helped Basic in a case like this, because it was only through discovery that the plaintiffs were able to get their hands on the bits of evidence that led the Sixth Circuit to believe that serious merger discussions were occurring between the two companies.[22] Yet as many have pointed out, the heightened pleading standard may impose an unrealistic pre-discovery evidentiary burden in cases where fraud reasonably is suspected. Assessing how well these imperfect mechanisms perform quickly gets us into hard questions about the efficacy of fraud-on-the-market suits as compensation or deterrence devices. We turn to this in the next part.

One lingering question in the *Basic* story has to do with scienter, not in terms of pleading but in terms of definition. Perhaps because scienter is so rarely addressed by courts outside of the heightened pleading requirements, it remains a surprisingly murky construct. As law students quickly find in their first year when encountering state of mind issues in torts or criminal law, there is a blurry continuum that runs from malice aforethought to complete innocence, taking in such familiar words and phrases as negligence, gross negligence, recklessness, deliberate disregard, bad faith and so on. The Supreme Court in the *Hochfelder* case ruled out negligence liability under Rule 10b–5 but left open all possibilities above that.[23] Today recklessness (and everything on a higher order of intent) is taken as a form of scienter, at least so long as it is of the subjective variety: i.e., awareness of a high risk that the statement is misleading, even if the defendant is not sure that it is a lie.

But while the law can be described fairly well in generalities, application is another thing entirely. Take *Basic* again, and assume that the company thought it was being asked specifically whether there was a

---

21.5 Congress enacted the Private Securities Litigation Reform Act (PSLRA) in 1995. Under the PSLRA's heightened pleading standards, a plaintiff asserting a Rule 10b–5 claim must allege facts with particularity that give rise to a strong inference of scienter. Private Securities Litigation Reform Act of 1995 (PSLRA), Pub.L.No. 104–67, 109 Stat. 737 (1995).

22. This is not clear, however, because in Basic's announcement of the deal with Combustion, it acknowledged prior negotiations. This acknowledgement is what precipitated the filing of the class action lawsuits, and might have been enough for a court to make a strong inference of scienter.

23. *Ernst & Ernst v. Hochfelder*, 425 U.S. 185 (1976).

merger being negotiated that could explain the price moves. Assume further that Basic thought that negotiations has a meaning that excludes the kinds of contacts that had been going on with Combustion and decided, after consultation with counsel, that the appropriate answer was therefore no. Is it safe from liability? If scienter is understood in terms of *motivation* (and the trial judge may well have thought this)— i.e., did Basic desire or specifically intend to mislead investors—then Basic would almost surely not be liable. But despite occasional outliers, the standard reading of scienter emphasizes *awareness* rather than motive.[24] That is, was the defendant aware of the facts that would make what was said materially misleading, or did the defendant recklessly disregard that risk? Indeed recklessness makes little sense as an approach if motivation is really the test, yet recklessness has near-universal acceptance in the courts. Here, Basic would not necessarily be protected if a court thought that its statements were misleading for failing to mention the discussions with Combustion, simply because Basic was aware of the discussions.

So, neither materiality nor the scienter requirement offers much protection to the company trying to do the right thing but (in hindsight) not getting it right. Which brings us to *Basic*'s lessons about talking to analysts and the press. What should Basic have said in response to either the press or stock exchange inquiries? No comment, perhaps, but the downsides to that approach were recognized by the Court in footnote 17 and widely appreciated. It works to preserve confidentiality only if it is a consistent practice, which hardly encourages open communications with investors. How about: "We are engaged is preliminary discussions regarding a merger with Combustion Engineering" (or "with a company we are not at liberty to name")? My guess is that this would have set off a great deal of speculative trading, because the background norm is that companies usually don't disclose preliminary merger discussions and hence this would have been taken as positive news. So maybe the prudent approach is a more textured disclosure about what had actually taken place between Combustion and Basic. But that would not be easy to compose, again remembering the hindsight bias: if a merger later takes place, all the negative signals will seem unduly dampening; if it doesn't, the positive signals will seem too provocative. Moreover, each additional fact must be verified, and under the half-truth doctrine, each additional fact raises new questions of what else now must be said to be complete.

Life is hard for the persons charged with disclosure. The Court was not persuaded, however, that making life easier for lawyers or business people was as important a value as pursuit of the truth. And so the Court moved on to the presumption of reliance. Before we move on to discuss the presumption of reliance, it is important to note the connection between the two. It is one thing if the consequence of not getting

---

24. See *AUSA Life Insurance Co. v. Ernst & Young*, 206 F.3d 202 (2d Cir. 2000); James D. Cox et al., Securities Regula- tion: Cases and Materials 671–72 (5th ed. 2006).

the disclosure right is an SEC cease and desist order or civil penalty, or even damage liability confined to a small class of investors who prove actual reliance on the alleged misstatement. Make it an open-ended class easily able to claim hundreds of millions of dollars in aggregate damages, however, and what's at stake goes up dramatically. That's what the reliance issue is all about, and so we now turn to the second half of *Basic*.

B. THE PRESUMPTION OF RELIANCE

When, as in *Basic*, an alleged misstatement or omission is addressed to the market as a whole instead of particular investors, the question of who can or should recover damages becomes central. By the time the case began in the early 1980s, certain propositions under Rule 10b–5 had become fairly clear: the defendant need not have itself been a purchaser or seller of securities, but rather owes a duty of honesty to all foreseeable marketplace traders;[25] defendants are liable only when they act with scienter;[26] etc. This doctrinal structure readily invited class action treatment for all traders similarly situated as the most efficient way of compensating for the presumed injuries, because nearly all the relevant questions were common ones involving defendants' conduct. The one exception was reliance, where the law of fraud has long insisted that plaintiff show that the misrepresentation had, in a "but for" sense, caused the transaction that produced the injury. Class actions simply cannot accommodate a reliance inquiry if the distinct accounts of tens of thousands of investors have to be evaluated, either as a matter of practicability or (because of Rule 23(b)(3)'s requirement that common issues predominate) as a matter of law. By the early 1980's, the courts had made substantial and imaginative efforts to solve this problem, usually by finding some way to "presume" reliance rather than inquire into it. The Supreme Court had twice, in other contexts, endorsed presumptions of reliance in securities fraud cases.[27]

In Rule 10b–5 cases involving allegations of false corporate publicity, the name given to the solution was the "fraud-on-the-market" theory. First fully articulated by the Ninth Circuit in *Blackie v. Barrack*[28] in 1976, the idea was that reliance could be presumed because the false publicity distorts the price of the stock, so that investors who relied on the "integrity" of the stock price were at least indirectly deceived. The idea that fraud can distort market price was simple common sense but was bolstered in *Blackie* and its progeny by reference to the efficient market hypothesis, which had formalized and offered empirical support for the idea that information is impounded in price remarkably quickly with respect to widely-traded securities. By the time *Basic* got to the Supreme Court, *Blackie* was pretty much the law; there was little if any

---

25. *See Texas Gulf Sulphur, supra* note 12.

26. *See Ernst & Ernst v. Hochfelder, supra* note 23.

27. *Mills v. Electric Auto–Lite Co.,* 396 U.S. 375 (1970); *Affiliated Ute Citizens v. United States,* 406 U.S. 128 (1972).

28. 524 F.2d 891 (9th Cir. 1975), *cert. denied,* 429 U.S. 816 (1976).

precedent going the other way. Hence the district court in *Basic* had readily certified the class of sellers by using the presumption, and the Sixth Circuit joined the other courts without much doubt in agreeing that the presumption was appropriate. When the Supreme Court granted certiorari on this as well as the materiality question, it was not in the face of any conflict in the circuits: the Solicitor General's office did not even think that certiorari was warranted—it advised the Court that materiality was the only important question.

The business community, however, plainly saw the threat that aggressive private securities litigation posed to the fraud-on-the-market theory, and joined Basic in arguing that it was important to shut the door on it. In this, Basic encountered some bad luck. Justice Lewis Powell, who had dominated the Court's corporate and business cases with a concern for predictability and restraint in the application of federal law,[29] had just retired from the Court. And remarkably, three of the Court's more conservative remaining members, Chief Justice Rehnquist, Justice Scalia and Justice Kennedy (Justice Powell's successor), took no part in the case, leaving just six Justices to decide it.

Interestingly, the SEC and the Solicitor General sided with the plaintiffs in endorsing the presumption of reliance and the fraud-on-the-market theory.[30] Given the business community's opposition, this was not a foregone conclusion—this was, after all, late in the Reagan Administration, hardly a time of liberal embrace of lawsuits threatening business interests. The SEC's amicus brief was ultimately influential on both the materiality and reliance issues. Justice Blackmun's opinion in *Basic* follows the SEC's analysis and recommendations almost to the letter.

The opinion marches through the reliance issue with little sense of doubt about the right outcome. It begins by saying that it is not addressing the fraud-on-the-market theory in general, only the presumption of reliance. That seems a bit disingenuous, however, because the theory depends entirely on the presumption. The opinion then turns to justification, and after predictable references to two cases where the Court had previously endorsed a presumption of reliance, the opinion simply follows *Blackie's* script. What is important, said the Court, is reliance on the market price rather than reliance on the specific misinformation, because information affects the price and fraud can thus readily distort it. In this sense, the Court says, the presumption is not only a practical solution to class action certification but conceptually sound. The majority then moves on to say that the presumption is rebuttable, offering examples of situations where rebutting is appropriate—where the fraud does not actually fool the market (in which case the fraud-on-the-market theory doesn't apply in the first place), or where

29. See Adam C. Pritchard, *Justice Lewis F. Powell, Jr., and the Counterrevolution in the Federal Securities Laws*, 62 Duke L.J. 841 (2003).

30. Brief for the Securities and Exchange Comm'n as Amicus Curiae Supporting Respondents, Basic Inc. v. Levinson, 485 U.S. 224 (1988) (No. 86–279), 1986 U.S. Briefs 279.

it is clear that plaintiffs would have made the same trade even if they had known of the fraud.

What is most interesting about this part of *Basic* is the role of market efficiency in the presumption of reliance.[31] Left unclear in the analysis is a very big conceptual question: precisely what about the market price is the investor presumptively relying on? One could say, and there are hints in the pre-*Basic* case law and academic literature cited by the Court to this effect,[32] that the investors are presumed to be relying on the market price to be an accurate indication of the value of the company's stock. Many investors (index investors, for example) do indeed invest passively in a diversified portfolio, and the efficient market hypothesis says that they are reasonable in so doing—it is very hard for anyone, with perhaps the exception of very sophisticated market professionals like hedge funds, to consistently beat the market. This is an important example of the kind of reliance the Court seems inclined to protect, but passive investors are probably a minority of traders. Many others are bargain hunters, seeking an above-normal return through savvy stock-picking, either personally or through actively managed mutual funds. They may be fools in chasing supra-normal returns, but they persist. If mere passive investing is what the Court was thinking of, the presumption is seriously over-inclusive to the extent that it covers the population of active investors as well.

But there is another reading that avoids this problem. A close look at the opinion suggests that the presumed reliance is not on the accuracy of the price necessarily, but simply on its "integrity." That is, even the active trader trying to beat the market still *refers* to the market price as a baseline, and at least may be assuming that the price is undistorted by fraud. The majority quotes an earlier case wondering who would willingly throw the dice in a crooked craps game?[33] This is probably the better reading of *Basic*, but such a reading immediately raises two questions. First, why should an investor assume that the market price is undistorted by fraud? Fraud, after all, has been frequent enough over the centuries that its risk is palpable. Indeed, in a truly efficient market, that residual fraud risk is priced; it is not assumed away.

What may really be going on, though, is that through the presumption of reliance, the plurality is recognizing an *entitlement* for investors to make this assumption about stock price integrity. That's justifiable, and as the opinion points out, consistent with the history and philosophy of the securities laws. But if the point is just to make stock prices reliable reference points via an integrity entitlement, we confront the second question: why should efficiency matter so much?[34] After all, fraud

---

31. *See* Donald Langevoort, *Theories, Assumptions and Securities Regulation: Market Efficiency Revisited*, 140 U. Pa. L. Rev. 851 (1992).

32. *See In re LTV Sec. Litig.*, 88 F.R.D. 134, 144 (N.D. Tex. 1980) (citing studies).

33. 485 U.S. at 246–47, quoting *Schlanger v. Four-Phase Systems Inc.*, 555 F. Supp. 535, 538 (S.D.N.Y. 1982).

34. See Jonathan Macey et al., *Lessons from Financial Economics: Materiality, Reliance and Extending the Reach of* Basic v. Levinson, 77 Va. L. Rev. 1017, 1018 (1991);

can distort the integrity of prices in markets whether thick or thin; investors would no more roll the dice in a crooked investment game involving stocks quoted in the pink sheets than with respect to those in the Dow Jones index. And in fact, there is little evidence that the Court was placing that much weight to the idea of an efficient market except as a synonym for markets that are sufficiently well-organized as to use reported prices or quotes as a reference point for subsequent trading. Pre-*Basic* cases made little serious factual inquiry into the efficiency question in open market cases. The hard questions arose only when there was no organized market at all, as with respect to initial public offerings, and even there courts sometimes stretched to justify a presumption of reliance.[35]

There is no reason to suspect that *Basic's* references to market efficiency were meant to insist on all that much in the way of efficiency. But there was enough confusion in the opinion to make it a litigable issue. Now that the strong, practically irrefutable, presumption of reliance in fraud-on-the-market cases was established, defense lawyers' tactics changed from fighting this as a matter of law to contesting it factually at the class certification stage, and the rapidly expanding understanding—and emerging doubts—about market efficiency gave them ample grist.

Judicial usage of "market efficiency" makes it seem as if this is a binary, yes-no question: as if markets divide neatly into the efficient and the inefficient. But that certainly isn't true. Tests of efficiency are largely tests of speed of adjustment, and speed varies based on type of stock, type of information, type of market and so on. There is no such thing as perfect efficiency except as an ideal-type model. There are only degrees of efficiency. Yet, based on judicial usage of "market efficiency", defense lawyers started looking for arguments that some kinds of markets weren't efficient enough, and started asking courts to draw a line beneath which the presumption would not apply. They then tried to push that line higher and higher.

And courts started taking efficiency more and more seriously.[36] No doubt this impulse was bolstered by growing concerns about the legitimacy of fraud-on-the-market lawsuits, concerns that seven years later led Congress to enact the Private Securities Litigation Reform Act of 1995. Judges skeptical of the merits of the lawsuit but (especially before

Langevoort, *supra* note 31. *See also* Zohar Goshen & Gideon Parchomovsky, *The Essential Role of Securities Regulation*, 55 Duke L.J. 711, 768–71 (2006).

35. *See Shores v. Sklar*, 647 F.2d 462 (5th Cir. 1981) (en banc), *cert. denied*, 459 U.S. 1102 (1983). For a critique of this case law in light of *Basic*, see William Carney, *Limits of the Fraud on the Market Doctrine*, 44 Bus. Law. 1259 (1989).

36. The most thorough discussion of this development is *In re PolyMedica Corp. Sec. Lit.*, 432 F.3d 1 (1st Cir. 2005), criticized in *Note—Recent Cases: Securities Law—First Circuit Defines an Efficient Market for Fraud-on-the-Market Purposes*, 119 Harv. L. Rev. 2284 (2006).

the PSLRA) lacking in other ways of getting rid of these cases might like the idea of denial of certifications on "insufficient efficiency" grounds.[37]

With this point we should turn for a minute to Justice White's dissent in *Basic* on the presumption of reliance. The dissent is rightly remembered for its doubts about whether market efficiency was well-enough established to justify the majority's presumption. But it is actually much more an expression of doubts about private securities class actions. Justice White challenges the basic principle that defendants who do not buy or sell stock should ever be liable under Rule 10b–5. But with the absence of natural allies like Rehnquist and Scalia from the case, White could only find one other justice to persuade, Justice O'Connor. As noted earlier, the Reagan Administration SEC and the Solicitor General weighed in on the other side, giving strong support to the majority's position.

Why did the government end up on the "anti-business" side? It is hard to know for sure. But it is at least interesting to note that the conservative law and economics types at the time had embraced the fraud-on-the-market theory, perhaps enraptured with the extent to which courts were actually paying attention to literature in financial economics. Daniel Fischel, soon to be Frank Easterbrook's colleague and co-author at the University of Chicago, wrote an influential endorsement of the fraud-on-the-market presumption in *The Business Lawyer* in 1982[38] and continued to defend it after *Basic* was decided, dismissing White's dissent as woefully misinformed.[39] One of Easterbrook's first major securities cases after he was appointed to the Seventh Circuit, *Flamm v. Eberstadt*,[40] treated the fraud-on-the-market theory as both good law and good economics.

But after *Basic* was handed down, others on the more conservative side started expressing severe doubts about fraud-on-the-market. The criticism was partly driven by the sense that agency costs infected the bringing of these lawsuits, making them settlement vehicles rather than ways of compensating investors for real fraud.[41] Others emphasized that the presumption of reliance expanded the scope of likely damages in ways that were far in excess of the social harm fraud causes, and such damages generated severe precaution costs that are borne by company shareholders.[42] Some tied the issues of materiality and reliance together,

37. *See* Paul Ferrillo et al., *The "Less than Efficient" Capital Markets Hypothesis: Requiring More Proof from Plaintiffs in Fraud-on-the-Market Cases*, 78 St. John's L. Rev. 81 (2004).

38. Daniel Fischel, *Use of Modern Finance Theory in Securities Fraud Cases Involving Actively Traded Securities*, 38 Bus. Law. 1 (1982).

39. Daniel Fischel, *Efficient Capital Markets, the Crash and the Fraud on the Market Theory*, 74 Cornell L. Rev. 907 (1989).

40. 814 F.2d 1169 (7th Cir. 1987). This was the same case in which Easterbrook took a "bright-line" position on materiality that the Court rejected in *Basic*.

41. *See* Roberta Romano, *The Shareholder Suit: Litigation Without Foundation?*, 7 J. L. Econ. & Org. 55 (1991).

42. *See* Paul Mahoney, *Precaution Costs and the Law of Fraud in Impersonal Markets*, 78 Va. L. Rev. 623 (1992).

pointing out that the massive liability threat created by fraud-on-the-market cases, coupled with the broad definition of materiality adopted in the first part of the Court's decision, undermines the legitimate corporate needs for secrecy in settings like confidential merger negotiations.[43]

An entirely different critique of *Basic* came from those who thought, like Justice White, that the plurality had bought too heavily into a strong vision of market efficiency. Just a couple of weeks before *Basic* was argued, the stock market suffered the largest single day drop in decades, on no obvious bad economic news, leading many to suggest that the stock market can often be more manic that rational. Indeed, counsel for Basic made reference to the crash in oral argument. This brought attention to research in financial economics that doubted the fundamental efficiency of the markets, and even its informational efficiency with respect to harder-to-evaluate kinds of information. What if the markets aren't really as efficient as theory posited?

That debate still rages today; market efficiency is very much a contestable hypothesis among financial economists, even though there are still plenty of strong defenders. And there are many who argue that because *Basic* requires plaintiffs to establish the efficiency of the market for the issuer's stock, evidence of market inefficiency as a general matter can and should be invoked to deny the presumption and, accordingly, reject class certification, especially when there is suspicion of a market bubble.[44]

As we saw earlier, this probably takes *Basic's* teachings too far. So far as the Court's likely vision of justifiable reliance is concerned, all that is needed is some confidence that the price was in fact distorted, and that can be as true with respect to manic markets as with well-disciplined ones. But once we lose confidence in efficient markets, the tools used to assess materiality and measure damages—the event study techniques—do inspire less confidence. Materiality becomes anything that moves markets, sensibly or not, and the abnormal returns following corrective disclosure captures market over or under reaction as easily as precise readjustment.

A good illustration of the contemporary dilemma is a Third Circuit decision, *In re Merck & Co. Securities Litigation*.[45] Merck is one of the world's most visible blue-chip stocks; if its market is not efficient, it's hard to imagine what would be. It filed a registration statement with the SEC for a spin-off of a subsidiary, in which it disclosed some revenue recognition adjustments that essentially acknowledged that the prior practice was incorrect. But this corrective disclosure was not highlighted and very obscure, leaving the math to the reader to figure out the nature and extent of the problem. There was no discernable market price

43. See Macey & Miller, *supra* note 18.

44. *See, e.g.*, Frederick Dunbar & Dana Heller, *Fraud on the Market Meets Behavioral Finance*, 31 Del. J. Corp. L. 455 (2006); *see also* Larry Ribstein, *Fraud on a Noisy Market*, 10 Lewis & Clark L. Rev. 137 (2006).

For a case rejecting a challenge based on noise trading, *see In re Xcelera.com Sec. Litig.*, 430 F.3d 503 (1st Cir. 2005).

45. 432 F.3d 261 (3d Cir. 2005).

reaction that day or the day after. But a month or so later, the *Wall Street Journal* published an article on the correction, doing the math, and Merck stock dropped significantly.

The Third Circuit dismissed the case by declaring that the revenue recognition issue was immaterial as a matter of law because there had been no price drop when the information first became available: absence of market effect *conclusively* demonstrates immateriality under the efficient market hypothesis. Is that right? Even in an efficient markets setting there is the possibility that professionals had already learned of the problems, from leaks or otherwise, so that the price had already corrected for the misrepresentations. After all, one of the main teachings of the efficient market hypothesis—to which the Third Circuit had declared its faithful "commitment"[46]—is that smart money doesn't wait for formal disclosure. One the other hand, is it beyond imagination that the market really didn't appreciate the truth until the *Journal* publicized it? There is doubt in the literature how quickly stock prices adjust to hard-to-interpret information about which there is likely disagreement even for large-cap issuers, and recognition that publicity may well play a role in price reactions.[47] The court's only response here was that if that were so, it would simply prove the inefficiency of the market for Merck's stock, and if so, under *Basic* there couldn't be a presumption of reliance in the first place. Either way, plaintiffs lose. Again, that obsession with efficiency is probably not what *Basic* intended, but well illustrates how the Court's muddle about reliance twenty years ago produces very different kinds of results today.

C. CONCLUSION

The materiality and reliance portions of *Basic* should be read together. That is the only way to appreciate what is really at stake when disclosure decisions are made in real time. *Basic's* presumption of reliance opened the door to massive liability exposure for violations of Rule 10b–5. That might be comfortable if the category of violations can readily be confined to lies and omissions that inappropriately distort stock prices. But once we introduce both legal indeterminacy and the risk of fact-finder error (the hindsight bias), the massive liability threat becomes more troubling. Even assuming accurate liability judgments, the fact that corporate actors will sometimes misjudge their disclosure responsibilities precisely because of the murky nature of the materiality and duty to disclose standards means that there will at least be a disproportion between what was done and what plaintiffs seek in compensation.

---

46. *Id.* at 269 ("Our court has one of the clearest commitments to the efficient market hypothesis").

47. For a discussion of this literature, see Harrison Hong & Jeremy Stein, *Disagreement and the Stock Market*, 21 J. ECON.

PERSPECTIVES 109 (2007). On publicity, see Gur Huberman & Tomer Regev, *Contagious Speculation and a Cure for Cancer: A Nonevent that Made Stock Prices Soar*, 56 J. FIN. 387 (2001).

One response might be that liability can be avoided by erring on the side of caution—disclose everything that might be material. That is essentially what the plaintiffs said Basic had to do when the stock exchange officials asked that it respond to the unusual stock price movements in the company's stock. If disclosure is unambiguously beneficial and not costly, that is probably right. But disclosure is costly and can sometimes be harmful to the company and its shareholders (even though *Basic* is probably not that good an illustration of the latter). That is why the norm is that companies can keep secrets and only have to divulge pursuant to specific SEC instruction or when necessary to make what they do say (or have said) not misleading. The market presumably understands and accepts the risk of informational asymmetry. Against that background it is not so easy to deflect hard questions by telling managers to "just disclose it." The perils of speaking out in the world that *Basic* created are unavoidable.

None of this calls into question *Basic's* result if one believes—as do many—that compensating investors who bought or sold at distorted prices and deterring fraud are important enough objectives. Yet there are still hard questions even putting aside the indeterminacy problem: Does the measure of damages under *Basic's* presumption systematically overcompensate investors?[48] And how well does the threat of liability deter managerial lies when settlements and judgments are borne by company shareholders (or D & O insurers) rather than managers themselves?[49] These are difficult issues with no easy answers, deserving far more time and attention to explore than we have here. Just don't lose sight of them when reading *Basic*.

48. *See* Frank Easterbrook & Daniel Fischel, *Optimal Damages in Securities Cases*, 52 U. Chi. L. Rev. 611 (1985); Donald C. Langevoort, *Capping Damages for Open-Market Securities Fraud*, 38 Ariz. L. Rev. 639 (1996). *But see* Goshen & Parchamovsky, *supra* note 34.

49. *See, e.g.*, John C. Coffee, *Reforming the Securities Class Action: An Essay on Deterrence and its Implementation*, 106 Colum. L. Rev. 1534 (2006); Jennifer Arlen & William Carney, *Vicarious Liability for Fraud on Securities Markets: Theory and Evidence*, 1992 U. Ill. L. Rev. 691.

Chapter 14

GOOD FAITH'S PROCEDURE AND SUBSTANCE: *IN RE CAREMARK INTERNATIONAL INC., DERIVATIVE LITIGATION*

By
Hillary A. Sale[*]

Good faith produces good procedures and good procedures produce good outcomes. These statements are descriptive of much of Delaware's corporate law as well as the Delaware courts' approach to fiduciary duties. *In re Caremark International Inc., Derivative Litigation*,[1] an important case in the annals of corporate law, exemplifies this good-faith approach both through its emphasis on monitoring and good-faith processes and procedures as well as through its own procedural place in history. This chapter explores the "procedural" elements of *Caremark* and the cases that followed and expanded its contours while focusing on the ways in which *Caremark*'s procedure and substance are intertwined.

Caremark exemplifies the connections between procedure and substance in several ways. For example, *Caremark*, in combination with a set of cases following the *Smith v. Van Gorkom*[2] opinion and the enactment of Delaware's exculpation statute, which allows companies to adopt exculpation clauses, created room for cases to survive motions to dismiss. Exculpation clauses eliminate damages for directors' breaches of the duty of care. Thus, if the plaintiffs were unable to allege a traditional loyalty violation, involving a conflict of interest or other financial breach, their complaint was likely to be dismissed. In essence, complaints with claims for damages grounded solely in care-based allegations were subject to dismissal because exculpation clauses eliminated the damages.

[*] F. Arnold Daum Professor of Corporate Finance and Law. Thanks to Bob Thompson for helpful comments and to Amy Koopmann for research assistance. This chapter is based, in part, on the author's Pileggi Lecture and the corresponding article on *Caremark, Monitoring* Caremark's *Good Faith*, 32 Del. J. Corp. L. 719 (2007).

1. 698 A.2d 959, 961 (Del. 1996).

2. 488 A.2d 858 (Del. 1985).

Caremark and its progeny shifted the focus from exculpable care claims to non-exculpable good-faith claims. It took several opinions to change the motion-to-dismiss pleading standards, but *Caremark* initiated this transition. It did so both by inserting the rhetoric of good faith into what was, in prior cases, an analysis focused solely on the duty of care and also by pressing on good faith's role in board processes and procedures. The result was room for plaintiffs to plead good-faith allegations in their complaints. Furthermore, as the pleading process changed and cases survived the motion to dismiss, good faith evolved from a procedural pleading mechanism to a defined, substantive directorial obligation. Indeed, with the infusion of good faith, the duty of loyalty has expanded from its traditional, financial-conflict-based focus to one that now incorporates both good faith generally and the good-faith monitoring obligation specifically. Thus, the pleading process changed first; then over time, the law followed, and *Caremark* contributed a great deal to this change.

This chapter also considers some of the other procedural issues surrounding the *Caremark* opinion. The pressure for the settlement scrutinized by the *Caremark* court arose, in part, out of the power of the then-recent federal organizational sentencing guidelines: a set of rules created through a process designed to diminish perceived inequities and judicial discretion. Further, *Caremark* itself is a procedural opinion. It is an opinion approving a proposed and agreed-upon settlement (thus generally eliminating the likelihood of appeal), but rather than simply evaluating the claims and terms, it actually develops and sets forth descriptions of director obligations in an era of tremendous corporate growth and expansion.[3] Sarbanes–Oxley's section 404, although several years later in time, creates federal disclosure requirements around internal controls and procedures—the same type of systems at issue in *Caremark*. By doing so, Congress and the Securities and Exchange Commission put pressure on Delaware to respond with its own updates for directorial roles. Thus, when the other good-faith opinions covered in this chapter were issued, their more substantive focus on good faith arose in part from that federal process and pressure.

Finally, *Caremark* is emblematic of Delaware's process-based corporate law. It pushes fiduciaries to focus on processes and procedures, while avoiding the delineation of specifics (because when circumstances change, specifics are less useful). This procedural focus is connected to a belief that good process leads to good outcomes, or that procedure and substance are intertwined. Thus, in several ways, *Caremark* illustrates how procedure and process both create and dominate the substance of corporate law.

---

3. Stone v. Ritter, 911 A.2d 362 (Del. 2006), a case decided ten years later, is the first case to hold that *Caremark* is the "law," of Delaware. *Id.* at 370. Prior to the date of *Stone*, the Delaware Supreme Court had cited *Caremark* with approval, but had never squarely faced the question of adopting it. *See, e.g., In re* Walt Disney Co. Derivative Litig., 906 A.2d 27, 67 n.111 (Del. 2006).

A. *IN RE CAREMARK INTERNATIONAL, INC., DERIVATIVE LITIGATION*[4]

To understand *Caremark* and its place, it is necessary first to examine the facts and the court's use of them to update general fiduciary conduct and duties and to push directors to pay attention to monitoring and good-faith obligations.[5] The main issue in *Caremark* was whether the company had failed to comply with health care regulations.[6] Although noncompliance with the provisions was criminal, the derivative claim focused on whether the directors had paid sufficient attention to, or had disregarded, the importance of the company's compliance with patient-care regulations. Compliance with layers of law and regulation is common for companies engaged in heavily regulated industries, like banks and utility companies or, as seen here, a healthcare company. In the context of fiduciary duties, the framework for ensuring compliance is referred to as a duty to monitor, a process in itself.[7]

The specific regulatory concern in *Caremark* was whether the company had made "kickback" payments to physicians in exchange for referrals to Caremark facilities for treatments. Because these sorts of payments could create incentives for referrals for unnecessary, inappropriate, or even simply less competent services, these payments are illegal.[8] Liability for making them thus carries both civil and criminal ramifications.

Caremark had a policy against *quid pro quo* payments, the most obvious form of illegal kickback payments.[9] However, the company had consulting and research contracts with physicians who recommended or prescribed Caremark services and products.[10] As a result, although prohibiting *quid pro quo* payments, the consulting arrangements increased the possibility that such payments might occur.[11]

The facts presented in the settlement opinion revealed that the company understood the potential for regulatory infractions. Thus, for example, the company issued a booklet with guidelines delimiting appropriate contractual relationships with doctors and facilities as well as stating that *quid pro quo* payments were barred.[12] According to Chancellor Allen's opinion, Caremark's lawyers "tended" to review and update the guide on an annual basis.[13] Of course, the landscape of allowable relationships changed over time. In response, the company amended its guidelines and standard contractual forms.[14] Throughout this period,

---

4. 698 A.2d 961 (Del. Ch. 1996).

5. *See*, Hillary A. Sale, *Delaware's Good Faith*, 89 CORNELL L. REV. 456, 467–69 (2004) (describing *Caremark* and its place in the growth of the good-faith doctrine).

6. 698 A.2d at 961–62.

7. *See* ROBERT C. CLARK, CORPORATE LAW § 3.4.2 (1986) (preceding *Caremark* and summarizing and analyzing monitoring duties and role of board).

8. 698 A.2d at 961–62.

9. *Id.* at 962.

10. *Id.* at 962.

11. *Id.* at 962.

12. *Id.* at 962.

13. *Id.* at 962.

14. *Id.* at 962.

inside and outside counsel advised the board of directors about the issues, stating, in particular, that the company's contracts were "in accord with the law."[15] The board, however, did recognize that the "law" was subject to different interpretations.[16]

Although, the Sarbanes–Oxley Act was many years in the future, the Caremark board had its own internal control structure. Management informed the board about education and training programs for the sales force designed to ensure compliance with the regulations.[17] The company revised its policies over time and provided the new policies to employees along with regular training sessions.[18] There may well have been more that the company could have done, but the factual recitation in the *Caremark* opinion revealed that the company was paying attention to the issue and to the potential for violations.

Despite these efforts, the company found itself faced with an investigation by the Health and Human Services Office of the Inspector General.[19] Within about a year, the Department of Justice joined the investigation, and over time, additional federal and state agencies also became involved.[20] Altogether, Caremark was under investigation for four years.[21] The company responded to the Inspector General's investigation by announcing that it would no longer pay certain fees to physicians.[22] The board also began reviewing its internal procedures and published a revised booklet of guidelines for appropriate contractual relationships with doctors and facilities. It also established an additional approval process for any such contracts.[23] Further, the board received a report from the company's outside auditors stating that the company had no "material" weaknesses.[24]

Despite that report, the board's Audit and Ethics Committee decided to require a thorough review of the company's compliance policies and a new employee handbook detailing those policies.[25] The board received reports on these issues and on others, including education and training programs for the sales force that introduced mandatory reporting of any illegal conduct through a confidential hotline designed to protect the identity of anyone making such reports.[26]

Caremark's efforts to ensure compliance both before and after the inspections did not prevent indictments. In fact, there were several indictments charging both the company and some officers.[27] The indictments included charges for the time period after the company had adopted some of the revised compliance measures.[28] The explanation for

15. *Id.* at 962.

16. *Id.* at 962.

17. *Id.* at 963.

18. *Id.* at 963.

19. *Id.* at 962. In fact, when initiated, the investigation was of Caremark's corporate predecessor. *Id.*

20. *Id.* at 962.

21. *Id.* at 960.

22. *Id.* at 962.

23. *Id.* at 963.

24. *Id.* at 963.

25. *Id.* at 963.

26. *Id.* at 963.

27. *Id.* at 963.

28. *Id.* at 964.

this timing issue was that the company continued to make problematic payments after the board was consulted and involved and while it was trying to respond to the federal and state investigations.[29] In response to the indictment, the company announced that it would terminate many of its programs, further restrict others, and no longer attempt to create agreements, even those that would be legally acceptable under the federal regulations.[30]

Caremark settled the federal and state matters pending against it, by pleading guilty to one felony count, making reimbursements to private and public parties, and by paying approximately $250 million in fines and other payments.[31] No senior officers or directors were cited for wrongdoing, and the Department of Justice stipulated that no "senior executive of Caremark participated in, condoned, or was willfully ignorant of wrongdoing in connection with the home infusion business practices."[32] The company, however, paid large criminal and civil fines.[33] In addition to paying large civil and criminal fines, Caremark agreed to make internal changes to enhance its compliance with the various laws and regulations.[34]

Among the civil cases that followed the indictment were the derivative cases filed and consolidated in the Delaware Chancery Court.[35] By its nature, derivative litigation raises a claim on behalf of the company. Here, the allegations were focused on whether Caremark had adequately supervised its employees and instituted corrective measures. The alleged harms were the fines and liability.[36]

After negotiations, the parties proposed a settlement.[37] This settlement contained a variety of proposed governance changes, many of which the company had already implemented through its settlements with federal and state officials. The *Caremark* opinion that resulted evaluated the proposed settlement to determine whether settlement was appropriate, and if so, whether the proposed terms were appropriate as well. According to Chancellor Allen, the settlement contained one significant proposal: the formation of a Compliance and Ethics Committee with four directors, two of whom were to be outside directors, who would report to the Caremark board on monitoring and compliance systems.[38]

At this stage of the proceedings, procedure again became very important, though here it is not the board's process, but the judge's that is at issue. Chancellor Allen was tasked with a fiduciary-like responsibility for reviewing the settlement to determine whether it was fair and reasonable to the class.[39] His job was to counteract the agency problems that exist both when the litigation is primarily lawyer-driven and when

29. *Id.* at 964.
30. *Id.* at 965.
31. *Id.* at 960–61, 964.
32. *Id.* at 965.
33. *Id.* at 965 n.10.
34. *Id.* at 965.
35. *Id.* at 964.

36. *Id.* at 964. Amended versions of this complaint were filed over the next several months. *Id.*
37. *Id.* at 965.
38. *Id.* at 966.
39. *Id.* at 966.

the plaintiffs have small stakes in the company. He was not, of course, faced with a complete set of facts. Instead, he had to take the litigation as it was, with the discovery incomplete, and place the facts in context. He also had to analyze the claims to determine whether the facts as presented supported a claim, and if so, whether the settlement was fair and reasonable in light of that claim and the likelihood of success.

Chancellor Allen found the allegation to be as follows: that the directors allowed a situation to develop and continue, thus exposing the company to significant legal liability.[40] If that statement were accurate, the board would have failed to engage in conscientious monitoring and in its oversight role. As a result, this portion of the opinion is perhaps the most interesting because Chancellor Allen set out the "law" so to speak, developing the concept of "active" monitoring into two categories. The first is comprised of those with bad outcomes but with processes that were only negligent or ill-advised.[41] The second are those with bad results *and* bad processes, like an "unconsidered failure of the board to act" where, presumably, action may have prevented the loss.[42] For the first group, Chancellor Allen concluded that business-judgment-rule review is appropriate "assuming the decision made was the product of a *process* that was *either* deliberately considered in good faith or was otherwise rational."[43] As applied elsewhere, the business judgment rule prevents a focus on the content of the business decision and the use of hindsight to criticize or second-guess decisions made at a prior point in time. Indeed, the business judgment rule is a procedural mechanism designed to encourage and protect process (on the theory that good processes produce substance) and to keep outsiders from making after-the-fact business judgments.[44] Here again, this judicially invoked presumption creates a procedural focus on the board's actions or lack thereof.

Importantly, the division of the cases in this manner also allows for a focus on the good faith and rationality of the process utilized in making the decision.[45] "Stupid," "egregious," "irrational," or "substantively wrong" decisions receive protection from the business judgment rule and are insulated from liability, "so long as the court determines that the process employed was either rational or employed in a *good faith* effort to advance corporate interests."[46] The result is a focus on whether, how, and when decisions were made. If the board's process meets the test, its decisions are protected.[47] And, directors who *"in fact exercise[] a good faith effort to be informed and to exercise appropriate judgment ... satisfy their"* fiduciary duties and obligations.[48]

---

40. *Id.* at 967.

41. *Id.* at 967.

42. *Id.* at 967.

43. *Id.* at 967 (citing Aronson v. Lewis, 473 A2d 805 (Del. 1984); Gagliardi v. Tri-Foods Int'l, Inc., 683 A.2d 1049 (Del. Ch. 1996)).

44. 698 A.2d at 967.

45. *Id.* at 967.

46. *Id.* at 967.

47. *Id.* at 967.

48. *Id.* at 968.

Caremark, then, updated the business judgment rule with its application to compliance situations and shifted the rhetoric from a focus on the fiduciary duty of care and adherence to it, to the place of good faith.[49] In doing so, Chancellor Allen reaffirmed that shareholders are not entitled to run companies themselves, to make business decisions, or to expect more than good-faith informed decisions made with the "exercise of appropriate judgment."[50] "Monitoring" failures occur, then, either through a bad decision, which with a good process is likely to be protected, or from "unconsidered inaction." The lack of a decision, to be distinguished from a decision not to decide, can result in liability. Yet of course, directors do not run the corporation on a day-to-day basis. They are instead charged with major business decisions along with some responsibility for "the organization and monitoring of the enterprise to assure that the corporation functions within the law to achieve its purposes."[51] Liability rooted in "monitoring" is then more likely to occur from a failure to set up, for example, appropriate compliance and internal controls systems to ensure that the corporation is not distracted from achieving its goals by the acts of officers and "employees deeper in the interior of the organization."[52]

As noted before, *Caremark* arose in the wake of the 1991 revisions to the United States Sentencing Guidelines that adopted Organizational Sentencing Guidelines.[53] These guidelines provided for penalties that had the potential to be dramatic, including, at the extreme, divesting a corporation of all of its assets. They were also designed to create incentives for organizations to prevent, detect, and report problems by rewarding them for doing so. Recall that the *Caremark* issue was patient-care regulatory compliance with potential criminal liability and sentencing implications looming in the background. As is the case with common law generally, *Caremark* also arose in the context of precedents, particularly the *Graham v. Allis–Chalmers Manufacturing Company* opinion.[54] Thirty years earlier, in the *Graham* opinion, the court had addressed whether board members should be liable for corporate losses resulting from antitrust criminal violations by employees. The *Graham* court found that the plaintiffs had not alleged the directors were aware of problems and failed to address them, but that, as in *Caremark*, the directors should have known about the issues and dealt with them. Concluding that there was no basis to find that the directors had failed in their duty to be informed, the court went on to hold that "absent cause for suspicion there is no duty upon the directors to install and

---

49. The update is, of course, a partial response to the effect of Delaware's exculpation clause, referred to as 102(b)(7). In response to the finding of liability in *Smith v. Van Gorkom*, 488 A.2d 858 (Del. 1985), the Delaware legislature adopted an exculpation statute. This statute allows corporations to place a provision in the Articles of Incorporation eliminating liability for directors who breach their duty of care. The statute, however, specifically states that acts not in good faith cannot be exculpated, thus leaving the window for liability open and allowing courts to occupy the space with good-faith rhetoric, if not liability.

50. *Id.* at 968.

51. *Id.* at 969.

52. *Id.* at 968–69.

53. U.S. Sentencing Guidelines Manual § 8.

54. 188 A.2d 125 (Del. 1963).

operate a corporate system of espionage to ferret out wrongdoing which they have no reason to suspect exists."[55]

Chancellor Allen, then, faced the *Graham* court's holding and strong language. His response was to update it, finding that taken literally, the language was too broad. Therefore, Chancellor Allen stressed that a more fitting interpretation of the language was that directors needed to establish information and reporting systems to satisfy their good-faith obligations to be reasonably informed. In reaching this conclusion, the Chancellor pointed to the Organizational Sentencing Guidelines and their potential impact on corporate liability. Thus, the Guidelines became in part a mechanism for updating the monitoring message. As prescribed in *Caremark*, the duty to monitor requires directors to implement appropriate "information gathering and reporting systems" designed, in good faith, to surface information about "material acts, events or conditions within the corporation, including compliance with applicable statutes and regulations[.]"[56] The systems must also allow the board to assess the company's business performance.[57]

Of course, no system, regardless of its design, can prevent all bad acts or ensure that those acts will be caught. Systems are not foolproof, and directors' fiduciary duties do not extend to that level. Instead, the obligation is to "exercise a good faith judgment" that the system is "in concept and design" sufficient to ensure appropriate and timely information in the ordinary course.[58] Thus, as delineated in *Caremark*, the board's good-faith obligation requires it to ensure both that such a system exists and that it is adequate.[59] It does not require directors "to possess detailed information about all aspects of the operation of the enterprise."[60] Conceived this way, the obligation, like the business judgment rule itself, incorporates cost benefit analysis. Chancellor Allen's approach to the monitoring duty implicitly weighs the costs of requiring directors to design systems with the benefits of what those systems might produce. "Perfect" systems, whatever they might be, would be prohibitively expensive, as well as, arguably, disruptive. Well-designed systems, however, will provide directors with the information necessary to make decisions and to catch problems earlier rather than later and will provide the ongoing information directors need to fulfill their strategic roles. More is not required. Indeed, according to *Caremark*, any failure to monitor must be "sustained or systematic" before liability is implicated.[61]

55. *Id.* at 130.

56. 698 A.2d at 969. The original statement is phrased in the negative and as a question, i.e. can it be said that directors need not establish such systems. Chancellor Allen answers it in the negative. *Id.*

57. *Id.* at 970.

58. *Id.* at 970.

59. *Id.* at 970.

60. *Id.* at 971.

61. *Id.* at 971. *See, e.g.,* Melvin A. Eisenberg, *The Duty of Good Faith in Corporate Law,* 31 Del. J. Corp. L. 1, 62–63 (2006) ("*Caremark* ... concerned disregard of the board's duty to install monitoring and information systems"); Donald C. Langevoort, *The Human Nature of Corporate Boards: Law, Norms, and the Unintended Consequences of Independence and Accountability,* 89 Geo. L.J. 797, 819–20 (2001) (stating that *Caremark* requires "affirma-

Interestingly for our study of procedure and substance, the *Caremark* opinion is also unique because of its procedural posture. As noted above, it is a settlement opinion and given its derivative nature was unlikely to be appealed. Derivative litigation is lawyer-driven. Thus, generally, even though representative plaintiffs play a role in the litigation, their lawyers play a particularly strong role and are often the ones who conceived of the litigation in the first place. Any proposed settlement would not only attempt to provide some relief, financial or otherwise, to the plaintiffs but would also include attorneys' fees. This case was no exception, with a request for fees of $1,025,000. Chancellor Allen did grant attorneys' fees, but reduced the amount to $816,000 plus expenses. This change was presumably sufficiently small that it did not prompt discontent, but did allow him to make the point about reigning in fees where the litigation appeared to provide the plaintiffs with less than their attorneys.

In *Caremark*, as in many other cases, the court approved an agreed-upon settlement with few changes and, therefore, appeal was unlikely. The result is that *Caremark* serves not only as an important opinion about monitoring obligations, but also as an opinion that reveals the power and uses of procedure in a strategic sense. The Chancellor's choice to update the law in a settlement opinion with minimal chance for appeal resulted in a shift in the substantive understanding of directorial obligations that, given the timing and context, turned out to be very powerful.

B. *SMITH v. VAN GORKOM*[62] AND ITS PROCEDURAL PROGENY

In between *Caremark* and later cases developing the doctrine of good faith were a series of cases that were procedurally very important and that, in fact, made the later cases possible. Although *Smith v. VanGorkom* preceded *Caremark* and was not a good-faith opinion, it prompted significant changes in, first, the Delaware corporation statute and then, over time, the common law. The cases in this section were responses to *Van Gorkom*, the exculpation clause that followed it, and *Caremark*.

In *Van Gorkom*, the Delaware Supreme Court found the directors liable for breaching their duty of care, noting that there was no bad-faith allegation. This case was unusual for several reasons. First, it was issued with dissenting opinions. The Delaware Supreme Court rarely issues such opinions, instead focusing on achieving unanimity. Second, it was one of only a few cases in which personal liability for directors had been assessed.[63] And third, it created a clamor for reform and, in fact, resulted

tive monitoring by boards to assure compliance with the law even in the absence of specific warning signs, particularly in settings where the temptations toward illegal behavior are strong"); *cf.* Lawrence E. Mitchell, *The Sarbanes–Oxley Act and the Reinvention of Corporate Governance?*, 48 VILL. L. REV. 1189, 1203 (2003) (discussing *Caremark* as a monitoring case and criticizing it as "incredibly weak" while comparing it to Sarbanes–Oxley).

62. 488 A.2d 858 (Del. 1985).

63. *See* Bernard S. Black, Brian R. Cheffins & Michael Klausner, *Outside Di-*

in quick legislative discussion and reform. Specifically, the Delaware legislature adopted the exculpation provision, referred to as 102(b)(7). This statute allows corporations to place a clause in the articles of incorporation eliminating monetary liability for directors who breach their duty of care.

The impact of the exculpation clause, however, was as much procedural as it was substantive. Although the clause exempts directors from damages for breaches of the duty of care, and is in that sense substantive, its early impact was at the motion-to-dismiss stage of litigation. A complaint alleging a breach of the duty of care and requesting damages is subject to dismissal in a company with such a clause (virtually all public companies now have such clauses in their articles), because the acts are exculpated.[64] It is easy to imagine that the response of any defense lawyer faced with claims of breaches of fiduciary duty would be to argue that the claims amounted to no more than care-based claims subject to exculpation and therefore, that the complaint should be dismissed. Indeed, that is what happened, and many cases were dismissed.

The statute, however, specifically states that acts not in good faith cannot be exculpated. Here again, it is easy to imagine the litigation response to this provision. Any complaints alleging non-financial, non-conflicting-interest breaches were presented as raising good-faith issues and not simple care concerns. Good faith, in essence, became a tool for surviving a motion to dismiss. Of course, the defendants responded with care-focused arguments, leaving the courts to either sort the claims into piles or to develop alternative solutions. The courts did so, developing a line of cases making it clear that complaints pleading good faith and loyalty concerns intertwined with exculpable care allegations can survive the motion to dismiss, garner discovery, and perhaps even make it to trial.[65] The result is a series of cases that arise from the lack of a definition of the term "good faith," a very powerful, but likely unintended, consequence of the legislative change.

Good faith's early impact was then both substantive, resulting in a revised pleading doctrine, and procedural, creating room for complaints to survive motions to dismiss. Of course for the cases later tried, good faith's impact was again substantive as the modern development of the good-faith obligation began. The *Disney* litigation is an example of a case that both survived the procedural hurdles and contributed to the development of the good-faith obligation.

rector Liability, 58 STANFORD L. REV. 1055 (2006).

64. *See* Emerald Partners v. Berlin, 726 A.2d 1215, 1224 (Del. 1999) (holding that exculpation clause supports dismissal if claims are solely due-care based).

65. *See* Malpiede v. Townson, 780 A.2d 1075, 1093 (Del. 2001) (dismissal appropriate where complaint alleges claims amounting only to care violations); McMullin v. Beran, 765 A.2d 910, 926 (Del. 2000) (where due care is intertwined with loyalty claims, dismissal based on exculpation clause is inappropriate).

C. *IN RE THE WALT DISNEY CO. DERIVATIVE LIT-IGATION*[66]

One of the most interesting recent cases to expound on good faith and to help to develop its boundaries was the case involving Michael Ovitz, Michael Eisner, and the Walt Disney Company board of directors. Prior to this case, good faith had not been squarely presented. The *Disney* plaintiffs questioned whether the directors had, in fact, performed certain required functions, raising the specter of conscious disregard of responsibilities or even abdication. The case is also procedurally unusual because it survived a motion to dismiss and proceeded to trial, allowing for later opinions in which the court could examine evidence, not just pleadings. The result is an opinion developing the substantive law regarding what good faith might mean, rather than how one pleads it.[67] Finally, this is the case that laid the foundation for the Delaware Supreme Court's more recent opinion in *Stone v. Ritter*[68] and the elocution of the good-faith obligation as linked to the duty of loyalty.

The legal issues in *Disney* centered on whether the board and appropriate committees had fulfilled their fiduciary duties or wasted company assets by hiring Michael Ovitz as President and terminating him just over a year later with a severance package alleged to be worth $130 million.[69] The key to the plaintiffs' allegations was the claim that the board did not discuss these decisions or in fact make them, and, thereby, abdicated its duties. Further, the plaintiffs alleged that Michael Eisner, then the Chair and CEO, personally selected Ovitz for his successor, negotiating and implementing both the employment and termination agreements on his own.[70] Specifically, the plaintiffs alleged that the board neither saw nor asked to see copies of either agreement prior to its execution. And, with respect to the non-fault termination agreement, the board's failure violated a bylaw requiring it to do so.[71] The Chancery Court's response to these allegations was to find that they were sufficient to raise questions of good faith, i.e., not simply exculpable care allegations, and to deny the motion to dismiss.[72] This step, of course, is attributable to the line of cases discussed in the prior section. Ultimately, however, the result after trial was a finding that the breach, if one occurred, was one only of the duty of care, protected by Disney's exculpation clause.[73] In short, the facts at trial did not implicate good faith.[74]

66. 906 A.2d 27 (Del. 2006).

67. *See* Hillary A. Sale, *Judging Heuristics*, 35 U.C. DAV. L. REV. 903, 953–54 (2002) (discussing how the use of heuristics in federal securities cases allows for dismissal and prevents the development of substantive standards of scienter); Jonathan R. Macey, *Judicial Preferences, Public Choice and the Rules of Procedure*, 23 J. LEGAL STUD. 627, 644–45 (1994) (noting use of procedural rules by Delaware judges and its effect on the development of substantive law).

68. 911 A.2d 362, 370 (Del. 2006).

69. 906 A.2d at 35.

70. Brehm v. Eisner, 825 A.2d 275, 281–87 (Del. Ch. 2003).

71. *Id.* at 281–82.

72. *Id.* at 289–90.

73. *In re* Walt Disney Co. Deriv. Litig., 907 A.2d 693 (Del. Ch. 2005).

74. *Id.* at 693.

The plaintiffs appealed the case to the Delaware Supreme Court, which affirmed the Chancellor's opinion. The appellate opinion, however, set forth important "conceptual guidance" on the good-faith obligation.[75] In doing so, the Delaware Supreme Court laid out a nonexclusive list of examples of conduct implicating good faith, noting that they "echo[ed] pronouncements" the Delaware courts had "made throughout the decades."[76] As described by the court, a fiduciary can fail to act in good faith "where the fiduciary intentionally acts with a purpose other than that of advancing the best interests of the corporation[,] . . . with the intent to violate applicable positive law[, or] . . . intentionally fails to act in the face of a known duty to act, demonstrating a conscious disregard for his duties."[77] Thus, the *Disney* opinion is the first one holding that good faith is in fact a director obligation and that severe recklessness, as opposed to gross negligence, might implicate that obligation.[78]

D. *STONE v. RITTER*[79]

In 2006, the Delaware Supreme Court issued an opinion clarifying good faith's place in the constellation of fiduciary responsibilities and directly applied it to monitoring duties. The complaint at issue raised *Caremark* allegations about a bank's compliance with banking regulations.[80] The key holding in *Stone* was that good-faith conduct is required of fiduciaries as an obligation pursuant to the duty of loyalty.[81] Prior to *Stone*, there had been debate and uncertainty about whether good faith was a separate fiduciary duty, not a fiduciary duty at all, or an aspect of either care or loyalty.[82] Post-*Stone*, however, it is now clear that directors who fail to act in good faith face allegations of and liability for a breach of the duty of loyalty.[83] *Stone* also provides the contours of possible violations of the good-faith obligation, at least in the context of the directors' oversight and monitoring role.[84]

75. 906 A.2d 27, 64 (Del. 2006).

76. *Id.* at 67 n.111.

77. *Id.* at 67.

78. *Compare* 906 A.2d at 67, *with* 906 A.2d at 64–65 (Del. 2006).

79. 911 A.2d 362, 370 (Del. 2006).

80. *Id.* at 370.

81. *Id.* at 370.

82. *See generally* Christopher M. Bruner, *Good Faith, State of Mind, and the Outer Boundaries of Director Liability*, 41 Wake Forest L. Rev. 1131 (2006); Melvin A. Eisenberg, *The Duty of Good Faith in Corporate Law*, 31 Del. J. Corp. L. 1 (2006); Sean J. Griffith, *Good Faith Business Judgment: A Theory of Rhetoric in Corporate Law Jurisprudence*, 55 Duke L.J. 1 (2005); Hillary A. Sale, *Delaware's Good Faith*, 89 Cornell L. Rev. 456 (2004). *See also*, Hon.

E. Norman Veasey, *Weil Briefing: Corporate Governance—Delaware Supreme Court Affirms Chancellor's Judgement of No Liability for Directors in Ovitz Case*, in Corporate Governance 2007, at 155 (PLI Corporate Law 7 Practice, Course Handbook Series, no. 10874, 2007) (describing *Disney* ruling and its implications for directors' good-faith obligations).

83. 911 A.2d 362, 370 (Del. 2006); ATR-Kim Eng Fin. Corp. v. Araneta, No. CIV. A. 489–N, 2006 WL 3783520, *19 (Del.Ch. Dec. 21, 2006) (finding two outside directors breached duty of loyalty by acting as "stooges" and failing to monitor); *see also* Ryan v. Gifford, No. CIV. A. 2214–N, 2007 WL 4161621 (Feb. 6, 2007) (finding options backdating allegations rooted in good-faith and sufficient to survive motion to dismiss); *In re* Tyson Foods, Inc., No. CIV.A. 1106–N, 2007 WL 416132 (Feb. 6, 2007) (same).

84. 911 A.2d at 370.

The case first appeared in Chancery Court, where the defendants filed a motion to dismiss for failure to plead demand futility. The Chancery Court granted the motion and described the complaint as one raising a "classic *Caremark* claim."[85] On appeal, the Delaware Supreme Court began its analysis by pointing out that the "plaintiffs acknowl-edge[d] that the directors neither 'knew [n]or should have known that violations of the law were occurring,' *i.e.,* that there were no 'red flags' before the directors."[86] Despite the absence of such allegations, the court held that the complaint did allege that "the defendants had utterly failed to implement any sort of statutorily required monitoring, reporting or information controls that would have enabled them to learn of problems requiring their attention."[87] This allegation, of course, is the so-called *Caremark* claim, in this case raised about a bank subject to extensive federal regulations, including some mandating the reporting of suspi-cious activities and others requiring systems designed to curb money laundering.[88]

Again, as in *Caremark*, this lawsuit emerged after federal and state government investigations resulted in fines for a Ponzi scheme operated through a Tennessee bank.[89] According to the plaintiffs, the perpetrators of the scheme opened custodial "investor" accounts that were supposed to receive monthly interest payments at a branch bank.[90] When the payments did not occur, some investors reported the two people who developed the scheme. Investigations and civil litigation then ensued.[91] Eventually, the perpetrators were indicted and pled guilty.[92]

The government investigated the bank's compliance with various regulations and reporting obligations.[93] The result was a Deferred Prose-cution Agreement that included the filing of a one-count Information charge against the company for failing to file required suspicious activity reports resulting in a fine of $40 million.[94] The accompanying "State-ment of Facts" indicated that although these problems were not discov-ered until 2002, at least one employee suspected the perpetrators of an illegal scheme in 2000.[95] This Statement of Facts "ascribe[d] no blame" to the board or to any director.[96]

In addition to the above-described agreement, in 2004 the Federal Reserve and state banking regulators issued a Cease and Desist Order requiring the bank to improve its compliance efforts[97] and hire an independent consultant to review the compliance programs and recom-mend appropriate changes.[98] FinCEN and the Federal Reserve also assessed a $10 million fine. Accompanying the fine was a determination

---

85. *Id.* at 362.

86. *Id.* at 364.

87. *Id.* at 364.

88. *Id.* at 365.

89. *Id.* at 365.

90. *Id.* at 365.

91. *Id.* at 365–66.

92. *Id.* at 366.

93. *Id.* at 366.

94. *Id.* at 366.

95. *Id.* at 366.

96. *Id.* at 366.

97. *Id.* at 366.

98. *Id.* at 366.

that the bank had violated statutes and its existing compliance programs lacked sufficient board and management oversight.[99] The company neither admitted nor denied the findings.[100] Those findings, however, were the basis of the *Stone* plaintiffs' allegations that the board had failed to fulfill both its good-faith monitoring and oversight responsibilities.[101]

To analyze the claim, the court turned to *Caremark*, stating that boards must "exercise a good faith judgment that the corporations' information and reporting system is in concept and design adequate to assure the board that appropriate information will come to its attention in a timely manner as a matter of ordinary operations."[102] Again, pointing to *Caremark*, the court noted that the board can meet this obligation without knowing in detail all aspects of the company or its operations, and that only sustained and systematic oversight failures, " 'such as an utter failure to attempt to assure a reasonable information and reporting system exists—will establish the lack of good faith that is a necessary condition to liability.' "[103] The court specifically located the oversight function, and liability for its breach, in the good-faith obligation.[104]

Before turning to the facts as pleaded, the court addressed the three types of good-faith violations noted in *Disney*, stating that they are the most "salient" types of violations and specifically reserved room for others. It then locates *Caremark* violations in the third *Disney* category: intentional failures to act in the face of a known duty to do so, in a manner that demonstrates a conscious disregard for one's duties.[105] Thus, a sustained or systematic oversight failure could occur either when a board fails to implement a reporting or control system or when it fails to monitor or oversee operations sufficiently.[106] These types of failures also amount to the sort of intentional failure that demonstrates conscious disregard for duties.[107] In addition, the court places the good-faith obligation within the duty of loyalty, settling the question of its place and clarifying that loyalty is capacious enough to expand beyond the traditional financial conflicts associated with it.[108]

The court then examined the plaintiffs' allegations in light of this good-faith standard, holding that the complaint and the documents attached to it belied their claims.[109] Specifically, the court held that the complaint, through its reliance on a report prepared by KPMG, actually showed that the bank's board had established "numerous" systems, including a compliance officer who presented regularly to the board and trained other security personnel, a compliance department staffed with nineteen people, a security department responsible for detection and

99. *Id.* at 366.

100. *Id.* at 366.

101. *See* 911 A.2d 362, 370–71.

102. *Id.* at 368.

103. *Id.* at 369 (quoting *In re* Caremark Int'l, Inc. Deriv. Litig., 698 A.2d 961, 971 (Del. Ch. 1996)).

104. *Id.* at 369.

105. *Id.* at 369.

106. *Id.* at 369.

107. *Id.* at 369.

108. *Id.* at 370.

109. *Id.* at 372–73.

reporting of activities, and a committee charged with oversight of suspicious activities.[110] The court also held that the board received regular reports on compliance matters, its audit committee "oversaw" the compliance efforts on a quarterly basis, and the board received both training and reports on training on an annual basis.[111] Furthermore, the court noted that the board enacted policies and procedures over time to assist with legal compliance.[112] All these efforts, the court held, revealed a board actively engaged in oversight and monitoring and not, therefore, susceptible to a claim that it failed to act in good-faith.[113]

The court also pointed out that oversight, no matter how thorough, cannot prevent criminal or civil violations.[114] Thus, for *Caremark* liability to exist, either the board must fail to create or monitor control systems or fail to act in the face of a "red flag." Both are breaches of the duty to monitor. Neither circumstance existed in *Stone*. Notably, neither circumstance existed in *Caremark* or its monitoring predecessor, *Graham*.

E. "RED FLAGS"

The fact that there were no "red flags" in these key cases, leaves practitioners as well as the reader of this chapter wondering what they are. Other cases reveal that red flags present in at least two ways. The first is when a significant incident occurs within the firm, perhaps only once, that makes clear that the internal controls are not functioning as designed. The second is when a situation repeats itself or "suggests" irregularity over time and should, therefore, filter up to the board's attention. Indeed, the longer the problem persists, the more likely a court is to find that it presents a "red-flag" issue.[115] The key is whether the court will find that a fiduciary "demonstrates a faithlessness or lack of true devotion to the interests of the corporation and its shareholders."[116]

To determine whether a red flag is present, the court will look to whether the fiduciaries either actually knew or should have known about the alleged problems. Several different types of situations can present red flags. For example, if a company's audits reveal problematic practices, and the board does not address them, the existence of the audit reports can be a red flag.[117] In a similar vein, allegations in litigation against the company might present red flags.[118] Newspaper or other media reports of specific company problems or pending government investigations should also attract board attention, and if unaddressed, might be treated as red flags.[119] In addition, general media stories of

---

110. *Id.* at 372.

111. *Id.* at 372.

112. *Id.* at 372.

113. *Id.* at 373.

114. *Id.* at 373.

115. *See In re* Abbott Labs. Derivative S'holders Litig., 325 F.3d 795, 806 (7th Cir. 2003) (pointing to allegations of long-term problems in red-flag analysis).

116. Ryan v. Gifford, 918 A.2d 341, 357 (Del. Ch. 2007).

117. *See* McCall v. Scott, 239 F.3d 808, 820 (6th Cir. 2001).

118. *See id.* at 822.

119. *See id.* at 823. *See also In re* Abbott Labs., 325 F.3d at 800 (noting existence of *Wall Street Journal* and *Bloomberg News* coverage in red-flag analysis).

significant industry or broad-based governance or accounting issues, like the 2006 stories on stock-options backdating, can also serve as red flags.[120] Such reports should prompt fiduciaries to determine whether their company faces the same or a similar issue. Notice to the company of negative government inspections of companies in, for example, a regulated industry may also meet the red-flag test.[121] Further, the resignations of fellow directors, depending on the circumstances, can raise issues requiring action.[122] The key is for directors to be active and engaged, asking questions and insisting on boardroom discussions when presented with such issues.[123] Finally, of course, isolated incidents, even those of the type described above, may not be sufficient by themselves. In a particular context or in combination, however, they can present a red flag question.[124]

F. CONCLUSION

Caremark and *Stone* make clear that monitoring and oversight are key to the good-faith obligation of fiduciaries and to the role of boards of directors as managers of managers.[125] The losses to corporations from the bad acts of officers and employees, even those much lower down in the operation, can be dramatic. Further, the acts of employees can actually inhibit the board from achieving its goals for the company.[126] Thus, the board must set up appropriate monitoring systems to surface the acts and prevent them where possible. It cannot, however—nor should it—monitor all of those acts on a daily basis. Instead, under *Caremark*, the board's responsibility is to create the systems, or processes, necessary "to assure that the corporation functions within the law to achieve its purposes."[127] *Stone* clarifies that a board that fails to either implement the appropriate system *or* fails to respond to red flags, is not a good-faith or loyal monitor.[128]

The duty to monitor, now clearly established as a good-faith obligation, also connects in important ways to the federal governance debate. Although not directly discussed as the duty to monitor, it is

---

120. *See* Hillary A. Sale, *Monitoring Caremark's Good Faith,* 32 Del. J. Corp. L. 719, 744–47 (describing press coverage of backdating issues and arguing that boards who had failed to investigate their companies' grants were at risk of ignoring a red flag).

121. *See In re* Abbott Labs, 325 F.3d at 799.

122. *See* Sale, *Monitoring Caremark's Good Faith,* 32 Del. J. Corp. L. at 743–44 (describing Jerome York's resignation letter from the General Motors board and arguing that the letter itself is a red flag).

123. *See id.* at 806 (criticizing board for failing to discuss certain issues at board meetings and for signing company filings without asking questions).

124. *See* McCall v. Scott, 239 F.3d at 823 (noting that some allegations in isolation might be insufficient, but that context matters).

125. *In re* Caremark Int'l, Inc., Deriv. Litig., 698 A.2d 959, 969 (Del. Ch. 1996).

126. 698 A.2d at 968.

127. 698 A.2d at 968–69. At bottom, this statement is about the board's overarching monitoring and managerial role in the corporation, with legal compliance in the background. *See, e.g.,* 698 A.2d at 969 (discussing sentencing guidelines).

128. For a critique of the *Stone* decision and this particular aspect of it, see Professor Bainbridge.com, *Stone v. Ritter & Directors' Caremark Oversight Duties,* Jan. 3, 2007, http://www.professorbainbridge.com/2007/01/stone_v_ritter_.html.

implicated in many of the securities-fraud complaints in which directors are accused of engaging in conscious disregard with respect to the company's revenue-recognition or other accounting practices. And, of course, Sarbanes–Oxley's section 404, the provision requiring public companies to establish internal control measures, is a federalized version of the duty to monitor. Recent press on the Sarbanes–Oxley Act indicates that companies have found it useful not only for setting up required systems but also for empowering directors to insist on the information that they need and increasing accountability both at the board level and below.[129] In particular, information is surfacing sooner and allowing for the resolution of issues before they become larger. In part, that is the goal of the duty to monitor. It is also an example of how procedures can produce substantive changes and outcomes.

Monitoring does, however, have its limits. Directors are not charged with daily decision-making. They are charged with oversight. Even though they make relatively few decisions when compared with their officer counterparts, oversight means more than "blind faith reliance" on officers or management-prepared documents.[130] Instead, their monitoring and good-faith obligations require them to ask questions and question answers. Federal securities law supports the same sorts of duties and obligations for directors in the context of public disclosures and filings. The theory undergirding the federal securities laws' disclosure premise is that the process of requiring the disclosure of information will produce substantive change. In essence, the federal securities laws establish a choice for boards—either create certain systems or disclose that you do not have them. When the absence is problematic, boards create systems.[131] Here again, process produces substance and change.

The duty to monitor also figures in the debates about the agency costs inherent in the separation of ownership and control.[132] The good-faith obligation of directors is central to these debates. This obligation, along with the general fiduciary duties, is designed to combat basic agency costs.[133] Although individual and institutional purchasers are the

---

129. *See* Joann S. Lublin & Kara Scannell, *Theory & Practice: Critics See Some Good From Sarbanes–Oxley—As Law Turns Five, They say It's Too Costly, But It Exposes Problems Before They Explode*, Wall St. J., July 30, 2007, at B1.

130. Official Comm. of Unsecured Creditors of Integrated Health Mgmt. v. Elkins, 2004 WL 1949290, at *15 (Aug. 24, 2004).

131. *See generally* Robert B. Thompson & Hillary A. Sale, *Securities Fraud as Corporate Governance: Reflections Upon Federalism*, 56 V and. L. Rev. 859, 872–74 (2003) (describing information-forcing-substance nature of federal disclosure requirements).

132. *See, e.g.,* Michael C. Jensen & William H. Meckling, *Theory of the Firm, Man-*

agerial Behavior, Agency Costs and Ownership Structure, 3 J. Fin. Econ. 305 (1976); *see also* Donald C. Langevoort, *The Human Nature of Corporate Boards: Law, Norms, and the Unintended Consequences of Independence and Accountability*, 89 Geo. L. J. 797, 802 (2000) (noting that board's monitoring functions are "the heart of what the agency cost model of the firm identifies as the central role for the board" preventing shirking and overreaching); Robert H. Sitkoff, *Trust Law, Corporate Law, and Capital Market Efficiency*, 28 J. Corp. L. 565 (2003) (comparing and contrasting agency cost models for corporations and trusts).

133. *See, e.g.,* Robert C. Clark, *Agency Costs Versus Fiduciary Duties, in* Principals and Agents: The Structure of Business 55

owners of the companies, their stakes are often too small, or their portfolios too diversified, to justify regular monitoring of the officers charged with running the corporations. The directors are assigned, indeed hired for, that role. The procedurally focused law, which emphasizes discussions about and the creation of systems for monitoring, if adhered to, builds trust in the director monitors—with potential liability as a backstop to ensure that they fulfill the trust and, thereby, the substantive duty. It also limits the debate to whether there was a good-faith process, rather than a hindsight examination of the underlying substantive decision.

Finally, all of the opinions addressed in this chapter share the emphasis on process and its substantive role. The Delaware judiciary's process-focused emphasis is its trademark. The cases from *Caremark* to *Stone* reveal several layers of process and procedure, including the process from pleading rules to post-trial opinions, through which the good-faith obligation evolved. Those cases also reveal the courts' preference for a good-faith obligation that is connected to the process of decision making, rather than the substantive outcomes. In tying the obligation to process, the court has made a statement about how good faith should and should not be measured. Furthermore, by requiring process, the court also made an effort to ensure that the underlying goal (informed decisions, even if risky) will be achieved and protected.[134] Of course, as part *B* of the chapter explores, the court also created the process, or the case law, that delineated the pleading rules that created room for the evolution of the good-faith obligation. Each procedural move, like the shift in pleading from care-based claims to claims intertwined with good-faith and loyalty issues, creates room for the law and the process to grow.[135] The result is a more fully defined obligation of good faith, located in the duty of loyalty.

Thus, the cases reveal how procedure informs substance, albeit slowly and over time. Procedure, of course, can also inhibit substance, or worse, replace it. The general role of procedure is to balance the costs and benefits of adjudication with substantive outcomes.[136] In corporate law, this tradeoff is fairly explicit. Although agency costs are accepted as an issue to be managed, their existence is balanced against underlying corporate goals and the need for decisions and risk taking. Authority is balanced with accountability, with a thumb on the authority side of the

(John W. Pratt & Richard J. Zeckhauser eds., 1985) (describing role of fiduciary duties in decreasing agency costs).

134. The theory is similar to that of due process for substantive constitutional rights, with process being accorded to assure protection of the underlying rights. *See, e.g.*, Frank H. Easterbrook, *Substance*

and Due Process, 1982 Sup. Ct. Rev. 85, 112–113.

135. Of course, when pleading rules become too strict, they stop the growth.

136. *See* Mathews v. Eldridge, 424 U.S. 319 (1976); Lawrence B. Solum, *Procedural Justice,* 78 S. Cal. L. Rev. 181, 191 (2004).

scale. The business judgment rule, through its presumption-shifting nature, makes these cost-benefit tradeoffs explicit. The court's elucidation of the good-faith obligation generally, and in the monitoring context specifically, as being process focused does so as well.

†